INTRODUCING APPLIED ETHICS

D1605924

INTRODUCING APPLIED ETHICS

edited by
Brenda Almond

BLACKWELL
Oxford UK & Cambridge USA

Copyright © Blackwell Publishers 1995
Chapter 2 copyright © Paul Gregory 1995

First published 1995

Blackwell Publishers Ltd
108 Cowley Road
Oxford OX4 1JF
UK

Blackwell Publishers Inc.
238 Main Street
Cambridge, Massachusetts 02142
USA

British Library Cataloguing in Publication Data

A CIP catalogue record for this book is available from the British Library.

Library of Congress Cataloging-in-Publication Data
Introducing applied ethics/edited by Brenda Almond.
     p.   cm.
    Includes bibliographical references and index.
    ISBN 0-631-19389-8 (alk. paper). – ISBN 0-631-19391-X (pbk.: alk. paper)
    1. Applied ethics.   I. Almond, Brenda.
BJ1031.I58   1995
170 – dc20

Typeset in Ehrhardt 10$\frac{1}{2}$ on 12 pt by Best-set Typesetter Ltd., Hong Kong
Printed in Great Britain by Hartnolls Ltd, Bodmin, Cornwall

This book is printed on acid-free paper.

Contents

Contributors

Brenda Almond is Professor of Moral and Social Philosophy at the University of Hull. She is Chair of the Society for Applied Philosophy and Joint Editor of the *Journal of Applied Philosophy*. Her books include *Moral Concerns* and *Exploring Philosophy*.

Robin Attfield is Professor of Philosophy at the University of Wales College of Cardiff. He has also taught in Nigeria and Kenya. He is the author of *God and the Secular, The Ethics of Environmental Concern, A Theory of Value and Obligation* and *Environmental Philosophy: Principles and Prospects*.

Michael Bavidge is Head of the Adult Education Programme at the Centre for Continuing Education at the University of Newcastle upon Tyne. He is the author of *Mad or Bad?* and co-author of *Can We Understand Animal Minds?*

Andrew Belsey is lecturer in Philosophy and Honorary Secretary of the Centre for Applied Ethics, University of Wales, Cardiff. With Ruth Chadwick he edits the Professional Ethics book series published by Routledge.

Robert Campbell is Principal Lecturer in Philosophy and Deputy Head of the Humanities Division of Bolton Institute. He is co-author (with D. Collinson) of *Ending Lives* and has published articles on suicide, responsibility, accidents, and the treatment of the critically ill. He is currently preparing a book on business ethics.

Ruth Chadwick is Professor of Moral Philosophy at the Centre for Professional Ethics in the University of Central Lancashire. She edited *Ethics, Reproduction and Genetic Control* and is co-ordinator of a European Union research project on ethical and philosophical perspectives on genetic screening.

Stephen R. L. Clark is Professor of Philosophy at Liverpool University. His books include *The Moral Status of Animals*, *The Nature of the Beast*, *Civil Peace and Sacred Order*, and *How to Think about the Earth*. He is married, with three children (and four cats).

C. A. J. (Tony) Coady is Boyce Gibson Professor of Philosophy, and founding Director of the Centre for Philosophy and Public Issues at the University of Melbourne, Australia. His book, *Testimony: a Philosophical Inquiry*, was published by Oxford University Press in 1992, and he is presently writing a book on 'The Morality of Political Violence'.

Andrew J. Cole is a Consultant Psychiatrist in Newcastle City Health NHS Trust and an Honorary Lecturer in the Department of Psychiatry at the University of Newcastle upon Tyne. He works within the community-based psychiatric service and has a special interest in cognitive therapy.

Donna Dickenson is a medical ethicist in the Department of Health and Social Welfare at the Open University, where she chairs an innovative course on Death and Dying. Her publications include *Moral Luck in Medical Ethics and Practical Politics* and *Death, Dying and Bereavement* (co-edited with Malcolm Johnson). She is preparing a volume of case-studies in psychiatric ethics, based on her 'clinical-ethical rounds' at an Oxford teaching hospital.

K. W. M. Fulford is Professor of Philosophy and Mental Health, University of Warwick, and was formerly a Research Psychiatrist and Honorary Consultant in the University Department of Psychiatry at the Warneford Hospital in Oxford. He is the founder Chairman of the Philosophy Group in the Royal College of Psychiatrists and the author of *Moral Theory and Medical Practice*.

Moira Gatens is Senior Lecturer in Philosophy at the University of Sydney. She is author of *Feminism and Philosophy: Perspectives on Difference and Equality* and *Imaginary Bodies and their Practices: Gender, Corporeality and Desire*. She was Visiting Fellow to Philosophy, in the Research School of Social Sciences at the Australian National University during 1994.

Paul Gregory is a graduate of the University of Kent and lives in Germany, where he works freelance as a commercial translator. His published articles include 'Against couples', 'The two sides of love' and 'Personhood and eroticism'.

John Haldane is Professor of Moral Philosophy and Director of the Centre for Philosophy and Public Affairs at the University of St Andrews. He has published widely in aesthetics, history of philosophy, philosophy of mind and social philosophy. He has contributed to several of the Blackwell philosophy *Companions* and is co-author, with J. J. C. Smart, of *Atheism and Theism*.

Jennifer Jackson is Senior Lecturer in Philosophy and Director of the Centre for Business and Professional Ethics at the University of Leeds. She has written a number of articles on aspects of theoretical and applied ethics.

John Kleinig is Professor of Philosophy in the Department of Law and Police Science, John Jay College of Criminal Justice, City University of New York, and editor of the journal *Criminal Justice Ethics*. His books include *Valuing Life*, *Professional Law Enforcement Codes: a Documentary Collection* and *The Ethics of Policing*.

Dick Holdsworth is Head of the STOA (Scientific and Technological Options Assessment) team in the Directorate-General for Research of the European Parliament, based in Luxembourg.

Judith Hughes is a Director of the Newcastle Centre for Applied Philosophy. She was co-author, with Mary Midgley, of *Women's Choices*, and has written a number of articles on children and philosophy.

Tibor Machan is Professor of Philosophy at Auburn University. He has written many books, including *The Pseudo-Science of B. F. Skinner*, *Individuals and Their Rights*, and *Capitalism and Individualism*. Among other works, he has edited *The Libertarian Reader* and *Commerce and Morality*. His most recent book is *The Virtue of Liberty*.

Mary Midgley was formerly Senior Lecturer in Philosophy at the University of Newcastle on Tyne, where she still lives. She is married and has three sons. Author of *Beast and Man* and *Animals and Why They Matter*, her recent books include *Can't We Make Moral Judgements?* and *Science as Salvation*.

Michael Parker is a lecturer at the Centre for Professional Ethics at the University of Central Lancashire. He worked for several years with the young homeless at one of Centrepoint's supportive hostels in central London. He is the Information Officer of the Society for Applied Philosophy.

Henry Tam is a Director of the Cambridge-based Centre for Citizenship Development. He is also the Assistant Chief Executive of an East Anglian local authority, with responsibilities which include the development of community crime reduction policies. He is the author of *A Philosophical Study of the Criteria for Responsibility Ascriptions*.

Jennifer Trusted teaches philosophy in the Department of Continuing and Adult Education at the University of Exeter and is a tutor for the Open University. She is also Chief Examiner for Philosophy A level. Among her publications are *Free Will and Responsibility*, *Moral Principles and Social Values*, *Physics and Metaphysics*, and various articles on bioethical and environmental themes.

Gerry Wallace studied at Leeds and Oxford Universities and teaches philosophy at the University of Hull. He has written on topics in moral and political philosophy and the philosophy of religion.

Introduction: Ethical Theory and Ethical Practice

Brenda Almond

Philosophy has traditionally been concerned with the most fundamental questions about how we should live and how we should conduct our social life and political affairs. Current interest in applied ethics, then, can justifiably be seen as a return to what have always been proper preoccupations of philosophers, questions about ends or ideals as opposed to means or techniques. It can also be seen as a return to a more holistic and humanistic approach to philosophy, trends which have been submerged under the prevailing scientism – the preoccupation with experiment and with manipulation of the material world – that has dominated the greater part of the twentieth century.

It is true, though, that the questions with which contemporary applied ethics is concerned tend to be posed in specific and concrete terms rather than in broad general ones, and that the applied philosopher most typically engages directly with issues of current concern and debate. But this, too, is no new development. As another commentator has remarked, 'I can think of no British philosopher until this century . . . who was not deeply immersed in social and political and economic issues, none who were not "applied philosophers."'[1] Some of these preoccupations are old and could be said to have a perennial interest: the intimate relationships of family life, for example, or the issues of peace and war that are never far from the consciousness of human beings. Others are of more recent origin. They are the product of new technologies, revolutions in communication, new weapons of indiscriminate destruction, and an unprecedented increase in the impact of humans on their environment and support systems. Surprisingly, despite the vast explosion of the media, the ubiquitous presence of television, the ever-increasing facility in producing and reproducing data, and the expansion of communications, opportunities for genuinely open public debate on these matters are rarer than might be supposed. In radio and television, this is the era of the sound-bite, of carefully staged debates between extremists of known views measured in minutes and, even so, punctuated by the distracting, often inconsequential, interventions of an interviewer. It is a period when major newspapers and journals have their known political and ideological leanings, and publish, on the whole, only columns and correspondence which will please or interest their already committed readers. Applied ethics, in contrast, yields scope and space for discussion of issues of public policy which is conducted on the established philosophical principle of following the argument where it leads. Thus it represents not only an internal movement in philosophy, but also an opportunity for philosophy to play a role in public debate, addressing questions that are seldom treated in the depth they deserve, and not often from an impartial as opposed to a *parti pris* standpoint.

Of course, this is not the only contribution that philosophy can make in relation to practical moral problems: it can also bring clarity, critical analysis, and ingrained habits of careful evaluation of argument to debates and policy discussions. The applied philosopher, however, cannot accept this as a complete account of the role of philosophy, and is thus more likely to be associated with the 'popular' view of philosophy as partially normative: that is to say, as involving considered examination not only of what one is doing but also of what one *ought* to be doing. In terms of its theoretical underpinning, this may seem to generate another difficulty, since philosophy is often understood or even defined as the most abstract of human investigations, so that the use of the term 'applied' needs some justification. In the case of *moral* philosophy, it is now common to provide this by drawing a distinction between applied and theoretical ethics (sometimes called *metaethics*), the line being drawn at the point where analysis of moral concepts such as 'right' and 'good', 'responsibility' and 'blame' gives place to normative recommendations. In other words, ethical theory is limited to a kind of moral ontology or epistemology: a theory of moral knowledge which concerns itself with ethical language and its uses and conventions, while applied ethics is confined to the particular and the concrete. The first of these will include discussion of such metaethical theories as ethical realism, subjectivism, and relativism, while the second will, at its most particular, shrink to a focus on the individual case-study, and reasoning procedures resembling the ancient science of casuistry.[2] According to this account, the place of the major normative ethical theories – utilitarianism, virtue ethics, etc. – lies somewhere between these two extremes.

There is no doubt that drawing a line in this way may be useful for certain purposes: for arranging academic courses, for example, or for planning an orderly progression of private study. But this should not be allowed to obscure the fact that applied and theoretical ethics are not discrete but lie on a continuum from the particular to the general, the concrete to the abstract. There is, then, an underlying continuity. Nevertheless, applied ethics is marked out in style and approach from the kind of moral philosophy that has been dominant for the greater part of the twentieth century and is, indeed, still favoured by some of the more technicist linguistic philosophers. Two important reasons for this have already been mentioned: first of all, applied ethics gives greater attention to context and to the detailed texture of the situations in which ethical problems arise; and, second, its approach is more generously holistic; that is to say, it is much more ready to include the insights of psychology, sociology and other relevant areas of knowledge in its deliberations, and its practitioners are willing to work with others – in particular, professionals and those experienced in other fields – to arrive at solutions to ethical problems which are genuinely *informed* by the relevant facts.

These are recent developments but before exploring further the question of applied ethics in the present day and the ways in which it represents a new 'turn' in philosophy, some justification must be given for the claim that, despite this novelty, applied ethics has deep roots in the mainstream traditions of western philosophy.

The Roots of Applied Ethics

There are good grounds for claiming – if perhaps a little paradoxically – that the inception of applied philosophy coincides with that of the western philosophical tradition as a whole. Indeed, the first of the early Greek philosophers, Thales (*c*.585 BC), could well qualify as an applied philosopher, for he is recorded as having combined economic acumen with an interest in legal and political reform. Having been scorned for his speculative and impractical interests – he was so preoccupied with studying the stars that he fell down a well! – he decided, very successfully, to go into business to demonstrate that philosophical abstraction had its uses, and even a potential cash value.

Later schools of philosophy in ancient times – Pythagoreans, Epicureans, Stoics – offered their followers principles for living and even indeed distinctive codes of practice and guidance on life-style. Socrates, too, while he avoided preaching any dogma, did offer an imitable and influential example of a way of living appropriate to the pursuit of philosophy.

For both Plato (*c*.428–348 BC) and Aristotle (384–322 BC), ethical and political questions were posed in terms of such notions as the good for man, the ultimate good, or what is good in itself and ought to exist for its own sake. They believed that this enquiry would lead both to a way of life for the individual and to a conception of the good society. Plato set out his blueprint for the good society in detail in his dialogue the *Republic*, which covered not only political arrangements, but also the details of social living: education, sex and reproduction, art, literature and censorship.[3] While Plato believed that individuals could not fail to live by the ethical insights they gained, Aristotle, unlike Plato, allowed for the intervention of weakness of will to divert the person who has recognized the good from pursuing it. Even more than Plato, then, he had good reason to believe that an individual needed a good society in order to be both virtuous and happy.

There was, then, a flowering of ethical and social reflection in ancient times. But in the modern period, too, most philosophers sought to apply their ethical insights to particular issues. To mention only some of the most renowned, St Thomas Aquinas (1225–74) treated a range of practical topics including marriage and the family in his *Summa Theologiae*; John Locke (1632–1704) wrote on the issue of toleration and also on education; Immanuel Kant (1724–1804) treated the subject of suicide, and also the question of whether it is ever right to tell a lie from benevolent motives, questions which continue to be extremely pertinent in the area of medical ethics. Kant's 'applied ethics' is developed also in his *Metaphysic of Morals*: important themes there are the dignity of human nature, and the primacy of reason.

Jeremy Bentham (1748–1832) wrote on punishment, even formulating detailed plans for a new type of prison, to be called the Panopticon. He also wrote on legal and political reform and worked out a complex system for applying utilitarian theory to particular cases, the 'felicific calculus', by means of which pleasures could be weighed against each other, and long-term considerations could be balanced against short-term desires. Hegel (1770–1831) wrote on the family, and on punishment, and his dialectical system and philosophy of history inspired Karl Marx's (1818–83) political philosophy which, although in a rather different way from that of the philosophers so far mentioned here, could certainly be said to have important practical influence in the world.

The essay *On Liberty* by John Stuart Mill (1806–73) is generally considered the classic exposition of liberalism, expressing the spirit of open and pluralistic societies, and his writings on toleration, on paternalism and on feminism continue to be of interest in the present day. Mill also attempted to work out the detailed application of his influential distinction between self-regarding and other-regarding actions to such highly specific issues as alcohol abuse and the sale of poisons.[4] Finally, the views of the American pragmatist John Dewey (1859–1952) on education, which derived from a democratic and egalitarian political philosophy, exercised great practical influence on education systems in the USA and Britain, particularly shaping the progressive movement and the trend to child-centred learning. Dewey, however, lived long enough also to criticize the way in which the ideas of his early work *Democracy and Education* were applied in practice and to publish a later critique of progressivism entitled *Experience and Education*. This, too, continues to be a living debate.

Applied Ethics Today

Applied ethics, then, is not a *new* subject, as these and many other possible examples illustrate. Nevertheless, it suffered a period of neglect as the pendulum in philosophy swung from the speculative metaphysics of the nineteenth century to the materialistic scientism of the twentieth. A number of factors contributed to this return to applied ethics, dating from the mid-twentieth century and later. Perhaps the most important of these was the development of new kinds of medical technology, particularly those involving new methods of reproduction, and those affecting the end of life; another was the political controversy involved in America's participation in the Vietnam War, and the moral dilemmas felt by young Americans who faced the draft whilst disagreeing with its purpose. This led to new interest in issues such as civil disobedience and the limits of protest, as well as theories about when war is justified, and the legitimacy of using violence for political ends. Generating another strand of the evolving picture of applied ethics was the movement for animal rights launched in the 1970s with the publication of Peter Singer's *Animal Liberation* while, roughly contemporaneous with this, was dawning public awareness of environmental threats on a global scale which eventually made environmental ethics a subject of more than philosophical interest. Finally, and more recently, has been the growth of business and corporate ethics following a series of scandals of public and business life. Exposures of insider trading and doubts and dilemmas associated with whistle-blowing have been influential. Of course, malpractices and the publicity given to them are not the whole story: there is also a wish, in a more public world, to secure customer loyalty on the old-fashioned principle that honesty pays. For all these reasons, then, and many others, applied philosophy has today entered a new, more self-conscious and better-defined phase of development. It is this new image that dictates the structure and approach of this book.

The first section deals with immediate personal concerns, family and relationships, as well as with some of those who are excluded from the family, the young homeless; the second with ethics in relation to such professional areas as education, journalism and medicine; the third and fourth with the wider social and political dimensions in which public policy is most clearly involved; while the final section takes the broadest view of ethical obligation, including international obligations and the claims of future generations and of other species. Some of the views expressed here may be controversial – they are the views of the individual author in each case – but the object of the volume as a whole is to provide a basis for informed debate on the issues rather than to establish specific conclusions. It is also to demonstrate how, for many personal and individual decisions, as well as for many aspects of political policy, both national and international, a basic direction emerges from what is essentially a philosophical stance.

A certain consensus, then – ethical if not political – emerges about the way in which solutions are to be sought. Most of the writers represented here would reject the view that issues can be settled by a simple cost-benefit calculation – the utilitarian approach – nor, on the other hand, would they seek for answers in the kind of religious or ideological approach in which someone else's authority is substituted for the authority of one's own reason. Such a comment, however, only reinforces the point that 'applied' issues belong very closely in a context of underlying theoretical assumptions. Without a theoretical underpinning, arguments in applied ethics would be merely arbitrary, the outcome of the idiosyncratic preferences of their originator. *Ad hoc* solutions are, of course, perfectly legitimate contributions to public debate, but they do not belong under the heading of philosophy, nor even under the narrower heading of philosophical or applied ethics. Something must be said, therefore, about this background of ethical theory, since authors here presuppose knowledge of certain distinctions, which play an important if unarticulated role in their evaluation of issues.

Ethical Theories

First, what *is* ethics? And what is its relation to morality? And how is applied ethics distinguished from either of these? Views on these key definitions differ, but it is reasonable to say that if morality involves judging what is good or right, and ethics is more concerned with the reasoning behind such a judgement, applied ethics has more in common with the former than the latter. That is to say, it is willing to confront substantial questions of the form: what is it right or wrong to do in *this* situation? It is not, however, confined to this basic level of particularity, but moves on readily to the level of codes of practice, rules and principles, and ultimately to that of overarching ethical theories. It is important to notice that the questions it asks at these higher levels of generality are not, What codes or principles *do* people in fact adopt? or, What theory is most widely supported? This would be sociology or social anthropology rather than ethics. Instead, at the level of principles it will ask which principles we *ought* to adopt, and at the level of theory, which theory is to be accepted and which rejected.

Until relatively recently, despite differences of religious or ideological background, it might have been possible to assume a common moral approach, and accepted norms of moral behaviour could, in general, have been taken as a starting-point for ethical reasoning. In the present day, such moral consensus cannot be presupposed and it is more common to find (sometimes tacit and unconscious) rejection of the very notion of moral principles and moral values. An uncritical empiricism may lead to a presumption in favour of pragmatism and utilitarianism. But absolutist approaches are by no means inconsistent with mainstream philosophical ethics, even if in practice the defence of an absolute conception of morality against relativist, subjectivist and utilitarian approaches is often associated with a religious perspective. There is no theoretical reason why this should be so, but in practice many writers on applied ethics do adopt an approach which is both utilitarian and secular. These include such well-known writers as the Australian philosopher Peter Singer and the Oxford philosopher R. M. Hare, whose prescriptivist theory combines utilitarianism with Kantian universalizability.[5]

Part of the reason for the dominance of utilitarianism may be that this is an approach in which self-interest plays a key role, and self-interest, of course, needs little justification. For the utilitarian, however, a multiplicity of individual interests – what is good for each member of society – make up the *common* interest – what is good for all, or at least for most. For the utilitarian, then, the ethically right action is whatever maximizes the welfare or happiness of the greatest number of people affected by it. Utilitarianism is a form of ethical *consequentialism* in that it makes right or wrong depend on the consequences or outcome of an action, as opposed to either the means by which it is achieved or the nature of the action itself. Against such a view may be set the perception of morality as imposing some constraints on the *way* in which we try to achieve our aims, and even as setting some kinds of action beyond the boundaries of ethical consideration. Thus killing, lying, stealing, are not, according to this more traditional view, to be justified by appeal to any good results they may produce.

Some forms of utilitarianism seek to avoid these difficulties by pointing out that rules such as those against lying, promise-breaking or killing are themselves beneficial, and therefore are themselves capable of being justified by appeal to the 'greatest happiness' principle; this was the position taken by J. S. Mill in his essay *Utilitarianism*. Others posit an imaginary 'social contract' in which people, from self-interest, agree on the rules likely to be most generally satisfactory, even if this sometimes means some personal sacrifice for the individual. John Rawls's *A Theory of Justice* (1971), which adopted a position of this type, inaugurated a new era in ethics, in its exploration of the implications of such a theory for economics, law and political theory.

In contrast, the idea of morality as absolutely binding is especially associated with Kant's moral philosophy; its basis was the principle of univerzalisability, expressed by Kant in his Categorical Imperative: Act only on a maxim which you can at the same time will to be a universal law.[6] For Kant, too, the question of motive was primary, and he distinguished between actions which *conformed* to the moral law and those done from duty or *for the sake of* the law. This doctrine presents the rigorous and binding nature of morality in terms of principles; but that idea can also be expressed by other moral notions: Kant himself also expressed it in terms of the important notion of people as deserving respect as ends in themselves rather than merely as means to other people's ends. But it is also embodied in the idea of universal rights which set absolute limits to the ways in which people or any other rational beings may treat each other.

A quite different but extremely influential approach is the ethic of care associated with some feminist philosophers: on the basis of research revealing that women tend to approach ethical dilemmas in a way which pays more account to context and detail and less to abstract principle and justice, a number of writers, most prominently Carol Gilligan, have argued that there is a theoretical ethic of care – of responsibility to particular others – that represents a feminist alternative to an abstract morality of principles, rights and justice. This approach is sometimes favoured for dealing with the kind of 'hard cases' encountered in, for example, health care and social work. Similarly, the approach known as 'virtue ethics' with its emphasis on seeking the good in particular situations, and seeking to develop virtues of character, may seem well adapted to many of the areas of interest to applied ethics, including the workplace and the hospital. Contemporary writers, including, for example, Elizabeth Anscombe and Philippa Foot, are associated with the view that morality relates to human well-being – 'flourishing' – and that this gives moral claims objective status: a right to be assessed as true or false.

Underlying all the practical issues, then, that will be considered here, are questions about justice, rights, utility, virtue and community. In a sense, it is true, as some commentators have remarked, that there cannot be an ethics which is *not* 'applied' since on the one hand, theoretical concepts like these are not to be viewed as mere abstractions, and, on the other, 'applications' of moral theory need to be rooted in the soil of a richer and more abstract awareness. It is not, however, the whole story: there is room for a conception of applied ethics as an area of enquiry which aims to supply clearer perceptions of right and wrong, with a view to embodying these insights in manners and institutions.

Is applied ethics, then, conservative or radical? Reactionary or revolutionary? The answer to this is that it can be either. Reflection may lead to a desire to seek to change things for the better, but it can also lead to a wish to guard what is best from the past against change. The methods which applied ethics can make its own may be compared to those of a designer who starts with a blueprint, but has to adapt it to the materials to hand and to the situations in which it is required, a method described by a number of philosophers – in particular Rawls – as that of *reflective equilibrium*. The intuitions of the ordinary person who has a basic regard for morality are measured against principles, which then have to be revised in the light of those intuitions. This is to be distinguished from the process favoured by orthodox utilitarian applied philosophers, who begin with a broad theory, possibly one entailing more specific principles, and then seek to apply this to particular cases.

One obstacle to pursuing many of these approaches is what has been called the fact/value distinction. In a famous passage of his *Treatise*, David Hume (1711–76) attacked arguments which seek to derive an *ought* from an *is*.[7] Later, too, G. E. Moore (1873–1958) argued that to identify moral characteristics with 'natural' or empirical ones is to commit a 'naturalistic fallacy'.[8] But the idea that facts and values are to be kept apart is less prevalent outside the English-speaking world; the notion of *praxis* is familiar from various continental traditions, including for example, the theories of Karl Marx, the philosophy of the Frankfurt School, and the writings of Jurgen Habermas (b.1929); while the idea of the philosopher as *engagé* – as playing a part in the world – is an important assumption of French existentialist philosophers such as Jean-Paul Sartre (1905–80), as well as of more recent French philosophers of the New Right. But these sources have also produced a different kind of challenge to the notion of applied ethics as an impartial and essentially reason-based approach to ethical and social issues – the analytic approach common to most of the contributors to this volume. Objections to the conception of universal moral norms and to foundationalist procedures in reasoning (the 'postmodernist' challenge) are associated with recent developments in Marxist theory, with certain feminist approaches to ethics and epistemology, and with the deconstructionist movement. These schools of thought may also adopt an analysis of power-structures in society incompatible with belief in individual freedom of action, which is itself a necessary condition of morality.

The reader will not be able to explore this rich mine of theory and basic philosophy further in the present volume, but will be wise to bear it in mind whilst engaging with the specific concerns of each individual chapter.

The Contributions

Applied ethics is presented here as an expanding area of thought and concern, and this is reflected in the arrangement of the chapters, which follow a logical development from the more personal and immediate concerns of the individual to the broadest and most extensive issues of public and political life. One of the main arenas of applied ethics, the ethics of the professions, is seen here as occupying a central and key position in this progression; for this is the area where the individual functions in an intermediate organization between the personal domains of family and neighbourhood, and the public domains of state or political community.

Most societies, however, throughout human history have turned on the linchpin of the family, and this is the starting-point here. Today, many of the most common assumptions about the relations between men and women and the raising of children are subjects of debate. In the opening chapter, Mary Midgley and Judith Hughes describe two models of the family: the traditionalist model based on the idea of the family as a solid unit consisting of man, woman and dependent children, and an individualist model which regards each person as a separate autonomous social atom with rights against all others. The authors argue that both models are unrealistic and that the new element today is that our age combines romantic individualism with a high degree of transitoriness and mobility. Whilst accepting that households break up under these circumstances, they point out that children, and most adults, too, still need lasting relationships.

Some would say that when the talk is of personal relationships, the key concept is that of love. This is the theme of Paul Gregory's contribution. In the West, he suggests, the idea of love has come to occupy a predominant position in value systems, jostling for supremacy with the notion of the good. The philosophical problems that today are most likely to impose themselves on any reflective, sensitive person have to do in the first place with the recognition of love and its differentiation from counterfeits, such as infatuation, or possessiveness. There are also darker questions. How does love relate to power? To hatred? Is love indeed, even the real thing, always desirable, always good?

These controversies about the family, and the re-evaluation of personal relationships, are closely linked to new social understandings of gender and its implications for sexual relations between men and women. In the light of recent policy developments on sexual harassment, Moira Gatens argues that there is a need for a rethinking of present possibilities for new ethical relations between men and women – relations that are not simply extensions of the familial, paternalist, etc., but which place greater emphasis on women's ethical responsibility for themselves.

But however relationships are structured, there will always be some people who for one reason or another are excluded from the network of family relations. Michael Parker discusses these issues by focusing on the problem of youth homelessness as it affects those who have left care, or are mentally ill, and who are estranged from their families. He explores the ethical and philosophical considerations resulting from the rising incidence of youth homelessness in the countries of Western Europe and the United States, pointing out that there is little agreement about either the rights of the young people themselves, or about the allocation of responsibility for their protection.

Education is often put forward as a panacea for the problems considered in Part I, and at the beginning of Part II, which is concerned with various areas of professional or public life, John Haldane discusses the nature of education as a social practice concerned with the transmission of certain traditional values. He argues that education is a matter of conserving bodies of knowledge, sentiment and conduct as these are embodied in traditional practices.

Another area of public life which reflects social values and attitudes is the world of journalism and the media. In Chapter 6, Andrew Belsey discusses the relation between the free circulation of information and opinion on the one hand, and the democratic process on the other. His discussion focuses, in particular, on the contrasting reporting practices of the United States and Britain.

The media are frequently involved in scrutiny of the world of business. Is this perhaps, because life in business (and commerce) puts a special strain on virtuous living? This question is central to Jennifer Jackson's discussion in the next chapter. She argues that two features of business life are responsible for this: its inherent competitiveness, and its promotion of consumerism. She finds, however, that when the virtues of justice, charity and temperance are looked at more closely in a business context, the apparent difficulties vanish, and that, after all, business life is not necessarily incompatible with virtue.

Dick Holdsworth considers the role of science and technology in society and argues that utilitarian calculation is particularly inappropriate as an ethical approach to the problems that arise in these areas. This is because, in these areas, the future is essentially open. The scientist, by definition, investigates the unknown, so that policy decisions must, of necessity, be taken from behind a kind of Rawlsian 'veil of ignorance'.

Science policy and medical practice are involved, too, in the subject of the next chapter, in which Ruth Chadwick discusses the wide-ranging implications of the project of analysing the human genome. She argues that the gene revolution has revolutionary implications for (a) how we regard ourselves as a species and (b) for bioethics itself. In particular, she points out that Human Genome Analysis raises ethical issues regarding the acquisition, control, applications, and meaning of genetic information about human beings, and that these have implications for such practices as genetic screening, counselling and gene therapy. Chadwick suggests that the ethical principle of autonomy has an important application in this area, but that genetics, with its emphasis on relatedness, points the way to a new communitarian perspective.

K. W. M. Fulford discusses the issue of non-voluntary treatment in the context of psychiatric medicine. He rejects a narrow 'medical' model, and argues that values and value judgements are implicit within the concept of mental illness.

The life of the community is protected and ordered by a framework of law. In Part III, Henry Tam discusses the condition essential to the administration of justice: that we should know what it is to attribute responsibility for a crime. This is also an issue of particular relevance to the problem of how to deal with the psychopathic criminal, and Michael Bavidge and Andrew Cole ask whether it is right to regard psychopathy as morally neutral, and explore some of the difficulties involved in treating psychopaths in the community. Rehabilitation, they point out, must inevitably take the form of reintegration into communal ways of living. But is the appropriate way to secure this punishment, or is it therapy?

In the next chapter Robert Campbell considers some of the issues most frequently discussed in another important area of medical practice. These include problems also relevant to the earlier discussion of psychiatric medicine, such as the model of medical treatment adopted: the medico-scientific one which sees disease and illness as technical problems, and the 'nursing' or 'caring' model. Campbell, however, applies this distinction to a number of sensitive problems surrounding the end of life: the treatment of the terminally ill or those in irreversible coma.

Finally, the ethical problems facing those who must enforce the legal system and bring criminals to justice, the police, is seldom given the attention it deserves. In Chapter 14 John Kleinig identifies a number of these issues, including the police use of deadly force (shooting and high speed pursuits), the use of non-deadly force: handcuffing, use of batons, tear gas, dogs, etc. He suggests that the moral considerations here relate to questions of necessity and proportionality. There are also, he points out, important questions of fairness, and questions about the legitimacy of using deception, and also means such as wire-tapping and the use of informers, to gain information.

These issues point in the direction of a wider discussion of the social and political dimensions of social controversies and this forms the focus for Part IV. Tony Coady discusses the issue of nationality and ethnicity, and the chapters by Brenda Almond and Tibor Machan address the wider political agenda in terms of the issue of liberty or community. Brenda Almond argues that liberalism is often viewed as a philosophy promoting moral neutralism, and in consequence the decline in social conditions today, e.g. crime, family breakdown and deteriorating cultural and moral standards, are often attributed to liberalism. She argues that this critique and consequent moves to communitarian alternatives, are unnecessary: liberalism is fully able, even in its minimalist classical formulation, to deal with these ills on the basis of supporting individual rights and enforcing contracts between individuals.

In his contribution, Tibor Machan points out that capitalism is often thought to be morally inferior to socialist alternatives, even though, he suggests, it has in fact served human beings well. Apart from its usefulness as a system in which productivity is encouraged, Machan argues that capitalism is also the economic organization that is most consistent with the requirements of a decent, just human community. He goes on to take up several moral challenges raised against capitalism, arguing that it is the system that allows humans to live *well*, to make the most of their lives.

One major area in which the debate between communitarians and free marketeers is crystallized is that of health. Many nations are asking, in view of spiralling costs and demands, what should be the role of the state in relation to the health-care needs of its citizens. Donna Dickenson points out that markets in health and social care are usually advocated on grounds that they are more efficient than central planning. She asks both whether this is so and whether efficiency is the right criterion to apply, in terms of social justice and individual needs. She points out that efficiency is a utilitarian goal, and that a common philosophical argument against utilitarianism is that it may disadvantage minorities. In the health field, these disadvantaged groups may include the elderly and the mentally ill.

Part V moves out into the wider context. First, in considering national and international obligations of the more advantaged groups or nations, Jennifer Trusted points out that 'rich' and 'poor' are relative and ambiguous terms, but argues that this is not a reason for dismissing poverty as unimportant. Nevertheless, she suggests that it would be wrong to make facile assumptions about its causes, as these have implications for the answer that might be given to such questions as, Is moral obligation in relation to the poor, particularly the distant poor, based on duty or compassion? Should the focus, in any case, of either duty or compassion be need at home, or need abroad? And are the obligations that are recognized here the kind that should be discharged by individuals, or by governments, or by aid agencies and charities?

Unfortunately it is war and sometimes terrorism rather than peaceful assistance to each other that often characterize the relations of nations and groups, and it is this that forms the focus of Gerry Wallace's contribution. Since it seems that war is sometimes seen as morally justified but terrorism not, he asks whether terrorism involves some extra dimension of evil. Much of our thinking about the morality of war, he points out, is based on the Just War doctrine which divides questions about the morality of war into questions about (a) the justice of the cause of the war and (b) justice in the conduct of war, a key requirement being that no matter how just the cause, non-combatants can never be targeted. In his chapter, Wallace discusses the commonly held view that terrorism inevitably violates this condition and therefore is always immoral.

These issues of peace and war, wide though they are, still concern in the main only human beings. Many people today believe that the scope of the moral community is wider than this, and in his chapter, Stephen Clark argues against making a firm distinction between human and non-human objects – between Beast and Human. This inherited attitude, he suggests, is the product of the history of humans as hunter-gatherers and of imperial and now industrial societies. He proposes a deconstruction of the notion of Humanity, opening the way for a new construction of moral community.

Such a construction is implicit in the final contribution, that of Robin Attfield, who considers ecological problems, and the need for an appropriate, possibly transformed value-theory. In particular, he discusses Aldo Leopold's proposal for a new ethic and the way in which this has been developed in the movement known as Deep Ecology. He argues for an internationalist and cosmopolitan approach which is related to the aim of sustainable development and the approach of 'comprehensive weighing'.

Whilst the authors represented here, then, have all treated some particular issue in depth and from a particular point of view, readers will find that each chapter is intended to be comprehensively informative about the area with which it deals. Some of the information, however, may be contained not in the text, but in the detailed Notes and Reading Guides accompanying each chapter. Authors also indicate, in their Reading Guide, where relevant discussions in classical philosophical literature are to be found. There are also separate bibliographies at the end of the volume for each subject-area. The field of applied ethics is wide, but we hope that the reader will find that this volume opens up its rich vistas in many different and specific areas of practical enquiry.

NOTES

1 Skillen, 'Welfare State vs. Welfare Society?', in Almond and Hill (eds), p. 209. Compare also Von Wright's comment: 'Anyone who thinks that a sharp distinction can be maintained between metaethics and normative ethics is invited to consider the nature of such works as Aristotle's *Nicomachean Ethics*, Kant's *Grundlegung zur Metaphysik der Sitten* or John Stuart Mill's *Utilitarianism*' (*Varieties of Goodness*, p. 3).
2 While 'casuistry' is today a derogatory term meaning sophistry or quibbling, the tradition is a respectable one which developed from the efforts of theologians to work out the detailed applications of religious texts and teachings. War, sexual ethics and usury were all thought appropriate areas for this exercise.
3 Plato was criticized for the totalitarian nature of his proposals by Karl Popper in *The Open Society and its Enemies*, and also by J. Talmon in *The Origins of Totalitarian Democracy*.
4 Mill's essay *On Liberty* is gathered with *On the Subjection of Women*, *Considerations on Representative Government* and *Utilitarianism* in a volume edited by John Gray.
5 See Singer, *Practical Ethics*, 2nd edn and Hare, *Moral Thinking*.
6 See Kant, in Paton, *The Moral Law*.
7 Hume, *Treatise of Human Nature*.
8 Moore, *Principia Ethica*.

READING GUIDE

For guidance in the areas of applied ethics covered in this volume, see the separate Reading Guides at the end of each chapter. Amongst a number of collections of more specialized readings which could be useful are: *Applied Philosophy: Morals and Metaphysics in Contemporary Debate*, edited by B. Almond and D. Hill; *Applied Ethics* edited by E. R. Winkler and J. R. Coombs; and *Moral Problems*, edited by J. Rachels.

P. Singer's edited volume *Applied Ethics* reprints some classic writings, including Hume on suicide and Mill on the death penalty.

For a general introduction to ethical theory see *Good and Evil: an Absolute Conception* by R. Gaita or *Living the Good Life: Introduction to Moral Philosophy* by G. Graham. Richard Norman has written a clear and readable account of some classical ethical theories in *The Moral Philosophers*.

PART I

The Personal Dimension: Family and Relationships

1

Trouble with Families?

Mary Midgley and Judith Hughes

Distress Signals

The family, it is said, is in a state of crisis. From the right and from the left the lamentations pour thick and fast. Agreeing that the family has 'broken down', experts lay the blame, singly or severally, on irresponsible fathers, selfish mothers, poverty and deprivation, politicians, the decline of religious belief, incompetent teachers, lax law courts or junk food. Whatever the cause or causes, the state, it is said, can no longer support feckless women who have babies out of wedlock. And in any case, there is something terribly wrong going on in contemporary western societies. We need (these critics argue) a return to basics, which includes a return to the image – projected in a thousand Hollywood movies of the mid-twentieth century – of happy wedded couples producing children in their twenties and staying together in conjugal bliss until death do them part. This is recommended as the main, perhaps the only, way to solve the problem of juvenile crime and to cut the rising social security bill at a stroke. It will also make the children happy and self-fulfilled.

That, anyway, is the story. And even those who do not share the partisan beliefs fuelling parts of it may still share a general unease and suspect a moral decline. Old values of respect for age, privacy and property, care of the young, politeness to those in authority, loyalty, truthfulness and patriotism are seen every day to have lost their force. And now we mourn them.

It is the job of sociologists, not philosophers, to enquire into the facts supporting these allegations, and the job of historians to decide how far the golden past age that is now invoked ever existed. But when the decline of the family is identified with a moral decline, philosophers need to ask what such a thing would be. They need, too, to question just what model or ideal of the family is at issue here. For when we think of moral decline as identical with the decline of traditional family structures, values and practices we need first to note that all these have been under attack from many quarters, at least since the time of Plato.

The firm pronouncements of public figures today rarely reflect those past criticisms. For instance, the British Home Secretary Michael Howard, speaking at the Conservative Party Conference in October 1993, said flatly, 'We must emphasize our belief that the traditional two-parent family is best. Best for the parents, best for society, and above all best for children.' But many philosophers, political theorists, psychologists and social reformers have not shared that confidence. From all these quarters, families have been castigated as undermining the state and society and as causing harm to the individuals within them. Precisely because the family is seen as a powerful element in society, it has the resources to subvert it; precisely because it is thought to hold so much sway over individuals, it has the power to oppress them. More recently, the premisses, though not the conclusion, have changed to suggest that, far from being all-powerful, the family is positively incompetent to undertake those roles which its advocates claim it fulfils.

Plato's suggestion in the *Republic* that the Guardians, though not the general populace, should hold wives and children in common was prompted partly by his eugenic beliefs, but mainly by his hope that eliminating family ties and interests would remove a major cause of quarrels.[1] Quarrels debilitate not just the individuals but the state itself, for the good state, like the good man, is a harmonious whole. What binds the state is that individuals in a community experience pleasures and pains in unison. And this is indeed a phenomenon which we see repeatedly in contemporary communities who have a common reaction of horror to a child murder or a terrorist bombing, a shared sense of jubilation as the local football team makes good. Communities bound, as Plato says, by shared pleasure or pain are strong and united and remain so as long as the individuals within them do not cut the bonds by the simple expedient of having each 'his own feelings apart'.

That city, says Plato, is best managed 'in which the greatest number say "mine" and "not mine" with the same meaning about the same thing'. Hence the Guardians would couple only at the behest of the state and would not know who their own parents or children were. Women would suckle any baby as it was handed to them. All would treat all as fathers, mothers, sons and daughters. They would then 'not use the word "mine" each of different things, but of the same; one will not drag into his own house whatever goods he can get apart from the rest; another will not drag into his own separate house a separate wife and separate children'. This is to make them 'free from quarrels and factions, as far as human quarrels come from possessing wealth or children or kindred'.

Plato is not saying that we should not say 'mine' and 'not mine' at all, but that we should say these things of the same things, not different ones. This is the thinking behind all genuine movements which aim to establish communes. The idea is not to abolish the family but to extend it. The same values of loyalty and concern, affection and responsibility are not removed but applied to a wider community.

These values run into serious trouble only when the community is extended beyond the grasp of the moral imagination so that the language of family relationship can no longer signify, or when the state itself claims entirely to replace the other individuals with whom one is in community. There is then a corresponding shift in values. Communism and fascism reduce the terminology of relationship to 'brother' and 'sister' or replace it with words like 'citizen', or 'comrade' or 'fellow countryman'. At this point, concepts such as filial duty, parental protectiveness, family loyalty finally vanish.

These moves can be, and usually are, made on nationalistic or party grounds. But there is a different, more drastic kind of rationale which has developed along philosophical rather than political lines and which attacks more deeply the insidiousness of the possessive 'my' and 'mine'. On this account, the problem with strong personal emotions such as love, which are known to occur sometimes in families, is that they destroy the impartiality needed for being a truly moral agent. A graphic illustration of this view is the celebrated ruling of the political philosopher William Godwin that 'pure unadulterated justice' compels one to save from a burning building a gifted benefactor of mankind, such as Archbishop Fénelon, rather than his chambermaid, even if that chambermaid happens to be one's own wife or mother. Godwin asks,

> What magic is there in the pronoun 'my', to overturn the decision of everlasting truth? My wife or my mother may be a fool or a prostitute, malicious, lying or dishonest. If they be, of what consequence is it that they are mine?[2]

This second line of attack shifts the focus from the harm which families may do to outsiders to their power to corrupt their own members, though some people might think that the denial of such ties was itself also a form of corruption.

Bad for Everybody?

Other theorists, however, have taken a still more drastic line, seeing family ties, not just as corrupting, but as deadly to the whole personality. Thus the British 'anti-psychiatrist' R. D. Laing argued, in his study of neuroses, that families, far from helping to cure the mental breakdowns of their members, were to a large extent the cause of them. Even schizophrenia and other psychoses were, in Laing's view, to be understood as simply natural responses to unbearable family pressures.

Plenty of other arguments have been used to show how unsuitable a social environment families can provide for men, for women and for children – how they can destroy all three. Until recently, sympathy was usually reserved for the males, for whom marriage was held to mark the end of most of the desirable features of life. 'Times are changed with him who marries,' wrote R. L. Stevenson; 'there are no more by-path meadows, where you may innocently linger, but the road lies long and straight and dusty to the grave.' But it is not only pleasure which flees. 'In marriage, a man becomes slack and selfish, and undergoes a fatty degeneration of his moral being.'[3] Disraeli's maxim that 'Every woman should marry – and no man' echoed this view. Not until the twentieth century was there a popular and sustained counter-claim made by women themselves. But if the family limits and represses creativity and individuality in men, how much more must it do this to women? For women not only take on extra responsibilities at marriage but change their names, may lose their jobs, and are likely to bear and rear children. Married women, it is claimed, are more likely to suffer mental breakdown than married men, while unmarried women are less likely than bachelors to suffer the same fate.

As for children, more of them are abused by members of their own families than by outsiders. For them, the family is a dangerous lottery whose closeness and privacy can hide and protect abuses just as surely as it can provide a safe and reassuring haven. Cycles of abuse and of criminality may perpetuate themselves through generations. According to this argument, if the family can be a force for great moral good through its inculcation of high moral standards, so it can be an equal force for bad, and it often is.

As if all this were not enough, the family also faces the opposite charge, not that it does bad things well, but that it does good things badly. The professionalization of education and child-rearing has steadily undermined the role of parents in the upbringing of children to the point where they have been deliberately excluded from playing traditional roles. For centuries, parents who could do so taught their children to read, inculcated moral values, socialized infants and passed on skills and folk wisdom. The state, quite rightly, stepped in to help those whose own skills or knowledge were deficient in these areas. But of course, it did not stop there. The professionals, not content merely to fill the gaps, began to claim exclusive rights and expertise over the whole business. Parents are still often discouraged from teaching their pre-school children to read, and sometimes expressly forbidden to do so. Nursery education is increasingly seen, not just as a desirable option for children without siblings or for children of working parents, but as a prerequisite of anyone's happy and successful development. State and Church sometimes ignore the role of parents in disputing over which of them ought to be teaching moral values to children.

Through increasing professionalization, then, the family escapes the charge of wickedness only to face the lesser accusation of incompetence.

Locating the Trouble

So, if families are damaging, damaged or both, we may wonder why there should now be complaints that all these efforts to destroy or undermine them seem to have succeeded. Yet the 'breakdown of the family' is indeed now seen as the central problem. Is it emerging that the benefits which families bestow on individuals and society do, after all, outweigh the catalogue of ills which we have been considering? This 'breakdown' is currently often identified with the increase in divorce, separation and single parenthood, but we should notice that the concern is not new. In an earlier generation, the move from the extended to the nuclear family was seen as a cause of isolation, bad manners and a diminishing sense of respect for the old. It then seemed that it was not the absence of a particular individual, father or mother, which was the problem but the absence of a network of related individuals. Moreover, the messages of distress are mixed; is the family too extended or too nuclear? Divorce sometimes helps to recreate extended families by generating wider, looser networks of step-relatives. But far from being welcomed, divorce is in general blamed as a cause of disaster.

Modern Mobility

What, then, is the central trouble? It is certainly not only that the state has to pay more for the upkeep of children. People do feel that something important is fading. Essentially, this important thing is surely the closeness, the emotional security, the firm sense of belonging that families everywhere have usually had.

But if we ask what has loosened that closeness, we see at once that huge changes in the wider world during the last two centuries were bound to weaken such links. Before the Industrial Revolution, nearly all human beings stayed put throughout their lives with a single set of people. Though there were always some traders and travellers and administrators who knew about matters at a distance, most people neither saw nor envisaged any other way of life than that of their parents. Now, most people in the wealthier nations feel mobile from the very start of their lives. They see many alternative ways of life and meet any number of strangers. They are brought up knowing that they may go anywhere, and also that customs in their own lands are constantly changing.

All this mobility is no doubt seen as a welcome freedom, but of course people do not move just for pleasure. Industry sucks people from place to place, dropping them at its own convenience, not theirs. Workless people drift into big towns. And the sheer numbers who are swirling around in this way are constantly growing. Neighbourhoods, which used to back and strengthen family bonds, are weakened and replaced by crowds of strangers. Networks of various sizes, both formal and informal, that used to structure life in clans, villages, churches, schools, clubs, societies, political parties and other group-ings have become weaker, more transient, harder to maintain. Workplaces have an increasingly fast turnover of staff. As all these wider patterns shift around, families are tending to be left as the last remaining unit that is available to maintain whatever stability is needed. This naturally puts great strain on personal affection, which is often left to do, in isolation, the connective work that used to be shared over a whole social network.

Individualist Euphoria

In this way, practical changes tend strongly to break up groups and to loosen bonds of all kinds. But at the level of theory too, powerful ideas have been working to justify, encourage and celebrate this shift. Since the early Enlight-enment, individualism has had great influence both in right-wing and left-wing thought. Western civilization has, in fact, developed a most unusual ideal of personal freedom, an ideal which often startles people from other sophisticated civilizations such as those of Asia. This ideal of freedom has powered the West's highest achievements and has certainly also produced theorists from Rousseau through Mill to Sartre, and modern right-wing thinkers have cel-ebrated the value of independence and the dignity of isolation. As Nietzsche put it,

> Do I counsel you to love your neighbour? I rather counsel you to flee from your neighbour and to love that which is farthest.
> Higher than love for one's neighbour is love for the remote and for the future. And I hold love for things and phantoms higher than love for men.[4]

In that spirit, during the twentieth century, a whole flood of anti-family novels, plays and films has warned the young of the need to isolate themselves and to reject interfering relatives, particularly parents. As Samuel Butler complained in *The Way of All Flesh*,

> Why should the generations overlap one another at all? Why cannot we be buried as eggs in neat little cells with ten or twenty thousand pounds each wrapped round us in Bank of England notes, and wake up, as the sphex wasp does, to find that its papa and mamma have not only left ample provision at its elbow, but have been eaten by sparrows some time before it began to live consciously on its own account?[5]

More seriously, the sociologist Edmund Leach laid it down in his 1967 Reith Lecture that, 'far from being the basis of the good society, the family, with all its narrow privacy and tawdry secrets, is the source of all our discontent'. Or, as the English poet Philip Larkin put it (in 'This Be The Verse'),

> They fuck you up, your mum and dad.
> They may not mean to, but they do.
> They fill you with the faults they had
> And add some extra, just for you.

This warning is certainly worth having. They may indeed do so. But if they were not there, would whoever else was in charge of us have done things any better? The memoirs of those brought up in orphanages do not suggest so. Small children everywhere form strong attachments, invariably expecting more attention than their carers can possibly give, and absorbing their faults as well as their virtues. They cannot, however, be left alone. Unlike wasps, we human beings need to be looked after and inducted into a culture. This is a most difficult, complex and exhausting process, one which stretches many parents' endurance beyond its limit. And culture itself is not an assault on our freedom, as romantics have often suggested. Without a culture, we would not be human at all. It is the deep, indispensable mine from which we draw most of our treasures, including, of course, our distinctive conception of freedom itself, and the concepts we use in criticizing current customs.

Should Families be Wider?

One-sided moralizing of the kind we have been considering is common. There is nothing unusual even about the individualistic humbug of claiming that radically dependent creatures such as ourselves can exist in social isolation. Pendulums, however, need to come back gently from these extremes if the point of the original campaign is not to be lost. Today, we certainly do still value individual freedom highly. We want to control domestic as well as political tyranny. But that does not mean we must endorse the violent exaltation of solitude urged on us by philosophical prophets of individualism.

Not all philosophical attacks on 'the family', however, have aimed at this complete isolation of the individual. Instead, theorists such as Plato and Marx wanted to widen the sense of belonging to include the whole community. They were protesting against the narrow, exclusive selfishness of the bourgeois family, which wasted people's efforts in strife. It was *in order to* cure this quarrelsome narrowness that Plato wanted all his Guardians to form one vast, undifferentiated family. His methods were extreme, but not his aims. Many of those who set up the Israeli kibbutzim and other communal groups have also wished to widen family feeling rather than to destroy it. So do many feminists, though some of them are indeed more radical, more individualistic libertarians.

Notoriously, however, actual attempts to put Plato's principles into practice always founder on the unregenerate partiality of human emotions. Neither parents nor children can play their roles without strong individual attachments. In orphanages, carers who try to be impartial find that the babies themselves frustrate them by attaching themselves firmly from the earliest age to one particular carer. We are born profoundly partial. Stoic philosophers tried very hard to eradicate these special attachments, calling for *apatheia*, a general, equable absence of passion. Thus Epictetus:

> The will of nature is to be learnt from matters which do not concern ourselves . . . Has another man's child died, or his wife? Who is there will not say, *It is the lot of humanity?* But when his own may die, then straightway it is, *Alas, wretched that I am!* But we should bethink ourselves of what we felt on hearing of others in the same plight.[6]

The Stoic idea was not that we should extend our strong feeling to include others, but that we should extend indifference from their case to our own. This singularly negative ideal had a deep and long-lasting effect on Enlightenment thinking, an effect that is most obvious in Spinoza (1632–77) but is still potent in Kant (1724–1804). Bishop Butler (1692–1752), however, shrewdly remarked that it is much easier to suppress affection in this way than it is to produce justice. As he put it,

> In general, experience will show that, as want of appetite to food supposes and proceeds from some bodily disease, so the apathy the Stoics talk of as much supposes or is accompanied with somewhat amiss in the moral character, in that which is the health of the mind. Those who formerly aimed at this upon the foot of philosophy appear to have had better success in eradicating the affections of tenderness and compassion than they had with the passions of envy, pride and resentment: these latter, at best, were but concealed, and that imperfectly too.[7]

Humans, it seems, can reach wider loyalties only through a gradual, careful expansion which has to start from vigorous personal and local bonds. Genuine, Buddhist-style non-attachment which converts affection into universal compassion may be the terminus of human striving, but it cannot possibly be its starting-point.

Normally, human loyalties must develop through a widening series of interlinked circles, starting with those around one, who are usually relatives, and following out wider networks of connections. Explicit reasons for preferring one network over another only emerge later when conflicts arise between different loyalties. Thus, someone brought up inside a positive, articulate family, political party, Church and state is likely to be provided with plenty of conflicts between the various ideals which these units represent, but also with plenty of material for resolving these conflicts and finding a way forward. Frictions between the various units can be fruitful sources of reform. By contrast, people who are brought up in a family that is socially isolated will lack that material, and they may have much more difficulty in understanding their whole social situation.

What is it to be mine or yours?

The dilemma about families is, then, a real one. Close personal relations do involve ambivalence. They make possible the worst as well as the best in human life. People brought near to each other do collide and often hurt one another gravely. The psychiatrist R. D. Laing and the campaigners against child-abuse are right to stress the risks involved in individual parenting. The difficulty is that no one has ever found a real alternative, an infallible, impartial, non-intimate way of rearing babies.

Can the concept of intimacy be cleared of its connection with the notion of *possession*? Is there, as Godwin suggested, something hopelessly corrupting about the use of the pronoun 'my' here? Is there something wrong with the whole concept of 'belonging' when it is applied to people?

Certainly owning or possessing people can sound wrong. Yet nobody, surely, wants to be 'disowned', or to belong nowhere? The trouble seems to be that this idea of possession or belonging covers an enormously wide spectrum. Plato was right to draw attention to the use of possessive pronouns such as 'mine'. These words range from unalarming examples such as *my shoes* and *my cup*, through *my house, my trees* and *my land* to much more mysterious cases like *my cat, my colleagues, my friends, my mother, my children* and *my country*. At one end, there seems to be a simple property relation based on contract, a relation that gives total control and no duties. At the other end lies a set of most complex personal relations involving deep respect and responsibility. And these relations unavoidably bind us to the wider community.

But even at the narrow end – the apparently neutral relation with shoes and cups – matters are not really so simple. Attachment comes in and plays its part. A small child who does not learn to care for its belongings, a child who is encouraged to treat them with casual contempt, misses something vital. Our shoes and cups are not just items that we have bought by contract so that we can smash them when we feel like it. They link us with the wider community. Perhaps Kant was wrong to rule that respect belongs only to persons, not to things. Things have meaning. They are tokens binding us into our culture, and also into the wider realm of nature. Contempt for things has in fact played a great part in our recent destruction of the environment. Perhaps the whole notion of belonging is one that we should treat more seriously.

Can Individualism be made Family-friendly?

Individualism is certainly here to stay, and we have reason to be thankful for that. When individuals are harmed, by their families or anything else, we do need to insist that they matter, that they should not be sacrificed to an ideal, however lofty, that their freedom is indeed a precious thing for which it is worth struggling. For those who are oppressed, freedom comes first, because without it nothing else seems possible. But there are other goods to consider as well as freedom. 'Bonds' are not just fetters; they are also life-lines.

Enlightenment thinking has tended to ignore the deep human need to balance freedom by love and co-operation, independence by sociability. In particular, certain philosophers, themselves celibate, have been disastrously blind to the intense, specific social needs of small children – and indeed of their parents too.[8]

Britain, like some other western societies, seems now to be reaching a stage where many people fear the evils of loneliness and emotional insecurity more than the pains of traditional constraint. Philosophers need to help in articulating this feeling, in rephrasing individualism in more human, less antisocial terms. They need to talk less about freedom in the abstract and more about the balance between particular freedoms and between the particular evils from which people need to be free. In our view, that is perhaps the main philosophical issue emerging from this topic.

The idea that life would be better without close, lasting attachments such as those that arise in families seems a foolish one. But how can people today organize the individualistic world in a less isolating way? How can we control our civilization's current fluidity so as to leave pockets of refuge in which people can safely bring up their children?

Various suggestions seem to surface as important. For instance, since children do make these intense demands for stable support, we surely need to help adolescents who cannot yet provide that support to avoid having babies too early. Unwanted and unconsidered teenage pregnancies are a real and serious evil. So it seems to us that making contraception, and an understanding of it, freely available to the young ought to be considered as among the duties of a responsible government. It is extremely unfortunate that, in some countries, governments have attempted to do this in a heavy-handed and overbearing manner which has discredited the whole project. But there are also countries, such as Mexico, where family-planning campaigns conducted by local people have proved both popular and effective. Their example should surely be followed.

For older people who already have children, the question is rather whether the parents will stay together. Here again, the conventions that used to enforce this stability undoubtedly caused a good deal of misery. It is neither possible nor desirable to revive them. Even within those conventions, however, it was not necessarily thought that upbringing by a mother alone – say, a widow or a sailor's wife – must be disastrous, though it was always recognized that her work was hard and she would need outside support.

The reformers who made divorce and separation easier no doubt thought that children would do better if the parents parted than if they stayed together while quarrelling. And it does seem that what upsets children most is not so much absence as discord. Unfortunately, however, current arrangements tend to provide both these things, since separated parents tend to continue to quarrel over the difficulties of disentangling their lives, and particularly over the children themselves. The importance of conciliation services here does now seem to be being recognized, along with the danger of letting adversarial lawyers inflame disputes. Family courts, devoted to resolving difficulties rather than allotting blame, are now being established. All this is surely a step in the right direction.

Undoubtedly, however, there is still a general dilemma here. At many points we today, in all kinds of societies, have to ask which we want more: secure social bonding or complete individual freedom? How shall we balance these ideals? It is not a single black-or-white choice between going into moral decline and returning to old ways. Instead, each society has a range of problems, some much harder than others, concerned with finding ways in which people can live together. Those ways will not necessarily produce familiar patterns. In many countries, family arrangements have changed a great deal over the ages, and they can very well change again.

Bring Back the Fathers?

Recently, discussions of family 'breakdown' have mainly treated the absence of fathers as the central cause. In particular, apparent increases in the criminality and irresponsibility of young males have been attributed to the absence of their fathers. The existence and strength of this particular causal link are at present much disputed, and, unfortunately, ideological commitments on both sides make considerable caution necessary in interpreting the evidence.[9] Recent attempts by administrators to extract maintenance from these fathers have become a political issue in a number of western countries, including Britain and the USA. But these moves seem aimed rather at saving public money than at domesticating these young men.

More seriously, however, it begins to seem that many young women are not prepared to take the trouble of domesticating them either. Substantial numbers of mothers do now seem to be choosing to be lone parents, rather than relying on the support of a man. We need to ask why they should make this choice.

In the economic climate of industrialized countries today, one answer is obvious. High unemployment means that many men are simply unable to provide financial support. And the kind of unemployment now prevailing, in which low-paid, insecure, part-time jobs for women replace full-time ones for men, has an evident tendency to break up families. But it seems that more is at stake than money. After all, men and women have always lived together in situations of extreme poverty and deprivation. Women do not refuse to live with men simply because they are poor. The reasons they are now giving have more to do with the attitudes of the men themselves than with their inability to be providers.

One young woman interviewed on a British television programme in September 1993 described how the father of her child occasionally came round to visit, stayed a while and then went off to his mother's house when he felt like it. She complained that he had no sense of responsibility and just wanted to do as he pleased. She was clear that he did not play a significant part in her life or the life of her child. She did not seem to think this a desirable situation, but rather a sorry fact. And no doubt she had reason to be sorry. When the two parent arrangement does work it has obvious great advantages. Effort and worry can then be divided, the partners can support each other, and the children can get two satisfactory role models. But when it doesn't work, all this fails to happen.

Does the young male's inability to be a financial provider somehow deprive him of that sense of responsibility in any walk of life which comes with having a real role to play in the family? This surely cannot be inevitable. Many men have learnt to take on other responsibilities in the family than that of breadwinner. What does seem to have happened is that young men are facing these responsibilities earlier and earlier and are finding that they simply are not ready to handle them.

There was perhaps some common sense behind Aristotle's recommendation that a man should marry and begin to produce children at the age of 37 while a woman should do so at 18.[10] Aristotle may have been wrong to think that these respective ages indicated the physical peak of the two sexes, but his suggestion that men need to mature – in other words, grow up – before taking on family responsibilities is one which is echoed through the ages. It has appeared in many forms. When men were obliged to soldier or to save or to learn before they were in a position to support a family, they married at a suitably late age. The need to delay starting a family became celebrated and tied to a notion of carefree bachelorhood which was tolerantly regarded as a necessary period of 'sowing wild oats'.

Obviously, a great deal of hypocrisy surrounded these attitudes. Men were not expected to do without sexual activity during this period and they were not legally obliged to provide for the children that they then fathered. But what was recognized, in the case of men, was that sexual proclivity and readiness to discharge family obligations do not necessarily go hand in hand. Neither, perhaps do they with women, and the concern about teenage pregnancies and motherhood is sometimes tied to a concern that 14- or 15-year-old girls are not psychologically or practically fitted to motherhood.

Modern western society adds a special difficulty here for both sexes in its remarkable segregation of different age-groups, which tends to keep current teenagers more ignorant than they are in most societies about what child-rearing will actually involve. Girls as well as boys now confront this problem, but they seem to manage their responsibilities better and at an earlier age than men do. They do not, on the whole, choose to give up their children for adoption or abandon them, nor to abuse them. Nor do these young single mothers produce an undue proportion of criminals or psychopaths.

The problem seems to be, not so much that we in the West are demanding less of young men but that we are demanding considerably more of them than previous ages did, and that they simply do not or cannot meet those demands. This is a serious difficulty, and it is certainly not going to go away quickly. Like the tendency of marriages to break down, it results in large part from a general, deliberate loosening of bonds and it is therefore an integral part of the current culture.

Conclusion

Whatever may eventually be done about these things, it seems clear that for some considerable time many children in Britain, the USA, and similar countries will be being brought up in one-parent families, or in what has been described as 'the mother-state-child family'.[11] We need, therefore, to find ways of making life tolerable for them, as well as ways of helping parents to stay together. Everything that tends to revive neighbourhoods, to reintegrate social contexts, to provide some sort of permanence within which these networks can grow and prosper, is urgently called for.

This support is not just a pragmatic, economic need, a device for keeping down crime, disease and protest. It is needed morally. The sort of provision that a society makes for families is indeed a moral matter, an aspect of its structure of ideals. If some kind of social Darwinist belief in the universal value of competition leads us to treat families as just one kind of unit among many, a unit that will survive or not according as it is fit to do so, then we shall be handing on an unbalanced, absurdly individualistic morality to our children.

If, too, that kind of competitive ethic leads us to treat the interests of men and women as necessarily competing, then we shall fail to look for ways in which they can be reconciled and can live harmoniously together. But living together is something absolutely essential for humans. It has to be made possible for the two sexes, just as it does across every other division where people often find it hard to understand one another. It is surely open to us to look for a more balanced form of individualism, a more human kind of freedom, that can make this possible.

NOTES

1 Plato, *Republic*, Book V, sect. 445–66, criticized by Aristotle in his *Politics*.
2 Godwin, *Enquiry Concerning Political Justice*, Book II, ch. 2, p. 71. In his second edition, Godwin altered this passage to refer to Fénelon's valet, who might be 'my brother, my father', thus opening further vistas of extraordinary speculations on class and gender which we cannot pursue here.
3 Stevenson, *Virginibus Puerisque*, 1. i and ii.
4 Nietzsche, *Thus Spake Zarathustra*, Part One, sect. 'Of love for one's neighbour'.
5 *The Way of All Flesh*, ch. 18.
6 Epictetus, *Encheiridion* or *Teachings*, Book II, ch. 25. See also Book III, chs 8 and 9.
7 Bishop Joseph Butler, *Fifteen Sermons*, Sermon V, 'Upon Compassion', sect. 11. The whole of this sermon and the following one is relevant – as, indeed, is Butler's entire position, since he completely rejects this polarization of reason and feeling.
8 See Hughes, 'The Philosopher's Child'. Also Okin, *Women in Western Political Thought*, index, under 'Child-rearing'.
9 See Berger *et al.*, *The Family: Is It Just Another Life-style Choice?* and Dennis, *Rising Crime and the Dismembered Family*.
10 Aristotle, *Politics*, Book VII, ch. 16, 1335a.
11 See Berger *et al.*, *The Family*, p. 45.

The first verse of Philip Larkin's Poem 'This Be The Verse' is reprinted by permission of Faber and Faber Ltd. Every effort has been made by the publishers to trace copyright holders.

READING GUIDE

Until lately, few philosophers attended at all systematically to questions about the family. Those who mentioned it mainly did so in order to discuss its relation to the state. In more recent times, there has been increasing interest in a number of issues which do bear on families: topics such as education, children's rights, abortion, euthanasia, fertility and other bioethical matters. But, in keeping with the individualistic temper of the age, writers have often tended to treat these issues separately, as matters affecting particular family members. It is still somewhat hard to bring in focus questions about the family as a whole.

Illuminating comments on it can, however, be drawn both from recent work, including J. Blustein's *Parents and Children: the Ethics of the family* and Susan M. Okin's *Justice, Gender and the Family*, and from the earlier tradition. See also G. Scarre (ed.), *Children, Parents and Politics*. In reading the earlier tradition, the most interesting points to notice often concern things which the theorists unquestioningly take for granted. Plato's anti-family manifesto in the *Republic* caused general alarm, and he himself withdrew most of it in the *Laws*. Aristotle answered the manifesto at some length, giving instead a rather conventional account which is interesting simply as an indication of views that were long and widely accepted. The Stoics supported Plato in that they thought personal affection irrational and disapproved of sorrow at the death of relations, especially of children. (This disapproval, expressed by Epictetus and often repeated, surely indicates that such sorrow was in fact strongly felt.) But in general Stoic sages accepted the family as a normal focus of duties. Christian thinkers did so too, though their exaltation of celibacy, along with some remarks in the Gospels (such as Matthew 12: 49 and 23: 9) tended to put family virtues in second place. Thus, throughout antiquity and the Middle Ages, the family was usually taken for granted as a natural grouping, imposing definite duties on its members, just as lordships and kingdoms did on rulers and their subjects. Indeed, the family often figured as the most fundamental of these models. Obedience to kings and to God himself was demanded *because* they stood as fathers to their people. No serious question was usually raised about the source of these duties, still less about the special position of the father. From the time of the Renaissance, however, social contract theorists did begin to raise these questions about political duty. But many of them, notably Rousseau, refused to extend their questioning to the level of the family. This meant that, though Man was indeed now held to be born free and could be bound only by contracts of his own choosing, Woman and Child remained bound, just as they always had been, by many unchosen bonds.

That anomaly left a striking piece of unfinished business on the Enlightenment agenda. It still gives us endless trouble today, and it has been a central reason why feminist critiques have been needed. Mary Wollstonecraft – who directly answered Rousseau – and J. S. Mill in his *Subjection of Women* urged that libertarian thought must be extended consistently into the private sphere. This campaign was carried further both in Marxist thought (see Engels and Shulamith Firestone) and by more individualistic thinkers influenced by Existentialism (see R. D. Laing and Simone de Beauvoir). The first line of argument emphasizes the need for equality, the second concentrates on autonomy.

Converging with these two campaigns, a separate but influential attack on families was also launched by behaviourist psychologists, on the quite different grounds that parents were too unscientific to be allowed to bring up their children. This idea may be studied, along with other strange and relevant proposals for child-rearing, in Christina Hardyment's *Dream Babies* and *For Her Own Good* edited by B. Ehrenreich and D. English, and, more directly, in B. F. Skinner's Utopia, *Walden Two*.

Philosophers have not taken much interest in this remarkable treatment of child-rearing as a specialized science. Instead, the main line of philosophical debate has concerned complaints – such as those of Bernard Williams – that autonomy and equality cannot possibly be the only ideals to aim at when considering families. In general, both these ideals have clearly begun to look inadequate, simply because too much has been expected of them. In a number of contexts, but perhaps above all in family matters, they are felt to have been urged too simple-mindedly, to the neglect of other equally important considerations.

Current philosophical debate, both inside and outside feminism, now centres on attempts to correct this one-sidedness without losing the real values represented by these ideals. We ourselves discussed this general clash of ideals in our book *Women's Choices*, and it is still a crucial contemporary issue.

CLASSICAL SOURCES

Aristotle: *Politics*; *Oeconomica*
Engels: *On the Origin of the Family, Private Property and the State*

Epictetus: *Discourses*
Plato: *Republic*, Book V; *Laws*, Books VI and XI
Rousseau: *Émile or On Education*, Book V
J. S. Mill: *On the Subjection of Women*

2

Love and Personal Relationships

Paul Gregory

> The difficulties become very great indeed and few rules can be reasonably set down
> beyond saying that it is important not to hurt the other person . . . There is little that can
> be stated that cannot be shown to be inappropriate in certain circumstances.
>
> *Debrett's Etiquette & Modern Manners*

It will not be disputed that our sense of identity, of who we are, is, in part at least, constituted by the relationships we have with other individuals, and that our potential for happiness is a function of how those relationships fare. One aspect moreover that is crucial for people in their relationships, that is indeed the measure for the importance of other matters, is the way they actually feel towards each other, including their perception of the attitude the other has towards them. In other words, to flourish, a personal relationship must be a community of affection.

Now there are two key concepts implied here: those of a degree of reciprocity and of a degree of love. How much reciprocity, and, first, what exactly is involved in love?

Affection, Caring and Attachment

A first thought might be to equate love only with a variety of feeling. In some colloquial contexts, the words are indeed used almost interchangeably: to have feelings for someone is to harbour love, at least of a kind.

One problem with classifying love as a feeling is that feeling can be so very unreliable, while love, to count as love, requires a considerable persistence over time.

Further reflection soon shows that love is never a single, solitary feeling, but that a whole pattern of emotions is involved. Love may show itself, for example, in anxiety about someone or in missing them, as well as in the sentiment of affection. Nor are these feelings (or any feelings) uninterruptedly present in the consciousness.[1]

More telling, though, than these somewhat introspective observations, is our objective assessment of the situation where someone else attests to feeling love. Sometimes we may take their word for it, but usually we will also have close regard to the way they act.

Might love be equated then solely with a pattern of action? No, because this supposition would make affection superfluous to the existence of love. Caring action on its own is not enough for us to say there is love, though it may often be an excellent indicator. Someone may for instance care, i.e. perform the actions of care, out of a sense of duty. Think of a nurse, or else of a dutiful husband who no longer feels anything for his wife.

In summary, love can be said neither to be simply a pattern of feeling, nor a pattern of action. A working metaphor is to see it as an undercurrent which sometimes manifests itself in feelings of various kinds, especially the sentiment of affection, and sometimes in actions.[2]

For our next step, let me introduce a notion of what I shall call bonding, although the alternative terms 'attachment' and 'focus' would not be far off the mark (there are subtle differences, which will become apparent by substituting in the following one or both of these words for 'bond').

Let us say that bonding is the way in which an individual's sense of self involves the thought of a person or persons to whom he or she relates. Now it is arguably the case that our sense of self is always associated with perceptions of others, and in their absence, with thoughts of others (including often thoughts of their perception of ourselves). This means that even the hermit will engage in some kind of imagined dialogue with others, although these may be only remembered or else composite or fictional persons. Bonding goes beyond this minimal orientation on others through the fixity of the persons in mind. That is, we do not quickly or easily stop thinking periodically about the particular persons we are attached to, if only because we think of ourselves *via* those persons. They will change with time, but the change is *necessarily* gradual. The process of bonding, i.e. the process through which someone acquires this status for us, may also be assumed to be gradual.

Note that this concept of bonding does not yet involve mutuality or reciprocity. It is not necessarily the case that we play a similar role or a similarly important role for the persons we bond to.

The existence of a relationship, and therefore the existence of a bond, does not necessarily mean that there is love exactly. Conversely, the existence of individual love does not necessarily mean that there is a relationship, although there must be a bond in at least one direction (think of cases of estrangement). This is because a relationship is necessarily mutual; it is observable and involves exchanges of various kinds and does not exist 'only in the mind' whereas a bond might well exist 'only in the mind' (though it must have a great deal more fixity than a figment of the imagination – a bond involving recurrent thought of the other individual concerned).

We said at the outset that, in order to flourish, a personal relationship must be a community of affection; and that this implied a degree of love, which we have just explored, and a degree of reciprocity. How much reciprocity?

Claims, Commitments and Presumptions

One of the things someone might say within a close relationship is, 'You are the most important person in my life, and I want to be the most important person in yours, too.'

Philosophically and ethically, this statement presents a number of issues. At first sight, it may seem to be a declaration of love, but note that it could equally well, in principle, be said within a relationship of enmity. On closer examination, the statement, assuming it is sincere, emerges as neither a sufficient condition for there to be love, nor a necessary condition, for you can surely love more than one other person. It may nevertheless very well be an expression of love, but as an expression it is incomplete, or else the expression of an incomplete love.

Imagine a moment how the world would be if this were the only form that love could take.[3] Only in a world that was miraculously ordered would each and every person have such a love. It would, necessarily, be a world full of couples (though not necessarily sexually intimate couples; the sexual component is a separate matter). In a world not miraculously ordered, it might conceivably be possible for everyone to belong to such a couple, but it would not be possible for that relationship to be always either freely chosen or one of a meeting of minds.

There are two components to our phrase. First there is a statement about how the speaker feels toward (or relates to) the person being addressed. (Or is it a vow?) Then there is the expression of a wish, though it may sound more like a demand, a demand that seems to follow from the initial declaration. But it does not follow. A child may be the most important person in her father's life, but, if he is a good father, he will not wish to be the most important person in her life.

This counter-example is of a relationship which by its nature is asymmetrical, and radically so. Perhaps we must focus instead on basically symmetrical relationships, between adults who are equals. Is the demand (for supreme importance in the life of the other) now justified on the grounds that the other is for me, the speaker, the most important individual in my life?

It is, surely, as a demand, presumptuous. Part of the problem comes from the superlatives involved. Note how the situation is transformed as these are qualified or withdrawn: 'You are the most important (or: a most important) person in my life, and I want to be important for you, too.' Or, going further, 'You count for me, and I want to count for you, too.'

The request which before was presumptuous now seems modest, so much so that it would seem heartless to reject it out of hand. The wish (or plea) comes closer to being a declaration of love to the extent that it has moderated and renounced the stronger claim for exclusive possession. Indeed, the nature of love is such, surely, that it does not pose, properly, any conditions. A declaration of love is not a contractual undertaking to the effect 'I will love this other person if (and only if) she loves me'. That would be an offer of commitment, which is not to be scorned, may indeed in various practical ways be more attractive, but is different. (The declaration of love includes a statement of commitment, and so is more than an offer of commitment. It says, 'You can call on me. I will make time and effort and attentiveness available for you.')

The commitment implied in a declaration of love may of course be exploited. The person loving must have faith that the other will not exploit their feelings, at least not in certain ways, and they can be mistaken in this conviction, as they can be mistaken in their perception of the other in a more general sense. The person who loves becomes vulnerable, necessarily.

Let us return for a moment to the totalitarian tone of the original utterance. The exclusive implication ('most important') opens up the way for a near-total vulnerability. Where love is more diffuse, the variety of commitments may itself provide fuel for conflict (including or especially ethical conflict), but the other commitments can also provide a check and a balance.

There is a topical question about how diffuse or how focused love should ideally be. Our real range of personal choice in this respect is doubtless somewhat limited. We cannot readily command our feelings (or the commitment in our hearts). And even where the psychological capacity for a more focused – or alternatively a more diffuse love – is present, social pressures can be restrictive. Others must go along with our choice, and they will often fail to do so, especially if it means going against prevailing norms, for example in the area of sexual intimacy.

This said, and notwithstanding how little room we may, psychologically or socially speaking, have as individuals to focus or spread our love, there is choice at another level. Thus you might choose to put your young child in a playgroup all day or alternatively sacrifice career and prosperity to spend much more time with her. The evidence seems to show that, accordingly, the child will relate to others in a more diffuse or a more focused way. (Whether the total capacity for love will be different is another matter, and one fraught with conceptual and normative difficulties.)

There is embedded in the original declaration ('and I want to be the most important person in your life, too') a desire for total reciprocity. I have suggested that, as a claim, this is presumptuous, which means that it is not legitimate. The argument for this was that love (and we have assumed the declaration to be one of love) does not properly set conditions. Now this is true, but it does not mean that love does not *have* conditions. Assuming love is a certain pattern equally of feeling and action, it needs for its realization the presence of its object, i.e. in order to perform the actions of love. Even in the case of separation, love may express itself in the efforts made to overcome that absence, i.e. to create presence. As a feeling (and as a readiness to act accordingly) love may long persist, but it is of course then a frustrated, an unhappy love. So the proper statement of the situation is that love does not set conditions in the sense of adopting a bargaining position – of, say, threatening withdrawal if the other fails to respond in kind. Such withdrawal would be unthinkable, i.e. conceptually inappropriate, always assuming the attitude involved is indeed one of love (though it would be conceptually appropriate in the case of commitment, which in some – especially Christian – quarters is often confused with love). (The situation is surely similar to – albeit much more serious than – that involved in liking; to stop liking someone just because they fail to like you back is not only childish, but inappropriate.) But although love does not set conditions, it does have need of circumstances in which it can flourish.[4] (The exact constellation of those circumstances is another matter.)

The conclusion these considerations provide is that, although the *claim* or *demand* 'I want to be the *most* important person in your life' is indeed presumptuous, the *desire* to be *an* important person in the life of the other remains of course entirely legitimate. The desire for a degree of reciprocity is indeed, since love has acute need of circumstances in which it can flourish, necessary.

What is it exactly that is to be reciprocated? The argument so far has spoken generally of love. It sounds then as if there has to be a degree of reciprocation, but that it is not legitimate to expect or demand that this be in equal measure, i.e. that the extent or intensity of the love be equal in both directions. Now there are circumstances in which it makes reasonable sense to speak in such terms, where a rough comparative measure of the intensity of love is possible. But talk of love and of its role in relationships usually requires more subtle concepts. When we ask precisely what is reciprocated, we become aware of the asymmetry in relationships. (It is pertinent that the word relationship conjures up most readily the image of a close companionship between members of the opposite sex. Quite apart from the aspect of sexual attraction and intimacies, this image is of a relationship between importantly different persons, such that close symmetry is difficult or impossible.)

To get a hold on the dynamics of love and relationships, we have other concepts, those of compatibility and complementarity. Compatibility may exist in the somewhat negative sense that serious conflict does not arise. We usually go a step further, especially when reflecting on a close relationship, and ask for complementarity, which implies that the one person supplies what the other lacks.[5]

The notion of complementarity, i.e. the ideal balance of give and take, is open to two interpretations. It may be that at one moment one thing is given, from Anne to Bert, and at the next another thing is given, this time from Bert to Anne. Another, more subtle scenario is that what from Anne's point of view is being given to her is from Bert's point of view being given to him. Anne wants to tell a story, and Bert wants to listen (to a story). (It may also occur that Bert wants to be told a story by Anne, and that Anne wants to tell a story to Bert, which is different and much more complex. The *depth*, the resonance, the aura of meaningfulness, that exchange can take on surely has to do with the recursive possibilities of such situations.)

Complementarity rarely comes of its own and even in propitious circumstances has to be worked at. There is here the idea of attending to a relationship, tending the relationship, seeing that the relationship as such thrives.

This conception seems to involve an essential shift away from concentration on the person loved; the specialness of the other may now appear to be a matter of secondary importance, and the pursuit of the *relationship* – or of *a* relationship – moves to centre-stage. It is possibly the relationship itself that is appreciated, rather than the person who is related to. A moment's reflection on the social and hence psychological importance of 'relationships' in determining the sense of social worth and social identity, i.e. of relationships which typically take the 'most important person' form, shows how easily a preoccupation with the relationship itself may degenerate. A way out of the difficulty is to insist that tending to the relationship necessarily involves attending to the person (as a person, and in their specialness), or to say that both are equally important. These reflections are not as abstruse as they may seem. If you attend to a relationship alone, you may fall into scheming, and become preoccupied with, for example, how the other perceives you (as the other pole in the relationship) rather than, say, communicating how *you* really are or feel towards the other. Quickly, cosmetics come to the fore. You come to 'manage' the relationship, even manage it well, rather than live it.

A focus is needed, which is neither just the benevolence of the person loving, nor the relationship within which that person stands, although both of these must be implicated, since without them it is not clear who is doing the loving where. (Love must not be reduced to well-wishing, least of all general well-wishing.)

One such focus would be the happiness of the person loved. Love might then be the will for the happiness of the person loved, such that the person loving wishes not only the happiness of the person they love, but also themselves to be a source of this happiness.

This would mean that there is a presumption at the heart of love. The person who loves assumes and insists that they themselves are capable of so contributing to the other's happiness. This presumption betrays a fundamental faith in oneself, a faith which we will generally want to say is a good and necessary thing.[6]

Note now how the presumption can turn tyrannical when the subject concerned endeavours to be not one source, but the sole source of the happiness of the other.

In place of the promotion of happiness, which is a somewhat grandiose term, perhaps inappropriate for characterizing all but the most ambitious relationships of love, we might speak equally of the furtherance of the well-being or the flourishing of the other. Or else simply of the good for them.

The latter formulation provides at once an explanation of the sense in which love may be said to be a force for good and the way in which it may nevertheless come into conflict with morality. The good for one person, who is loved, may well clash with that of another, who is not loved. Moreover, there may be error as to what is good for another, or else an error in the perceived complementarity. You could genuinely be mistaken in believing that your company will benefit the other; equally she could be mistaken that her company would not be for your good, or yours for hers.

We might discover that the person we are attached to (and feel for, and care for) is different from how we perceived them. What happens to love in such a case, and what should happen to it? Is such a change in perception a justification for giving notice to the relationship? Must the attachment transfer to the new person, or be abandoned? Here there is, surely, a distinct role for an ethical stance, which insists on commitments being honoured up to a point, even if they have been made in error. An attachment or an affection may wane, and may not be forced, but neither can felt love (or its absence) be the sole guide in such circumstances. There is, at the least, a need for gentleness and well-intentioned support, if only for a time, and perhaps a long time. Love implies commitment, and some of the obligation generated by the commitment remains even when love has vanished.

Prior to love, then, there is a virtue in being critical and attentive in our perceptions of others. Though precisely these strengths, in excess, can be destructive of the generous impulse to love someone, which involves trusting them to be something like we believe and hope them to be. Indeed, we may only be able to come to know someone by first investing our feelings and generating an attachment. Note that this also involves a faith that the other will be responsive, even rising above themselves to meet our expectations. Consideration of what it is to know a person, and of the possibility of being mistaken in one's perceptions of another (quite apart from the possibilities of being rejected or oneself misperceived) reveals the very real precariousness involved in love, at least at the outset.

'At the outset' relationships, and the love that informs them or else is lacking, have histories, as too do those who enter into relationships. This is not an incidental aspect, but essential. Attachments grow from a sequence of encounters and exchanges. This is why it is sometimes puzzling to an outsider that some couples are so attached to each other when objectively they seem so far apart. Whether what is involved is love exactly, and the extent to which the relationship is mutually beneficial, is a separate matter. Familiarity is not the same as love.

NOTES

1 There is a parallel situation in epistemology, or rather, in the theory of perception. Our perceptions even of an everyday object are varied and discontinuous.
2 Consider here also the double-edged nature of words such as 'concern' and 'caring'. Concern is an emotional response, but the word implies that the subject feeling concern is anxious to act on their concern in so far as this is possible. Care straddles the divide between action and feeling even more ambiguously, denoting – according to context and intonation – sometimes action, sometimes feeling, and often both.
3 A thought experiment of this kind is of course what Kant proposed in order to provide a criterion of whether a category of action is compliant with the moral law.
4 When an offer of love is rejected, the person loving is popularly consoled – or cajoled – with statements such as 'If you really loved her, you would accept her decision and leave her alone.' But whatever independent force an injunction to accept the rejection may have, it is unconnected with love.
5 There is a philosophical tradition going back to Plato of interpreting love in terms of a lack or deficiency on the part of the person loving. But a more appealing view of love is to see it as expressing an abundance, as a need to give rather than to take. This is interestingly explored in the work of Georges Bataille, who takes his cue from Nietzsche.
6 Such faith is one clear meaning that might be attributed to the otherwise obscure but popular notion of self-love or love of self. In psychological and theological writing, reference is often made to a 'good' self-love, which is contrasted starkly with egoism. One writer who makes a serious attempt to elucidate the distinction is Denis de Rougemont, in his *Les Mythes de l'amour*. But I remain unconvinced that the notion of self-love can be made genuinely fruitful for normative and philosophical discourse. In the final analysis, it always runs up against the imponderable nature of the self, and so ends by explaining neither love nor self nor anything else.

READING GUIDE

The classic discussion of love is Plato's dialogue the *Symposium*, but Plato also discusses the tendency of the passions to become dominant in the *Phaedrus*. Aristotle discusses friendship in the *Nicomachean Ethics*, Books VIII and IX.

Irving Singer's *The Nature of Love* is a standard work in three volumes: Plato to Luther; Courtly and Romantic Love; The Modern World. This work includes extensive notes giving guidance to further reading. Denis de Rougemont's *Les Mythes de l'amour* is relevant to much of the discussion in this chapter, as is also the work of Georges Bataille. See also *The History of Sexuality* by Michel Foucault. Simone de Beauvoir's *The Second Sex* presents a rather different and more personal viewpoint.

These and related subjects are discussed by Roger Scruton in his book *Sexual Desire* and by Paul Gilbert in *Human Relationships*. The philosophical aspects of love are also discussed by Ilham Dilman in *Love and Human Separateness* and by Mark Fisher in *Personal Love*. Brenda Almond discusses some of the issues in her article 'Human bonds'. *Philosophy and Sex*, edited by R. Baker and F. Elliston is a useful collection of articles on a variety of related themes.

CLASSICAL SOURCES

Plato: *Symposium*; *Phaedrus*
Aristotle: *Ethics*

3

Between the Sexes: Care or Justice?

Moira Gatens

Introduction: Different Realities?

In 1949, some decades ago, Simone de Beauvoir wrote, 'There is a whole region of human experience which the male deliberately chooses to ignore because he fails to *think* it; this experience woman *lives*.'[1] The region of human experience to which de Beauvoir was referring is, of course, the sphere of personal relations, including familial and sexual relations, love, reproduction and those aspects of existence that have defined the social, economic and political situation of women. In schematic terms, it concerns that which has traditionally fallen under the rubric of the private sphere. Much about the situation of women has changed since 1949 and that which woman once merely 'lived' has now been thoroughly 'thought', or theorized. One important consequence of feminist thought and political practice about notions of the private, the family and the personal, is the unsettling effect which this has had on the standard categories of thought which underpin traditional political and moral theory (see the table of oppositions below). The articulation of a region of peculiarly female experience thus has had the effect of challenging the assumed disembodied and universal subject central to traditional political and moral thought. This subject does not tally with the lived experience of most women.

From the perspective of feminist theory, long-held distinctions between the private and the public, nature and culture, the personal and the political, the family and the state, do not so much capture truths about universal human experience, as they reveal the partial perspective of male theorists, who consistently mistake their experience of social, political and moral life for the totality of human experience. Feminist theory has devoted considerable energy to an analysis of the private–public split. One consequence of this analysis has been

The dualism of private and public

Private	Public
nature	culture
necessity	freedom
family	state
pre-formed status	contract
embodied	abstract
particular	universal
partial	impartial
personal	political
unregulated (?)	regulated
ethic of care (Gilligan)	ethic of justice (Rawls)
self-sacrifice	self-interest

to show that the dualism of private versus public, along with all its associate dualisms (as shown in the table below), are much less sharply demarcated than liberal political theory assumes.

Feminist thought has brought so-called private issues on to the public and political agenda, often demanding that the state regulate and otherwise intervene – for example, by providing public education on issues such as domestic violence – in practices and ways of life that many philosophers and political theorists had declared private and so 'off-limits' to governmental intervention. Feminists have argued that refraining from regulative intervention in private or personal relations does not amount to being apolitical. Refraining from regulation can itself be a political act by tacitly supporting existing social and economic inequalities. The recent legal recognition, in some jurisdictions, of rape within marriage is a case in point. Such legislation increases the difficulty of maintaining the sharp distinction between public and private concerns given that the private is often defined, for example in the Wolfenden Report, as that which is 'in brief and crude terms, not the law's business'.[2] Feminist analyses of the operations of power between the sexes have significantly altered conceptions of that which the law takes to be its 'business'.[3]

Rape within marriage, sexual harassment, domestic violence, 'stalking' and 'date-rape' are all instances of the sorts of harm that feminists recently have brought to the attention of the public. Institutions such as law, schools, universities and workplaces have been targeted as requiring radical change through education and regulation. The unequal relations of power between men and women in the home and in the workplace have far-reaching effects. They not only leave women economically disadvantaged but further place them in situations of physical and psychological vulnerability. Both Catharine MacKinnon[4] and Carole Pateman[5] have questioned whether women's consent, under such conditions, can be genuinely free. Women, they suggest, simply do not fit the liberal description of the abstract citizen who enters freely chosen contractual relations. Hence, they claim that the just treatment of women cannot be achieved simply by admitting them to equal standing with men. When applied to relations between men and women, the standard liberal notions of universal and impartial rules which govern the interactions of abstract social actors, are understood to result in the unjust treatment of women. All women are symbolically, and most women are empirically, associated with the realm of the family, which is a realm of pre-formed status – rather than contract – in which women as wives, mothers and houseworkers are defined in relation to the services they provide for men. In many situations women's well-being depends upon their responsiveness to the needs of men who structurally occupy positions of power in relation to women: the husband at home, the boss at work.

Moreover, since MacKinnon argues that gender (as distinct from biological sexual difference) is itself an effect of these relations of domination and subordination, power is implicated at the very heart of male–female relations. When MacKinnon's view of power is coupled with another influential view concerning the different, and incompatible perceptions of social reality of men and women, the possibility of the sexes sharing a moral community appear very bleak. These increasingly influential views do indeed render problematic any notion of free association between the sexes.

In her controversial book, *The Morning After: Sex, Fear and Feminism*,[6] Katie Roiphe offers a sceptical analysis of an example of men's and women's incompatible understandings of a common social phenomenon: dating. The example is taken from a pamphlet, widely distributed in Australian and Anglo-American university campuses, entitled *Acquaintance Rape: Is Dating Dangerous?.*

> The pamphlet tells us what 'she' is thinking and what 'he' is thinking as the date progresses. She thinks: 'He was really handsome and he had a great smile. We talked and found we had a lot in common. When he asked me over to his place for a drink I thought it would be OK. He was such a good listener and I wanted him to ask me out again' . . . he is thinking: 'She looked really hot, wearing a sexy dress that showed off her great body.' . . . He notes, 'She seemed pretty relaxed so I asked her back to my place for a drink . . . When she said "yes" I knew that I was going to be lucky.' When they get to his room the bed turns out to be the only place to sit. . . . He begins by kissing. She says she really liked him so the kissing was nice. But then he pushes her down on the bed. She tries to get up and tells him to stop, but 'he was so much bigger and stronger.'[7]

This narrative is offered as a typical 'date-rape' scenario. The front of the pamphlet graphically makes its point: a photograph (taken prior to the bedroom scene), which shows the two young people having fun together, is ripped in two, she on one torn half, he on the other. What looked like a shared social event between two participants, is in fact two events, now separated by a violence or tearing. The patterns of communication between the sexes are shown as hopelessly confused and each assumes that her or his perception of the situation is how the situation *really* is. This failure of communication results in harm to the woman since the unequal power relation between them means that the man's perception dominates.

There is much truth in such stories and feminists are right to draw attention to the systemic effects of unequal power between the sexes. These effects are felt at the level of our day-to-day interactions as well as in the broader arenas of employment. However, the proposition that the *source* of much violent behaviour toward women is men's and women's radically different perceptions of their interactions with each other, is highly contentious. What does it mean to claim that while one party believes he is having consensual intercourse, the other party believes she is being raped? Further, what would count as just and fair treatment for each party involved in such situations? Do such situations amount to a form of *de facto* perceptual sexual apartheid, where men and women have incommensurable perceptions? If men and women do tend to experience the same event differently, what does this imply for juridical and ethical relations between them? For example does it mean that liberal universal moral principles should be rejected in favour of specific moralities for specific contexts, for example, one set of principles for ethical relations within the same sex and another set for ethical relations between the sexes? Certainly, this is not a novel idea in the history of moral thought.[8]

Many philosophers have subscribed to the view that men and women do, and *should*, occupy different spheres governed by a sex-specific morality. They have argued that love has a different meaning for men and women and that one's sense of justice and morality varies, depending on one's sex. This was one of the strongest arguments of Enlightenment philosophers, such as Rousseau, for excluding women from political and civil life. This is not particularly surprising: the 'great' philosophers are notorious for their insistence on women's difference from, and inferiority to, men. What is surprising is the number of feminist philosophers in the present who agree that women have different notions of morality while making the further claim that such notions are superior to the traditional moral notions produced by male philosophers. Some feminist philosophers have posited the existence of 'male' and 'female' styles of thought that influence male and female behaviour in all contexts. Some claim that these different styles of thought have their basis in the different biologies of men and women, others that they derive from structural and institutional differences that are socially and historically specific. In this paper I will focus on the political implications of the claim of some feminists that men and women entertain essentially different notions of morality. The paper falls into three sections: section one considers some contemporary examples of the argument for sexually-specific moralities; section two offers a critical historical perspective on this argument; and the third and final section will return to the question of present and future possibilities for satisfactory moral relations between the sexes.

An Ethic of Care versus an Ethic of Justice: Duties versus Rights

More than two centuries ago Mary Wollstonecraft drew attention to a paradox in men's reasoning about women, morality and politics. She argued that although political theorists acknowledge the co-implication of notions of rights and duties, many nevertheless expected women to honour their duties whilst denying them their rights. Wollstonecraft denied the coherence of such an expectation. By her lights, the ability to act dutifully or morally (rather than, say, obediently), presupposes individuals who possesses both the capacity and the opportunity to develop their reason and claim their rights. Women, she pointed out, possess the capacity but have been denied the opportunity.[9]

Other feminists in the present have drawn attention to the manner in which men's publicly authorized human rights depend upon women's acceptance of a grossly unequal share of responsibilities, particularly the responsibility for the care of those who cannot care for themselves (children, the aged, the infirm). It is a marked feature of contemporary liberal democracies (as well as socialist societies) that although women have gained many benefits and rights formerly denied them, men have failed to take up their share of social burdens and responsiblilities. In contemporary moral philosophy this feature of modern liberal democracies has crystallized around two competing and, according to some, incompatible moral theories: an ethic of care (closely identified with the work of Carol Gilligan) and an ethic of justice (often represented by the work of John Rawls). It is pertinent here that the former theory is concerned with responsiveness to the needs of others and the latter with an abstract model which provides a frame for just action. I will offer a very brief account of each moral theory in turn before offering criticisms of both.

In her book, *In a Different Voice: Psychological Theory and Women's Development*, Gilligan presents an argument for sexually specific forms of moral reasoning. Several feminist theorists have developed this argument further in the context of moral philosophy, including Sara Ruddick,[10] Virginia Held[11] and Nel Noddings.[12] Gilligan posits that in their consideration of moral issues, females employ a mode of reasoning different from that used by males. She claims that for women

> the moral problem arises from conflicting responsibilities rather than from competing rights and requires for its resolution a mode of thinking that is contextual and

narrative rather than formal and abstract. This conception of morality as concerned with the activity of care centres moral development around the understanding of responsibility and relationships, just as the conception of morality as fairness ties moral development to the understanding of rights and rules.[13]

Those who think that women do indeed reason differently about moral issues do not necessarily thereby commit themselves to an essentialist view of sexual difference. Many contemporary moral philosophers argue that women's responsiveness to the context in which a moral issue arises, and to the particularity of those for whom it arises, is due to the mothering activities in which they engage or for which they are trained, whether they engage in it or not. In fact some, for example Held, claim that since mothering is a social rather than biological role, men could in principle 'mother' as readily as women.[14] Held hypothesizes that if men did take an equal share in caring tasks, and especially child-rearing, then they too would be likely to develop a more contextualized and 'caring' approach both in their responses to moral situations and in their moral theorizing.

Held asks us to imagine the effect it would have on our moral and political reasoning if we were to displace the self-sufficient, individual rational contractor from centre-stage and posit instead the relation between mother and child. This relation, she argues, is both conceptually and causally, *the* primary social relation.[15] She suggests that one consequence would be that traditional moral and political conceptions of respecting others by not interfering with them would be 'dramatically shown up as inadequate'. According to Held, traditional views assume

> that people can fend for the themselves and provide through their own initiatives and efforts what they need. This Robinson Crusoe image of 'economic man' is false for almost everyone, but is totally false in the case of infants and children, and recognising this can be salutary. It can lead us to see very vividly how unsatisfactory are those prevalent political views according to which we fulfill our obligations merely by refraining from interference and having laws and governments which only protect us from incursions by others. The arguments for government to provide positive enablements to those in need are at least as strong as those for government to protect us from interference.[16]

One should pause a moment and take stock of the 'reversal' of the usual feminist strategy that Held here performs. Traditionally feminists have drawn attention to the covert regulation of familial relations. They have argued that the family is neither a wholly natural nor a simply private association. The unpaid domestic tasks of child-rearing and housework that women have traditionally performed have been shown to be socially and economically necessary rather than simply a personal service. Arguments, in the 1970s, for wages for housework or the recent introduction in many western economies of the so-called 'carer's allowance' both stress the non-private and non-personal aspects of women's traditional work. In other words, feminists have attempted to import at least some of the practices and norms of contractual and public relations into the family by acknowledging that women's work is economically necessary work. Held, on the other hand, recommends exporting the practices and norms of the family into the public. The caring and concern, taken to characterize the family, is offered as a general model for conduct in moral and political life. I will have more to say about this below.

For now, I will offer a summary of the most important features of the ethic of care stance. An ethic of care may be characterized by three main points. First, it is a stance that is responsive to the specific character and context of any given moral issue, including its affective elements. Second, moral attitudes are seen to have their origins in the experience of oneself and one's values as formed in and by dependent relations with others, paradigmatically, the mother–child relation. Third, the care stance takes as its focus responsibilities and duties of care to others.

Many of those who subscribe to the ethic of care oppose it to an ethic of justice, such as that developed by John Rawls in *A Theory of Justice*. This is an opposition that Rawls himself does not assume. I do not intend discussing Rawls's views in any detail. The interest of his work here concerns the use to which it has been put by those theorists who desire to promote the care stance over moral theories of justice. Rawls understands justice to be concerned with the fair distribution of social goods. A just society for him is one in which 'all social primary goods – liberty and opportunity, income and wealth, and the bases of self-respect – are . . . distributed equally unless an unequal distribution of any or all of these goods is to the advantage of the least favoured'.[17] Unlike the ethic of care this moral stance may be characterized by the following three points. First, the justice stance is concerned with determining the appropriate *principles* of justice. Second, the self capable of applying these principles is one who will not be influenced by the particulars of the case or by any affective relations relevant to that case. Third, justice is concerned with the rights of the individual.[18]

Even from this necessarily brief description, one can readily glean the extent to which the 'care' stance and the 'justice' stance are almost mirror reversals of each other. These two stances are consistent with the left and right hand side of the table of dualisms at the beginning of this paper and map on to traditional understandings of sexual difference. Feminists have rightly criticized Rawls's view of justice for its failure to bring the family into the moral arena. It is commonly held that families are governed by love and care and that it would be inappropriate to raise issues of justice in the 'private' realm of the family. However, as Iris Young points out, distributive theories of justice tend to presume that the units among which basic distributions take place are families, and that it is as family members, often heads of families, that individuals enter the public realm where justice operates. Thus they neglect issues of justice within families – for example the issue of whether the traditional sexual division of labour still presupposed by much law and employment policy is just.[19]

I think Young is right about the limits of distributive theories of justice. However, this is not the only instance of the blindness of moral theorists to the question of the sexual division of labour. Those who argue for an ethic of care in opposition to an ethic of justice seem unaware of the extent to which the traditional sexual division of labour is repeating itself in moral theory. Marilyn Friedman has noted this tendency:

> The tasks of governing, regulating social order, and managing other 'public' institutions have been monopolized by men as their privileged domain, and the tasks of sustaining privatized personal relationships have been undertaken by or imposed on women. The genders have thus been conceived in terms of special and distinctive moral projects. Justice and rights have structured male moral norms, values, and virtues, while care and responsiveness have defined female moral norms, values, and virtues.[20]

Such a division of labour reflects and repeats the institutionalized roles and status of men and women in contemporary society. It also runs the risk of entrenching sexual differences in theory just at the moment when such differences are under challenge from social change.

Can a convincing case for the historical determination of such differences between the sexes be made? Two questions arise in this context. The first concerns whether the opposition between care and justice is historical, that is, whether the opposition arises as a result of the functioning of specific social institutions that are opposed to each other, such as the family, headed by an individual citizen, and the state. The second, and related, question concerns the cause of the gendering of these oppositions. It is in the context of such questions that feminists have asked whether the characteristics of the so-called impartial actor in the public domain are dependent upon his access to, and command of, a private household, which includes a wife. What undergirds the individual's capacity to pursue his self-interest in a society based on free contract? What 'private' arrangements must be in place before public dealings between individuals can be understood as regulated by impartial and just norms? Feminist political theorists have argued that the exclusion of women and children was central in the formation of modern conceptions of the public.[21] As many have argued, the notion of the 'individual' in liberal political theory invariably turns out to be a male head of a household.

Care and Justice in Historical Context: 'The Personal is Political'

'Men make their own history but under circumstances directly encountered, given and transmitted from the past.'[22] Whether we like it or not we are all compelled to live our lives within institutions governed by normative assumptions to which we did not give our consent. These normative parameters affect our relations with others and our capacity to act in certain ways. Presumably, it is this fact of our social existences which underlies the famous feminist slogan, 'The personal is political'. I take this to mean that our personal relations are lived in political structures that form and limit how we may act. Feminists have argued that even, or especially, the most private of our feelings are affected by our political context. A well-known feminist, writing in 1972, argued that a 'book on radical feminism that did not deal with love would be a political failure. For love . . . is the pivot of women's oppression today.'[23] Those relations which we enter through personal or private choice, for example, marriage, are often as prescriptive as those in which we merely find ourselves, for example, the family and the society to which we are born. Legal institutions prescribe what we can and also what we cannot do within such voluntary associations. These legal norms may generate new, as well as legitimate existing, informal norms of habit and custom which then operate to sanction and constrain transgressive behaviour and actions.

Marriage is the institution which governs most heterosexual love relations in the present. Historically, laws governing marriage denied wives any civil existence at all. Women, upon marriage, were placed under the coverture of their husbands. Vestiges of the historical notion of women's 'civil death' upon marriage remain in our present marriage laws. An understanding of men's and women's present legal status requires some understanding of the past.

John Stuart Mill was painfully aware of the rights and powers conferred upon him, independently of his will, by the marriage contract. Mill felt strongly enough about the injustice of laws governing marriage to draw up a counter-document on the occasion of his own marriage. This document reads, in part,

> the whole character of the marriage relation as constituted by law being such that both she and I entirely and conscientiously disapprove, for this among other reasons, that it confers upon one of the parties to the contract, legal power and control over the person, property, and freedom of action of the other party, independent of her wishes and will; I, having no means of legally divesting myself of these odious powers . . . feel it my duty to put on record a formal protest against the existing law of marriage, in so far as conferring such powers; and a solemn promise never in any case or under any circumstances to use them.[24]

Mill's comments draw attention to the extent to which our private and personal relations are bound by regulation. Such legal sanctioning of relations of power and subservience establishes a differentiation between the sexes in terms of economic and social status *independently* of the will of the spouses. This, in turn, will inevitably affect the character of love and justice as it is lived and theorized by men and women. For women, love all too frequently can involve sacrificing one's own needs for the needs of others. This may be seen as a structural requirement of many women's lives rather than any innate tendency to self-denial. To quote Mill again: 'If women are better than men in anything it surely is in individual self-sacrifice for those of their own family. But I lay little stress on this, so long as they are universally taught that they are born and created for self-sacrifice.'[25] That women's love often *comes to mean* care for other has everything to do with their training *as women*.

The marriage contract has certainly changed since John Stuart Mill and Harriet Taylor were married, yet it is still, as many feminists have argued, a contract that can be viewed as a feudal or pre-modern relic.[26] Susan Moller Okin, for example, observes that if we are to achieve justice between the sexes then we must recognize that personal relations within the family adversely effect women's freedom of action in all other institutional settings, especially the contractual public sphere, understood by liberals to be the paradigm of free and equal association. Marriage, she maintains, is a very peculiar contract,

> that does not conform with the *principles* . . . of liberal contract doctrine. It is a preformed status contract which restricts the parties' freedom to choose their partners (for example, there must be only one partner, and of the opposite sex) and of which they are *not free to choose the terms*. The courts' refusal to enforce explicit contracts between husband and wife . . . has been due to the fact that the courts have regarded the *terms of marriage as already established*. When, for example, they have refused to enforce intramarital agreements in which wives have agreed to forgo support for other consideration, and in which husbands have agreed to pay their wives for work done in a family business, they have done so on the grounds that the *wife's right to support* in the former case, and her *obligation to provide services* for her husband, in the latter, are *fixed by the marriage contract itself* . . . Gender-structured marriage is a clear case of socially created and reinforced inequality.[27]

Such views present a serious challenge to the common assumption that the private sphere is unregulated. They also challenge the individualist's claim that the institution in which heterosexual love most often makes its 'home' is private and so may be entirely shaped by the values and preferences of those who enter it. The simple fact is that love plus marriage equals a legal *obligation*, on the part of the wife, to provide 'services' that centre on the care of her husband and children, and on the part of the husband, to provide economic support. In this sense, the formation of individual preferences (to be the child-rearer rather than the wage-earner, for example) can not be seen as wholly exogenous to one's social position, including one's sex.

Love, as it is lived in the contemporary institution of marriage and the family, is bound to have quite different consequences and a quite different meaning for women than for men. Moreover, since almost all of us were raised in families, those who never marry do not thereby escape the formative influences of marriage. The family is a crucial site for the acquisition and development of notions of fairness and socially acceptable attitudes and behaviour. Relations beween husband and wife have profound effects on children raised in that context. Conscious and unconscious expectations surrounding sexual difference and self-worth have their origins in the family. Families reproduce not just physical beings, they also reproduce the values and customs which govern the behaviour of human beings in specific social and political contexts.

This different placement of men and women does not merely affect their conceptions of love but will, in a general sense at least, colour the character and development of all their moral values, including justice. It is an implicit feature of the marriage contract and an explicit feature of common social perceptions of marriage that husbands 'provide for' their wives by participating in wage work whereas wives perform a set of unpaid 'services' for their husbands and children.[28] However, the provision of such services cannot be seen simply as a 'job', since the care that women provide in the home is understood as a way of showing their love for their families. As Hanne Haavind argues, 'there are differences between what the male and the female are supposed to and willing to do *because* of love.'[29] One common consequence then of love and marriage in contemporary society is that it turns women inward, towards the needs of a particular household, which is conceived as a realm of care, whereas it turns men outwards, toward the public world of wage-labour governed by universal principles intended to 'check' the self-interest of actors in that world.

Women who are mothers and who also participate in wage-labour are thus arguably put in a 'double-bind'. The values, attitudes and behaviour appropriate to the family, along with the time and energy expended there, renders many women vulnerable to a range of harms in the context of paid employment.[30] Her habitual attentiveness to the affective needs and states of others as well as her tendency to value co-operation may leave her vulnerable to more competitive attitudes, such as that of 'every man for himself'. Her responsiveness to the needs of others may make women less able to deal with unwanted sexual advances in the workplace. Under these circumstances, that which each sex perceives as just and fair treatment may well vary.

Quite simply, the conceptions of love, care and justice which we have inherited from history and which have become embedded in our institutions, will take on markedly different interpretations for those whose actions are circumscribed by sexually specific day-to-day practices and institutionally de-marcated roles. Were it the case that men and women occupied different spheres, the promotion of sexually specific ethical relations would be be seen as a plausible solution to the conflicts between private interests and public good. However, such difference is inevitably hierarchized into relations of superiority and inferiority where public authority subordinates private interest. Clearly, the contemporary situation of women and men in western societies is not divided in this manner. It is matter of some urgency then, that men and women come to some agreement concerning the form of moral community in which both feel that they can live. My contribution to the ongoing task of forming such a community is to argue against some current trends in feminist theory and practice which recommend the extension of the care stance from the family to *all* our relations.

Between the Sexes

The tendency in some contemporary feminist moral theory to present the 'care stance' and the 'justice stance' as both exclusive and exhaustive approaches, functions to entrench further the very oppositions which feminists have suc-cessfully challenged: those between the personal and the political, the private and the public, the particular and the universal. The plausibility of the oppo-sition between care and justice is parasitic on these other oppositions. More-over, to fail to acknowledge this parasitic relation amounts to a tacit endorsement of the very oppositions that have historically come between the sexes and which function to keep them apart. In this sense the care stance, taken alone, is a conservative moral position that harks back to an ideology of 'sepa-rate spheres' for the sexes. It is also a stance that operates by a double standard since it assumes that the inadequacies of the justice stance may be traced to men's domination of women without acknowledging the implications of such a claim for the moral values which women have developed in a situation of subordination.

Both femininity and masculinity as they are presently constituted are partial and distorted ways of being female and male in contemporary society. To assert the superiority of one over the other is to ignore their highly interdependent relation. Feminine ways of being moral do not have an automatically superior value simply by virtue of their association with women. Nor should we expect to produce a satisfactory moral stance simply by treating care and justice as complementary – as forming a neutral 'androgynous' moral theory when com-bined. If both women's and men's experience has been distorted and biased by their respective institutional and historical placement then adding the two perspectives together will not cancel out that distortion. As Genevieve Lloyd has argued,

The idea that women have their own distinctive kind of intellectual or moral character has itself been partly formed within the philosophical traditon to which it may now appear to be a reaction . . . 'the feminine' . . . occur[s] in a space already prepared for it by the intellectual tradition it seeks to reject.[31]

Given the gendered history of these concepts, we may well hold prejudicial expectations that men's and women's moral behaviour will be governed by one or the other stance, but in practice most people employ aspects of both care and justice in familial, work and friendship settings. Marilyn Friedman, arguing along similar lines, has claimed that 'the care–justice dichotomy is rationally implausible and that the two concepts are conceptually compatible'.[32]

In order to address the problem of men who abuse their positions of power or who fail to give adequate care, we require an analysis of power rather than the assertion of sexually differentiated moral perspectives. Stereotypical understandings of femininity and masculinity may well be implicated in the power relations between the sexes. Femininity is often characterized by terms such as responsiveness, submissiveness and passivity but that which is taken to characterize femininity should not be confused with how women actually behave and neither femininity nor women's perspectives should be confused with feminist theory. Even if it were the case that many women tend to take a care stance in their moral judgements, this would not, in itself, be any reason for feminists to value that stance over others. To do so is to risk affirming those very qualities that have become associated with women through their subordination. It is appropriate, at this point, to return to the example of 'different realities' with which this paper began.

An adequate analysis of the 'date-rape' story is hampered by the fact that it is a brief and fictional recreation of a phenomenon which according to some is very common. At face value it is a clear case of a man raping a woman, since we are told that she tells him to stop and he does not. However, the highly stylized and stereotyped portrayal of the sexes tells another story. She is interested in his personality ('he was a great listener'), he is interested in her body ('she looked really hot'; 'great body'). She is portrayed as seeking a relationship, he is portrayed as seeking his own self-interest. The pamphlet does not simply convey a message about rape or the dangers of dating, it offers a sketch of male and female preferences and behaviours that tells a story about female vulnerability and male strength. It also raises a more general concern about the tendency in some contemporary feminist thought to see (hetero)sexual intercourse as inherently oppressive or harmful to women.[33] Sexual intercourse certainly can be, and often is, a metaphor for the power play between the sexes. However, the tendency to assume that the victor and the victim are always pre-scripted can function to invalidate those occasions on which women *do* consent.[34] This hunter/hunted pre-scripting should be of concern to feminists. It runs the risk of returning women to a legal category from which they have recently, and perhaps only partially, escaped: the category which includes children and the mentally incompetent whose testimony and consent can not be taken seriously. Such persons' perceptions are seen not only as different but as unreliable.

MacKinnon argues for special rights of protection for women partly on the basis on their inability to care for themselves. In this sense she supports a contextual ethic of care, administered through the law, which takes account of the specificities of women's situation.[35] She argues that legal assumptions concerning adult status – that adults are autonomous, self-defining, free, equal – are systematically denied by women's treatment in society and particularly by their depiction in pornography. From this basis, she argues,

> Some of the same reasons *children* are granted some specific legal avenues for redress – relative lack of power, inability to command respect for their consent and self-determination, in some cases less physical strength or lowered legitimacy in using it, specific credibility problems, and lack of access to resources for meaningful self-expression – also hold true for the social positon of *women* compared to men.[36]

MacKinnon maintains that gender differences should be understood as differences in power. Feminine and masculine traits are socially constructed in contexts of male power over women. MacKinnon's strategy in the face of this power imbalance is to impose an ethic of care on the state that is realized through the law. The result is that all women are denied autonomy and infantilized. They are seen as lacking the qualities that define adults. This strategy fails to take account of the problematic demarcation of the dualisms mentioned at the beginning of this paper. The simple fact is that every adult person who is autonomous necessarily is involved in a variety of relations of interdependency. Moreover, some men, as well as women, are not autonomous even in this qualified interdependent sense. However, this is not sufficient justification to treat women as a blanket category and infantilize them *all*. As a public and legal attempt to redress the power imbalance between the sexes, MacKinnon's strategy empowers women only to the extent that they occupy the role of the victim or the wronged party.

MacKinnon's strategy is one which opposes care and protection (administered through the law) to power and so fails to acknowledge the exercise of power that is involved in care. Even in an idealized situation of care, one party is exercising his or her power to affect what she or he *takes to be* the well-being of the other. This is not to argue that all power relations are bad, it is rather to argue that power, understood as the capacity to affect the actions of others, is present in all human relations. In adult–child relations this power is necessarily unequally distributed. The exercise of the power to protect in relation to children need not be an exercise in domination since they lack certain capacities crucial to self-determination. As Spinoza pointed out, if childhood were a permanent state, we would feel very sorry for children. However, adults can be deprived of the opportunity to develop skills of self-protection and self-care if they are treated like children. There is some reason to regard with caution feminist strategies that attempt legally to encode perceptions of women's weakness. The institutionalization of notions which infantilize women may function to entrench traditional ideas about their need for special protection. In this sense, the application of the care stance to public institutions, such as law, may function conservatively.

The tendency to see either care or justice as providing an exhaustive account of morality impoverishes our ability to think beyond either the family (dispenser of care) or the state (dispenser of justice).[37] It is precisely this dichotomy that we need to think beyond if we are to build a moral community between men and women that is neither a maternalized state nor a masculinized private sphere.[38]

NOTES

1 de Beauvoir, *The Second Sex*, p. 624.
2 The *Wolfenden Report* (1957) is a report on the proper scope of the law, particularly in relation to homosexuality and prostitution. Quoted in Lacey, 'Theory into practice?', p. 97.
3 Perhaps the best-known work on this subject is Catharine MacKinnon's *Feminism Unmodified: Discourses on Life and Law*.
4 MacKinnon, *Feminism Unmodified*, esp. pp. 180–3.
5 See Pateman, *Sexual Contract* and *Disorder of Women*.
6 Roiphe, *The Morning After*.
7 Ibid., pp. 58–9.
8 See, for example, Aristotle, *Nicomachean Ethics* and Rousseau, *Émile*. For an example of feminist criticisms made of the sex-specific moralities of Aristotle and Rousseau respectively, see Saxonhouse, 'Aristotle: defective males, hierarchy, and the limits of politics'. *Theory*. See also Gatens, *Feminism and Philosophy*.
9 See Gatens, *Feminism and Philosophy*, ch. 1.
10 Ruddick, *Maternal Thinking*.
11 Held, *Feminist Morality*.
12 Noddings, *Caring: a Feminist Approach*.
13 Gilligan, *In a Different Voice*, p. 19.
14 Held, *Feminist Morality*, p. 80.
15 Ibid., p. 195.
16 Ibid., p. 207
17 Quoted in Kymlicka, *Contemporary Political Philosophy*, p. 52.
18 See Kymlica, *Contemporary Political Philosophy*, pp. 265 and 270 for comparable lists.
19 Young, *Justice and the Politics of Difference*, p. 21.
20 Friedman, *What Are Friends For?*, pp. 122–3.
21 See, for example, Landes, *Women and the Public Sphere*.
22 Marx, quoted in Okin, *Justice, Gender and the Family*, p. 140.

23 From Firestone's *Dialectic of Sex*, quoted in Solomon and Higgins, *Philosophy of (Erotic) Love*, p. 247.
24 Quoted in Rossi, *Eassys on Sex Equality*, p. 45.
25 Quoted in McCloskey, 'Some consequences of a conjective economics', p. 79.
26 Compare with the view expressed by Pateman in *Sexual Contract*.
27 Okin, *Justice, Gender and the Family*, pp. 122–3, emphasis added.
28 Ibid., p. 139.
29 Haavind, 'Love and power in marriage', p. 145.
30 See Game and Pringle, *Gender at Work*, especially ch. 6.
31 Lloyd, *The Man of Reason*, 2nd edn, p. 105
32 Friedman, *What Are Friends For?*, p. 126.
33 See, for example, Dworkin, *Intercourse*.
34 For a challenging critique of the victim–victor pre-scripting of women and men see Marcus, 'Fighting bodies, fighting words'.
35 This claim may seem odd given that MacKinnon sharply dismisses Gilligan's views. (See MacKinnon, *Feminism Unmodified*, pp. 38–9.) My argument here is that MacKinnon is unaware of how closely her views on the appropriate role of the law approximate and tacitly accept Gilligan's stance.
36 MacKinnon, *Feminism Unmodified*, p. 181.
37 For an alternative model of ethical community see Friedman, *What Are Friends For?*.
38 An earlier version of this paper was delivered to the Philosophy Department at the Research School of Social Sciences, The Australian National University. I would like to thank participants for their comments. For helpful criticisms on an early draft of this paper thanks are due to Brenda Almond, Barbara Caine, Robert Goodin, Duncan Ivison, Alison MacKinnon, Michael Smith, Susan Wolf and especially, Paul Patton.

READING GUIDE

A clear and (critically) sympathetic introduction to feminist moral philosophies of care is Will Kymlicka's *Contemporary Political Philosophy*, chapter 7. Kymlicka's text offers an accessible introduction to a number of moral theories (utilitarianism, Rawls, Marxism and communitarianism) in contemporary philosophy which is very useful for providing the context for current debates in feminist moral theory.

The diversity of feminist moral philosophical stances may be gleaned from a collection of essays edited by Eva Kittay and Diana Meyers, *Women and Moral Theory*. This collection includes several critical discussions of the notion that men and women reason differently about moral issues.

The most cogent account of the care–justice debate may be found in Marilyn Friedman's *What Are Friends For?*, especially Part II. Virginia Held in *Feminist Morality: Transforming Culture, Society and Politics*, chapter 10, offers a sketch of what society might look like were it to take familial rather than contractual relations as its model. Susan Moller Okin, who is not convinced of the validity of the care–justice dichotomy, offers an alternative view of the sorts of social, economic and political change needed in order for relations between the sexes to become just, in *Justice, Gender and the Family*.

4

Children Who Run: Ethics and Homelessness

Michael Parker

The Problem

The rising incidence of homelessness in the countries of Western Europe and the United States, together with the fact that among the homeless the very young are increasingly highly represented, raises a number of ethical and social issues which must be confronted by the whole community: by the homeless themselves, by their relatives, those professionally involved and by the public at large.[1] The effect of homelessness upon the lives of very young children is of particular concern and also where the ethical issues are at their most intense.[2] Despite the substantial and growing number of children who currently run away from home or from local authority care, going on to become homeless, there is no consensus about either the rights of the children themselves or about the allocation of responsibility for their protection.[3] Indeed, I shall be going on to argue that this lack of consensus is itself one of the causes of the increase in homelessness among children. For it allows children as young as 9 or 10 to 'fall through the net' and to end up living on the streets of major cities or, increasingly, rural towns and villages.[4]

The present chapter falls into two parts. In the first part I introduce the problem of homelessness among children, partly on the basis of my own experience and partly on the basis of recent empirical research.[5] I then elaborate some of the ethical and social issues raised by the problem. In the second part of the chapter I go on to look at what philosophy can have to say about the ethical issues raised in the first part and I attempt to give pointers towards a conceptual framework which might help in the clarification of such issues. Finally, in my conclusion, I attempt, in a limited way, to propose practical ways in which, using the conceptual framework I have sketched, some of the underlying causes of homelessness among children might begin to be eliminated.

Homelessness

Homelessness enters most people's lives, if it does so at all, through their television screen, their newspaper or perhaps, if they live in one of our larger cities, because they happen to trip over beggars on their way to work or as they leave the theatre at night. The rising incidence of homelessness means that fewer people can be unaware that it exists and that it is an aspect of their own community and the way of life of those around them. In this sense youth homelessness and indeed all homelessness presents itself as an issue of concern and a *problem for the whole community*.

On the face of it, a good solution to the problem of homelessness might be seen to be one which simply got people off the streets. This certainly can be a worthwhile activity and the British government's Rough Sleepers Initiative was a positive move in this sense.[6] However, the question which needs surely to be answered is why it is that so many children are ending up on the streets in the first place, and this question retains its importance even when an emergency shelter is substituted for the street. Clearly, every homeless child has his or her own story to be told. However, in my experience, homelessness has less to do with the details of the individual's circumstances, tragic as these may be, than with what happens as the tragedy unfolds. For it is ambivalence about the resolution of certain central questions of responsibility which constitutes the 'hole in the net' through which children at risk fall, ending up on the street. It should not seem strange therefore that I begin my consideration of homelessness not with people on the street but by looking at the breakdown of the relationships between children and those who are responsible for their welfare. For this is where homelessness begins.

Children Who Run

In most cases children live and grow up with those family members who take responsibility for them from birth. This usually means a member, or members, of the child's biological family, or perhaps a stepparent. A significant number of children, however, will spend their childhood in the care of foster parents, social workers or those by whom they have been adopted. Whichever of these is the case, under normal circumstances, children usually remain the responsibility of their 'family' throughout their childhood, this relationship of dependence ending naturally, though not without difficulty, as the child becomes an adult and achieves something like independence.

The first step on the way to a child becoming homeless inevitably involves the breakdown of these forms of support and there are three general ways in which this might come about. These are:

1 When the child runs away from the family home. Approximately 30,000 children aged 17 or under ran away from their family home in England and Scotland in 1990.[7]
2 When the child runs away from care. In 1990, 13,000 children ran away from care in England and Scotland.[8]
3 When the parent or legal guardian evicts the child from the household.[9]

Most runaways cite arguments within the family as a significant reason for running away from home.[10] Most are in their mid-teens. This is inevitably a time of transition and some conflict for most children as they move toward independence and adulthood. The conflicts which occur at this time are not all, however, of the kind that lead children to leave home and most get resolved one way or another within the family itself.[11] There are times when as a teenager it is tempting and natural to want to run away but probably wrong to do so. Few children would leave home because they hadn't got the gift they wanted for Christmas or because they had been told to be in by ten o'clock at night. But there are times, it seems to me, when it clearly is right for a child seriously to consider running away from home or from care. Recent accounts in the news of cases of the sexual and physical abuse of children and of their severe neglect by parents, and indeed by social workers, often make one wonder why the children concerned hadn't run away sooner than they did.

The difference in importance between the kinds of reasons a child might give for considering leaving home or care is clear in the cases I have described but there most also be borderline cases; perhaps where a child feels that she is being restrained unreasonably from doing what she wants to do or where she has been beaten for breaking a house rule and is unsure whether she is at risk in the longer term. In such cases it must be extremely difficult for a child to decide whether to stay or run away. In general, children find it hard to leave home even when their mistreatment has been very serious, often staying in an abusive situation for many years before gaining the courage, or perhaps sufficient fear, to leave. Family loyalty, fear of homelessness and the threat of punishment, even in abusive families, are often so powerful that it is reasonable to assume that if a child does run away and stay away there is almost inevitably *something* wrong even if it is not in fact abuse. Research by the National Children's Home[12] suggests that just over three-quarters of those children who do run away from home or care return of their own accord within forty-eight hours; but there is also research showing that of those who turned up at one particular shelter – that of Centrepoint in London – 31 percent said that they were running from abuse.[13] If one takes into account the difficulty involved in talking about such things to strangers, it is possible that the numbers are actually higher than this.

The question of when it is right for a child to run away from home or care is not one that admits of a general and conclusive answer. The decision about whether or not to leave has ultimately to be the child's. It will tend to be based upon something like the extent to which she feels that she is a genuine participant *for herself* in her relationships with those who are responsible for her, measured against the degree to which she feels she is no longer a participant in this sense but rather the victim of an abuse of power on the part of those who are her 'carers'. Children run away because they have been denied the opportunity to participate in defining their own identity and the nature of the relationships they have with those around them. That they have run away is sufficient ground for concern. For they have chosen the dangers of the street over those of home.

When children run away, most stay in their local area but all are clearly at serious risk.[14] One can imagine the places they end up sleeping and the dangers they face in so doing; these dangers are increased by the fact that they will know that if they present themselves at a police station or at a night shelter they run the further risk of being returned to the 'care' of those from whom they have run. Perhaps they have run away before and this has happened. For this reason runaways have, aside from their age, been at particular risk. The reason for this added risk has been that until recently, under Section 2 of the Child Abduction Act 1984, it has been an offence for anyone to take away or detain anyone under 16 years of age, and this has meant that agencies working with runaways have faced the risk of prosecution and have had to turn them over to the police. A consequence of this has been that those children who are afraid of going home or afraid of the police, have commonly ended up on the street and in this sense have fallen through even the safety net provided for other (older) homeless people by the voluntary organizations.

One of the practical aspects of working with such vulnerable children is that when they arrive at a shelter or hostel they are often frightened and tired and tend to have very little reason to believe that adults are to be trusted. The balance between staying with unknown adults in a hostel and sleeping rough on the street may be extremely fine, given the child's experiences. This means that in a one-off interview or even within the space of a day, hostel workers are often unlikely to hear the child's account of why she has run away, let alone any details of where she is from or who she is. The child's fear at this stage may simply be the result of nights on the street or of experiences she has had since she left home and it *may* turn out that the reason she left home is insufficient ground for her not to be returned home fairly promptly. She may, however, have been subjected to years of horrifying abuse by those responsible for her welfare and may have been terrified into keeping her secret. If the child is saying nothing, or perhaps nothing other than that she does not want to go home, what ought hostel workers to do? In practice, the immediate physical and emotional welfare of the child will provide a priority and this will involve an assessment of what is in her longer-term interest, to be arrived at on the basis (partly) of what the child herself reveals as she comes to trust those who are working on her behalf. But such a process inevitably takes time, and for this there must be a 'safe place' where a child might be helped to feel at her ease and encouraged to tell her story in her own time to people she could come to trust. Section 2 of the Child Abduction Act 1982 however has meant that in the UK such places have until recently been illegal.

Notwithstanding the legal context, the existence of a 'refuge' of this kind clearly raises all sorts of ethical questions about the rights of parents and other agencies. For, whilst it seems sensible that the primary and immediate responsibility of those who come into contact with runaways ought to be the child's safety, they must also be subject to responsibilities in addition to those they have to the child. The hostel and its employees are in addition responsible to a wider community which includes the police, the social services and indeed the child's parents or guardians. In many cases, if not all, these responsibilities will pull in opposite directions and this tension creates a number of practical ethical problems for those who come into contact with homeless runaways. To what extent then, given that the child has in fact chosen to run away, ought parents or carers to continue to be allowed access to the child? Ought the parent or carer ever to be able to demand that the child is returned home immediately and, in cases where this is ruled out, ought the parent to know where the child is and be allowed to have contact? There will be occasions, say in cases where a child is making accusations of sexual abuse, when the question of the parents' right to manage their own affairs and the lives of the children concerned will have to be given very serious consideration. The details of any particular case can only be assessed in the light of the facts of that case but it could be argued that, in these more serious cases, the parent or carer ought not to be allowed, at least in the short term, to see the child. For, in such cases, it may be important to keep her location a secret from them in order to prevent her once again from becoming a victim.

On the other hand, it also seems clear that there may well be occasions, certainly not in cases of abuse but perhaps in cases of other kinds of mistreatment, when the family ought to be able to maintain a certain amount of contact and possibly after some counselling, acquire the right to be reunited. There may, further, be far less serious cases of disputes where the child ought to be returned to the family or carer as a matter of course.

In the short term, however, when a particular child is discovered to be at risk, it may well not be possible to decide quickly which of these descriptions applies, and this poses a dilemma. For, if it is argued that families ought only to lose their right to manage their affairs, in this kind of case, if there is evidence that members of that family have been mistreated and if, as is often the case at this early stage, there is no actual evidence of any kind (other than the fact that the child has run away from home), should not the hostel's primary responsibility then be to return the child immediately to his or her family? For the child's parents or carer, the right to have the child returned to them if nothing incriminating comes out is the least that can be demanded. Having come indirectly into contact with the hostel, they have a broader and more general right to be treated fairly in its work. Their right to be contacted and told that the child is well and in safe hands is, then, beyond dispute but should they have any rights in addition to these? This is the other horn of the dilemma. For the claims of parents and carers, important as these may be, need to be weighed against the fact that there may well be reason to believe the child to be at risk *from* her family. There may also turn out to be some serious criminal consequences, for the parents or social workers, of the child telling her story. How are we to balance the child's need for refuge against the rights of the parent or carer?

The need for a resolution of this dilemma and of these ethical questions is clearly of great urgency. For the consequence of the current ambivalence is that children, fearing that they will not be taken seriously and fearing that they will be returned to those from whom they have run, are avoiding contact with those who, under different circumstances, might be able to help them. In this way, this very ambivalence can be said to be a contributing factor to the problem of runaways who are homeless and consequently at risk.

The Ethical Issues

It is clear at the outset that solutions to the problem of homelessness can in the end only come about as a result of concerted practical and political measures. Nevertheless, finding the right practical measures depends upon first laying open the unspoken ethical and conceptual assumptions which inform our understanding of particular social problems, thereby making policy decisions, if not easier certainly more clearly delineated. It is here that philosophy is able to make a distinctive contribution. Philosophers are essentially concerned with the use of argument and the pursuit of clarity. Many of the arguments in everyday use are bedevilled by a lack of clarity, much of which springs from the ambivalence of key concepts. This ambivalence often has practical consequences, as in the present case, when ambiguities about rights and responsibilities compound the problems of runaways.

If philosophy is going to make a useful contribution to such ethical debates, however, it will not be by attempting, as philosophy often has, to stand outside the everyday processes of dialogue and negotiation which together constitute the means by which people work out meaningful ways of living together. Moral philosophers, believing, rightly, that the putting aside of one's own interests must be central to ethics, have sometimes implied that the making of objective moral judgments must involve, in addition, finding a standpoint outside the community and indeed outside what it is to be human at all. They have attempted to achieve this in many ways. Some have advocated the adoption of the position of an 'Ideal Observer' who must, by standing aside from the affairs of the world, attempt to take on all preferences, interests or pleasures and make a decision on the basis of satisfying the greater number of these.[15] Others, in particular John Rawls, have suggested that a position ought to be adopted 'behind a veil of ignorance' from where an approach to ethical problems could be arrived at by the drawing up of an impartial contract or set of rules.[16] However, the problem with approaches which depend on this kind of radical detachment is that they tend to obscure the truth that problems like homelessness arise *just because* of our social embeddedness, i.e. because we are human and because both homeless people and we ourselves are part of the ways of life from which we draw our identity. Philosophy, then, is of more use in practical affairs when, instead of encouraging us to step back from the problem at hand, it is willing for us to get involved more deeply with these problems in their specificity.

I have throughout this chapter referred to homelessness as a problem for 'communities' and before moving on to look at homelessness itself, a little needs to be said about just what is meant by a 'community' here. When asked by a philosopher, such a question is often once again a demand that one steps back from the particulars of one's own social embeddedness, but the definition I have in mind here is a practical one and one with which I believe most people would identify. One's 'community' in the sense in which I shall be using the term in this chapter is to be loosely defined as being constituted by all those people with whom we have to work out meaningful ways of living together. The nature of these negotiations may vary both in form and in intensity but the existence of negotiation of some kind is fundamental to the possibility of social, and ultimately of individual, life itself. This 'negotiational' account of community allows for the sense of degrees of community or identification which we all tend to feel.[17] Within the family, people enter into complex and extended negotiation about a whole range of aspects of how to live meaningfully together (or separately) *as* a family. There is often a great sense of reciprocity here, even in disputes, and feelings of community within the family are often by far the strongest sense of community many people are likely to experience. Even within the family however, decisions about communal life cannot be isolated from the individual's sense of also belonging to a wider community. This might be a matter, for example, of deciding whether to recycle our refuse in response to our concern for future generations or in contrast, it might be a matter of dealing with accusations of abuse when social workers and police arrive on the doorstep in the middle of the night to take our children away. In the modern world, via television, there is also a sense in which, for example, homeless children on the streets of Soho become *de facto* members of our community. Do we join a charity, give a donation, worry about the safety of our own children or simply ignore the problem? Any of these responses may be meaningful ways of dealing with a newly arrived-at sense of being human beings together, of sharing in a community or rather a range of communities.[18]

A common difficulty faced by accounts of ethics which are based in notions of 'community' is that they tend to have difficulty explaining just what would be wrong with, say sexual abuse, were a particular community universally to see it as right. The problem arises because 'communitarian' approaches tend to see the community as the primary source of notions of goodness and the rights of individuals as secondary to the maintenance of communal life. It seems to me that in general such criticisms of communitarianism are valid. Any useful ethical approach must be capable, at least sometimes, of upholding the rights of individuals *against* their community.[19] By defining 'community' as consisting of those with whom I enter into negotiation about how we are to live meaningfully together, I tie it both to the importance and the meaningfulness of an individual life and to the importance, for the very existence of both the community and of the individual, of meaningful dialogue between the two. Thus the identity of persons is seen to be bound up, at least to some extent, with their ability to engage in meaningful relationships with others, having been thrown by birth and circumstance into networks of relationships within which they must negotiate both their identity and the meaningfulness of the world around them.

In the previous paragraph I introduced the concept of 'rights' and described some of the problems which arise from too abstract interpretations of rights in contrast to stressing the notion of 'community'. Whilst philosophical discussion of the concept of 'rights' has a relatively short history linguistically, it is true that rights belong to a well-established tradition of ethical reasoning.[20] Their origins can be traced to the recognition by the Stoic philosophers in ancient Greece of the possibility that the actual laws in a particular community might be seen to be unjust when contrasted with a 'natural law' which is not itself relative to a particular community, and to which everyone has access through individual reflection. For this reason the concept of 'universal human rights' which grew out of the 'natural law' tradition has often appealed to those who have felt themselves to be oppressed. It may be argued that it is this appeal to universal human rights transcending any particular community that makes it possible to uphold the rights of individuals *against* their community, and it must be admitted that in recent years the concept of universal human rights has come to play an important role in the practice of international relations and in the critique of government.

But whilst the appeal to universal human rights has great power in a pragmatic sense, just how far can one identify 'rights' intelligibly with the concept of an individual over and above her community? To what extent does it make sense to talk of human beings, and consequently their rights, transcending community in this way? I argued earlier that it is not possible to conceive of individuals who are able in some sense to step outside of their community. The intelligibility of the concept of universal human rights, in so far as this is understood in terms of the rights of the universal individual, rests ultimately upon the possibility of a similar radical detachment of the individual from human concerns. For it requires an appeal to something like the concept of an 'inner person' independent of social context. The appeal to universal human rights in this individualistic sense is made possible by the contrast between the needs of the community and those of this 'inner person'.

However, as I pointed out earlier, the problem with any approach which demands the radical detachment of the person from his or her community and consequently from all meaningful interaction with others, is that it requires one to lose sight of the fact that human concerns are *concerns for us* just because of our social embeddedness, because we are human and because our humanity is framed by the fact that we share in ways of life with other people out of which we draw our identity. It is our social embeddedness which makes it possible for us to *be* individuals. For it is in our social interactions that we negotiate our identity and it is here also that we play our role in the maintenance and transformation of our community. Both individuals and communities appear to be made possible by their interrelatedness and their interaction.[21]

In the light of these considerations it seems that any satisfactory analysis of rights[22] must begin from the recognition that rights are to be located neither in the individual nor in the community, but in the nature of the ethical negotiations between them. Ethical problems arise with respect not simply to individuals or communities in themselves but to the forms of negotiation they undertake, to work out meaningful ways of living together; that is, the ways in which they treat each other. This means that if there is to be a justification of the use of a vocabulary of rights, this cannot lie in a commitment to the existence of an abstract 'individual' but must lie instead in a commitment to particular ways of living with others, to particular 'ethical' ways of living. The best expression of this kind of commitment, it seems to me, is Kant's maxim that we should treat each other not as 'means' but as 'ends'.[23] One can see how such a commitment might lead, in a fruitful way, to a different analysis of rights, in a more socially embedded language, and comprising, on the one hand, a positive right to have an active role in the creation of a meaningful identity *for oneself* in one's negotiations with others, and on the other hand, a complementary negative right not to be objectified in such negotiations; that is, not to be fixed by it *despite oneself*.

Such an account could I believe, lead to an enriching of the link between the question of who can be the subject of a right and the question of the duties which such rights imply for others. For consideration of the link between duties and rights in this context must again bring one back to communities, that is, to the idea that both rights and duties are tied in some sense to the nature of our relations to those with whom we have to work out meaningful ways of living together: our community.

This is not necessarily a narrow or restrictive conclusion, for the extended concept of community which I described in the earlier part of this discussion included, deliberately, not only members of a person's immediate family, or his or her town, culture or nation, but all those with whom it is necessary to work out meaningful ways of living together. Whilst this allows for the notion of degrees of community which most people feel, it is also a reminder of the fact that we do have meaningful relations with a community, whose constituency is diverse and extended, and that these wider relations too bring with them responsibilities and difficulties. This is why, as I argued earlier, homelessness is a *problem for everyone*.

For this issue, then, the concepts of the 'social embeddedness of individuals', 'community' and the 'negotiation of meaning' are fundamental, and are to be preferred to a theory of rights framed in individualistic terms; for it leads not to the call for freedom *from* community but to the call for the right to a *voice within one's community*. It is for want of a voice, it seems to me, that children run away from home or care in the first place and it is the fear that their voice will not be heard that forces them to remain at risk. It is their community – and the rest of us form that community – which denies them that voice.

Concluding Remarks

Homelessness enters the lives of most people, even if indirectly, and when this happens, homeless children become *de facto* members and victims of *our* community and hence a *problem for us*. As participants in such a community, we acquire a duty to do what we can to bring about the empowerment of the children concerned. What our responsibility is depends to some extent upon us, the nature of our lives and our ability to intervene. If all my time is taken up working for an AIDS charity for example, or if I am immobile, perhaps my obligation to the homeless might be satisfied by donations to a charity: I can not save everyone. But to ignore the issue is to continue to participate in a dialogue of victimization.

Homelessness is also and primarily both a personal issue for the children involved and their families and a professional issue for those who come into contact with the homeless through their work (hostel workers, the police, social workers, hospital staff, and others). Some of the problems raised by homelessness for those concerned are unique to this social issue: the combination of working with children, on the edge of the law and often against the wishes of the child's legal guardians, gives rise to a range of problems not previously encountered in combination. For many, the idea of third parties becoming involved in the relations between parents and their children or between the social services and a child in its care will be deeply worrying. However, the price we pay if we ignore this possibility (given sufficient safeguards) is a continuing rise in the number of children on the street, itself a deeply worrying prospect. Children, indeed all people, ought to be able to participate, that is to have a voice, in the everyday processes of dialogue which constitute the means by which people work out meaningful ways of living together and out of which they draw their identities. It may be the failure to allow children to take their full part in such processes, and the fact that they feel this so deeply, that causes them to run away in the first place, and if so, it may be the continued denial of this right that encourages them to stay away from those who might otherwise help them.

What is required, it seems to me, is the establishment, at many levels, of forums where children will feel safe and where they will be able to begin to participate in the dialogues which frame their lives. In the UK the Children Act of 1989 has made it possible, subject to stringent supervision, for approved agencies to work for a limited period with children who run away in something like the ways I have indicated. This can only be a good thing.[24] Establishing such refuges would not, of course, stop children running away from home or from care, nor would it stop them ending up on the street, but it would ensure that once there they would very quickly have access to the safety and support they are going to need to re-establish something like a healthy life-style.[25]

Youth homelessness itself will continue as long as we fail to reconstruct the nature of family life and life in our community in general in such a way that children feel themselves to be participating in the development of their own and their community's way of life rather than feeling themselves to be its victims. Perhaps the true measure of whether or not one's work with a child, or a parent (or anyone else for that matter), has been ethical is the extent to which they come through the experience feeling that their story has been heard and that they have been taken seriously. This is very different from having everything they say accepted as true!

NOTES

1 Research by the British charity Shelter, *Homelessness: the Facts*, published in 1992, shows that in 1991, 146,790 households were accepted as 'homeless' by local councils. Shelter estimates that this represents 420,000 individuals. But this can only be the tip of the iceberg because these figures only include those defined as 'in priority need'. Shelter estimates that up to 2 million people in the UK are either homeless or at risk of becoming homeless.

2 For the purposes of this chapter I shall be using the term 'child' to refer to young people under the age of 16 though much of what I have to say will also be of relevance to those of 16 and 17 years of age. This is because, in the UK at least, there is structural ambiguity about whether these are children or adults. This is apparent in the way social security

benefits are distributed, for example, where those under 18 have no automatic right to income support.

3 Abrahams and Mungall, *Runaways*.
4 See Button, *Rural Housing for Youth*.
5 I have been working with the young homeless in London, in a range of capacities, for the past decade. Most of this work has been with the charity Centrepoint.
6 For details see Strathdee, *No Way Back*.
7 National Children's Home, *Runaways*.
8 National Children's Home, *Runaways*.
9 Centrepoint's in-house statistics for April to September 1993 show that 22 per cent of those interviewed (387) said that they left home because they were told to leave.
10 See Strathdee, *Children Who Run*.
11 In this chapter I shall often refer to 'families', 'parents', 'home' and 'carers'. In each case note should be taken of my comments at the beginning of this chapter about the variety of environments in which children grow up and from which they run.
12 National Children's Home, *Runaways*.
13 Strathdee, *Children Who Run*.
14 National Children's Home, *Runaways*, showed that 98 per cent of runaways stay in their local area as defined by police force boundaries.
15 For a fuller discussion of these theories, see Williams, *Ethics and the limits of philosophy*, pp. 71–92.
16 Rawls, *A Theory of Justice*.
17 I have elaborated this idea more fully in my 'The growth of understanding'.
18 It is possible for those one does not know personally to become a part of one's community. For example, an advertisement in *The Times*, London, 17 May 1994 by Amnesty International achieved this in detailing allegations of killings of street children in Columbia.
19 See Bell, *Communitarianism and its Critics*.
20 For a discussion of the history and analysis of rights, see Almond, 'Rights'.
21 See, for example, Vygotsky, *Mind in Society*.
22 See Almond, 'Rights'.
23 *The Moral Law* (Kant's *Groundwork of the Metaphysics of Morals*), p. 91.
24 The Centrepoint refuge (the Glaxo Refuge for Children and Young People) was in 1994 still the only example.
25 Given that research seems to suggest that most runaways tend to stay in their local area there are grounds perhaps for the establishment of a network of such refuges.

READING GUIDE

This chapter looks at the problem of youth homelessness from a perspective which locates the roots of morality in the social lives of human beings and in the necessity for people to work out meaningful ways of living together. It does this by arguing that ethical problems arise just *because* of our social embeddedness and that philosophical approaches which involve finding a standpoint external to the concerns of actual human beings inevitably lose sight of why homelessness is a problem. These considerations are part of the current debate between communitarians and liberals, and a good account of this can be found in Daniel Bell's *Communitarianism and its Critics*. The issue of community is also discussed by Almond in chapter 16 of the present volume, and further references are to be found in the Reading Guide for that chapter.

There are many papers and reports on the issue of homelessness itself. A good place to start would be Susan Hutson and Mark Liddiard's *Youth Homelessness: the Construction of a Social Issue*. The rights of children and of parents have been explored in two publications from the Institute of Economic Affairs: *The Family: Is it Just Another Lifestyle choice?* edited by J. Davies and *Rising Crime and the Dismembered Family* by N. Dennis. The same issue is approached from a different direction in Mary Midgley's 'Rights talk will not sort out child abuse', *Journal of Applied Philosophy*, vol. 8, 1991, and Jill Jones's *Young People in and out of the Housing Market*. For a philosophical discussion of the idea of home, see A. Tucker, 'In search of home', *Journal of Applied Philosophy*, vol. 10, 1994.

PART II

Public and Professional Dimensions: Ethics and the Professions

5

Education: Conserving Tradition

John Haldane

I

Let me begin with a quotation from a figure not generally regarded as an educational thinker but one who, I believe, has provided some of the wisest counsel on the central questions of education of any author in this century. He writes,

> The trouble in too many of our modern schools is that the State, being controlled so specially by the few, allows cranks and experiments to go straight to the school-room when they have never passed through the Parliament, the public house, the private house, the church or the market place. Obviously it ought to be the oldest things that are taught to the youngest people; the assured and experienced truths that are put first to the baby. But in a school today the baby has to submit to a system that is younger than himself.

This spirited passage comes from a chapter headed 'Authority the unavoidable', in a section entitled 'Education; or, The Mistake About The Child' in G. K. Chesterton's *What's Wrong with the World* – a book first published in 1910.[1] As is detectable in this passage, Chesterton's interest includes a political concern about the distribution of power in society. However, the point I want to focus on is that signalled by the chapter title, i.e. the unavoidability of authority, and, related to this, the importance of seeing that education is (or includes, as a major part) a process of authoritative transmission of beliefs, attitudes and abilities from those who possess them to those who lack them. Chesterton makes this point with characteristic style a few pages prior to that from which I quoted above. He writes,

Education is only truth in a state of transmission; and how can we pass on truth if it has never come into our hand . . .

I know that certain crazy pedants have attempted to counter this difficulty by maintaining that education is not instruction at all. They present the process as coming not from outside, from the teacher, but entirely from inside the boy. Education, they say, is the Latin for leading out or drawing out the dormant faculties of each person . . . There is, indeed, in each living creature a collection of forces and functions; but education means producing these in particular shapes and training them to particular purposes, or it means nothing at all. Speaking is the most practical instance of the whole situation. You may indeed 'draw out' squeals and grunts from the child by simply poking him and pulling him about . . . But you will wait and watch very patiently indeed before you draw the English language out of him. That you have got to put into him; and there's an end on the matter.[2]

I am almost tempted to leave the issue there, confident that anyone reading Chesterton's words will be convinced of their truth; but a philosophical essay calls for a more elaborate articulation and defence of a thesis than these quotations provide. In the following sections, therefore, I shall say something about the philosophy of education as an area of systematic thought, and then embark upon the task of giving an account of education itself as a norm-bearing and norm-constrained social practice.

Before proceeding, however, I want to anticipate a possible response prompted by my title. It might reasonably be supposed that the conjunction of 'education', 'conservation' and 'tradition' signals the presentation of a conservative philosophy of education. As will become clear, I do think that in some sense education is conservative, indeed that it *must* be so. But this very assumption of necessity indicates that the conservatism in question is not that of a reactionary politics. I shall argue that of its nature education involves a commitment to the transmission from one generation to the next of a set of cognitive and social values; otherwise expressed, it involves inculcating in its recipients understanding of, and respect for, certain traditions. However that does not imply (but nor does it exclude) a commitment to educational practices designed to instil an unquestioning respect for the established political order, or for political authority more generally, or for market liberalism. Arguments for and against these views rest on moral, social, historical and economic premises additional to those which I claim establish the case for a tradition-conserving idea of education. For those with a Chestertonian appetite for paradox, the main point could be put by saying that reason makes conservative traditionalists of us all–even those of us who are, for example, radical socialists. Equivalently, an anti-conservative philosophy of education is a confusion potentially injurious to the minds of those it would seek to have educated by its lights.

II

As a branch of academic study analytical philosophy of education is a very new subject, going back perhaps to the Second World War but not much before then and not taking its present form until the 1960s.[3] Of course many major philosophers have thought and written about education in earlier periods, most famously Plato in the *Republic*, St Augustine in *De Magistro*, Descartes in his *Discourse on Method*, Kant in his *Pedagogical Lectures*, Rousseau in *Émile*, and Dewey in *Democracy and Education*; and other figures such as Comenius, Pestalozzi, Herbart, Froebel and Montessori set out systematic theories of educational aims and methods. None the less, it is only in the second half of the twentieth century that philosophy of education has established itself as an area of organized philosophical speculation.

This establishment and the future prospects for the subject depend upon a number of factors of which I shall only comment on two, both of which are related to more general developments in philosophy. First, in the post-war years, and in the English-speaking world, there developed within academic philosophy a certain understanding of its own competence and of its proper methods of enquiry which involved the idea that it is an essentially second order activity concerned with the task of clarifying confusions in various areas of thought, such as the natural and social sciences, religion, morality and less organized regions of recurrent thinking about the world and our experience of it. Given this conception of philosophical reflection as thought about thought and about the practices that thought informs, it was not long before some philosophers began to examine the central ideas and assumptions of education. So was born and grew *analytical philosophy of education*, the leading proponents of which included Israel Scheffler, Richard Peters and Paul Hirst at Harvard, London and Cambridge, respectively.[4]

True to its conception of philosophy this approach saw its aim as being that of understanding the nature of education in its most general structure: not studying the particularities of this or that teaching method or proposing specific educational goals, but discerning the overall form of educational activity and distinguishing within this the supporting framework of concepts and values. Typically this involved analysing the notions of teaching and of learning, of education, socialization and indoctrination, of knowledge and commitment and so on. However, although such a study was primarily reflective, aiming at understanding practice rather than at supporting or changing it, there were several points where theory touched upon policy.

First, analysis sometimes reveals confusions both in pre-reflective ways of thinking and in theories. For example, although he was not concerned with educational issues, Peter Geach's arguments against so called 'abstractionist' accounts of concept formation were taken up by philosophers of education and used in criticism of certain educational theories and methods.[5] Second, and relatedly, a familiar conclusion of philosophical analysis is the demonstration of inconsistency and fallacious reasoning in people's thinking. One area of education in which this sort of result has important implications is that of moral and religious instruction where issues of rationality and justification are to the fore. The question of whether the inculcation of virtue and of religious commitment is consistent with educational goals, as contrasted with the aim of indoctrination, is clearly an important one, the answer to which should bear upon actual practice. This leads to the third point of contact. The analysis of educational concepts often showed them to be, in part or in whole, evaluatively or normatively laden. I mean by this that the processes and outcomes they describe are implicitly held to be desirable (or undesirable), required (or prohibited). This has sometimes been put in terms of a contrast between internal and external features and relations. For example, the fact that the injection into a human body of certain chemicals leads to the destruction of particular kinds of tissue leaves unanswered the question whether to do so is good, bad or indifferent. By contrast, it is not an 'open question' whether medical treatment is a desirable practice; so that if administering the chemical is part of such a treatment we can assume, other things being equal, that what is going on is good. This is because the description 'providing medical treatment' is internally related to the idea of bringing about or restoring health. This aim is a non-contingent feature of medicine. Similarly, it is a non-contingent goal of education to bring about understanding, and it is a conceptual truth (as contrasted with a purely empirical one) that, other things being equal, understanding is worth attaining, not merely as an instrument to some further end but for its own sake.

This sort of analytical reasoning was deployed to good effect in writings by Peters and others and revealed the extent to which education expresses a commitment to the value of human development. In his book *Ethics and Education*, for example, Peters argued that, of its very nature, education involves processes leading to the development of a desirable state of mind in which one attains some understanding and cares about what is held to be of value. Of course, this is not to say that education is necessarily successful, or that it cannot be perverted to bad ends. Just as medical skills can prove inadequate to the restoration of health, or even be used to inflict injury, so education can fail or be abused; but the point remains that these constitute failures or perversions precisely because of the defining goals of medicine and of education: health and virtue, respectively.

Critics of analytical philosophy of education of the 1960s and 1970s often seem to forget that it had these practical and normative connections. They write as if it simply constructed conceptual maps while remaining studiously neutral on issues of policy. This is simply not so. However it is true to say that philosophy of education in this style had a detached, impersonal quality as contrasted with writings influenced by phenomenology and existentialism,[6] and that it lacked the political commitment of left- and right-wing theories and critiques.[7] As economic, demographic and political developments brought about changes in the organization and funding of schools, colleges and institutes of education, an attitude of reflective detachment seemed to some to be a serious failing in educational thought, and perhaps even to be expressive of the moral and social outlook of a privileged class. Thus it was argued that analytical philosophy was no longer able to provide the inspiration and methodology for serious thinking about education.[8] Additionally, and ironically, the very changes in the educational policies of governments, to which its critics accused it of failing to respond, themselves resulted in reductions in the number of academic posts available to philosophers of education and so the subject began to go into something of a decline.

III

At this point, however, I want to turn to the second factor bearing upon the position of the subject, and to suggest that continuing developments within analytical philosophy are contributing to the resurgence of philosophical thinking about education. This trend, however, is not back towards the analysis of educational concepts. For one thing, the results achieved by Peters and others remain available (though we may need to be reminded of them). The trend is towards the development of philosophy of education as an aspect of applied, or as I should prefer to say, 'practical' philosophy.[9]

I remarked that some critics of the analytical approach accused it of having neglected the ethics and politics of education, and suggested that this may overlook the extent to which analysis may bear upon practice. Nevertheless there is justice in the charge, though it is also somewhat ironic inasmuch as what it reveals is not a slavish attachment to orthodoxies within the main body of academic philosophy but, on the contrary, a failure of philosophy of education to keep pace with trends in the parent discipline. For during the period that Peters and his followers were applying the methods of conceptual analysis developed within the 'pure' philosophy of the 1950s and 1960s, moral and political philosophers were re-examining and frequently rejecting the assumption associated with those methods, namely, that philosophy can only describe the structure of thought and action and not judge it to be good or bad, right or wrong.

By the early 1970s, however, there was emerging a new sense of the potential of philosophical enquiry in areas of individual conduct and social policy. The decade began with the publication of John Rawls's defence of a liberal-egalitarian political order in *A Theory of Justice* (1971), and in political philosophy this was joined by other major works such as Robert Nozick's *Anarchy, State and Utopia* (1974) and Michael Walzer's *Spheres of Justice* (1980). In moral philosophy several authors attempted to derive substantial moral claims and even entire ethical systems from principles of practical reason. Important contributions of this sort were made by moral rationalists such as Thomas Nagel, Alan Donagan and Alan Gewirth, and in the 1980s their works were joined by studies which argued that values cannot be understood or justified save in their historical context. The most important contribution in this genre was Alasdair MacIntyre's *After Virtue*.[10]

There is no single preferred method employed by these moral and political philosophers, but they share a belief in the possibility of reasoning about values and policies. Although such reasoning takes different forms, a recurrent tendency in keeping with the analytical heritage is to demonstrate the conceptual and normative structure of an idea or way of thinking and to show its relation to other notions and practices. In his very influential writings Rawls, for example, tries to show how our thinking about political issues, in particular justice, is shaped by an ideal common in western societies of citizens as free and equal persons.[11] On this account we do not begin political philosophy in a moral vacuum but start with certain shared commitments and concerns and try to work out in the light of these, or of critically refined versions of them, acceptable forms of justification. As the process proceeds more values come into view, and standards, for example of the public defensibility of policy, begin to take definite form and become compelling. Those writers such as MacIntyre and Charles Taylor[12] who lay stress upon the historical and cultural contexts of moral and political thought use their explorations of the past to locate the sources of our normative assumptions and to relate them to our evolving sense of ourselves and of our many and various relations with others.

Reflection upon education and the issues surrounding it needs to absorb more extensively the products of recent moral and social philosophy and to draw upon the full range of concepts and methods (re)discovered and developed since the early 1970s. There is no shortage of issues requiring attention: How do the claims of universal liberal education stand when challenged by the particular values and limitations associated with national and other cultural identities? What is to be made of the idea that education is a form of personal development when some philosophers of mind are attacking the central notions of common-sense ('folk') psychology, including that of persons as unified moral subjects, and others are arguing that personhood is a projected construct? Are there universal educational values or is the best we can arrive at a set of socially relative norms? How are we to conceive language learning in the face of philosophical critiques of the very idea of objective meaning and relatedly of correct and incorrect usage? How can the state justify funding public education out of taxes levied from childless individuals? How, if at all, can the allocation of resources for the provision of art and sport education be justified in societies whose industrial economies are in need of scientists and engineers, and in a world where millions live out their short lives in ignorance and pain? How should educators respond to the cognitive and moral values of popular culture, particularly as this is influenced through the various news and entertainment media? In what sense, if any, are clever and educated people better and more admirable than unintelligent and ignorant ones?

This is not the occasion to try to answer these questions, though in the following sections the first two – concerning liberal education and particular values, and the nature of persons – will be discussed further. For the moment, however, I want to stress the practical importance and philosophical character of all the issues listed. We need to formulate views and policies concerning them, however qualified and provisional these might be, and philosophers of education who have nothing to say about them cannot expect to command the interest, let alone the respect, of other applied philosophers, or, more important, of those who feel the need of understanding and resolution but who recognize their own inability to achieve them. To date, educational theorists have not shown sufficient interest in the challenges and opportunities presented by the best of recent work in moral and social philosophy and in the philosophies of mind, action and language. But as writers in these latter fields find themselves engaging with aspects of educational principles and policies, and some philosophers of education acquire a command of the more general philosophical literature, the situation will improve.[13]

IV

So much then for the general question of philosophy of education and its relation to applied or practical philosophy. I want now to return to the specific issue signalled by my title and introduced in section I, that of the nature of education as a social practice concerned with the transmission of certain traditional values. To describe education in these terms may seem to beg the question against other possible accounts, or if it fails to do this that may suggest that the description is so accommodating as to be vacuous. Earlier I concluded, somewhat provocatively, that reason must make 'conservative traditionalists' of us all; now I need to explain and substantiate that claim while ensuring that it does not in the process reduce to triviality.

Unlike his teacher Plato, Aristotle wrote no work in which reflections on education play a major part. However his preoccupations with philosophical method and with the structure of reasoning, and his theories of nature and of value have bequeathed to us sets of ideas that are of the first importance in trying to understand education. Both before and after Aristotle, some philosophers have viewed the empirical world as consisting of independent, and only contingently related, elements: atoms (or whatever was the preferred alternative) moving in the void. On this account of nature there can be no understanding of structures and processes as intelligible; at best objects and events might be explained in terms of repeated patterns of combination and consequence. The occurrence of an event of a certain type, say, could be viewed as 'to be expected' in a given set of circumstances because it has been observed in the past that similar antecedents preface events of that sort. Notice that in this scheme, which in modern times is almost always associated with Hume, one cannot say that the antecedents 'produce' or 'give rise' to the event because that would involve attributing to them certain causal powers which would be partly or wholly constitutive of their natures, and which would license claims to the effect that relations between objects go beyond contingency and merely statistical probability and amount to tendencies rooted in the essential natures of things.

Carrying the 'atomistic' view further, various consequences follow for philosophical anthropology and for the theories of knowledge and value. Human beings are complexes compounded out of more basic natural elements and their behaviour, whether individually or collectively, is only amenable to explanation in terms of observed regularities. This much follows from the basic metaphysics of nature, but the point about explanation is reinforced when one considers the kind of epistemology that goes with atomism. Just as the objects of experience are only contingently related, so experiences themselves and their contents are distinct items. Apart, perhaps, from matters of strict logic, such as entailment and contradiction, the relations between the elements of perception, thought and feeling can only be sequential and associative: one impression or idea following upon another; and, in due course, contents of various sorts coming to be associated with each other in the 'mind' of the 'subject' (whatever on this view these latter entities might be). Similarly, issues of reason and value as these arise in the explanation of action become part of the mechanics of psychology. In and of themselves the existence of an object or the occurrence of an event are not things that can intelligibly be regarded as good. Instead, one might say that these were desirable inasmuch as they were actual or potential objects of desire. It is not difficult to see how the atomist picture develops or how it might be further elaborated in relation to educational issues. To the extent that they seem relevant at all, the central concepts of instruction, learning and understanding, and of reasons, goals and values will be the concern of individual and social psychology, and, so far as practice is concerned, of some species of cognitive and behavioural science.

Presumably few readers will find this general prospect or the position that underlies it attractive; but the philosophical question is whether or not it is true. In considering this, one may wonder what the alternatives might be and how the issue between them could be resolved. At this level of opposition between general and comprehensive philosophical positions one is sometimes reduced to making judgements of overall plausibility or appeal. But a more satisfactory resolution would be achieved if it could be shown that one or more positions are internally inconsistent or otherwise incoherent; and it would be even better if it could be demonstrated that to the extent that they seem to make sense that is because they tacitly assume certain of the ideas of a rival account. In effect this is the method of transcendental dialectic: demonstrating that a claim or theory presupposes that which it denies, and that these presuppositions form part of a coherent alternative.

Such, I suggest, is how an Aristotelian position stands in relation to the atomistic view. The latter tacitly depends in its descriptions upon a non-atomistic set of assumptions about nature and our knowledge of it. This dependency is in part a matter of an underlying framework of causal intelligibility and unifying natures and in part one of non-associative rationality and objective values. Consider, for example, the ways in which someone might be led to develop the atomistic view. He or she observes the behaviour of various objects and tries to understand this. Such observation might involve experimental instruments or unaided perception, and might be short term or considerably extended. For any of this to make sense it has to be assumed that the objects under study are distinguishable from others of different kinds. This presupposes that there are principles of individuation and re-identification that allow one to pick out things of the relevant type and keep track of them over time. Next, it needs to be assumed that it is possible, at least in principle, to distinguish typical behaviour and effects from untypical phenomena, and to ascribe the former to the objects as proper to them, rather than as belonging to other elements in the situation. If instrumentation is involved it has to be determined whether this is operating normally, in accord, that is to say, with the ends for which it has been designed. That in turn requires certain assumptions about the nature and causal powers of the instruments, and about possible sources of malfunction or of external interference – themselves being conceived of in terms of certain constitutions and natural effects. Similarly, assumptions have to be made about one's own sense organs, about their proper objects and their reliability. Beyond these lie various presuppositions concerning the character of thought and action. Establishing the circumstances of any empirical study involves planning and arranging the situation and oneself within it, remembering past experiences, recalling and relying upon the testimony of others, forming hypotheses, and constraining these by rational criteria more restrictive than that of the mere avoidance of logical contradiction but also more demanding than mere consistency. And in all of this it is assumed that some procedures have instrumental value and that the end they serve, or the end served by it – understanding, say – is worth pursuing in and of itself.

Thus, by examining the situation in which someone advances and claims to offer support for the atomistic perspective it is shown that this involves presuppositions incompatible with that view. More to the point, an alternative account is intimated, and it is this that is developed in the writings of Aristotle and of his medieval and contemporary followers. In this latter scheme neither the world nor our knowledge of it is atomistic. Things, ourselves included, are possessed of natures that are their principles of organization and activity. These are the objects of study, and study itself is the exercise of a set of natural powers, namely those of perception and rationality. Moreover an understanding of a thing as being of this or that sort, as having this or that structure and capacities, brings with it an appreciation of what it is to be a good or bad specimen, i.e. to be a well organized and proper functioning instance of that kind. Here of course the values are not necessarily moral ones, though they might be implicated in moral judgements. But the point remains that understanding natures implicitly involves an appreciation of norms pertaining to them. Moreover understanding is itself normative with respect to enquiry. That is to say, it specifies its end as something to be achieved, the attainment of which is thereby conceived of as good.

V

With these ideas in mind let me return to the issue of education. Earlier I claimed that this has, as a non-contingent goal, the aim of bringing about understanding. There are important and difficult philosophical and empirical questions concerning the relative contribution to this process of teacher and pupil. I cannot explore these now but it is clear enough that no activities on the part of the teacher could produce understanding, as contrasted with behavioural responses, unless the pupil had the potentiality to acquire and exercise concepts and practical skills. This in turn raises questions about the nature and extent of human intellectual predispositions. Whatever these, however, it is also obvious that if left to his or her own devices a child will not self-generate understanding. Put in terms of the ancient and medieval vocabularies in which these issues were once debated, the growth of knowledge depends upon innate structures but these are 'potentialities' not 'actualities'. And in order for these potentialities to be realized and given determinate content there need to be external sources of formation and instruction. To repeat Chesterton's telling observation:

> There is indeed, in each living creature a collection of forces and functions; but education means producing these in particular shapes and training them to particular purposes or it means nothing at all. Speaking is the most practical instance of the whole situation . . . You will wait and watch very patiently indeed before you draw the English language out of [a child]. That you have got to put into him.

Chesterton's example of language is particular apposite. Along with co-ordinated movement speech is the first thing we try to teach a child. That is because we regard it as the primary mode of expression and communication for rational, social animals. We try to establish contact with an infant as a potential participant in ongoing social and personal practices that are largely mediated by language. But it is important to see that the child's acquisition of its first language is not a matter of coming to possess a medium *externally* related to the various activities, traditions and institutions that shape the infant's social environment. Rather, the language is itself part of the social fabric and is shaped by, and in turn influences, the development of these various ways of thinking and acting. To acquire a language is to acquire a culture. It is to become part of a socially and historically extended tradition.

Moreover, what is true of socially embedded natural languages is also true of other symbolic forms. When a child learns to use numerals or to draw pictures it is not acquiring a medium of representation that is neutral with respect to its primary exercises. A child simply has not mastered the use of the numeral 2, or of a basic pictorial element unless it can deploy these in ways that make sense to those who instructed him or her in them. To learn English, or arithmetic, or drawing, or basic morality, is to be inducted into a complex set of rule- or norm-governed practices. It simply makes no sense at this stage to regard instructor and pupil as equals with respect to the content that might be expressed through the system of representations. It is not just that the art teacher can draw better than the child what lies on the table before them, but that through acquiring and gaining some mastery of the tradition of draughtsmanship the teacher sees the objects in ways as yet unavailable to the child. Learning to draw is a way of learning to see and understand; learning to read and write is a way of coming to organize experience and imagine possibilities; learning moral values is a way of developing a respect for others.

Since learning, as I am concerned with it here, is the correlative of being taught, what one learns is to a greater or lesser degree ways of seeing, understanding, valuing, imagining and behaving that are antecedently possessed by the teacher who is thereby authoritatively qualified with respect to them. Of course this is not to say that education is or should be a process of social cloning. Differences in experience, ability, temperament and imagination will lead both to extensions of existing practices and to criticisms of them. But in the first instance education is a matter of conserving bodies of knowledge, sentiment and conduct, as these are incarnate in traditional practices. Even if it were not welcome, authority is unavoidable.

VI

What then of such questions as how to relate the values of liberal education to the claims of particular cultural communities, and the idea that traditional education rests on an outmoded view of human beings as rational animals? In a way these are linked, for they connect with another more general issue, namely that of the nature of persons. Philosophical reflection leads us to ask how we are related to our bodies and how we are related to one another. According to one tradition, contributed to in different ways by Descartes and by Kant, the answer is that the relations are *contingent* in both cases. Our existence as persons is distinct from that of our bodies and from the existence of other persons; at most we thinking subjects *happen* to be connected with middle-size organisms that *happen* to live in groups. Another possibility is that the relations in both cases are *constitutive*. We are comprised as persons out of our bodies and out of the complex relations in which we stand to others. I cannot pursue these interesting but difficult matters now, but let me observe that there are major problems blocking the way of any attempt to maintain either that we are entirely distinct from our bodies, or that we are strictly identical with them. On the one hand our understanding of empirical knowledge and action tells against dualism; on the other it hardly seems intelligible to say that thought is 'really' brain activity and that action is no more than bodily movement. In order to learn and to teach language we need to engage with a common environment and to recognize meaning in one another's behaviour. The application of such psychological concepts as those of belief, intention and desire is presupposed in the interpretation of human activity, and this fact undermines the idea that there is nothing more to us than neurophysiology. Paradoxically, the very possibility of reading about and discussing with others this radical materialist hypothesis serves to disprove it. As was observed earlier, study itself is the exercise of a set of natural powers of perception and reason. We are thinking, acting beings and our thinking and acting goes on for the most part in a public world.

What about the relation between individual and social life and its bearing upon the debate about our identities? Again two possibilities stand in opposition to one another: in this case *radical individualism* and *radical collectivism*. The former can be thought of first in terms of the atomist metaphor introduced earlier. It views individual persons as being in principle constituted at least in the essentials of personhood, independently of one another. That is to say, what makes a given person *A* the individual he or she is, with his or her distinctive knowledge and values, *need* owe nothing to the activities and influences of others. Of course, as a matter of nature there will be biological relations between individuals, and as a matter of fact there will be many social influences, but these are to be thought of as contingent dependencies. Changing metaphors, we might think of society as a voluntary association such as a club, the origins of which lie in the decisions of its founders and the continued existence of which depends upon the consent of its members. As in a club the members of society have a separate and prior individual identity.

In contrast to this the radical collectivist denies that persons have a non-social identity. Here the appropriate model might be that of a jigsaw puzzle none of whose pieces contains a complete image. Suppose further that what the constructed puzzle shows is a crowded scene with groups of individuals arranged so as to compose a pattern or design; let us say that they spell out the word 'SOCIETY'. Taken on their own the individual pieces certainly have a nature – being material objects of such and such shapes – but they entirely lack the compositional and pictorial significance bestowed upon them by the overall design. On this account we can say that individual human beings have no identity as *persons* save in the context of a social order that bestows significance upon them.

Once again it is impossible in the space available to try to resolve the dispute between such philosophical positions. None the less it is worth noting the implausibility of these extremes, and introducing a further and intermediate possibility. Clearly, in some sense, we are social animals. We are born of, and usually into, relationships; and the circumstances of our birth and life shape our understanding and our values. How I think of myself depends upon how others think of me, and on how in our society generally people think of others. As it happens there is in the English-speaking world a great interest in biography and autobiography. For various reasons the idea of a 'life' with a narrative structure of accomplishments and disappointments, joys and tragedies, etc., is an important interpretative and evaluative concept; most readers will understand themselves and others in terms of it. However it is not too difficult, at least in the abstract, to imagine that it might have been otherwise. In other times and in other places shared concepts of self-understanding may differ, and tied to that difference will be a multitude of further differences. On this basis it is possible to advance a moderate form of communitarianism, conceding to the collectivist something of the idea of the social constitution of persons, while agreeing with the individualist that much of what we are is a function of pre-social nature and intra-social self-determination.

The question for education is how it should respond to the fact that we are rational social animals. First, it needs to recognize that our identities combine primary and secondary elements. That is to say, while nature lays down a foundation of inclinations and abilities, the social circumstances of our lives shape and add to these in distinctive, and often deeply pervasive, ways. This suggests that education must combine an interest in what is universal in human nature with a respect for the culturally specific. The problem, of course, is when these seem to be in tension, or more likely (and more coherently) when the conceptions and values of distinct cultures seem to conflict. This would hardly be a practical problem if the case were that of separate and separated cultures, but these have domestic counterparts in multicultural societies.

One illustration of this problem is the conflict which has been felt to arise in societies such as Britain and the United States where the public culture is broadly liberal and agnostic about religious and moral doctrines, but which contain communities that are partly defined by their religious and ethical commitments. There are in fact two sorts of problems here. One concerns the question of whether it is compatible with the tradition of liberal education to permit or to enable such groups to run their own schools. The other bears upon the educational aims of the system of public schooling. These are large issues but it is in keeping with the earlier discussion to suggest that they admit of rational resolution, and that this can best be achieved by thinking about the nature of education as the transmission of knowledge and values from one generation to another. Given what else I have said about human nature it should be recognized that this is not an interaction between equals. Teachers have more fully realized their potential for personal development than the children in their charge, who are at much earlier stages of formation. Further, teachers teach with the authority of the societies they serve, imparting the knowledge and values that are the common possessions of their cultures. Thus, in Chesterton's words, 'it ought to be the oldest things that are taught to the youngest people; the assured and experienced truths that are put first to the baby'.

In considering the issues of education in multicultural societies one needs to find a tolerable balance between the general values, conception of knowledge and methods of enquiry dominant within society and the particular concerns of minority communities, be they Asian Muslim or recusant Catholic. This suggests the need for a broadly shaped educational policy insisting upon the transmission of the dominant cognitive and social values, such as the independence of truth from opinion and the general superiority of practised enquirers over untutored opinionators; the non-instrumental value of human life and the merits of autonomous action.[14] Within the area delineated by these and other commitments, however, there is space for a plurality of further educational aims. In presenting things in this way, though, it is important not to suppose that what really matters is the common and the general, with the diverse and the particular being optional ornaments. These are not separable elements any more than the particular dimensions and surface texture of an object are in reality separable from its general shape. A society's educational policy can only be concerned with general forms of human life; it is for particular schools and the communities they serve to determine more specific forms in accord with their own values. What must not be lost sight of at both levels, however, is the unavoidability in education of authority.

NOTES

1 Chesterton, *What's Wrong with the World*, p. 204. For an examination of Chesterton's ideas about education see Haldane, 'Chesterton's philosophy of education'.
2 Chesterton, *What's Wrong with the World*, pp. 200–1.
3 For an interesting account of its history as an academic subject see Dearden, 'Philosophy of Education'; and for surveys of earlier and later periods see O'Hear, 'History of

philosophy of education', Harris's review, 'Recent work in the philosophy of education'; and Carr, 'Recent work in the philosophy of education'.

4 See Scheffler, *Language of Education*. Peters's important early contributions include *Authority, Responsibility and Education* and *Ethics and Education*. Paul Hirst's influential essays are collected in *Knowledge and the Curriculum*. Characteristic samplings of the interests and methods adopted by analytical philosophers considering educational issues are to be found in two anthologies edited by Peters: *The Concept of Education* and *Philosophy of Education*. For a later set of essays some of which reflect back upon Peters's work see Cooper (ed.), *Education, Values and Mind*.

5 See Geach, *Mental Acts* and for the deployment of related considerations in connection with educational theory see Hamlyn, *Experience and the Growth of Understanding*.

6 See, for example, Morris, *Existentialism in Education*, Curtis and Mays (eds), *Phenomenology and Education* and Cooper, *Authenticity and Learning*.

7 See Harris, *Education and Knowledge* and Cooper, *Illusions of Equality*.

8 See, for example, Harris's review 'Recent work in the philosophy of education'.

9 For a brief discussion of the nature of applied ethics and its relation to earlier forms of philosophy such as casuistry see Haldane, 'Applied Ethics'.

10 For the main arguments of what I am here calling 'moral rationalists', see Nagel, *Possibility of Altruism*, Donagan, *Theory of Morality* and Gewirth, *Reason and Morality*. Alasdair MacIntyre's ideas have been further developed in two later works: *Whose Justice? Which Rationality?* and *Three Rival Versions of Moral Inquiry*.

11 For a full presentation of his later thinking about justice see Rawls, *Political Liberalism*.

12 See, for example, MacIntyre's *After Virtue* and Taylor's major study *Sources of the Self*.

13 For relevant recent contributions from moral and social philosophy see Nagel, *Equality and Partiality* and Taylor, *Multiculturalism and the Politics of Recognition*; and for educational studies informed by contemporary ethical and political theory see Callan, *Autonomy and Schooling* and Carr, *Educating the Virtues*. Important perspectives in the philosophy of mind, with implications for educational theory, are developed by Davidson, *Essays on Actions and Events*, Churchland, *Matter and Consciousness* and Dennett, *The Intentional Stance*. For applications of 'eliminative materialism' to philosophy of education see Walker and Evers, 'Towards a materialist pragmatist philosophy of education', and for a critical response see Haldane, 'Metaphysics in the philosophy of education'.

14 For further discussion of related issues, see Haldane 'Religious education in a pluralist Society'.

READING GUIDE

Some readings on the recent history of philosophy of education are given in the Notes for this chapter and in its bibliography at the end of the book. See in particular notes 3 and 4. Other books which explore issues related to education are *Means and Ends in Education* by Brenda Cohen, *Learning to be Moral* by Paul Crittenden, and Anthony O'Hear's *Education, Society and Human Nature*. See also G. Langford, *Education, Persons and Society* and *Educating Reason: Rationality, Critical Thinking and Education*.

While these all deal with teaching, curriculum matters, and the philosophy of education in general, Amy Gutmann's *Democratic Education* and K. Strike's *Liberal Justice and the*

Marxist Critique of Education are predominantly about its political and social context. *Education and the Good Life* by John White and *Beyond Domination: an Essay in the Political Philosophy of Education* by P. White also take up social and ethical issues.

John Dewey's *Democracy and Education*, which was published in 1912, strongly influenced the progressive movement this century, in both America and Europe, though Dewey also criticized its excesses in a later work, *Experience and Education*.

CLASSICAL SOURCES

Plato: *Republic*; *Laws*
Rousseau: *Émile, or On Education*
Kant: *Pedagogical Lectures*
Matthew Arnold: *Culture and Anarchy*

6

Ethics, Law and the Quality of the Media

Andrew Belsey

> Everyone has the right to freedom of opinion and expression; this right includes freedom to hold opinions without interference and to seek, receive and impart information and ideas through any media and regardless of frontiers.
>
> Article 19 of the Universal Declaration of Human Rights

> . . . there never can be one easy answer to all free speech questions.
>
> Lee, *The Cost of Free Speech*

Introduction

The free circulation of information and opinion is one of the vital elements that animate the democratic process. It is therefore in the interests of anyone who wishes to promote and enhance the democratic nature of society to be concerned about the quality, in an ethical sense, of that society's media. However, there is no overall pattern to the media in different democratic societies. There are, for example, very many contrasts between the British and American media. Newspapers, television stations and radio channels have different patterns of geographical distribution within their respective countries, and different structures of ownership. These differences have a significant effect on the output, but even more significant, I shall argue, are the different ethical and legal frameworks within which British and American journalists operate. I shall further argue that these different frameworks have consequences for the quality of the media, to the detriment of the British media, and therefore to the detriment of British political and public life. In a chapter like this the characterizations of the media in the United States and the United Kingdom are bound to be over-simplified, but this will not, I hope, destroy the main points that I shall discuss.

Press Freedom as a Background to Ethics?

The political justification of press freedom is the foundation for one of the most influential discussions of the principles of media ethics to have appeared in recent years, Klaidman and Beauchamp's *The Virtuous Journalist*. The authors suggest that the 'expectation in the United States and most Western democracies is that journalists will provide information the public needs to carry out the duties of citizenship and that the media will provide a forum for the circulation of ideas and opinions'.[1]

It is this function of the press in the democratic political process, Klaidman and Beauchamp further point out, that justifies the press having 'special legal privileges and protections to gather and publish or broadcast news and other information and opinion free from intimidation'.[2] This privilege is most notably present in the United States, where the First Amendment to the Constitution lays down that 'Congress shall make no law . . . abridging the freedom of speech, or of the press'. One point of great significance to draw from this is that among the targets of the First Amendment is intimidation of the press by the executive or any other branch of government.

Klaidman and Beauchamp are not so much concerned with constitutional and legal matters, however; their interest is in moral issues and arguments. But given their statement that 'the tradition of a legally protected free press forms an indispensable background against which we will interpret the moral rights and responsibilities of journalists',[3] it is possible to extrapolate a 'thesis': that a tradition of a legally protected free press is not just an indispensable *background* to but an indispensable *condition* for the practice of ethical journalism, for being, that is, a virtuous journalist. Furthermore, I suggest, it is the presence of such a tradition in the United States, and its absence in the United Kingdom, that accounts for many of the ethical differences between the American and the British press, and for many of the ethical deficiencies of the latter.

The United States

The First Amendment is enormously important to the practice of journalism in the United States. American journalists do not have to worry, or do not have to worry very much, about legal objections to what they are doing or proposing to do. The shower of writs and injunctions, or the threat of them, which forms such a substantial part of British media life, is largely absent in the United States. There the law is on the side of journalists and not, as in the United Kingdom, one of the forces against which they have to struggle. Furthermore in the United States there is the extra positive freedom conferred on journalists through freedom of information legislation in addition to the negative freedom from interference guaranteed by the First Amendment.

However, it is important not to exaggerate. Even the constitutional assurance of press freedom is not absolute: there are legal sanctions on or obstacles to what the press can publish. For example, American newspapers, radio and television channels, and other information outlets can be sued for libel. But the legal test for defamation, requiring statements damaging to a public person's reputation to be made maliciously or with reckless disregard for the truth, is much more severe than in the United Kingdom, and means that the American press can discuss and criticize public figures with great freedom – precisely the freedom that the spirit of the Constitution requires for a democracy.

Again, although the American press can publish much material that the government would prefer it not to publish (there being no equivalent of British 'Official Secrecy'), even the American legal system's objections to prior restraint can be overcome if there is sufficient cause, such as a genuine danger to national security or a real threat to life. For example, if an American paper obtained a list of active CIA agents in Iran and proposed to publish it, the American courts would not allow this. The freedom of the press guaranteed by the Constitution has to be balanced against other constitutional rights and freedoms and other values, and sometimes, as in the example, press freedom quite rightly has to take second place.

Furthermore, no doubt the Constitution does not protect American editors and journalists from informal attempts at intimidation: either sweet-talking or threats from lobbies representing powerful groups, whether in government, business or elsewhere, who do not see unrestricted press comment on their activities as in their interests, and who wish to impose their own forms of restriction. And no doubt American editors and journalists do not always find it easy or even possible to resist such inducements. Nevertheless, and this is the important point, the First Amendment provides solid support, a firm grounding from which editors and journalists can repel those who attempt to pervert the ideal of press freedom.

But even the First Amendment itself can be exploited in ways that will appear morally objectionable to many. Consider the following story:

> In 1991, a public television station based in San Francisco, KQED, sued the governor of San Quentin penitentiary for the right to film a forthcoming execution – of Robert Alton Harris, the first man to be executed in California since 1967. The station argued that the public had a right to see the sentence carried out in its name, as well as read about it; it was, they said, a First Amendment issue.[4]

But was this really a First Amendment issue, or just a clever manœuvre to obtain a sensational journalistic scoop? Although judicial executions were public when the American Constitution was enacted, it might well be thought that attempts by the media to recreate the practice are not in line with ethical journalism.

So it is important to realize that even though the First Amendment can be seen as a condition for ethical practice in journalism, it does not guarantee it. After all, nothing can guarantee ethical conduct in any area of human life; there are too many frailties and distractions to permit this. And if ethical journalism were guaranteed in the United States by its Constitution, there would have been no ethical dilemmas and unethical practices to provide the material for Klaidman and Beauchamp's book, nor indeed any need for such a book.

No, the thesis is not a Utopian one: it is that a constitutional right to press freedom is a requirement for the practice of ethical journalism, not a guarantee of it. In practice the ethics will always be less than perfect, but concentration on ethical issues not only keeps ethics under constant review, but also enables unethical behaviour to be eliminated by ethical improvement. So although there are plenty of examples of unethical behaviour by American journalists, they are exceptionable cases within an overall ethical practice. They give rise to much critical soul-searching within journalism itself.

So it is no exaggeration to say that American journalism takes ethics seriously and takes ethical practice seriously. Thus editors and columnists write and publish articles which not only discuss the principles involved but also their application in practice, especially after a case in which ethical standards have been put at risk. The lack of legal restraint and the constitutional protection of the press actually foregrounds the ethical issues and forces journalists to consider them. There can be no hiding place, no shrugging-off of responsibility because the law will look after such problems. Thus the onus is on journalists to develop ethical practices and on each journalist to behave ethically. As Klaidman and Beauchamp put it, 'freedom from legal constraints is a special privilege that demands increased awareness of moral obligation'.[5]

The reason for this is quite simple: the legal freedom to publish almost anything does not mean that publication is always morally justifiable.[6] Questions about obscenity, invasion of privacy, deception, breach of confidence, vulgarity, character assassination, racism, sexism, homophobia and many other moral issues can be raised even when there is no legal prohibition on publication. Thus there is an obligation on the journalist to become an applied ethicist, to understand at least something about ethical theory and how to apply it in practice. Is this, though, an unreal, over-optimistic expectation to have of journalists? No more so than of any other profession which intrinsically involves ethical dilemmas and decisions. If we expect, for example, doctors and other health-care professionals to be increasingly aware of the ethics of their practices (and we *do* have such expectations), then we should expect no less from journalists.

There is more than one way of approaching ethical theory. Some moral philosophers suggest that morality is based on rights, duties and respect for persons, while others are consequentialists or utilitarians of various sorts, arguing for the maximization of a desired outcome, such as happiness or social welfare. Without necessarily being incompatible with either of these approaches, Klaidman and Beauchamp's prescription for American journalism is in terms of virtue and the virtues: every journalist the virtuous journalist.

There are many virtues that contribute to ethical journalism. Klaidman and Beauchamp's account involves, among others, fairness, accuracy, honesty, integrity, objectivity, non-malevolence, benevolence, trustworthiness, sensitivity, humility, accountability and humour. (Some of these are clearly more journalism-specific than others.) They point out, though, that we 'should not look . . . for some finite list expressing the traits of virtuous journalists'.[7] This is because they are concerned not just with virtues but virtue, and the virtuous journalist is one who exhibits not some list of virtues but rather a virtuous character.

In spite of Klaidman and Beauchamp's slight defensiveness about the 'Victorian' sound of the words 'virtue' and 'character', there are some good reasons for taking this approach. One of the features of human social life is the absence of decision-procedures, algorithms to which to refer in times of ethical dilemma or difficulty. Human life constantly throws us into novel situations which might have some similarity with what we have experienced before but which are sufficiently different for us to be unsure how to proceed. The virtuous character is (by definition, I suggest) precisely the character that is best equipped to deal with novelty that is ethically problematic. The virtuous character is the one who can see the relevance of old principles to new situations, or can adapt old principles to new situations without losing what is essential to the principles. Such a combination of principle and pragmatism will be as valuable in journalism as in any other area of life which is certain to keep producing new ethical dilemmas.

Klaidman and Beauchamp conclude this part of the argument thus: 'Even journalists who are repelled by virtue language would probably agree that the public is better served when journalists perform well because of good character than because of sanctions, threats, rules, laws, regulations, and the like'.[8] This takes the argument back to the political, democratic defence of press freedom, and to the American situation of the First Amendment guarantee. Given the existence of this guarantee, it is not only possible but also morally obligatory for American journalists to take very seriously the question of what constitutes ethical practice in journalism. They have the freedom, and they have to find ways of using it well, and not abusing it. To put the matter briefly: freedom to practise journalism brings with it the obligation to be concerned with the ethical quality of the output.

The United Kingdom

The British situation is very different. Radio and television broadcasting is heavily regulated in a much more politicized way. All terrestrial stations are licensed, and licences are renewed periodically (and thus can fail to be renewed, as has happened to several radio and television companies). Everything that is broadcast on BBC or independent radio and television channels has to have the approval of the Board of Governors of the BBC, the Independent Television Commission or the Radio Authority (the members of which are political appointments). Of course, these bodies do not normally interfere with quotidian matters (the system would break down if they tried to too often), but their existence does in fact amount to an over-arching censorship mechanism that can (and does) step in when necessary. Nevertheless, in the broadcasting media, whether run by the BBC or independent, commercial companies, there is still a strong commitment to the ethos of public service broadcasting and the maintenance of high quality output.

But should viewers or listeners feel that quality has been compromised there are two further politically-appointed statutory bodies that can be appealed to, the Broadcasting Complaints Commission (BCC) and the Broadcasting Standards Council (BSC), which judge allegations from the public about lack of factual accuracy, unfairness in presentation and invasions of privacy (BCC), and lack of taste and decency in areas to do with sex, violence, foul language and the treatment of disasters (BSC). The adjudications of these bodies have, overall, satisfied neither the complainants nor the broadcasters, and this has produced all-round scepticism about their usefulness as quality-control mechanisms.

The British newspaper and periodical press is not statutorily controlled or regulated in the same way. Anyone with sufficient capital can start a newspaper. But in practice this is a large hurdle to overcome, and the weekday and Sunday national newspapers (and much of the rest of the press) tend to be owned by individual press barons or major corporations, most of whom take ownership to license editorial intervention. This is not conducive to quality. Many British journalists wish that their newspapers were owned by proprietors or companies solely interested in making profits and not propaganda, so that they (the journalists) could get on with the practice of their craft. Whether this would in fact allow the journalists to concentrate on the quality of the output is, however, surely open to doubt, since commercialism is itself a potentially distorting pressure.

Interestingly, the current lack of total commitment to quality is reflected in the division of British newspapers into the 'quality' press and the rest, the tabloids. It follows from this division that whereas part of the press is at least *aiming* at quality (whether it is hitting the target is another matter), the rest do not even have quality in their sights. However, there is a code of practice for all the newspaper and periodical media which is supposed to enshrine a commitment to ethical practice in journalism and quality of output. This is supervised by a non-statutory body, the Press Complaints Commission (PCC), and represents an attempt at self-regulation by the press, precisely in order to avoid statutory regulation. But again, the PCC's activities have been received with considerable scepticism in many quarters, although its claims to have raised the standards of journalist conduct are not without foundation.

But in addition to all these differences in the situation of the British media, there are the even greater legal differences. There is no 'First Amendment' or any equivalent constitutional assurance of press freedom. The European Convention for the Protection of Human Rights and Fundamental Freedoms (commonly called the European Convention on Human Rights), Article 10 of which contains a provision similar to Article 19 of the Universal Declaration of Human Rights, has not been incorporated into British law, and its status in British courts is not entirely clear. There is no Freedom of Information Act, and in spite of government claims to a commitment to openness, the practice remains at best half-hearted. British law affords journalists few privileges, and in one instance where it is able to, the right to protect the identity of confidential sources, courts have in general found reasons to override the right.

But as well as this rather unfriendly legal atmosphere, there are over fifty pieces of specific legislation restricting what can be published in the media.[9] Some of these are legitimate and have good justifications. Others do not, and are highly contentious. Some are rather obscure. But there are plenty of well-known and important restrictions: official secrets, libel, obscenity, confidence, contempt of court, reporting restrictions on terrorism, all of which have in practice considerable implications for journalism.

Again, some of these restrictions might have some justification. But what has been seen in recent years, in official secrecy cases such as *Spycatcher* and many others, has been a systematic attempt by the government to enforce its claim that everything is an official secret unless its publication is explicitly authorized by the government. What happened in the United Kingdom can be contrasted with what happens in the United States (already mentioned above) and what would have happened had the British government attempted to enforce its position in the American courts:

> Nor was any attempt made by the [British] Government to stop publication of *Spycatcher* in the USA. No doubt the government was mindful of the inconvenient First Amendment to the American Constitution which protects freedom of expression. In the Pentagon Papers case, the US Supreme Court held that the principle of freedom of expression required that no prior restraint could be placed on government information, except during war time or when the lives of government agents would be put at risk.[10]

The main point, then, is that British journalists are surrounded, hemmed in, by barrier after barrier of legal restriction. American journalists are almost entirely free from legal restrictions, and are thus free to think about the ethical aspects of their work.

And there is a much deeper underlying difference. Klaidman and Beauchamp referred to the 'expectation in the United States and most Western democracies . . . that journalists will provide information the public needs to carry out the duties of citizenship'.[11] But the United Kingdom is not a democracy in the American sense; it is a constitutional monarchy, without a written constitution, where there is still much executive privilege ('crown prerogative'), and with a population of subjects, not citizens. The established political tradition is deeply hostile to ideals of a free press and freedom of information. There is no acknowledged right to know but rather an executive right to keep the people in ignorance.

It is true that this harsh background has melted a bit in recent years, but it still has profound effects on the practice of journalism. With some exceptions, British journalists spend so much time seeing what they can get away with in a legal sense that they have little time for ethics.[12] I suggest that there is actually a causal relationship at work here. Journalists are faced by a combination of a hostile government and an unsympathetic judiciary. This creates conflict, and a mutually reinforcing sense of provocation on both sides. The result is an unhealthy situation for journalism, not least because it distracts attention from the ideal of the virtuous journalist which is found in the United States.

Quality: Law or Ethics?

Since the early 1980s there has been a constant and ever-developing struggle between the British media and the political establishment.[13] Part of this involved attempts by the government, usually backed by judges, to keep what it insisted were its own secrets, especially those concerning the Security Service (MI5) and the Secret Intelligence Service (MI6), out of the hands of the media and therefore out of the minds of the voters. These attempts resulted in a succession of court cases in which the government attempted to suppress publication of books, radio and television programmes and newspaper articles which included information about MI5 or MI6.[14] In spite of short-term victories, this was a campaign that the government could not win in the long run, and the fact that MI5 and MI6 are now publicly acknowledged, controlled by statute and the subjects of two information booklets,[15] represents something of a success by the media on behalf of democracy.[16]

The other site of struggle is quite different: it concerns the self-proclaimed 'right' of the tabloid press to keep feeding the British public with an endless diet of sex, lies and photographs, generally 'revealing' the scandalous private lives of numerous public figures, including cabinet ministers and other politicians, show-business personalities and members of the royal family (assuming that the last two categories are distinct). There is no real evidence that it is public opinion that is leading the fight against these excesses; the public continues to buy the newspapers in large numbers, and circulations increase when there is some new sensational revelation. The fuss about these matters has been largely generated by government ministers and other politicians, in a campaign which in First-Amendment terms would amount to intimidation. It could well be that part of the establishment's motive in throwing accusations of invasions of privacy against the media has been a desire to draw the public's attention away from the potentially much more serious threat to individual privacy and well-being presented by the state's secret services. Individuals and organizations with power do not welcome vigorous investigative journalism by a free press. The government's campaign against the press in the name of protection of privacy can therefore be seen as revenge for the media's victory in forcing some of the state's secrets a little further into the open.

The campaign for privacy legislation has not, however, proceeded smoothly, and a series of official inquiries and reports has merely highlighted the near impossibility of framing acceptable legislation. The problem has been caused partly by differences about the justification for further controls on the media, and partly by the sheer difficulty of drafting proposals which satisfactorily match the government's aspirations in this area. As has been pointed out by critics of further legislation, privacy is an issue which has wide consequences in many areas of society, and to single out the press could be not only difficult but also unjust.[17] Is it fair to shackle the press but not, for example, credit-rating agencies or direct-selling organizations, both of which collect personal information on individuals without their knowledge or consent?

However, in any discussion of possible legislation there are three main candidates for consideration. The first is that there should be a statutory body to control the press, with powers to fine offenders and require corrections and apologies to be published. The second is that there should be a new tort (a civil wrong) of infringement of privacy, with the complainant being able to recover damages through the courts. The third is that physical intrusions into private property to obtain information or photographs, and the use of electronic bugging devices, should be criminal offences.[18]

The third proposal is the easiest to justify; indeed, many people are surprised to discover that these activities are not already illegal. They are certainly not normally compatible with ethical journalistic practice, and with regard to such activities journalists should be in the same position as everyone else. No one wants their space invaded or their communications intercepted, whether by journalists or whoever, and the offences are so gross that there is a strong case for making them illegal. Nevertheless, some caution is advisable before rushing into legislation. First, the laws would need careful drafting to ensure fair treatment of borderline cases. And second, perhaps there are cases where such apparently unethical activities by journalists could be justifiable; for example, in a serious case of corruption. This raises the possibility that there should be a defence against criminal charges if intrusions into private property or electronic eavesdroppings could be shown to be in the public interest.

The other two proposals are less easy to justify, I claim. The general conduct of journalists, and their conduct in cases involving issues of privacy, are matters of ethics, not law. I argue this for three reasons. The first is that further laws in these areas would have a seriously inhibiting effect on the media, preventing them from investigating and reporting on matters of importance and significance.[19] The second reason puts the first into the context of the political, democratic defence of press freedom; in the words of the critics of further regulation, 'Our conclusion is that a privacy law or any further statutory regulation of the media on the lines proposed would be seriously detrimental to freedom of speech and freedom to publish, without which a democratic society cannot operate properly'.[20]

The third reason reverts to the thesis with which I have been concerned: that a tradition of a legally protected free press is not just an indispensable *back-ground* to but an indispensable *condition* for the practice of ethical journalism, for being, that is, a virtuous journalist. If there is anything in this analysis, then it follows that the last thing British journalism needs is more legal restriction. It would be merely a further excuse for not taking ethics seriously in the practice of journalism. The introduction of a new statutory body to regulate the press and a new civil privacy law would be counter-productive, and far from improving the quality of the British media would be a barrier to the development of ethical journalism.

Questions of Quality

This does not mean that there is nothing that should be done. There are many things wrong with the British media: in addition to too much legal restriction there is a narrow concentration of ownership and control, no context of freedom of information, and, more specifically as a subject for ethical concern, too much sensationalism, trivialization and lack of seriousness in the treatment of many issues in many cases on many occasions.

There are a number of things that should be done, therefore, on the ethical front. One is that not only should there be no increase in the amount of legal restrictions on the media, there should be a decrease. Proper freedom of information, less official secrecy and more open government would be a start. In a quite different area, there is a strong case for reforming the libel law, to give it a much severer test of defamation, so that there can be a more honest and open discussion of the dealings of, for example, a figure such as Robert Maxwell while he is still alive and doing damage to the interests of thousands of innocent people.

There is also a strong case in liberal democracies for self-regulation in the media, and in the British context this would include the reform and strengthening (and probably the renaming) of the Press Complaints Commission, while keeping it as a non-statutory body. Self-regulation of course includes supervising a code of conduct, but this is not enough. Codes of conduct tend to be negative, prohibiting unethical practices, rather than positively encouraging the raising of standards. Self-regulation therefore also includes engagement with the development of quality in journalism, and with the education of journalists in the ethics of their profession, with the producing, that is, of virtuous journalists. This in turn suggests a practical move: the enhancement of education in ethical theory and practice as part of training courses for journalists.

One way forward would be for this reformed body to concentrate on the issue of competence. Competence in a profession involves not just command of technical skills but also the ability to deploy moral qualities.[21] This is illustrated by the common notion that truth-telling is constitutive of journalism. A commitment to truth-telling implies honesty, integrity, tenaciousness and no doubt other virtues on the part of the journalist, all deployed in the quest for accuracy. In practice it issues in the somewhat notorious emphasis on fact-checking in American journalism. This is how one British journalist, on a fellowship at the *Washington Post*, experienced it:

> Both the fact-checking and velvet-gloved treatment of writers are facets of the same phenomenon: the deadly seriousness with which the Post – and American journalists in general – approach the business of journalism. In the Post's imposing 15th Street offices the atmosphere is more reminiscent of a university faculty or a government department than a British newsroom . . . At . . . times, American journalists talk like historians; the pressure is less to get something into the paper than to get it absolutely right.[22]

This is certainly taking seriousness seriously, but ethics is involved in many other facets of journalism too. I believe that all the recent tabloid stories about sexual indiscretions and failed marriages among the famous have not infringed privacy because the information was already in the public domain or was properly being placed there.[23] Nevertheless, the stories have mostly been unethical because otherwise legitimate information was presented in vulgar ways, showing complete lack of sensitivity and taste. Matters of presentation, language, register, style, format and layout actually come within the ethical definition of competence.

Media Ethics in an Unfree Society

There is an obvious objection to the thesis that a tradition of a legally protected free press is an indispensable condition for the practice of ethical journalism and for being a virtuous journalist. It is insulting to the many brave journalists in countries with just the opposite traditions, who strive against threats of general harassment, government persecution or even extra-judicial assassination to maintain ethical standards in everyday practice. I agree, and some qualification to the thesis is necessary. It is clear that journalism practised in such hostile circumstances is often far more virtuous than any performed in democratic countries. The journalists who preserved their integrity in South Africa while that country was still dominated by apartheid come to mind as obvious examples, and clearly there are many more working in even more difficult circumstances. What I suggest is that such journalists, although lacking any actual legal protection, are precisely working in the spirit of the First Amendment or Article 19 of the Universal Declaration of Human Rights. They are acknowledging the ideal of a free press, and are working to bring it about together with the democratic form of society from which it is inseparable.

Envoi: Towards the Superhighway Code?

If we look into the future, we can glimpse a world in which many of the issues discussed here will no longer have the same relevance.[24] Perhaps sensing intimations of their own mortality, British newspapers have published a spate of articles about the electronic future of global communications, and the ethical and political problems which it will bring – is already bringing, in fact. This calls for some speculation, although the situation is far too fluid for any definite conclusions to be drawn at this stage.[25] Newspapers and journals, terrestrial television channels, even telephones and faxes, will all give way to satellite television and the Internet, the global information superhighway which will link the personal computers that every individual will have.

This vision does indeed raise important ethical, legal and political questions, about ownership and control, copyright, censorship, and above all quality. On the one hand, it seems like the fulfilment of the Founding Fathers' hopes: the globalization of the First Amendment or Article 19 of the Universal Declaration. For the more advanced the technology, the more difficult it is to censor and control it. This is truly receiving and imparting information and ideas 'regardless of frontiers', as the information and images come straight on to the screen of your television or computer from anywhere in the world. On the other hand, what hope is there for quality control if these new media are used for exchanging pornography, Nazi propaganda and communications between international criminals and terrorists? Who, then, will own and control access to these new media? Who will, or can, ensure that unsuitable material is not transmitted?

As far as television is concerned, one possibility is to try to ban satellite dishes, as Iran has done. Fine, when the dishes are highly visible, but what happens when advances in technology reduce them and the receiving set to the size of a wrist-watch? The future world economy is going to be highly infor-mation-intensive, and many countries attempting to develop modern econo-mies, such as China, recognize this, and accept that divorce from global electronic networks will not be possible, but also plan to control access to and censor the information on the networks. This is likely to be a futile plan.

At the same time, the American government is proposing to combat inter-national crime on the Internet by ensuring that only encryption that can be read by intelligence agencies such as the CIA and MI5 will be permitted, using technology that will leave a 'window' in a coded message that allows entry to those with the technological key. This has been objected to by companies which believe that the system would be used to gather economic intelligence ('spying' is a simpler way of putting it), and by individuals who do not believe that access to their electronic mail by government agencies is in the spirit of the First Amendment.

If future technological developments make official control and censorship of information exchanges impossible, then there is little scope for legal restrictions and restraints. This glimpse into the future therefore reinforces the message of this chapter, that quality in the media is a matter not for law but for ethics.

NOTES

1 Klaidman and Beauchamp, *Virtuous Journalist*, p. 5.
2 Ibid.
3 Ibid.
4 Helen Birch, *Guardian*, 12 March 1994, reviewing Wendy Lesser, *Pictures at an Ex-ecution*, Cambridge, Mass., Harvard University Press, 1993.
5 Klaidman and Beauchamp, *Virtuous Journalist*, p. 12.
6 See Lee, *Cost of Free Speech*, p. 7 and *passim*.
7 Klaidman and Beauchamp, *Virtuous Journalist*, p. 19.
8 Ibid., p. 18.
9 Stephenson, *Media Freedom and Media Regulation*, p. 26.
10 Thornton, *Decade of Decline*, p. 6.
11 Klaidman and Beauchamp, *Virtuous Journalist*, p. 5.
12 As Robertson and Nichol put it, 'Journalists . . . are obliged to ask, not "what *should* I write" but "what *can* I write that will get past the lawyers?"', *Media Law*, p. xvii.
13 For some details of the most recent episodes in this struggle, see Peak, *The Media Guide 1994*, esp. pp. 11–14.
14 See Thornton, *Decade of Decline*, esp. ch. 2, and Ewing and Gearty, *Freedom under Thatcher*, esp. ch. 5.
15 *MI5: The Security Service* and *Central Intelligence Machinery*.
16 Nevertheless, this has produced only half-open government, since the official booklets conceal more than they reveal, and the whole area is still subject to the Official Secrets Act.
17 Stephenson, *Media Freedom and Media Regulation*, p. 10.

18 This is a summary of proposals emanating from various sources. For details, see Stephenson, *Media Freedom and Media Regulation*.

19 See Stephenson, *Media Freedom and Media Regulation, passim*.

20 Ibid., p. 25.

21 Cf. Klaidman and Beauchamp, *Virtuous Journalist*, p. 25.

22 Ian Katz, 'Postal codes', *Guardian*, 14 March 1994. Katz is also the author of a piece of investigative journalism written in this spirit: The bugging of an NHS doctor, *Guardian*, 1 April 1994. The *Guardian* is not always so scrupulous, however, or it would not have allowed a contributor to refer to Samuel Smiles as an American (5 April 1994).

23 See Belsey, 'Privacy, publicity and politics', in Belsey and Chadwick (eds), *Ethical Issues in Journalism*, pp. 77–92.

24 These remarks continue the brief discussion in Belsey and Chadwick, 'Ethics and politics of the media: the quest for quality', in Belsey and Chadwick (eds), *Ethical Issues in Journalism*, pp. 1–14, esp. pp. 4–5.

25 See, for example, Andrew Brown, 'Words speak louder than pictures on-line', *The Independent*, 14 April 1994 and Jonathan Freedland, 'A network heaven in your own front room', *Guardian*, 1 May 1994.

READING GUIDE

The book featured in this chapter about media ethics in the United States is Stephen Klaidman and Tom L. Beauchamp, *The Virtuous Journalist*. This can be contrasted with Andrew Belsey and Ruth Chadwick (eds), *Ethical Issues in Journalism and the Media*, which is more about the British situation. Other books originating in the United States are: Deni Elliott (ed.), *Responsible Journalism*, and Clifford G. Christians, Kim B. Rotzoll and Mark Fackler, *Media Ethics: Cases and Moral Reasoning*.

The text of the Constitution of the United States of America can be found in S. E. Finer (ed.), *Five Constitutions*. The texts of the Universal Declaration of Human Rights and the European Convention for the Protection of Human Rights and Fundamental Freedoms, together with discussion of the principles involved, can be found in Paul Sieghart, *The Lawful Rights of Mankind*.

The political issues are explored in Judith Lichtenberg (ed.), *Democracy and the Mass Media*, and John Keane, *The Media and Democracy*.

Simon Lee, *The Cost of Free Speech*, is an important critical examination of the conventional arguments for freedom of expression.

Geoffrey Robertson and Andrew Nichol, *Media Law*, is a 652-page compendium on the English law, with some Anglo–American comparisons.

The British controversies about press regulation and privacy can be followed in these official publications: *Report of the Committee on Privacy and Related Matters* (Chairman: Sir David Calcutt), June 1990; Sir David Calcutt, *Review of Press Self-Regulation*, January 1993; House of Commons National Heritage Select Committee, *Privacy and Media Intrusion*, March 1993; Lord Chancellor's Department, *Infringement of Privacy*, July 1993; and in the critical response, drafted by Hugh Stephenson, *Media Freedom and Media Regulation: an Alternative White Paper*, February 1994.

Other worthwhile works include: Eric Barendt, *Freedom of Speech*; Patrick Birkinshaw, *Freedom of Information: the Law, the Practice and the Ideal*; S. C. Jansen, *Censorship: the Knot that Binds Power and Knowledge.*

CLASSICAL SOURCES

John Milton, *Areopagitica, a Speech of Mr John Milton for the Liberty of Unlicensed Printing, to the Parliament of England.* This blast against the parliamentary ordinance of June 1643 imposing licensing and censorship on the press appeared as a pamphlet in 1644, twenty-three years before the publication of *Paradise Lost*.

John Stuart Mill, *On Liberty* (1859), contains some of the fundamental arguments for individual freedom, including freedom of thought, speech, discussion and publication.

7

Reconciling Business Imperatives and Moral Virtues

Jennifer Jackson

Is there any special difficulty about being truly virtuous while leading a life in business and commerce? Have we any more reason to suspect the virtues of enthusiastic and successful businessmen than of doctors, scientists or teachers? Maybe some occupations, though legitimate in themselves, pose a special threat to the moral character of those who engage in them.

One does not have to be a pacifist, for instance, to have qualms about the corrupting character of the military life of professional soldiers. To be sure, soldiers especially need to have ingrained in their character certain virtues such as courage and self-discipline. Yet, it is also the case thay they are trained to kill, to maim, to destroy property and lay to waste whole regions of terrain, all of which requires that they learn to suppress the civilian inhibitions that are bound up with sustaining respect for life and for property. Moreover, as an army of individualists would be ineffective, soldiers are expected to do these things, if ordered, unreflectively, accepting on trust that the use of force is necessary, hence legitimate – though the necessity on particular occasions may be neither obvious nor uncontroversial.

Similarly, one does not have to be a socialist to have qualms about the corrupting character of business life for those who engage in it. There are, I suggest, two aspects of business activity that may engender such qualms: (1) the competitive nature of business: the seeming unremitting need to be doing others down – which might appear to be subversive of the concerns both of justice and compassion and (2) the complicity of business in promoting consumerism and worldliness – which might appear to be subversive of the concerns of temperance (as that virtue was traditionally conceived).

Competitiveness in Business

Disadvantaging the opposition, one's rivals, is not just an incidental feature of business life; it has to be one's purpose: to study the opposition, spy out their weaknesses, to take advantage of them 'to steal a march' as they say. The military metaphor is perhaps indicative of the hostile attitude one adopts toward one's rivals: they are 'the enemy'. We expect enthusiastic and dedicated business people to take pride in, to delight in, their own successes. But characteristically their successes are others' failures.

Now both compassion and a sense of justice would appear to be impediments to avid and vigorous competitiveness. The compassionate do not exult in the failure of others, nor are they indifferent to it; rather, they seek to prevent or mitigate it. Those who have a sense of justice acknowledge the claims of the weak not to be taken advantage of and scorn to use their power to disadvantage them. Yet is not this precisely what the 'enterprising' in commerce are good at: spotting the weakness in the opposition and seeing how it can serve to strengthen their own position to the detriment of rivals?

Consumerism in Business

Temperateness has to do with moderation of appetites, a moderation which is supposed to reflect a low (and correct) estimation of the significance of worldly pastimes and possessions. Now it may be said that those who engage in business are especially susceptible to worldliness since their occupation is devoted simply to money-making and since, moreover, the imperatives of the market require that whatever levels of profit they achieve, they never rest content but continually strive after further growth.

This suggestion, though, conveys a wholly misleading picture. After all, most people in business are making money for others; they do not own the businesses for which they work. And whether or not the recipients of dividends spend these on silly extravagances is no more the concern of business people, it may be said, than is it the concern of doctors whether the patients whom they restore to health are going to lead worthy or unworthy lives.

Admittedly, people who are in the business of making money for others generally get paid quite handsomely themselves – as of course do medical consultants and lawyers. If it is true that the rich are especially prone to worldliness that is, then, an occupational hazard that is not peculiar to business life. In any case, arguably while riches may make one more susceptible to some vices it may make one less susceptible to others; the rich are not so likely to succumb to bribery, for example.[1]

Yet even if many business people live modestly themselves, are they not, most of them, implicated in actively promoting worldliness, hence intemperance, in society? To be sure not all business is so implicated, not even all trade and advertising. A business executive may be employed by a charity or be working for a government service such as Citizens' Advice. The advertiser may be promulgating health and safety; the salesmen, marketing courses on environmental ethics. All the same does not much of business thrive on what John Kenneth Galbraith calls 'the dependence effect': creating a market for new products by coaxing people into new desires, new dissatisfactions?[2]

Sellers, of course, do not have to believe in their own sales patter. All the same should we not expect that successful and enthusiastic sellers enjoy their job and take a pride in it? This is hardly laudable if they believe, as it appears that those who are temperate must, that anyone who falls for their patter is being harmed thereby or is at least risking harm?

It would appear then that if there is a special difficulty over reconciling temperance with a life in business and commerce that is not so much because those who engage in that life are personally liable to live intemperately, but because they are involved, generally speaking, in exploiting and fostering consumerism, hence intemperance, in others.

Are Justice, Compassion and Temperance Moral Virtues?

One obvious way out of the difficulty of reconciling being truly virtuous with a life in business is to challenge the assumption that justice, compassion and temperance are moral virtues. While compassion would appear to hold a place of central importance in Christian ethics, it gets no mention from Plato or Aristotle. Aristotle does stress the importance of friendship in a good life; but friendship in his view is ideally a relationship of mutual respect between equally superior persons: it has nothing to do with active pity for the wretched, for the losers, in a society. Aristotle deplores mean-spiritedness. But people who simply ignore the plight of the wretched in the world need not be mean-spirited. They may quite simply be indifferent.

Both Plato and Aristotle regard justice as a central moral virtue, but its status has come under attack on at least two fronts. Plato sketches out, albeit for refutation, one line of attack which he represents through the stances on justice he assigns to Thrasymachus in the *Republic* and to Callicles in the *Gorgias*. They contend that it is obviously irrational not to use to the full whatever strength one has *vis-à-vis* the weak, and that incantations against the strong taking advantage of the weak as 'shameful' and 'unjust' are specimens of mere self-serving rhetoric by which the clever should not be duped. In short, if only fools take justice seriously how can it be a moral virtue?

More recently another line of attack on justice as a virtue has been mounted by utilitarians (some, not all – not J. S. Mill), by Marxists and by (some) feminists, all of whom see our preoccupation with justice whether in the guise of respecting rights or of standing on a principle or of adhering to rules, as an impediment to social progress and the furtherance of the general good. Rights, principles and rules, they say, are at best only rough guides to virtuous choice. Not infrequently situations arise in which it is evident that more good would come of overriding a right, setting aside a principle, jettisoning a rule.

It may even be suggested that justice belongs to a juvenile phase of our moral education at which stage we think of morality as a matter of following certain rules. As we mature into adult morality these rules are superimposed or supplanted by the one ultimate principle of universal benevolence. Alternatively, it may be suggested that the rule mentality is appropriate in one place, namely when we are having to make choices in the thick of action, so to speak. The direct appeal to the ultimate principle of universal benevolence is appropriate in another place, when, in our quieter moments free from pressures, we are able to survey critically the rules on which we rely when making choices.

What about temperance? Is it a virtue? In Christian ethics as with Plato and Aristotle, temperance is treated as central among the virtues. Yet many post-Kantian moralists may consider its status as a moral virtue to be problematic. They may argue that morality only begins where prudence leaves off. But temperance seems so obviously a matter of prudence. There is no moral virtue, they may say, in the merely self-regarding discipline of the temperate.

Having noted that each of the virtues I am discussing has its status challenged from some quarter, I will proceed here on the assumption that all three so-called moral virtues can be successfully defended against such attacks. What is implied in such a claim? I will assume what I take to be a basically Aristotelian conception of moral virtues according to which each virtue is a disposition of character which can (only) be voluntarily acquired and with which we all of us need to equip ourselves if we are to make the most of our lives whatever vicissitudes of fortune happen to befall us. I am assuming, then, that we need to and can cultivate self-discipline in respect of our appetites and to learn not to set more store by their attendant pleasures than they merit. Similarly, we need to and can cultivate both compassion and justice so as to be able to live in peace and fellowship in human society (since we are social animals and a solitary life for us is pitiful). Both these virtues, I would suggest, are necessary and neither, rightly understood, is an impediment to the other. I shall further assume here that none of these virtues is strictly speaking incompatible with business life, that there is no inherent injustice, for example, in the relationship between employers and employees under capitalism.

What I propose rather to explore here is the less radical though still disturbing claim that these virtues though not impossible are especially *difficult* to accommodate in business life. To rebut this claim one might either deny that avidity in competition and in consumerism is characteristic of business activity or one might undertake to demonstrate, by making a closer inspection of each virtue, that avidity in competition and in consumerism is not after all subversive of any of them. It is the latter mode of rebuttal which I shall attempt.

Compassion

It is difficult to find a satisfactory name for the virtue under consideration here. 'Compassion' conveys better the importance of appropriate motivation; 'Charity', better the importance of appropriate action. In fixing on the former label, I do not mean to denigrate the critical importance of appropriate action. Let us understand, then, 'compassion' to involve not just passive but active sympathy for the plight of the unfortunate, a sympathy which engages the *will* in seeking to prevent or alleviate the suffering of others. Those who have the virtue not only care about the plight of the unfortunate, they believe that one has a duty to care. Thus, for example, moral education of the young should include teaching them to care. Now can we consistently strive to get people both to care, to accept a duty to care, and at the same time, encourage competitiveness in commerce?

What sort of constraints does the duty to care impose on those who are compassionate, who have the virtue? The duty to care is what is sometimes called an 'imperfect' duty. Imperfect duties bind us in an open-ended and somewhat indeterminate way: they allow us a certain discretion in how we act on them and they are not straightforwardly fulfillable. In contrast, perfect duties bind in specific and wholly determinate ways and they are straightforwardly fulfillable.[3]

Compare, for example, the imperfect duty of care parents have for their children with the perfect duty binding on witnesses not to commit perjury in the witness box. The former duty is open-ended in the sense that however conscientiously parents care for their children there is always more that they could do by way of caring. The duty is also somewhat indeterminate in that there are many alternative ways of caring for one's children and different ways which are mutually incompatible may be equally reasonable. Parents rightly and inevitably have a degree of discretion over how they care, provided that they care. In the case of perjury in the witness box there is no open-endedness, no indeterminacy (apart, of course, from the vagueness at the margin as to what counts as a lie), no scope for discretion: perjury is, quite simply, always contrary to duty. Witnesses can fulfil their duty whereas parents have never done 'fulfilling' theirs.

Let us consider further the *discretionary* element in the imperfect duty to care. Towards whom do we owe this duty? To everyone in need? Not so, since if those in need were entitled to our help as of right, the duty to provide it would turn out to be a requirement of justice not of charity. While this topic is discussed more extensively in this volume (Chapter 19), it is relevant to say here that at least if we assume a secular standpoint, we should not think of this duty as 'owed' to anyone, as based on a debt. Rather its basis may be nothing other than the recognition of need and the sympathy that need elicits in those who are compassionate – who have learned to care. If this is indeed the basis of concern, those who have it must feel it towards anyone in need. But it does not follow that they have a duty to help all those in need that they are able to help. The duty being 'imperfect' they have a degree of discretion over how and whom among those in need they do help. In other words, while the felt concern is not selective, the way that concern is addressed is.

As we have noted, in the case of an imperfect duty it does not really make sense to speak of 'fulfilling' our duty or 'doing' our duty. Rather we should regard the mark of those who have the virtue to be that they are dutiful, that they act in accordance with the duty (from the appropriate motive of course). There may be, as we have noted, various mutually incompatible ways of being dutiful and the fact that there are possibilities of being dutiful which we voluntarily pass up does not of itself show us to be undutiful. A doctor may be exemplary in his dutifulness in caring for his patients (caring in this case, of course, being a duty of justice not charity) though at this particular moment he is to be found idly strolling on a beach in Majorca while back home in Walsall where his practice is, patients of his are dying.

Might we then reconcile compassion with competitiveness in commerce by suggesting that those who are aggressively competitive exercise their discretion over whom they help and when, by excluding from their active concern anyone whose interests happen to be in conflict with their entrepreneurial interest? They could confine their deeds of compassion to their private as opposed to their working hours. Charity and business, they may say, do not mix. Thus the same individuals who make business prosper and prosper themselves thereby may be generous benefactors in their private lives and may devote their own time and energy to worthwhile causes (and, of course, be doing so because they genuinely care).

But this way of reconciling competitiveness in commerce with the duty to care will hardly do. Although the compassionate have some discretion over whom to help among those in need whom they could help, that is not to say that they can simply designate a whole portion of their daily life, their office hours, so to speak, an exclusion zone so far as compassion is concerned. Moral virtues do not admit of exclusionary zones. If honesty is a virtue, it must be needed and appropriate in all spheres of life and for all kinds of people however circumstanced, be they young or old, rich or poor, work-mates or play-mates, superiors or subordinates, healthy or ailing, friends or strangers, etc. Likewise with compassion.

To choose not to exercise one's compassion towards those with whom one has business dealings or those on whom one's business dealings impinge, one must have a reason: choice implies intentionality. What reason could a compassionate person have for adopting such a policy, namely not to mix business and charity? If one chooses to tolerate the plight of the unfortunate, this must either itself be one's aim or a means to some further aim. The former possibility is surely ruled out for the compassionate: wanting someone's misfortune as such necessarily demonstrates a failure of compassion.

What though of the latter possibility? Cannot the compassionate choose to tolerate someone's misfortune and even to cause it if it is the unavoidable consequence of, or means to, some other overriding aim? But while situations may *arise* in which the compassionate who are engaged in commerce are faced with hard choices which they may resolve in favour of commercial advantage without necessarily compromising their virtue, such situations rarely *do* arise. In the normal course of business activity executives are not faced with such hard choices since although they are continually seeking to get the competitive edge over others, that is not to say that they aim at, or even expect, serious misfortune to result for these others thereby. Compassion, it should be noted, is only appropriate *vis-à-vis* serious misfortune: it is not elicited simply by disadvantage (not even if it is unmerited disadvantage). In all manner of ways we continually and quite innocently compete with one another for advantage; for example, in queuing for a ticket, we put all those who queue behind us at a disadvantage.

The question of how executives can square their avid competitiveness with being compassionate is misleading, then, in so far as it embodies the suggestion that the aims of the compassionate and of the aggressively competitive in business are characteristically in conflict. They are not. Those who are competitive in business do not normally expect through their activities to drive their opponents into ruin. Even where ruin is foreseeable, it will usually be a consequence not just of being outsmarted in competition on this or that particular occasion but of other factors too, for example the parlous state of the economy and its ramifications, such as high interest rates. Hence, even if a rival's misfortune is acute and was predictable, it does not follow that because one contributed to it, one is responsible for it. Disadvantage may have been aimed at, ruin not.

All the same, while the aims of the compassionate and the competitive in business are not characteristically in conflict, they can on occasion conflict and force on business people hard choices, for example between abandoning a policy with consequent significant loss to those they are servicing (and indirectly to themselves) and pursuing a policy which has a ruinous consequence for someone else. Compassionate business people may be expected to find such situations harrowing and to cast around for a compromise solution.

Justice

It would appear, as I have suggested, that justice is an impediment to aggressive competitiveness in commerce inasmuch as those who have a sense of justice acknowledge the claims of the weak not to be taken advantage of and scorn to use their power to disadvantage them, whereas the 'enterprising' in commerce are skilled in doing precisely that: exploiting the weaknesses of their rivals. Let us then consider further what justice as a virtue involves, how, more precisely, it limits the exercise of power by the strong and whether on closer examination our suspicion is confirmed that those who are aggressively competitive in commerce must have especial difficulty in respecting the rights of the weak not to be taken advantage of.

Like J. S. Mill, I would locate justice in that part of morality in which the language of obligation, of rights and duties is appropriate: it concerns what we owe one another and what we are entitled to require of one another.[4] There is much else, of course, to morality that is not the concern of justice: attitudes and actions which are morally admirable or contemptible. Justice, as defined here, concerns the hard core of morality, so to speak, the constraints which are deemed to be an essential condition for living in peace and co-operation with one another. Basically such constraints are in respect of force and fraud. Justice, then, is the disposition of character which attaches our wills to up-holding and respecting these constraints. To be just is to recognize and embrace these constraints and live our lives by them. Whereas if we lack this virtue we are either prepared to use force or fraud to gain advantage over others or, if we refrain, we do so only out of fear of reprisal or because of other inconveniences, if we have the virtue we do not even entertain the possibility of gaining advantage in such ways and would dismiss the very idea with scorn if it arose.

If we are just we not only act justly ourselves and, as I have said, for preference not from fear or for convenience, but, being 'for justice', i.e. caring that justice be done, we acknowledge a duty to promote justice, to defend justice generally. Here again it is important to distinguish the perfect duty we are under ourselves to act justly and the imperfect duty we are under to defend and promote justice. In respect of the former duty we have no discrimination over if, when and how we act justly; we are bound *always* to act justly: not to lie, steal, cheat, murder. In respect of the latter duty we do have discrimination over if, when and how we promote or defend justice in the world at large.

Now is it not going to be difficult for people who are keenly competitive in commerce, who are adept at exploiting the weaknesses of their rivals, at the same time willingly to keep within the constraints embraced by those who are just? Is it not going to be difficult for the keenly competitive not only to demonstrate the commitment themselves always to act justly but also the genuine concern to advance the cause of justice in the world at large?

Just how difficult it is to promote the duties of justice alongside avid com-petitiveness in commerce depends partly of course on what precisely these duties encompass. Here let us confine our attention to an uncontroversially central aspect of these duties which would appear to constitute a substantial impediment to avid competitiveness: the requirement to be honest. Indeed, fraudulent practices may appear to be so much a part and parcel of daily business life as to cast doubt on our initial presumption that the combination of living virtuously and engaging in business life may be difficult but is not impossible.

This cynical suspicion perhaps rests at least in part on the casual assumption that deception in any shape or form is fraudulent, or dishonest. But is this true? To be sure, there are many familiar kinds of situations in our commercial (as in our social) dealings, where it is advantageous and also is common practice both to allow and even to cause other people's deception. We should not leap to the conclusion from this that all these deceptive practices are dishonest. Trust is the good that makes honesty a virtue. But not all deceptions, not even all intentional deceptions, involve a betrayal of trust. Trust is betrayed only in circumstances where (1) people actually rely on you (2) they are entitled to do so.

Thus, there are all sorts of stratagems and tricks that we play on one another, not just in business but generally in our social lives, which are innocent although they involve allowing or causing deception: innocent, only because trust is not betrayed. Is it dishonest to allow someone with whom you are chatting to believe that he is interesting you or amusing you? Does an honest person continually butt in to conversation to correct misunderstandings?

If honesty requires of those who possess it that they eschew deception altogether, then the honest must be rather boring, tiresome companions and, moreover, incapable of close friendship: don't we need to harbour and indulge some conceits about one another to sustain affection and fellowship? Virtues, Hume argues, must be amiable qualities such as make us useful or agreeable. But those who eschew deception altogether can be neither useful nor agreeable – certainly, not the latter. Thus if honesty does indeed require a complete renunciation of deception it should go the way of the 'monkish' virtues which, says Hume, are 'everywhere rejected by men of sense'; 'we justly, therefore, transfer them to the opposite column, and place them in the catalogue of vices'.[5] As in social life, so in business, we often innocently allow or cause deception. Thus, if we agree that it is not possible, and perhaps not even desirable, to do business without regular recourse to deception, we need not on that account concede that there is ever any necessity to perpetrate a fraud (i.e. a deception which involves a betrayal of trust).

All the same, even if the requirement to be honest does not oblige those who acknowledge it and act accordingly to eschew deceptive practices *as such* but only those which are also fraudulent, this in itself surely still puts them at a competitive disadvantage *vis-à-vis* those who are morally less fastidious. Other things being equal, the better armed in combat should fare better. The morally scrupulous forswear a weapon that their opponents are prepared to use. Moralizers may protest that the weapon in question is double-edged. But that might be reason to use it with caution and only as a last resort rather than a reason to rule it out altogether.

We should, then, admit that it is more difficult to be effectively competitive if one is honest – yet maybe not significantly so. Obstacles that are self-imposed rather than externally imposed are more easily faced and surmounted. For those who are honest, the constraints that the virtue imposes are willingly embraced. Those who are both honest and keenly competitive can be expected to exercise their resourcefulness in finding alternative ways of promoting growth that do not require the use of fraud.

Obviously, those who are honest and keenly competitive in commerce will demonstrate their attachment to honesty not only by their own scrupulous avoidance of fraudulent practice but also by their readiness to oppose and expose the fraudulent practices of others. We have commented on the discretionary character of imperfect duties such as the duty of charity. The discretionary element notwithstanding, there is truth in the saying 'Charity begins at home'. Those who have compassion will want to exercise it where they are in a position to do so effectively, which will normally include the home-front. Hence a conspicuous absence of charity there rather belies the presence of genuine concern. For similar reasons, we can expect those who are honest in business to be outspoken in their opposition to fraudulent business practices.[6]

Temperance

What are we to understand by temperance? Does it properly fall within the ambit of Hume's 'monkish' virtues? And, if it does, should we, like Hume, list it among the vices, not the virtues? Does being temperate require disdain for worldly pleasures and pursuits or merely self-discipline in their indulgence? Hume's denunciation of the 'monkish' virtues, of habits of self-denial that go beyond mere self-discipline, points up the need to demonstrate the good that temperance as a virtue might serve. Self-denial 'for its own sake' so to speak would appear to lack merit or even sense:

> Celibacy, fasting, penance, mortification, self-denial, humility, silence, solitude, and the whole train of monkish virtues; for what reason are they everywhere rejected by men of sense, but because they serve to no manner of purpose; neither advance a man's fortune in the world, nor render him a more valuable member of society; neither quality him for entertainment of company, nor increase his power of self-enjoyment? We observe, on the contrary, that they cross all these desirable ends; stupify the understanding and harden the heart, obscure the fancy and sour the temper. We justly, therefore, transfer them to the opposite column, and place them in the catalogue of vices; nor has any superstition force enough among men of the world, to pervert entirely these natural sentiments. A gloomy, hare-brained enthusiast, after his death, may have a place in the calendar; but will scarcely ever be admitted, when

alive, into intimacy and society, except by those who are as delirious and dismal as himself.[7]

Perhaps, though, we can recast our definition of temperance in a more Aristotelian mould so as to both salvage it as a virtue and render it a trait compatible with some degree, a modicum, of worldliness. The temperate person, according to Aristotle, desires (bodily) pleasures 'only to a moderate degree, and not more than he should, nor when he should not, and so on; but the things that, being pleasant, make for health and good condition, he will desire moderately and as he should, and also the pleasant things if they are not hindrances to these ends, or contrary to what is noble, or beyond his means'.[8]

On this account, temperance is not simply a matter of exercising self-control *vis-à-vis* bodily desires or worldly pursuits generally, but of possessing and showing sound judgement in the degree of importance we attach to these in our lives. A hedonist might display remarkable self-discipline, fasting for a feast; such behaviour would not manifest and might even belie the presence of virtue as pleasures would be foregone only for the sake of more pleasures of a similarly worldly type, and the effort involved in fasting might itself be a distraction from more important concerns. To this extent, I suggest, we should follow Plato who in the *Phaedo* (68cff.) repudiates the conception of temperance in which self-control is dictated merely by the appetite for self-indulgence. As with the virtues of compassion and justice, so with temperance, having the virtue is not simply a matter of acting appropriately. It is also a matter of acting with appropriate motivation – not, therefore, so as to achieve maximum overall indulgence (the hedonist's motivation for self-discipline), but because it is appreciated that these indulgences can easily absorb more of our attention then they merit at the expense of other valuable experiences and pursuits without which our lives would be impoverished.

Thus, even feats of extreme self-denial and austere living do not as such demonstrate temperance; it all depends on the soundness of the judgement that underlies and sustains the self-denial. Misers, for example, live most austerely, but not because they are devoting their lives to particularly worthwhile pursuits which require self-denial. On the other hand, it may be that temperance does require of us extreme self-denial. It would appear to do so, for example, if in truth all bodily indulgences are hazardous and liable to unhinge our critical powers. And we should perhaps expect those who believe both in original sin and an afterlife to support Plato's repudiation of all but the 'necessary pleasures' – eating only to avoid the distractions of hunger or infirmity etc. – rather than to approve of Aristotle's openness to the possibility of innocuous self-indulgence.

Let us proceed on the assumption that temperance is compatible with a modicum of acquisitiveness. In that case, have we any good reason to regard business life as especially difficult to reconcile with living temperately? As we have already noted, a great many managers are busy making money for others: they are not owner managers. If they are acquisitive it is on other people's behalf and, as we have also noted, how the beneficiaries of the service provided by managers spend their dividends, whether on frivolous living or not, is hardly the managers' responsibility.

There may, though, be certain types of business activity which do tend to undermine temperance. We have remarked that while riches may put a strain on temperance, riches are not peculiar to business life – nor, we should add, are riches achieved by all who are successful in business. But sudden fluctuations of fortune as opposed to a steady increase of income may be characteristic of certain types of business life and may put a special strain on the virtue. Then again, in some lines of business, executives are obliged to live ostentatiously so as to maintain for their firms an image of successfulness. Thus an executive who might be perfectly content to drive to work in a mini may be prevailed upon to accept a posher company car. Yet once a person gets used to a more luxurious life-style it may become difficult to revert to simpler living, e.g. on retirement.

Let us concede then that for some particular lines of business temperance may be especially difficult to maintain, though business people in general are under no more difficulty than people in other occupations over living temperately. Yet it may be said that many people in business who are not personally unduly acquisitive are none the less implicated in encouraging excessive acquisitiveness, hence intemperance, in others. Now the connection between being temperate oneself and being concerned that other people be temperate is not at all obvious – if it even exists. It is unlike the connection between being just oneself and caring that others be just. All the same is it not implausible to suppose that individuals who are temperate, who therefore deplore undue acquisitiveness and who are sensitive to the risks of bodily or worldly self-indulgences, should at the same time relish an occupation which is single-mindedly dedicated to promoting consumerism, hence intemperance?

But to what extent is marketing engaged in undermining people's temperance? Marketeers may be accused of deliberately creating in customers 'unnatural' desires so as to sell the products these desires establish a market for. And in so far as few of our desires qualify as natural – only, F. A. von Hayek suggests, the desires for food, for shelter, for sex – it would seem to be true that most products being marketed answer to unnatural desires.[9] But, as Hayek proceeds to argue, many such products enhance our lives and acquiring a taste for them is an important part of becoming civilized and educated. Thus there is no reason why the temperate who are in trade should have qualms about selling their products merely because the taste for them has to be acquired. What matters rather is whether once such a taste is acquired, it can be kept within bounds so as not to distract us from the other good things in life.

In any case, are not many products on the market (e.g. washing machines and refrigerators) genuinely labour-saving? They free those who buy them from some of the daily grind of worldly concerns. As we have already noted, whether customers use their extra freedom frivolously or not, is not the sellers' responsibility. In short, we should expect those who are temperate and who engage in business to be fastidious about the products they promote. But though this implies that they are restricted somewhat in what they market and how they market, it by no means debars them from successful and satisfying careers in marketing.

Conclusion

It is true that the virtuous are constrained in particular ways that debar them from seizing on certain opportunities of which less scrupulous persons would take advantage. The just do not lie or cheat; the compassionate reject plans which they foresee will precipitate other people into financial ruin; the temperate reject promotions of products which encourage dangerous addiction. But there is no reason to suppose that these constraints are not equally restrictive for the virtuous in other occupations, e.g. in medicine or education. Giving patients or students honest appraisals of their state of progress and prospects takes up much more time than does giving glib reassurances, time that could be spent on other patients or students. Maybe the specific virtues that typically pose impediments to our endeavours vary somewhat from one calling or type of career to another. But whatever way we happen to spend our working lives, virtues, if we have them, limit the means whereby we carry out our tasks. The notion, then, that 'business ethics' is peculiarly risible, unlike say 'medical ethics', is sheer prejudice.

NOTES

1 As Cephalus maintains in Book 1 of Plato's *Republic*.
2 Galbraith, *The Affluent Society*.
3 J. S. Mill discusses the traditional distinction between duties of perfect and imperfect obligation from a utilitarian perspective in ch. 5 of his essay *Utilitarianism*.
4 See Mill's *Utilitarianism*, ch. 5.
5 Hume, *Enquiry Concerning the Principles of Morals*, § 219.
6 For a fuller discussion of honesty in business, see Bok, *Lying* and *Secrets*, ch. 10. See also Jackson, 'Honesty in marketing'. On the importance of trust in business dealing, see 'Preserving trust in a pluralist culture'.
7 Hume, *Enquiry Concerning the Principles of Morals*, § 219.
8 Aristotle, *Nicomachean Ethics* as translated (1954) by W. D. Ross.
9 Hayek, 'The non-sequitor of the "Dependence Effect"'.

READING GUIDE

There is discussion of how business alters or affects what morality requires or permits in many compilations of articles on business ethics, e.g. Part 1 of A. Pablo Iannone (ed.), *Contemporary Moral Controversies in Business*. I particularly recommend Joan Callahan (ed.), *Ethical Issues in Professional Life*, in which morally problematic aspects of practice and policy are discussed over a range of different professional and business roles. For further discussion of the possibility of 'applying' ethics see Richard M. Fox and Joseph P. DeMarco (eds), *New Directions in Ethics*.

For general examination of moral virtues see: P. T. Geach, *The Virtues: the Stanton Lectures, 1973–74*; Philippa Foot. *Virtues and Vices*; James D. Wallace, *Virtues and Vices*: Alasdair MacIntyre, *After Virtue*; Michael Slote, *Goods and Virtues* and *From Morality to Virtue*.

For down-to-earth but thoughtful and wide-ranging discussion of the difficulties of reconciling the needs of business with moral imperatives see Laura L. Nash, *Good Intentions Aside*.

CLASSICAL SOURCES

Plato: *Phaedo*; *Charmides*; *Protagoras*; *Gorgias*; *Meno*
Aristotle: *Eudemian Ethics*; *Nicomachean Ethics*
Kant: *Metaphysics of Morals*, Part II
Hume: *Enquiry concerning the Principles of Morals*
J. S. Mill: *Utilitarianism*

8

The Gene Revolution

Ruth Chadwick

In Michael Ignatieff's novel *Scar Tissue* the narrator describes the collapse of his mother's personality caused by premature Alzheimer's disease, which runs in the family. Towards the end of the book he comes to terms with the probability that he himself is about to set out on the 'journey' towards the disintegration of his self. He says,

> My brother hates it when I use the word fate. But then he is a doctor. He believes that they are bringing fate around, getting it under control. Genetics, for example, now makes it possible to estimate, with varying degrees of accuracy, the time and manner of our dying. In Greek mythology, the Fates determined the length of human life, taking their scissors to our span. We may have the knowledge once reserved by these goddesses, but we haven't much idea how to live with what we know. Would ignorance be better? My brother wants to know.[1]

The predictive power of genetic tests is here somewhat exaggerated, but the quotation nevertheless asks an important question: What is the value of genetic information; would ignorance be better?

The Human Genome Project, the international attempt to produce a compete map and sequence of the human genome – the complete set of genes that human beings possess – is currently under way. It has been compared in its magnitude to the American Apollo project of putting a man on the moon and will cost billions of dollars. Both the National Institutes of Health in the USA and the European Commission have set aside parts of their research budget to examine the ethical issues that arise.

So what are the ethical issues? What is the point of mapping and sequencing the genome? Is it worthwhile or is it a wasteful use of resources? For example there are large parts of the genome – stretches of genes that have no known function – that are known as 'junk DNA'. So there has been dispute in the scientific community over whether it would be preferable to sequence parts of the genome rather than all of it, with the suggestion that funds are being diverted into areas which simply happen to be fashionable.[2] Against this it is argued that there is a big difference between 'junk' and 'garbage'.[3] People collect and keep junk; it might come in useful, whereas garbage is thrown away. Similarly, the parts of the genome which are labelled as junk may turn out to have some important function of which we are currently unaware. The main arguments in favour of the project are (1) the medical usefulness of the information and (2) the potential of genetic information for increasing our understanding of human beings. The results, however, will raise ethical issues connected with the acquisition (through screening and testing), control (e.g. in counselling), applications (medical uses) and meaning (for our understanding of human life) of genetic information.

Acquisition of Information: Genetic Screening

Whereas testing applies to the analysis of the genetic make-up of an individual, to establish whether or not he or she carries a certain gene, screening is applied to a particular population to determine the prevalence of a gene. Historically, screening tended to follow identification of an individual presenting as an 'index case', but greater genetic knowledge will facilitate the screening of individuals at the population level of risk. Different kinds of screening can be distinguished:

1 Neonatal screening, such as is currently in place for phenylketonuria, is primarily of use for identifying those suffering from diseases that can be ameliorated by early treatment.
2 Screening or testing in childhood will facilitate both the detection of those with a predisposition to develop late onset diseases such as Huntington's chorea, and the identification of carrier status prior to reproductive age. There are particular problems here, however, with consent, possible stigmatization, and the disclosure of information to the child.
3 Pre-conception screening of adults, it is said, will increase the possibilities of informed reproductive choice.
4 Prenatal screening will have particular relevance for assessing the status of the fetus, with the associated ethical dilemmas concerning abortion.

Screening of adults will increasingly have implications beyond reproductive choice. It may become possible to do 'broad spectrum' screening of individuals for a wide range of conditions, with the associated likelihood of increased anxiety arising from changes in self-image following testing, and the danger of stigmatization. Ignatieff's novel shows, however, that one's self-image can be affected by knowing what is 'in the family' irrespective of genetic testing. The question arises as to whether more precise knowledge will make the situation better or worse.

Several categories of ethical issues arise here: what are the implications here for an increase in techniques of surveillance? What criteria should be satisfied before the introduction of a particular screening programme? In accordance with what principles should a screening programme be carried out? What are the criteria for success, i.e. how should it be evaluated afterwards?

Historical precedents are not altogether reassuring. The implementation of sickle-cell screening in the USA led to stigmatization of carriers of the sickle-cell gene, despite the fact that they did not have sickle-cell disease. Further worry surrounds the use of screening and testing to identify people who have a genetic predisposition to develop a disease in later life which has a genetic component but which may require some environmental component to trigger it. Suppose, for example, that we could identify which individuals were at increased risk, because of their genetic make-up, of succumbing to cancer caused by a particular toxin in the workplace. Such individuals might find themselves unemployable or uninsurable. There is a question concerning what information about genetic predispositions ought to be made available to employers and insurers and a conceptual question about what counts as a predisposition. There is a danger that the distinction between 'predisposed' and 'predetermined' might become blurred. Ignatieff speaks of predicting the time of our dying, but there is a question as to whether this would ever be possible, even in principle.

Arguments against genetic discrimination, or 'geneticism', are analogous to those opposing racism and sexism. There are worries, however, that greater genetic knowledge may lead to less tolerance of genetic disease, which may come to be seen as avoidable, and thus someone's responsibility, rather than an 'act of God'. It is important therefore to distinguish between the evaluation of a particular genetic condition and the value of the individual who suffers from it. Hence there are issues about terminology: the choice between 'handicap', 'defect', 'disorder' and 'variant' is not ethically neutral.

Control of Information: Genetic Counselling

Genetic screening programmes will increase the need for associated counselling, and here what is at issue is control of information. Genetic counselling is commonly understood to include estimating the risk of having or propagating a genetic disorder; advising the counsellee at risk about the medical facts underlying the disorder; and facilitating and supporting a decision by the counsellee.[4]

The issue of control of information is related to both informed consent and confidentiality. Informed consent is particularly problematic in genetic counselling, when the problems associated with perceptions of risk are taken into account. To a couple being counselled about a 1 in 4 chance of giving birth to a child suffering from a recessive genetic condition, the numerical probability may be less meaningful than the nature of the condition itself. Further, individuals' perception of risk can be affected by the way in which information is presented, and by counsellees' attitudes to risk generally: whether they are 'risk neutral', 'risk averse' or 'risk lovers'.[5] The introduction of broad-spectrum screening will magnify the complexity of the issues. Informed consent, for example, will be trickier when a number of diseases are at issue at the same time.

There is also a question concerning the extent to which counselling can facilitate autonomous choice. It may be the case that the very existence of genetic screening and counselling encourages a culture which puts pressure on individuals to make particular reproductive decisions. In line with the importance, in medical ethics generally, commonly given to the principle of autonomy, the prevailing model in genetic counselling has been that counsellors should be non-directive. Counselling, in facilitating counsellee decision-making, is thus distinguished from advice. It has been suggested, however, by Angus Clarke[6] that the very structure of the counselling interview militates against the possibility of non-directiveness, and the fact that, for example, termination of an affected pregnancy is put on the table as an option may somehow suggest to clients that this is an option they ought to take.

The applicability of principles of medical ethics to genetic counselling is further complicated by the fact that the 'client' in this context is normally a couple or family rather than an individual. This raises issues concerning the duty of confidentiality, which are relevant to both screening and counselling. The discovery of non-paternity is an example of a dilemma that might arise; for example, genetic testing of a child and his or her parents might reveal that the male partner is not the genetic father of the child. Does he have a right to this information, or does the mother have a right to confidentiality?

Applications of Information: Gene therapy

Optimists take the view that genetic knowledge will facilitate treatments for genetic diseases in the form of gene therapy. It is important, however, to note that it cannot be assumed that identification of the genetic basis of a disease will necessarily lead to a genetic cure, at least not in the near future. Gene therapy has proved controversial because it involves actual alteration of an individual at the genetic level. An analogy is frequently drawn, however, between gene therapy and organ transplants – receiving a foreign gene is analogous to receiving a foreign kidney – and thus it is argued that it should be regarded in the same way as other forms of medical treatment, subject to the requirements of informed consent.

While this argument may hold for somatic therapy, germ-line therapy is more problematic. Somatic gene therapy is the treatment of the body cells of an individual; the genetic alteration will not be passed on to descendants of that individual. Germ-line therapy, however, will involve changes that directly affect subsequent generations. The 'directly' is an important qualification because somatic alterations may have an indirect effect on the germ-line. Many commentators see a moral difference between these two, and suggest that while somatic therapy is morally acceptable, germ-line therapy is not.[7] The arguments for this position are first, that whereas the individual undergoing somatic therapy has the opportunity to consent or refuse therapy, those affected by germ-line therapy will be as yet unborn generations, who cannot express a choice in the matter. This raises the general philosophical and ethical question about whether we have obligations to future generations. The issue is made more complicated by the second argument, that there is at present insufficient knowledge to justify taking risks that may be irrevocable. At the extreme the irrevocable intervention might be action taken to eliminate a particular gene from the gene pool altogether. Just as we have eliminated smallpox, we might decide to eradicate a particular gene thought undesirable, only to discover too late that it had some hidden advantage, thus losing valuable genetic diversity. Third, there is an argument to the effect that individuals have a right to a genetic inheritance that has not been tampered with, though this is sometimes modified to express the view there is a right to a genetic inheritance that has not been tampered with except to remove pathology.[8] A further moral problem associated with germ-line therapy is connected with the means of carrying it out. Such therapy has either to be able to target the germ cells of an adult or be carried out at the embryonic stage. Its development will therefore involve research on human embryos and give rise to the ethical issues associated with embryo research.

On the other hand there are arguments to suggest that there is a positive obligation to develop germ-line therapy. First, there is the general obligation to relieve suffering where we can, in this case by seeking treatments for genetic disease. Second, there is the argument from scientific freedom, though this argument is largely connected with a view that classifies gene therapy as research.[9] Third, there is an argument from reproductive autonomy. Germ-line therapy might be, for some couples, the only way they can achieve what Marcus Pembrey has called a 'winning combination' of genes.[10] While in theory most couples 'at risk' could avail themselves of pre-implantation diagnosis and embryo selection, there will be a few who cannot produce an embryo of their own which is free of debilitating disease. And even if this is not the case, there is an argument that if a woman can consent to somatic therapy on her child, why cannot she ensure that all her descendants should be free of a certain condition. For example, given the availability of gene therapy, if the mother in *Scar Tissue* had discovered prior to having children that she carried the gene for the disease from which she suffered, why should she not ensure that none of her children had to face it, rather than simply having somatic therapy on herself?

The potential use of the techniques of gene therapy for 'enhancement' raises further issues.[11] The debate over the distinction between therapy and enhancement raises the question of what should be the goals of medicine. Worries are often expressed in the media about designer babies, but a beneficial use of enhancement could be a kind of preventive genetic vaccination to protect against certain diseases. Søren Holm has pointed out that this could be particularly effective in developing countries, but that a consideration of political and social realities suggests that the techniques will be used to increase rather then reduce existing inequalities.[12] This point makes clear the importance of examining the technologies within social context.

Underlying many of the concerns about genetic screening, genetic counselling with the option of termination of affected fetuses, and gene therapy, is an anxiety about eugenics, the attempt to improve the human gene pool. This anxiety arises because of historical precedents which show the potential for abuse. It is also one factor in the drive towards the upholding of non-directiveness in counselling. The question arises as to the extent to which it is possible to advocate steps to improve genetic public health without the associations of discredited genetic eugenic policies. It is sometimes said that the important factor here is not the attempt to improve genetic quality *per se*, but the political arrangements that are in place, that it is totalitarian use of these techniques that we have to fear, but not their use in a democracy. While this point may be true to a large extent, it ignores the subtle influences of paradigm shifts in relation to both images of human beings and values.

From the overview of problems that I have given, it is clear that some themes recur, notably autonomy and its related themes of non-directiveness, choice and informed consent. Genetic information will, some say, allow us to choose to have healthy children, or at least to avoid the birth of unhealthy ones; to choose therapy for ourselves and possibly our descendants; to make informed choices as to whether or not we want to be tested.

When new developments are presented in terms of increasing choice, it is difficult to argue against them; it seems almost churlish to do so.[13] That is why it is important to look at the context in which choices are made. The context, in this case, depends on prevailing modes of thought. Developments in genetics have brought with them new paradigms which themselves represent challenges for ethics, particularly bioethics. These new paradigms concern our understanding of human beings and of the concept of health.

New Paradigms: Images of Human Beings

Elaine Draper has talked of a new 'genetic orthodoxy' (Abby Lippman makes a similar point about 'geneticization')[14] which, while on the face of it acknowledging that environmental influences are important, in fact allows genetic models to drive policy.

Sydney Brenner writes,

> What is most important about the enterprise [i.e. the Human Genome Project] is the scientific knowledge that it will generate, and the insights it will give us into our structure, function and origins . . . it is the most important, the most interesting and the most challenging scientific project that we have.[15]

What sort of insights? Evelyne Schuster has described a paradigm shift that has occurred with regard to the nature of human beings, which she ascribes to a worldview based on life seen as information, reproduction as the transmission of information, individuals as programmed by codes. This, argues Schuster, is no more objective than other theoretical models, but has been influential in guiding the social and ethical views of scientists working on the Human Genome Project.[16]

As Schuster points out, what is crucial is how the information is perceived by the public, because whether or not it is reasonable to accept the shift in paradigm towards an informational model of human life, if the public accepts it, it may well be what drives policy. This is particularly important with regard to public acceptance and interpretation of screening programmes, for the model has reductionist and determinist implications. It is reductionist in that it reduces explanations of human life to one level, that of genetic information. This is undesirable in so far as other significant explanatory factors are omitted from the picture. (Of course, geneticization is not the first model to do this; the mind–brain identity theory argues that all mental events can be reduced to physical ones, for example.) Those opposed to genetic reductionism claim that greater genetic knowledge will not necessarily lead to greater understanding of what it is to be a human being; there are aspects to this which must inevitably evade scientific explanation.

Reductionism in turn encourages determinism. The suggestion is that if we know the genetic information we can make predictions about the lives of individuals because the genetic code programmes individuals. This is why it is important, as stated above, to distinguish between predisposition and predetermination.

Some have gone as far as to claim that the Human Genome Project will 'solve' the nature–nurture debate. Evelyn Fox Keller gives this suggestion a new twist by suggesting that the ethical debate about the Human Genome Project has to be located in the historical context of the nature–nurture debate.[17] She says that in the aftermath of World War II, a sharp divide was made between culture and biology, in the revulsion against the eugenic abuses of that period, so that as far as human behaviour was concerned, interest was focused on culture and psychology. Now, however, in the light of the explosion of genetic technology, what makes respectable again the applicability of biological models to human beings is the rhetoric of genetic disease. She argues, therefore, that the construction of the concepts of genetic disease, and of genetic normality as the absence of such disease, has paved the way for the allocation of resources to the Human Genome Project, by moulding public perceptions of health and disease so that they are informed by genetics.

We have here an example of a paradigm shift, but one that cannot hope to explain the 'human condition' because it is not even trying to discover some human essence. This lack is due to the fact that the project is driven by the disease model, and by a geneticized disease model. The normal human being is simply one who does not suffer from genetic disease, and the aim of genetic medicine is to produce 'normal' human beings. In this way, Keller argues, what she calls the new 'eugenics of normalcy' is distanced from the old-style discredited eugenics. She notes too, that it is presented as facilitating individual choice.

The genetic model of health has potentially serious consequences for social health policies. Where the genetic orthodoxy prevails, there are understandable fears that less effort will be made for social provision for those who do suffer from genetic disease. The 'choice' to terminate a pregnancy in the knowledge of a social climate increasingly hostile to genetic disease then begins to look rather different. Statements such as the following, from a Royal College of Physicians report, are significant:

> The life-time cost to the NHS of one [Down syndrome] patient is double the cost of examining about one hundred amniotic fluids and terminating one affected fetus.[18]

Some might read this as encouraging termination in these circumstances, in which case the autonomy of the individual, understood in terms of self-determination, could begin to take on the aspect of self-reliance if the option not to terminate is taken.

The shift towards a geneticized concept of health includes a portrayal of genetic medicine as the ultimate in preventive medicine: by controlling the quality of children born; by gene therapy of a preventive nature; and by the introduction of 'smart cards' carrying genetic profiles of people, enabling appropriate preventive action to be taken.

Before rushing to the conclusion that this analysis is correct, namely that genetic orthodoxy is winning the day, it is important to look at evidence on the other side. As regards the point about prevention, ironically this may be a reason why genetic services will not be seen as a 'good buy' in the changed circumstances of the provision of health care in the UK, where health outcomes and health gain are used as measures of successful interventions. The health gains from genetic interventions (particularly terminations) are particularly difficult to measure.

Secondly, recognition of the link between social inequalities and health status suggests that it is far from being the case that genetic explanations have replaced others. Further, it would be a mistake to dismiss what benefit genetic explanations and interventions do have to offer. The important point is to avoid a reductionism that overlooks some significant factor.

Ethics

Changes in how we regard human beings inevitably have implications for ethics. Thus it is no surprise to find that along with developments in genetics have come suggestions that what are required are new ways of approaching the clinical implications, morally speaking.

The role of theory in bioethics is currently undergoing a considerable amount of scrutiny. The traditions of consequentialism and deontology, and the principlism of Beauchamp and Childress,[19] have come under attack in general, from virtue ethicists, feminist ethicists and the new casuistry.[20] But in genetics in particular it might be argued that the traditional approaches are unsatisfactory, This is not for the reason often given that old theories cannot easily cope with new technologies, but because the particular nature of genetics in the clinical setting introduces several complicating factors. The central one of these is the fact that while most traditional ethical theories in bioethics focus on the individual, genetics is concerned with relatedness. For example, in the counselling situation the clinician is likely to encounter a couple, or family; testing an individual may indicate that his or her genetic relatives are at risk. Now of course there are other situations in health-care ethics where the interests of individuals other than the client might properly be taken into account, but the point is that it is an essential feature of the clinical genetic context. This has not traditionally been the case in bioethics in our society, where it has been the autonomy or rights of the individual that have been supreme considerations. This contrasts very much with other societies, such as Japan, where the whole family is very much involved, reflected perhaps in the Japanese word for 'person' which literally translated means 'human between-ness'.[21]

In the UK, the 1991 report of the Royal College of Physicians, *Ethical Issues in Clinical Genetics*, took these points on board and suggested that there were reasons for considering whether, in certain limited cases, the rights of individuals to autonomy and confidentiality might be limited in clinical genetics. The reasons given for this position were two: first, the fact that decisions in clinical genetics were concerned with having children, and second, that there were considerations concerned with what might be called the ownership of genes.

Further consideration of their arguments makes it clear that the point here is that genetics always essentially involves other people. In deciding whether or not to have children, people other than the client, at the very least future children themselves, are affected. Further, information relevant to a reproductive decisions of yours may be relevant to a similar decision of one of your genetic relatives, such as a sister. The point about ownership is that it is not enough to say that information about your genes is yours, because they are your genes (and thus confidential if that is what you want), because other people share those genes. Thus genetic information does not have the same status as other information in your medical notes.

Despite the fact pointed out above, that Keller and others have noted the emphasis on individual choice in the debate, there is evidence of a shift away from autonomy in the genetic context. At the same time there are moves in bioethical theory generally to move away from the primacy of the principle of autonomy. Even within a morality based on principles, of course, autonomy has had to compete with the principle of justice, and thus the claims of some individuals have had to compete with the claims of other individuals, but the point here is precisely that these are seen as conflicts between the (justifiable) claims of individuals. The suggestion in moving away from autonomy would be that the individual choice is the wrong place to start.

The question has to be located within the prevailing debates about allocation of health care generally, and the ongoing discussion as to whether individuals' rights to health care should be subjected to limits. The values which should inform resource allocation are a matter of debate: desert, need, utility are competing candidates.[22] This debate, again, has to be engaged in within the general political philosophy debate about social justice. Individual autonomy is in tension with the values of community and solidarity.

Autonomy itself is a concept that is in dispute. Traditionally interpreted in terms of self-determination, as a 'local' concept, it indicates that it is up to the individual to decide what health-care interventions he or she wants. To this view there are certain limits. First, the choice takes place not only against a given social context which puts constraints on choice, but also against the background of the social construction of genetic diseases. What counts as a genetic disease is itself not clear. Second, the other side of choice is responsibility. Individuals who make the wrong 'choices' may be blamed for the fact that they have failed to prevent genetic disease.

What alternative strategies are there? One is to adopt a different interpretation of autonomy: another is to introduce limitations to it. These may not be mutually incompatible. Autonomy can be interpreted as a 'global concept' – interpreted, that is, not in terms of making particular choices in specific situations, but in terms of living an autonomous life. In this sense the autonomous individual has the capacity for some second order reflection on his or her first order choices.[23] This will be important in the counselling setting, where supply of information should facilitate reflection on significant life choices, in this case reproductive ones. In the context of screening, however, and other implications of human genome analysis, this may be insufficient. The human genome is in some sense the common heritage of all human beings, and thus poses issues beyond the individual. This suggests the desirability of mediating between the values of autonomy and community.

Communitarian ethics as applied to health care will suggest the limits within which genetic interventions should be carried out; according to Hub Zwart, it embodies a willingness to accept, as opposed to a constant readiness to intervene.[24] The place to start, then, in redressing the balance is by turning from questions of individualism to questions that affect the community, looking beyond the biological paradigms to the environmental causes of ill health: acknowledging the need for an appropriate level of social provision for genetic disease, and the value of preserving genetic diversity. It is the response given to these questions that will determine the social context within which individual choices are made. In the light of the pressing nature of these issues, the calls of bodies such as the Nuffield Council on Bioethics for programmes of raising public awareness of developments in genetics are to be welcomed.[25]

NOTES

1 Ignatieff, *Scar Tissue*, p. 5.
2 See, e.g., Skene, 'Mapping the human genome'.
3 See Brenner, 'The human genome'.
4 See, e.g., Royal College of Physicians, *Prenatal Diagnosis and Genetic Screening*.
5 See chapter on risk in Chadwick *et al.*, *Ethical Implications of Human Genome Analysis*, and references cited therein.
6 See Clarke's article, 'Is non-directive genetic counselling possible?'
7 See, e.g., the Clothier Report.
8 See de Wachter, *Experimental Gene Therapy*, pp. 90ff.
9 As the Clothier Report does.
10 Pembrey, 'Embryo therapy'.
11 See, e.g., Anderson, 'Human gene therapy'.
12 Holm, 'Genetic engineering'.
13 Marilyn Strathern made this point at the BMA conference on sex selection, 23 April 1993.
14 Draper, 'Genetic secrets'. Lippman, 'Prenatal genetic testing'.
15 Brenner, 'The human genome', p. 6.
16 Shuster, 'Determinism and reductionism: a greater threat because of the Human Genome Project?'
17 Keller, 'Nature, nurture, and the Human Genome Project'.
18 Royal College of Physicians, *Purchasers' Guide to Genetic Services*, para. 2.5.
19 Beauchamp and Childress, *Principles of Biomedical Ethics*.
20 See, e.g., Green, 'Method in bioethics'.

21 See the report on the International Seminar on Bioethics, Dunedin, New Zealand 22–6 November 1993 in *Philosophy Today*, 15 (January 1994), p. 9.
22 See, e.g., Chadwick, 'Justice in priority setting'.
23 See Dworkin, *Theory and Practice of Autonomy*.
24 Zwart, 'Rationing in the Netherlands'.
25 Nuffield Council on Bioethics, *Genetic Screening: Ethical Issues*, para. 10.17.

READING GUIDE

There are several useful collections of essays on ethical, social and scientific issues raised by the Human Genome Project. These include *The Code of Codes*, edited by D. J. Kevles and L. Hood; *Gene Mapping*, edited by G. J. Annas and S. Elias; *Human Genetic Information*, edited by D. Chadwick *et al*. The 1991 special issue of *Bioethics*, 5(3) on the Human Genome Project looks at both the project as a whole and at genetic counselling.

Darryl Macer's *Shaping Genes* provides an excellent survey of the literature. Another good introduction is the British Medical Association's book, *Our Genetic Future*. Bartha Maria Knoppers' report for the Law Reform Commission of Canada (*Human Dignity and Genetic Heritage*) explores legal issues, gene therapy, and the notions of human dignity and genetic heritage.

On specific issues, Angus Clarke's *Genetic Counselling: Practice and Principles* explores different perspectives on counselling; the Nuffield Council on Bioethics has produced a report entitled *Genetic Screening: Ethical Issues*. Maurice de Wachter's report (*Experimental (Somatic) Gene Therapy*) and the Clothier Report (on the ethics of gene therapy) provide good introductions to the issues.

9

Ethical Decision-making in Science and Technology

Dick Holdsworth

Is There Anything Special About Science?

The connection between science and philosophy has been extremely close in the history of western thought, ever since the period of ancient Greek history which Europeans consider to have seen the birth of both these types of intellectual discipline. During the twentieth century there have been moments when the links between mathematics, logic and epistemology have become so tight that the language of science became the only acceptable language in which to express propositions about the world. For many philosophers practising the analytical approach this tendency was a natural development of the empirical tradition. Indeed one could see much of the modern history of ideas in Britain – and therefore of the actual history of the interplay of science and technology with the country's experience of industrialization and its aftermath – as illuminated by the legacy of the empiricist philosopher, David Hume.

Having said that, many people would still not feel that science had been harmoniously woven into the close texture of today's culture and society. For example, although there are examples of novelists who have successfully integrated scientific ideas into their writing, they are (not counting the science-fiction community) conspicuously few in number. By comparison with our own state, we might envy the Pythagoreans, for whom mathematics, cosmology, numerology and even diet formed an integrated system of value and belief. Rightly or wrongly, it is common nowadays to conceive of science and technology as somehow separate from 'normal' human experience, perhaps as alien to it. So, before plunging into a discussion of the ethics of science and technology it is worth examining the question of whether there is anything special about these areas of human activity which either separates them from the rest of experience, or, which is not necessarily the same thing, marks them out for special treatment by the moral philosopher.

One answer might be that indeed there is, because of the great power which technology gives people to modify the physical world: to exert 'mastery' over nature. Sometimes the power is wielded by people with good intentions, and sometimes it is not, but this is only another way of saying that the wielding has ethical implications.

The use of power is a subject for ethics. This is not only true in a context where technology happens to be on the agenda. For example, the technical performance of weapons of mass destruction can be enhanced by an intensified effort in research and development. But when it actually comes to taking a decision about if and how to use the weapons, do we really want to say that the moral issues at stake have a special quality, peculiar to the domain of science? Do we want to compartmentalize those issues, to put them, as it were, into a scientific 'black box'? Many people would want to argue in the opposite sense, saying that, on the contrary, what we really need is to make a better job of integrating science and technology with the other elements of our moral universe.

Let me illustrate the argument with an analogy from environmental management, where practitioners often speak about the need to get away from 'end-of-pipe' solutions to problems of emissions. What they mean is that instead of running a process which we know will cause undesirable emissions and then trying to cobble together a cure for the problem once it has already occurred, it would be much better to design new types of system in which the 'cure' is integrated with the process. Similarly, I think we should beware of implicitly adopting a picture of science and technology as processes which continuously emit moral problems for moral philosophers to 'clean up' one by one as they come out of the end of the pipe. The alternative would be for moral philosophers to analyse the prerequisites for a scientific and technological practice in which the ethical dimension was integrated into the process from the outset.

In suggesting this, I have something different in mind from the requirement that individual scientists and technologists should heed the moral dimension of their activities. This is indeed an important matter, as most scientists and technologists are well aware. But a moment's thought will show that even if every scientist is a saint, the implications of their discoveries may yet give rise to problematical moral choices.[1] Those problems cannot be made to vanish. The objective that could be set, however, is that of defining an approach to the scientific process whereby all members of society, whether scientists or not, might feel that it had been successfully integrated with the other dimensions of their social being.

This is a legitimate task for applied philosophy. Here the object is not to find areas of application for ready-made ethical solutions, even supposing that such things could exist. That would truly be an 'end-of-pipe' approach. Neither is it the aim simply to do a kind of Linnaean classification, or taxonomy of ethical issues, marking out, for example, scientific-ethical issues from criminological-ethical issues or social-welfare-ethical ones. Perhaps it is not even enough to define the task as that of prospecting in the various evolving territories of self-renewing human experience for moral problems which, because of their novelty or intractability or complexity, suggest themselves as fruitful candidates for second-order analysis. Yet that formula may at least provide a clue, since it confronts us with the old question of whether there is any bridge for the moral philosopher to venture across between second-order ethical analysis and first-order morals.

Some philosophers answer that question by pointing out that one of the worst things about the moral problems which afflict people is the muddle which so often surrounds them, and that therefore all clarification of ethical arguments is helpful. I would agree with that proposition but suggest that, as far as science policy is concerned the argument needs to be located in the context of critical rationalism. That is to say, I would maintain that in a knowledge community which lives by the critical analysis of hypotheses every increment in the quality of criticism, at whatever level of analysis or discourse, contributes to the overall quality of the knowledge in the community. Notice this emphasis on quality. When one is discussing the contribution of advances in science to society, it is natural enough to think in quantitative terms: what the concept of criticism brings is a focus on the qualitative aspect of our assessment.

The Myth of Prometheus

The Greek myth of creation tells how Prometheus, one of the race of giants known as Titans, made man out of earth and water. Prometheus, whose name means 'forethought', then angered Zeus by going up to heaven and stealing fire from the chariot of the sun, which he took back to earth and gave to man, enabling him to develop the technical means to establish his mastery over nature. Zeus, goes the legend, created woman in revenge, to torment man with her beauty. Zeus punished Prometheus by chaining him to a rock, where his liver was perpetually devoured by an eagle.

The myth of Prometheus has worked in people's minds as a metaphor for invention. We can find an illustration of this in the period, in the late eighteenth and early nineteenth centuries, when scientific and technical knowledge underwent that rapid expansion which formed such an important part of the phenomenon known as the Industrial Revolution. This section of the present chapter will briefly evoke the social and intellectual setting in which the myth of Prometheus assumed a meaning for contemporaries caught up in the ferment of the new scientific ideas at that time. The purpose is to show how closely embedded scientific ideas always are in the social fabric of the day, and how impossible it is to consider the ethical dimension of scientific and technological practice in isolation from the systems of knowledge, belief and value which are woven into the texture of any given society at any given time. This point can be illustrated by some examples from the past. They involve attitudes which may seem in some ways alien to our present experience and ideas. Yet they do reflect social fact at those times, and the working through of those attitudes in the climate of the day helped to condition the nature of the industrialization process – a process which, to a significant degree, we are still experiencing today.

The late eighteenth and early nineteenth centuries was a time when the properties and uses of electricity were coming to be understood. The experiments then conducted were often spectacular, as for example those conducted with kites to test Benjamin Franklin's theory, developed as a result of experiments at Philadelphia in 1752, that lightning was electricity. Franklin wrote in his *Autobiography*,

> What gave my book the more sudden and general celebrity, was the success of one of its proposed experiments, made by Messrs. Dalibard and De Lor at Marly, for drawing lightning from the clouds. This engag'd the public attention every where. M. de Lor, who had an apparatus for experimental philosophy, and lectur'd in that branch of science, undertook to repeat what he called the *Philadelphia Experiments*; and, after they were performed before the king and court, all the curious of Paris flocked to see them.[2]

This reminder that empirical science used to be called 'experimental philosophy' is itself interesting, as is the evocation by Franklin, at an early date, of the 'gee-whizz' effect which has often been a factor in both the acceptance and the misunderstanding of science and technology by society at large. The anecdote also exemplifies the international character of science: Dalibard and de Lor were conducting in France experiments which had been designed in America in order to test a hypothesis which in future would be accepted on both sides of the Atlantic.

At a time when religion was firmly embedded in social and political institutions, an interest in experimental philosophy could represent a challenge to the established order. That challenge was made explicit in the life and writings of the scientist and radical thinker Joseph Priestley (1733–1804). Priestley belonged to an intellectual generation whose thinking combined non-conformist protestantism, attachment to the principles of the American and French revolutions and an interest in science. Another representative of this tendency was the mathematician, Richard Price. In his work, *Experiments and Observations on Different Kinds of Air*, Priestley wrote,

> The rapid process of knowledge, which, like the progress of a wave of the sea, of sound, or of light from the sun, extends itself not in this or that way only, but *in all*

directions, will, I doubt not, be the means, under God, of extirpating *all* error and prejudice, and of putting an end to all undue and usurped authority in the business of religion, as well as of *science*, and all the efforts of the interested friends of corrupt establishments of all kinds, will be ineffectual for their support in this enlightened age; though, by retarding their downfall, they may make the final ruin of them more complete and glorious . . . And the English hierarchy, if there be anything unsound in its constitution has equal reason to tremble before an air pump, or an electrical machine.[3]

The air-pump and the electrical machine were typical instruments of scientific experimentation during a period in the eighteenth and early nineteenth centuries which was also a time when the movement for political reform was gathering momentum. Another, slightly later character in the same story is the poet Percy Bysshe Shelley. Consider the description, written by his friend Thomas Jefferson Hogg, of a visit to Shelley's rooms during his first year at University College, Oxford, in 1810:

An electrical machine, an air-pump, the galvanic trough, a solar microscope and large glass jars and receivers, were conspicuous amidst the mass of matter.[4]

Shelley attached himself to the 'electrical machine' and told Hogg to turn the handle. In due course, Shelley's 'long, wild locks bristled and stood on end'. Shelley never completed his studies at Oxford. He was expelled on suspicion of writing a pamphlet entitled 'The necessity of atheism'. For him, as for Priestley, the objective character of scientific enquiry was a weapon to be employed in the fight against superstition, which is how he regarded religion. Like Priestley, he was a reformer who thought that religion reinforced the structures of political despotism and social oppression which characterized Britain in the early part of the nineteenth century. He thought the progress of science would have a liberating effect.

It is interesting to contrast this view with that which many people would hold nowadays, that it is science and technology which buttress the authority of the state. In support of the latter view, it is easy to see how technology could be portrayed as an instrument of social exclusion by drawing attention to the limits, financial or social, that may be set on access to medical technology, or to the information and communications technologies which today increasingly constitute the infrastructure of social life. On the other hand, though, technology can provide means for combating social exclusion: for example, by providing opportunities for distance working and distance learning, by providing new chances of employment to people with physical impairments, or simply by providing those means of communication and information which, as we have just noted, modern life does require. Whether the technology is used in one way rather than the other, then, depends on the wider characteristics of the society in which the choices are being made, and those characteristics can change. A significant new development in Europe has been the inclusion, in

1994, in the European Union's multi-annual Framework Programme for research and technical development activities of a set of objectives related to the fight against social exclusion.[5]

This helps to confirm the view that the opinions people form of the benefits and disadvantages of science, of the rights and obligations of scientists, and of their own rights and obligations in a society which is greatly influenced by science, are not static phenomena. They change and develop in the context of the general social, political and intellectual movements of the times, what Priestley called 'the rapid process of knowledge'.[6]

To return to the second example, Shelley's scientific connections can be sketched more widely. As a reformer and an iconoclast, he was deeply interested in the views of the anarchist philosopher William Godwin, whose friend he became. The friendship was interrupted when Shelley eloped with, and later married Mary, the daughter of Godwin and his wife Mary Wollstonecraft, author of *A Vindication of the Rights of Woman* (1792).[7]

Mary Shelley herself was to be the author of a famous book: *Frankenstein* (1818). The full title of the novel is: *Frankenstein or, the Modern Prometheus*. The reason for the subtitle is that it was the culminating achievement of Frankenstein's researches to 'infuse a spark of being' into the lifeless body that he had pieced together. The nature of the 'spark', the fire called down by Frankenstein, is not specified, but the reader can guess its nature. Recalling his youth, Frankenstein says that at the age of 15 he witnessed the destruction of a great tree by lightning, which provided the occasion for a conversation with 'a man of great research in natural philosophy', who 'entered on the explanation of a theory which he had formed on the subject of electricity and galvanism'.[8]

According to two modern commentators on Mary Shelley's novel, what begins in her story of Dr Frankenstein as a rationalist undertaking – a scientist's exercise in empirical investigation, informed by the latest knowledge concerning electricity – 'is transformed finally into the Romantic quest: modern man in search of his soul'.[9] Whether this is a suitable metaphor for our changing relationship with science in the industrial and post-industrial eras is something that may emerge from a more detailed examination of the ethical dimensions of contemporary practice in science and technology.

The Nature of Ethical Debate in Science and Technology

Turning to the contemporary scene, scientific magazines such as the British weekly *New Scientist* constantly report upon developments which, on analysis, turn out to raise underlying ethical issues of considerable social importance. A recent survey revealed a range of such issues, all raising the question of the moral evaluation of choices at the frontier of knowledge. For example:

- Should laws about privacy take priority over measures designed to encourage the supply of data to researchers trying to combat life-threatening disease?
- Has a government agency the right secretly to carry out radiation experiments on human subjects without their consent, for example by injecting plutonium into terminally-ill patients?
- Is it acceptable for the director of a national centre for genetic research in one country at the same time to be a leading figure in a biotechnology company in another, which might profit from the research results of the former?
- If homosexuality were shown to be genetically determined, would it be wrong to screen for the gene in unborn children?
- Even if global climate change is a serious threat to the planet, have we the right to initiate climate-engineering schemes which might run out of control?
- Would it be right to refuse funding to research into a possible genetic basis for violent behaviour, on the grounds that this diverted attention away from research into the social causes of violence?
- Have human beings the right to implement 'terraforming' on Mars, i.e. create an Earth-like environment on that planet? Would Martians have the right to consent to this?
- Ought the practical difficulty of labelling every single type of food product that may have been produced with the help of genetic engineering to influence our future practice in the matter, bearing in mind that some foods might contain copies of human genes, and that copies of animal genes could occur in food offered for consumption to persons with particular religious or other beliefs, including vegetarianism?
- If there are legitimate objections to cloning experiments using human embryos, would these be removed if scientists were to pick out for their research embryos which, it has been ascertained, already posses lethal defects which would in any case prevent their developing to maturity?
- Digital imaging is a form of computerized photography which makes it easier to remove blemishes from photographs and enhance their aesthetic qualities. It could also be used to falsify an image, for example by removing from, or adding to a group photograph the face of a criminal suspect. Where is the dividing line between improvement of the image and fraud?
- In the context of the debate about keeping animals in zoos, is animal captivity 'captivity'?
- If it is true that moral philosophers do not agree among themselves on ethical principles, is it pointless to ask them to sit on ethics committees monitoring the application of given types of science or technology?

One thing that emerges from the questions is that the ethical issues here fall into different types. An exhaustive analysis of each type will not be attempted here, but they need at least to be signalled. They can mostly be grouped in the following categories (in each case examples of the key issues are given):

1 The activities of the individual practitioner:
   evidence, method, originality, co-operation, rivalry, motivation, responsibilities to clients or patients.
2 Individual freedom and responsibility (not only of the scientists and technologists themselves):
   genetic determinism, nature/nurture, environmental/historical determinism, quantum indeterminism.
3 Social and political freedom and responsibility:
   freedom of expression and criticism, consultation, participation, social integration/exclusion/control, data ethics, legislating for individual moral choice, genetics, universal access to technologies, religion.
4 Technological risk:
   accountability, information, regulation or deregulation.

Accepting that the moral problems which can arise from science and technology are of different kinds, we see that some of them relate to the personal careers of scientists and technologists. These arise from the desire of individual practitioners for promotion, fame, position and wealth. They can involve issues of co-operation, the sharing of knowledge, falsifying of results, plagiarism, conflicts of interest, and so on. Other problems concern responsibilities to or for people outside the scientific community, and not only people but also animals, plants and objects in the environment. These responsibilities often relate either to the welfare of other people or to risks to which they may be exposed.

Since the want of welfare can also be interpreted as a risk, and since lapses of morality by individual practitioners can also entail risk – for example, when empirical data are tampered with to support a flawed hypothesis – technological risk is clearly of considerable ethical significance and can provide a suitable focus for the remainder of the discussion here. The subject is large, and it will be possible to do no more than sketch out for the reader an approach to the ethics of technological risk based on Popperian critical rationalism and (a variant of) the Rawlsian conception of social contract. A convenient term to describe this approach is critical contractualism.

The expression 'technological risk' is taken to cover risks attributable to science as well as technology, not because they are necessarily the same, nor because technology is merely applied science, but because it is when scientific and technical knowledge is embodied in a technology which will or may actually be used in real-world operations that the issue of what risks those operations carry becomes salient, and therefore that issues of right and wrong in the management of the risk merit analysis.

The term risk is used here to refer to the probability that a given state of affairs, deemed actually or potentially harmful, will arise. Merely to quantify a risk by giving it a numerical value does not entail that the state of affairs under consideration is 'risky'. Probabilities are expressed in values between 0 and 1. Something which carried no risk could be said to have a risk of 0.

Another question to consider is how science and technology stand in relation to one another and whether, for example, as far as risks to the wider community are concerned, the scientist can be deemed free from responsibility on the grounds that the discoveries of science can only impact on society or the environment after technologists have decided to apply them in real-world situations. Or is it perhaps the case that technologists only work with the intellectual materials that scientists put into their hands, and therefore the responsibility for the consequences of technology really lies with the scientists?

I have already suggested that technology cannot be defined simply as applied science. On the contrary, the relationship between scientist and technologist is interactive, and it can be the technologist who takes the lead.[10] An interesting thought is that it was a long time after engineers such as James Watt had begun making powerful steam engines that the science of thermodynamics was pioneered by Carnot, Clausius, Kelvin and others. Yet thermodynamics could be described as the scientific explanation of why steam engines work.[11] Again, there is the history of scientific instruments. In important cases, such as the invention of the telescope and the microscope, the technology was a prerequisite for the science. In many instances, such technology is invented by scientists who need it for their research. Equally, there are cases at the frontier of knowledge where technical modifications made by engineers to experimental machines in the light of experimentation feed back into the scientific research. Rather than seeing them as contrary ideas, then, it is more profitable to concentrate on what science and technology have in common, as dynamic systems of knowledge.

Science and Technology as Dynamic Systems of Knowledge

To return to the list of contemporary questions given earlier I should like to ask the reader to confront the following questions:

> Knowing that the list of questions just given is only a sample of a vast number of issues in the ethics of science and technology, how confident are you that there is a 'right' answer to each question? And if you say you are not confident, what reasons do you give for your uncertainty?

It would, I think, be an exceptional person who could honestly claim to know the 'right' answer to all the questions in the list and who could have a realistic prospect of making good that claim in the opinion of dispassionate yet skilful analysts. But if there is uncertainty about some or all of the answers, wherein does the uncertainty lie? Are we just going to say that people bring different values to the assessment of such issues? Or that the issues are very complex? All this would be true, but not necessarily helpful.

I would rather introduce a different perspective, and say that all the issues in our list are issues which involve *new knowledge*. They are all part of that phenomenon which Priestley called 'the rapid process of knowledge'. And then I would like to take the argument one stage further and say that there is something special about new knowledge, which is that it is soon going to become old knowledge and be superseded by *newer* new knowledge. I am going to argue that herein lies an in-principle objection to consequentialist analyses of the ethics of science and technology, and notably to utilitarian ones.

To introduce this argument, I first wish to explain the idea of science and technology as dynamic systems of knowledge. Sciences are systems of knowledge, and these systems are dynamic. That is to say, events inside them are continually being acted on by outside forces. These include environmental change, societal pressures and evolving cultural patterns, including the revolutionary transformations which are bound to occur at one time or another in the many other systems of knowledge with which one given science may interface. What is true of science, in this respect, also goes for technology. It is futile to discuss the ethics of science and technology unless this crucial aspect, their dynamic nature, is understood. People often refer to 'the frontier of knowledge'. They seldom talk about 'the frontier of ignorance', but by definition the two things are identical, and at any given moment there are always many parts of the frontier which are in flux.

Scientific research is always being pursued – and technologies are always being applied – in and by societies which are permanently involved in the process of reallocating resources and priorities in response to demographic, economic and political influences that for the most part lie beyond the control of decision-makers. What determines whether money from a national budget goes to one research project or another, or whether that research is conducted by a woman or a man, or whether it is done in a laboratory in Europe or in Africa, is not primarily the nature of the research task, but one of the types of external influence which have already been mentioned.

One consequence of this is that the non-scientist cannot pretend to hold the scientist or technologist at arm's length like a laboratory specimen, to be treated as an alien object for detached inspection and, perhaps, dissection. The respective roles of the scientist and the non-scientist only have meaning within the shared social context, and that context is changing imperceptibly around them, partly as a result of their own actions. From one moment to the next it may be impossible for them to tell whether they are antagonists or accomplices.

Every member of society is continuously acquiring new information: from personal experience, from culture or the media, from education and training, or from all the different types of research. Viewed in this light, all societies can be thought of as dynamic communities of knowledge.

Critical Rationalism

The idea that knowledge advances by a process of evolutionary growth has received its most authoritative statement in Popper's book *Objective Knowledge*. Popper sees a uniform process for the acquisition of knowledge which holds true 'from the amoeba to Einstein'.[12] The essence of this process is trial and error. Popper's view may be contrasted with that of the American philosopher of science, Thomas Kuhn. According to this, new scientific theories can be viewed as putative paradigms for the type of scientific practice which members of the scientific community will come to regard as 'normal science'.[13]

For purposes of my argument, however, I shall take Popperian critical rationalism as a starting-point. This is because it broadly projects the view of the evolutionary growth of knowledge as something which involves the view of the whole of society that I described earlier. It makes us see, that is, the whole of society as being involved in a permanent learning process. This is not, however, a simple picture of steady onward progress in one direction. Just as Priestley, in talking about the rapid *process* of knowledge, avoided giving a picture of all scientific knowledge pointing one way, towards what one might call 'Progress with a capital P', so the Popperian view of the growth of knowledge as being based on trial and error is first and foremost a theory of error. It advances the view that knowledge is gained by the elimination of false hypotheses. Making the same point in different language, it is a theory of negative feedback: a model in which a continuous flow of hypotheses are continually tested to destruction by criticism based on reason and experience.

I said earlier that the frontier of knowledge is the same thing as the frontier of ignorance. It follows that if what we *are* is conditioned by what we *know*, as individuals or collectively, then what we are is conditioned also by what we do *not* know. There is a story from the early days of the telephone about a man who said, 'This is a truly wonderful invention. I can foresee the day when there will be one in every city in America.' Statements like that help to give a picture of the social setting in which they were made. They help to show how utterly, at a given moment in time, people can fail to understand the implications for society of newly-acquired knowledge. One reason why, with hindsight, we can see this so clearly is because we know 'what happened next', in the sense that we know what subsequent acquisitions of knowledge occurred.

In an earlier work Popper used this kind of argument against theories of human society which infer the course of future events from a path discerned in history.[14] His intended target there was the Marxist view of history, but here I am not concerned with the polemical application of the argument, but with its logic. This could be paraphrased as follows: What people do depends on what they know; people do not yet know the things they are going to learn in the future; but what people do in the future will depend on these things that they do not yet know; therefore we cannot know how people are going to act in the future.

I would like to suggest that this argument can be used, at least in the context of the present discussion, against consequentialist ethics. This is not to rely on the argument that the empirical difficulty of ascertaining in advance the consequences of an action is a reason for not taking consequences into account when trying to weigh up the morality of the alternative courses of action. Let us agree that a moral actor doing a utilitarian calculus need not be paralysed into inaction because it is hard for her to determine exactly what quantity of happiness is going to be delivered to exactly what number of people as a result of her action. Let us agree that the operational difficulty of performing those precise quantifications does not in itself amount to a conceptual flaw in the theory of utilitarianism. But what I want to get at is a different point: that if a moral decision has to be taken in the specific context of 'the rapid process of knowledge' we cannot consistently make use of any form of consequentialist calculus. *If it is inherent to the situation that the locus of decision is poised on the frontier of ignorance, then it is absurd to claim to 'know' the consequences of action.*

What do I mean by 'inherent to the situation'? Well, in many situations in life we may say to ourselves that though we ourselves may have difficulty in working out the consequences of our actions there might be other, wiser or better-placed observers who could make a better job of it on our behalf. But if we are talking about a situation which is at the very edge of human knowledge – a situation in which, by its very nature, the existence of any 'wiser or better-placed observers' is an a priori impossibility – then the character of the problem changes.

I have been arguing that the process of the acquisition of knowledge is a joint enterprise in which all social actors are involved, and not only scientists or technologists. It is not hard to find practical illustrations of the truth of this. A good example, mentioned earlier, is provided by the development of information and communications technologies. The experience of people using these technologies becomes part of the feedback loop which helps to guide the future path of development. Information technology is an obvious example, because it is becoming integrated into almost all aspects of life in post-industrial societies. At the same time, we have to recognize that not every member of society becomes aware of, or needs to use every new advance in scientific or technical knowledge. For example, there are innovations going on all the time in the science and technology of the materials used in industrial and indeed consumer products of which only a tiny proportion ever emerge into the consciousness of the lay public.

But who are the lay public? Is it not wrong that the great majority of people are left in ignorance of important facts which can have an impact on their lives and well-being? Is it not unjust, this inequality of knowledge between those who are informed about science and technology and those who may feel that information-deprivation has trapped them into a passive role as consumers? Certainly there is a risk that these people with the valuable information in a given situation will try to use it to manipulate other people to their advantage. But trying to ensure that all of the people have all of the information all of the time is a bad strategy for managing that risk. The objective should be to improve the information flow in the particular settings where specific information is needed.

Social relations are characterized by inequalities of various kinds, for example the fact that some people have got more money than others. Is inequality of knowledge the same sort of inequality as inequality of material wealth? Does it give rise to the same sort of ethical problems? In particular, should the distribution of knowledge be subjected to the criteria of distributive justice? A typical situation where inequality of knowledge can be identified is the relation between what you might call the punter and the professional: between the house-purchaser and the surveyor, the music-lover and the manufacturer of expensive audio systems, the nervous air traveller and the aeronautical engineer, the patient and the surgeon.

However, the apparent unequal distribution of knowledge is to some extent counterbalanced by the division of labour in society. This is because it distributes different roles to us all to be enacted in the respective settings of the different dimensions of our social lives. Thus, the anxious house-purchaser who nervously calls in the surveyor to view his crumbling ruin is on the underside of an unequal distribution of knowledge. But tomorrow the same individual may be the confident doctor who instructs that identical surveyor to take the pills three times a day. We have all given up the claim to universality of knowledge. We specialize, and we rely on other specialists to supply us with the goods and services we no longer make any effort to provide for ourselves. If things work perfectly, then our ignorance in some settings is balanced by our expert knowledge in others. The unequal distribution of knowledge which it is easy to identify in one micro-situation evens itself out if we take a broad enough perspective on the total, macro-situation.

This versatility of roles connects in an interesting way with the starting assumptions of modern versions of the social contract theory. In the version advanced by the American philosopher, John Rawls, justice is understood as fairness. What is fair is whatever contract is negotiated by human beings who commence their deliberations by adopting a perspective called 'the original position'. This is chiefly characterized by equality and 'a veil of ignorance' which disguises from the parties to the contract the features of their own situation which might introduce bias into their decisions. In this conception, the state of equality is intended to correspond to the state of nature in the traditional theory of the social contract.[15]

The veil of ignorance is a subtle concept, and it stretches surprisingly far. Rawls says that in the original position 'no one knows his place in society, his class position or social status; nor does he know his fortune in the distribution of natural assets and abilities, his intelligence and strength, and the like'.[16] But more to the point in relation to the present argument, the parties do not know to what generation they severally belong. This is because Rawls has foreseen the difficulties which will arise when the discussion turns to such issues as genetics, environmental protection and the management of natural resources, where the consequences of action reach down the generations.

Critical Contractualism

Critical contractualism may be described as a theory which combines the Rawlsian method of reaching ethical decisions with the Popperian account of scientific knowledge. On the basis of that account, I have argued here that the growth of knowledge is a process, not merely a trajectory. We can speak of the *quality* of that process. That quality has at least three dimensions, which we can label as follows:

1 enhancing information flow;
2 facilitating negative feedback (criticism);
3 forcing mutual confrontation between different types of growing knowledge (itself a form of criticism).

I have suggested that the Rawlsian contract is important because, in the context of the growth of knowledge, any form of the consequentialist calculus is a priori unfeasible: science presupposes a moving edge of ignorance. For the Rawlsian parties in the original position, the reassurance of a consequentialist calculus would be illusory. All they can do is make a pact among themselves to adopt a risk-minimizing strategy for moving forward into unknown territory. The hypothesis at the heart of critical contractualism is that the best strategy for the parties to the Rawlsian contract is the one which maximizes the quality of the process of the growth of knowledge. The quality of that process depends on two interacting factors: information and criticism. Without information, the quality of criticism is diminished, and without criticism the utility of information is reduced.

In practice, this would mean using the law to enforce a high level of information disclosure by the practitioners of technologies where the level of risk is uncertain, but not using the law to ban such technologies unless and until the flow of information, appropriately criticized and evaluated, made it possible to reach a judgement on the level of risk involved. The logic of this approach would be the Popperian logic of trial and error: criticism can only establish the error if the trial has been made and information has been acquired from it. The apparent permissiveness of a system based on these principles would be compensated by the stringency of the requirement for the disclosure of information relevant to risk assessment.

The idea of a trade-off between a licence to operate for industry and the imposition by regulatory authorities of an enhanced requirement of information disclosure is not a new one. To a greater or lesser extent it is already incorporated in legislation. The question of which channels the resulting information flow is directed into is important. In different countries and varying circumstances there may be disclosure to official agencies, some of whose operations are secret, or there may be public disclosure. In parallel with the rise of official agencies for registering and perhaps assessing such items of information as safety reports, environmental impact assessments, eco-audits or inventories of dangerous substances, there has been the emergence of various types of technology assessment agency. Some of these are in the public sector,[17] some in the private and some in the category of NGO (non-governmental organization).

However, the argument being made here is not simply for a trade-off between industry and government. The Rawlsian parties do not know which side they are on, or even how many sides there are. Citizens of industrialized societies know from experience how complex these questions are. They are accustomed to public debates about new industrial projects in which many factors have to be weighed against each other: for example, justice to the investors in a company, justice to the inhabitants of an unpolluted region, justice to unemployed workers seeking jobs, and so on. The suggestion being made here is that one reason for the sterility of the debate in many cases is that the goal of an exact calculation of the utility of each available option is an a priori impossibility. It is rendered impossible by the moving edge of ignorance.

The alternative is the dynamic conception of justice obtained by locating the Rawlsian parties in their imaginary caucus on the very lip of that moving edge – by realizing that the locus of the Rawlsian pact is not stationary but moves with the Popperian flux of knowledge. The Rawlsian veil of ignorance, then, is particularly well adapted to solving issues requiring decision in the areas of science and technology. By acknowledging the necessary uncertainty of conditions of choice in these areas, we recognize the need imaginatively to place ourselves in the various roles, present or future, that will be affected by these choices.

In particular, we noted earlier how playing one role in a particular social context, a given individual may be the beneficiary of the knowledge-imbalance inherent to the situation, but that, playing a different role in a different context, the same individual human being may be forced into the role of the person who is disadvantaged in the knowledge-imbalance. Taking this idea into the context of the Rawlsian original position, it means that the parties to the pact, hidden behind the veil of ignorance, must contemplate the possibility that some or many of the others may be themselves in other social roles. If a pact can be concluded on that basis it will be something more significant than a trade-off between social entities which can be easily externalized like 'industry' and 'government'. It will be a concord between the different facets of each person's social being.

The idea that the interlocutors we encounter in some social situations might turn out to be ourselves in other roles is a disturbing one. It may even be the case that the individual in a complex society based on division of labour is condemned to an intrinsically impossible quest for consistency among his or her different social roles. But whether or not there is an a priori impossibility to the quest, people need to adopt a strategy for achieving at least some degree of moral quietus. For citizens of societies in which the task of decision-making in the areas of science and technology is becoming ever more pressing and more complex, one possible strategy is the one which has been sketched here.

NOTES

1 See the interesting discussion in Johnson 'Do engineers have social responsibilities?'.
2 Franklin, *Autobiography*, pp. 175–6.
3 The passage is given here as quoted in the chapter 'Joseph Priestley – Science, religion and politics in the age of revolution' by John Christie, in Porter, *Man Masters Nature: 25 Centuries of Science*, p. 91.
4 Blunden, *Shelley*, p. 51.
5 Commission of the European Communities, Proposals for Council Decisions concerning the Specific Programmes implementing the Fourth Framework Programme for Research, Technological Development and Demonstration Activities (1994–1998), COM(94)68 final, Brussels, 30 March 1994, p. 465. The objectives come under the proposed Specific Programme entitled 'A European programme of targeted socio-economic research for growth, employment and social integration'.
6 For a thoughtful analysis of the 'promise' of technology and the idea that it can have a liberating effect, the reader is referred to *Technology and the Character of Contemporary Life: a Philosophical Enquiry*, by A. Borgmann.
7 The story of this passage in Shelley's life is told in E. Blunden's book *Shelley: a Life Story*. See also D. Locke, *A Fantasy of Reason*, for an account of this interesting circle touching on the life of William Godwin.
8 Shelley, M. W., *Frankenstein or, the Modern Prometheus*, p. 32.
9 Robert E. Dowse and D. J. Palmer, editors of the 1963 Dent edition of *Frankenstein*.
10 For a discussion of 'The interaction of science and technology' see the passage under that title which serves as the editors' introduction to Part Three of *Science in Context*, edited by B. Barnes and D. Edge, pp. 147–85.

11 This example was given by Philip David in a workshop organized by the European Union's SPRINT Programme in Luxembourg on 8 June 1994.

12 Popper, *Objective Knowledge.*

13 The debate on these models has been a central issue in the philosophy of science. This chapter is not the place for an extended survey of the debate, but it is important to be aware of it. A good introduction to the subject is provided in *Criticism and the Growth of Knowledge*, edited by I. Lakatos and A. Musgrave.

14 Popper, *The Poverty of Historicism.*

15 Rawls, *A Theory of Justice*, p. 12. Rawls's account has been the subject of wide-ranging debate since the publication of *A Theory of Justice* in 1971. One useful collection of articles is N. Daniels (ed.), *Reading Rawls.*

16 Rawls, *A Theory of Justice*, p. 137.

17 For example, the parliamentary technology assessment organizations such as POST (Parliamentary Office of Science and Technology) in the United Kingdom, OTA (Office of Technology Assessment) at the US Congress and STOA at the European Parliament (Scientific and Technological Options Assessment).

READING GUIDE

For an exposition of critical rationalism, there is Popper's *Objective Knowledge* and for the debate on it there is Lakatos and Musgrave's *Criticism and the Growth of Knowledge*, which has papers by – among others – Kuhn, Popper, Lakatos and Feyerabend. See also Feyerabend, *Science in a Free Society.* Popper returned to his key themes in *In Search of a Better World.*

In *The Coming of Post-Industrial Society*, first published in 1973, the American sociologist Daniel Bell devoted a chapter to 'The dimensions of knowledge and technology: the new class structure of post-industrial society'. Since his book was planned as 'a venture in social forecasting' this analysis of the knowledge community makes interesting reading now. He dares to put the complex question: What is technological change? The reader in search of an answer will find Steven Yearley's *Science, Technology and Social Change* a thoughtful guide. He analyses the idea that scientific knowledge should be regarded as socially constructed. The reader interested in the sociological approach to science is referred to the work *Science in Context: Readings in the Sociology of Science*, edited by Barry Barnes and David Edge of the Science Studies department at the University of Edinburgh. For the structure of the scientific culture in Europe, see Ros Herman, *The European Scientific Community.*

The key work by the American philosopher John Rawls referred to in this chapter has been *A Theory of Justice.* For debate on his ideas, the reader is referred to *Reading Rawls*, edited by N. Daniels.

Popper desribed his epistemology as 'evolutionary'. The concept of evolution is often misunderstood. A fresh and interesting account is given by Richard Dawkins in *The Blind Watchmaker.*

In this chapter I have emphasized the value of looking at the attitudes and ideas of earlier periods. An evolutionary biologist and humanist who was extremely influential in the 1930s and 1940s was Julian Huxley, author of numerous books on the social impact of science, including *Essays of a Humanist.* Some of his themes were taken up in the 1960s by a Californian microbiologist, Catherine Roberts, who had spent the two decades since World

War II working for Carlsberg in Copenhagen. Her book is called *The Scientific Conscience.* But a key work of the 1960s is Rachel Carson's *Silent Spring*, which alerted people to the environmental damage caused by excessive use of synthetic insecticides.

A good introduction to the analysis, assessment and management of risk is *Technological Risk* by H. W. Lewis. The book benefits from the author's practical experience as an adviser to American government bodies as well as his academic knowledge. An interesting study which specifically analyses the public information requirements embodied in a piece of European Union legislation on industrial risk – the Seveso Directive – is that carried out for the European Commission in 1992 by Brian Wynne, *Empirical Evaluation of Public Information on Major Industrial Accident* Hazards.

All knowledge communities are not identical. The friction that can occur when diverse forms enter into contact can lead to the obliteration of cultural diversity to the disadvantage of people in 'developing' countries whose knowledge systems have already enabled them to develop an appropriate relationship with the local environment. This theme is taken up in Vandana Shiva's *Monocultures of the Mind: Perspectives on Biodiversity and Biotechnology.* She analyses the effects of international patent agreements on the availability of valuable indigenous plant species to people in Third World countries. For a clear and concise guide by a philosopher to North–South issues arising from the role in this area of GATT (General Agreement on Tariffs and Trade) and TRIPs (Trade Related Intellectual Property), see Louise Sarch, *The Effects of Patent Protection on Plant Biotechnologies in Developing Countries.*

10

Psychiatry, Compulsory Treatment and the Value-based Model of Mental Illness

K. W. M. Fulford

It is widely accepted that philosophy, particularly ethics, has a contribution to make in the area of medicine. Problems arising from technological advance have brought this into particular focus in recent decades. A whole new discipline, bioethics, has sprung up in response to these problems, reflecting the concerns not just of the medical profession, but of politicians, journalists and the general public.

Psychiatry has shared in the ethical problems raised by advances in medical technology. The findings of a recent report on genetic screening, for instance, are highly relevant in a general way to the ethical issues raised by new understanding of the genetics of severe mental disorders such as schizophrenia.[1] Of perhaps even greater concern in psychiatry, however, are ethical issues arising from changes in social policy and practice. These have been relatively neglected by bioethics. Yet they include such acute ethical issues as those raised by involuntary (compulsory) treatment of the mentally ill, the move to care and control in the community rather than in institutions, shrinking resources and the growing needs of the long-term mentally ill, and pressures on patient confidentiality between professionals working in a multidisciplinary team.

In this chapter, I will argue that a new and more ambitious vision of ethics in medicine will be needed if we are to make an adequate response to the ethical problems of day-to-day practice in psychiatry. Questions of fundamental ethical theory, as well as what is generally recognized under the term 'bioethics', will play a part here, as will issues which belong to the area of metaphysics. For, as we will find, there are a range of general philosophical problems, such as the nature of personal identity and rationality, which lie barely submerged beneath the surface ethical structure of practical psychiatry.

Consent to Treatment

Psychiatry shares with the rest of medicine that whole range of ethically challenging questions which bioethics has made its own.[2] Particularly acute, though, are problems of consent. This is because psychiatry is the only branch of medicine in which fully conscious, adult patients of normal intelligence can be treated against their express wishes, not (just) for the protection of others but in their own interests.

In a recent questionnaire study, doctors were asked for their reactions to a number of cases in which the question of whether to override a patient's unwillingness to be treated was at issue.[3] There are many limitations to the use of case vignettes for testing ethical intuitions, but the reactions provoked by the cases featured in this study threw light on the way in which the issues are viewed from the perspective of the professional psychiatrist.

Thus, one case from the study involved a young woman who was a novice in a convent:

Case 1: Miss H
Brought by her colleagues for an urgent outpatient appointment as they were unable to contain her bizarre and sexually uninhibited behaviour. Showed pressure of speech, grandiose delusions and auditory hallucinations. Refusing to stay.

This patient was suffering from a serious form of mental illness, hypomania, in which mood is pathologically elevated (as compared with depression in which it is pathologically depressed). With such disorders there is a widely held ethical intuition that the patient should be treated if necessary against his or her express wishes. This reflects the general ethical principle that doctors should act in the patient's best interests. Such cases, it is felt, are among those (also including small children and the mentally disadvantaged) whose express wishes, contrary to the general rule, are *not* a reliable guide to their best interests. Involuntary treatment has provoked strong opposition, not least from the perspective of philosophy.[4] But the intuition has deep historical roots and is shared by a wide variety of different cultures.[5] In the case of Miss H, there was almost complete agreement amongst those questioned that she should be admitted to hospital and treated as an involuntary patient under prevailing mental health legislation.

At first sight this degree of intuitive agreement in practice may appear highly satisfactory from an ethical point of view. The intuition that involuntary treatment is appropriate in such a case is, of course, not shared by everyone; notably it is not shared by the patient; and it is the (necessary) infringement of individual liberty inherent in involuntary treatment which has led authors such as the American psychiatrist Thomas Szasz to reject it. Yet from a practical point of view, it may be thought, surely what we have in a case like that of Miss H, is one of those well-grounded ethical intuitions upon which modern casuists have come to rely.[6]

This would be over-hasty, however. In the first place, psychiatry is notoriously vulnerable to abuse, to involuntary 'treatment' being used, not to help someone who is ill, but as a means of political or social control. Such abuses may become institutionalized, as in the former Soviet Union;[7] but sporadic cases occur all too frequently in every country. Again, on a more everyday basis, there is a genuine difficulty about just where to draw the line. There is a debate among moderates about this. Traditionally, the worry has been about over-use of compulsion. But in recent years there has been concern that professionals were not sufficiently *willing* to use compulsion![8] This difficulty, which is essentially a practical one, showed up clearly in the questionnaire study. Despite the homogeneity of the respondents – all were psychiatrists working in the same department – there was considerable disagreement over no less than two out of the thirteen cases reviewed. The two cases which provoked particular disagreement were these:

Case 2: Mr S
Aged 48. Bank manager. (Depression) Presented in casualty with biological symptoms of depression and a hypochondriacal delusion (that he had brain cancer). History of attempted suicide. Asking for something to 'help him sleep'. He refused to stay in hospital when he was told that he was suffering from depression.

Case 3: Miss A
Age 21. Student. (Anorexia nervosa) Four-year history of intermittent anorexia. Currently seriously underweight, exercising and using laxatives; amenorrhoeic. She refused to allow herself to be admitted, maintaining that she was 'too fat'.

In the case of Mr S, half the respondents were in favour of involuntary treatment, half against. In the case of Miss A, a quarter were in favour and three-quarters against. If, then, even under the well-controlled conditions of a questionnaire study, there can be this degree of disagreement, the problem in the hurly-burly of practice must be significant indeed.

Mental health professionals tend to assume that problems in this area reflect, essentially, medico-legal difficulties of applying the relevant mental health legislation. However, although such legislation provides a broad framework for involuntary treatment, it is not sufficiently fine-grained to explain the way in which involuntary treatment is actually used. The UK Mental Health Act, like that of other jurisdictions,[9] defines two central criteria for such treatment. The first is that the patient is suffering from a mental disorder (defined very widely as 'mental illness, arrested or incomplete development of mind, psychopathic disorder and any other disorder or disability of mind'); the second is that treatment is necessary in the interests of the patient's own health or safety, or for the protection of others. Applied to our questionnaire study, these broad criteria would encompass all thirteen cases. The Code of Practice,[10] moreover, although providing detailed and generally helpful guidance, fails in this case either to explain the pattern of results (nothing in it restricts the use of involuntary treatment to Case 1, for instance). Indeed to the extent that the code emphasizes the importance of risk of harm as an indication for involuntary treatment, it would suggest, contrary to the findings of the study, that Cases 2 and 3 are *better* candidates for involuntary treatment than Case 1, these being at risk of death, from suicide and starvation respectively.

Faced with difficulties of this kind, bioethics has sought to clarify the ethical grounds of involuntary psychiatric treatment, to look behind our ethical intuitions, as a guide to practice. Bioethics currently offers two main styles of ethical reasoning: casuistry and the principles approach. As to casuistry, this is *prima facie* relevant since it starts from the 'bottom up', as it is often put, seeking to help us clarify our ethical intuitions by comparing and contrasting actual cases. This is a powerful method for ethical training, increasing sensitivity to and awareness of ethical issues.[11] It has, though, an inherent weakness applied to psychiatry, namely its reliance on consensus. Jonsen and Toulmin's original advocacy of casuistry was based on their observation that a diverse group of practitioners and bioethicists could agree on *what* it was right to do, while disagreeing on *why* it was right. Hence they said, ethical intuition should come before ethical reasoning, not vice versa.[12] Yet this is a recipe for *consolidating* authority in just those cases in which authority can be misused. We will return to the reasons for this in more detail in the next section. But in psychiatry at least, casuistry could as well have been used to endorse as to oppose the abusive practices which developed in the former USSR.

The other main style of ethical reasoning is 'top down', from broad principles to individual cases. One paradigm of this approach is the four principles proposed by the American medical ethicists Beauchamp and Childress: beneficence, non-maleficence, autonomy and justice.[13] These are to be understood as *prima facie* principles, each having *prima facie* weight but none as of right trumping the others. Involuntary treatment, then, is directly analysable, up to a point, in terms of a balance between autonomy and beneficence. The good health-care professional should act both beneficently and with respect for the patient's autonomy. There are often profound difficulties in drawing this balance. But in the case of severe mental illness, at least, it seems that the patient's power of autonomous decision-making is so impaired that the principle of beneficence provides a clear justification for intervening in the patient's best interest.

This is the standard account. It is important in that it corresponds broadly with our ethical intuition about cases of this kind, and thus has a degree of face validity. But it is also important because its treatment of autonomy focuses attention on the ethical significance of *diagnosis*.

Conceptually, diagnosis and treatment are really two sides of the same coin.[14] And in relation to involuntary treatment at least, specific diagnoses do seem to be ethically significant. The Butler Committee,[15] whose report was an important influence on the Mental Health Act 1983, looked in detail at this question. They recognized that seriousness of disorder as such was not sufficient to mark out those who, in the relevant sense, were 'not responsible'. The traditional notion of 'psychotic disorder', on the other hand, especially as defined by the presence of delusions, seemed to meet the case. The Mental Health Act, as we have seen, defines mental disorder very broadly, and for this reason it fails to correlate with the ethical intuition that involuntary treatment is appropriate only for certain kinds of mental disorder. But the narrower Butler criterion coincides closely with this intuition. In our study, for instance, Miss H had florid delusions, while all those patients for whom involuntary treatment was not thought appropriate had no delusions; and of the two cases over which there was disagreement, Mr S (Case 2) had only one delusion, while Miss A (Case 3) was only equivocally deluded.

Beauchamp and Childress, then, bring us squarely to the ethical importance of *diagnosis* in relation to involuntary treatment. The difficulty, though, comes when we try to cash out the operative diagnostic notion of 'impairment of autonomy' in a clinically relevant way. Thus, these authors, in common with others, develop a detailed account of autonomy in terms of a series of competencies. Autonomous decision-making, they argue, requires intentionality, understanding, deliberative capacity, coherence and freedom from external controlling influences. Hence where one or more of these is lacking, involuntary treatment in the best interests of the person concerned may be justified on the grounds that he or she is not competent to make the required decisions autonomously.

This account certainly covers many kinds of mental disorder. In dementia, for instance, the disorder discussed in detail by Beauchamp and Childress, there is often *in*coherence and *lack* of understanding; and with severe mental deficiency, understanding and deliberative capacity may both be lacking. The competencies account, moreover, is consistent with the dominant model of disease in medicine, the so-called 'medical model'. Indeed it implies this model.[16] According to the medical model, disease is to be understood as an essentially factual notion, particular diseases being defined on the basis of scientific information about bodily and mental functioning. Psychiatric illness and its symptoms are therefore seen as the result of abnormalities in bodily and mental functioning. According to this model, 'disease' may have an evaluative element in its meaning, but this will be important only in the 'applied' part of medicine, in treatment. It will be peripheral to the core of purely scientific knowledge by which distinctively medical expertise is defined.[17] This is an attractive model from the point of view of psychiatric ethics, moreover, for as the philosopher Antony Flew has argued, writing of delusions, it holds out the prospect of defining the proper scope of involuntary psychiatric treatment objectively, by scientific tests of mental functioning.[18]

The medical model is not without its difficulties even in physical medicine, however. From a practical point of view, it marginalizes the perspective of the user of services, emphasizing the doctor's knowledge of disease at the expense of the patient's experience of illness.[19] Theoretically, it fails to explain many of the features of everyday medical usage, in particular the logical relationships between the three key medical concepts, illness, disease and dysfunction.[20]

Some of these difficulties will be considered in more detail later. But the key difficulty for now is that the analysis proposed by Beauchamp and Childress, although indeed covering some cases (such as dementia) simply fails to explain many other cases. In relation to the questionnaire study, for instance, the 'competencies' approach takes us no nearer to explaining the intuitive selection of cases than the approach embodied in the UK Mental Health Act.[21] Miss H (Case 1), for instance, may have lacked a degree of coherence; but amongst those cases which were firmly *rejected* as candidates for involuntary treatment, some scored much *higher* for loss of competencies (a case of hysterical paralysis, for instance, involving both loss of intentionality and of deliberative capacity). This is not to say that the Beauchamp and Childress analysis, and with it the medical model, is wrong. To repeat, some cases (like dementia) can be helpfully analysed in terms of the impaired competencies and disturbances of functioning that are central to the bioethical–medical model. That this account none the less fails with a wide range of other types of mental disorders suggests, therefore, not that it is wrong but that it is incomplete.

The Value-based Model of Mental Illness

What should we make of the incompleteness of the medical model? One possibility, the most natural from the standard medical point of view, is that it is a reflection of no more than the incompleteness of mental science – something that may be remedied by future scientific progress. However, as no less an advocate of the medical model than Boorse has pointed out, there are certain general features of the model that suggest that it will never be sufficient: for example, the concept of function, central to the model, attaches naturally to bodily and mental *parts and systems*, whereas psychosis, the central type of mental disorder, seems to involve the person *as a whole*.[22] A second possibility is that mental illnesses are, after all, not really mental illnesses, that despite appearances they are entities of a radically different kind from physical illnesses. Szasz and other 'anti-psychiatrists', emphasizing the more value-laden nature of mental illnesses, have argued that they are really moral rather than medical entities, that hysteria, for example, is really just malingering, that psychopathy is really just delinquency.[23]

This same feature of mental illnesses, however, viewed through the lens of meta- or theoretical ethics, suggests a third possibility, namely that, despite appearances, *physical* illnesses as well as mental illnesses are essentially evaluative concepts. Metaethics is that part of ethical theory which is concerned with the logic (the meanings and implications) of value terms. For a while, in the 1950s and 1960s, many philosophers, especially in the linguistic analytical tradition of Anglo-American philosophy, took this aspect of ethical theory to be coextensive with philosophical ethics. Philosophers, they argued, should be concerned with the form of valid ethical argument rather than with substantive moral questions. Modern moral philosophy, with certain notable exceptions.[24] has reacted against this position, concerning itself more with questions of substance than with logical form. In this section I will argue that in psychiatry at least, form and content, meaning and substance, are equal partners in applied ethical theory and that examination of the logic of value terms provides key insights into the meaning of mental illness. This in turn, as I will show later, has important implications for practice.

The key to the contribution of ethical theory in this area is the observation, emphasized by Hare, Urmson and others at the height of the linguistic analytical period in moral philosophy, that the strength of the evaluative connotations of value terms, including such all-purpose value terms as good and bad, varies with context.[25] An expression like 'good picture', for instance, has well-marked evaluative connotations; 'good' in this context sounds like a value term. 'Good apple' on the other hand has mainly descriptive connotations. In this context, 'good' conveys something like 'clean-skinned, sweet, etc.' This suggests that if 'illness' is a value term, the more value-laden 'mental illness' could be to the less value-laden 'physical illness' as 'good picture' is to 'good apple'. In neither case is the one expression, being more or less value laden, more or less valid than the other. In both cases, differences in the strengths of their evaluative connotations are a legitimate reflection of a logical property which 'illness' shares with 'good' and indeed with value terms in general.

The mechanism behind this logical property, as outlined by Hare and Urmson, is consistent with this possibility. There are a number of factors involved. But the most important from the point of view of psychiatric ethics is the way in which the descriptive criteria we adopt in making a value judgement vary with context. Where these descriptive criteria are relatively closed, where there is little variation from person to person and from case to case, they can become attached by association to the meaning of the value term in question; where on the other hand the criteria are relatively open, there is no stable descriptive meaning to become attached in this way. Thus in the case of apples, most people in most contexts judge clean-skinned, sweet, etc. apples to be good, and so 'clean-skinned, sweet, etc.' becomes attached by association to the meaning of 'good apple'. 'Good picture' on the other hand lacks a stable descriptive meaning because the descriptive criteria by which we judge pictures are relatively open.

We can now apply this mechanism direct to physical illness and mental illness. Thus anything other than the mildest of pain, a typical symptom of physical illness, is for most people in most contexts at best a necessary evil; pain is therefore a relatively closed phenomenon, evaluatively speaking. Anxiety on the other hand, a typical symptom of mental illness, is an experience which different people evaluate quite differently; some people enjoy the 'buzz of fear' in hang-gliding say, while for others this is highly aversive. Where pain is closed, then, anxiety is open, and this, to the extent that pain and anxiety are indeed typical symptoms of, respectively, physical illness and mental illness, is sufficient to explain the more descriptive connotations of physical illness and the more evaluative connotations of mental illness.

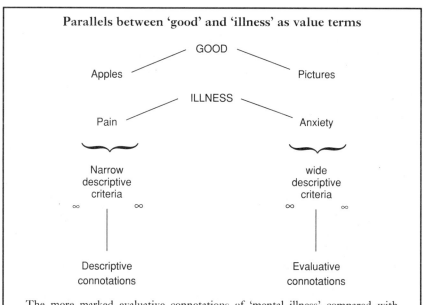

Parallels between 'good' and 'illness' as value terms

The more marked evaluative connotations of 'mental illness' compared with 'physical illness' reflect the fact that the descriptive criteria by which we evaluate typical symptoms of physical illness (such as pain) are more narrowly defined or agreed upon than those by which we evaluate typical symptoms of mental illness (such as anxiety). The figure makes the point that in this respect, 'illness' (mental or physical) is no different from any other value term, including 'good'.

The parallels between 'good' and 'illness' as value terms are summarized in the figure. It is important to see that there is nothing here which is special to illness. The two cases flow through in precisely the same way. It is important, too, to see that there is nothing here for science, as such, to do. All that is involved is the logic of value terms combined with the psychological facts of human nature. We could adopt different criteria of goodness in apples. There is no logical barrier to this, it would not be self-contradictory to judge a rotten apple to be good; indeed in some contexts, as in the case of cider making, rotten apples *are* judged to be good. But this is a matter of human nature, not something to be determined by scientific advance. Science may indeed help us to develop secondary criteria, more detailed, or more reliable, ways of defining our primary criteria – a chemical measure of the sweetness of an apple, say. Scientific advances may even change our value judgements: sweet apples could come to be judged bad if found to be carcinogenic. But in neither case is it the science as such that is operative. A scientific measure of sweetness could only be a criterion for goodness in apples if sweetness itself, human nature being what it is, is already a criterion. Similarly, sweet apples, if found to be carcinogenic, would only come to be judged 'bad apples' because, human nature being what it is, avoiding cancer is (generally) judged more important than enjoying sweet apples.

I emphasize these logical features of the model because it is from the pre-eminence it affords human nature, and the (psychological) openness of many of our value judgements, that many of its practical consequences for psychiatric ethics flow. In the next section I will review these briefly, first as they relate to involuntary treatment, then for psychiatry in general.

Theory and Practice

A first practical consequence of the model of mental illness derived from theoretical ethics, which I have called here the value-based model, is that it gives us a quite different picture of the difficulties raised by psychiatric diagnosis. As we saw earlier, diagnostic problems are central to the difficulties raised by involuntary treatment, but in the standard medical model in bioethics it has been assumed that these problems are, ultimately, scientific in nature. As already noted, there is nothing in the value-based model which is anti-scientific. Indeed given that the criteria for value judgements are *descriptive* criteria, it emphasizes the importance of good science. In so far as diagnostic questions in psychiatry turn on careful descriptions of symptoms, or indeed on knowledge of brain functioning, there is a clear obligation to exercise all due rigour and objectivity. But in psychiatry, the value-based model suggests, this will never be enough. Questions of value, as well as questions of fact, will always come in. Science, in the form of disease theory, can inform, in some cases even change, our values.[26] But if the value-based model is right, science can no more be the sole arbiter of judgements of mental illness, than it can of goodness in apples or indeed taste in pictures.

The importance of value judgements in psychiatric diagnosis is consistent with empirical work showing cross-cultural and gender biases in psychiatric diagnosis.[27] Such biases, though, have tended to be interpreted consistently with the medical–scientific model as representing a misuse or misapplication of objective categories of disorder, rather than as an integral feature of psychiatric diagnosis itself. Similarly, the importance of value judgements in assessments of rationality has been recognized in philosophy and in bioethics.[28] In the latter, though, again consistently with the bioethical–medical model, this has often been perceived as something separate from, rather than integral to, diagnosis. In Beauchamp and Childress's phrase, such judgements represent a 'moral and *not a medical*' consideration, one which would disappear if 'precise, nonevaluative criteria were available for making such determinations of competence'.[29]

A value-based model thus brings moral, or at any rate evaluative considerations in from the periphery to the centre of diagnosis in psychiatry. The same, of course, is true in principle, according to the model, in physical medicine. It is just that in physical medicine the value judgements in question are by and large unproblematic and hence can be ignored.

This leads us to a second practical consequence of the value-based model. For the difference between models on this point suggests a different way of understanding the vulnerability of psychiatry to abuse. It has been recognized for some time that the peculiar difficulties involved in psychiatric diagnosis were among the factors which rendered psychiatry vulnerable in this way. But it was assumed that these were, at base, difficulties arising from the underdeveloped state of the mental sciences.[30] What is shown by the present model is that important as these difficulties may be, differences of value could be important as well. Indeed transferring the simplified model of illness appropriate to physical medicine to psychiatry could be positively dangerous in the case of abuse. For this focuses attention on the scientific aspects of diagnosis *at the expense of* its evaluative aspects, and hence away from what on the value-based model could be the more important vulnerability factor. There is evidence that in the former USSR, in which a strongly medical–scientific model of mental illness was current, this played a critical role in allowing abuse to become widespread.[31]

Recognizing that our difficulties arise (partly) from the evaluatively open nature of judgements of mental illness is one thing; resolving these difficulties is another. Indeed a direct consequence of the value-based model is that, granted that there are *legitimate* differences between people's evaluations of experiences like anxiety, psychiatric diagnosis is *legitimately* less determinate than diagnosis in physical medicine. A third practical corollary of the model, then, is a marked shift towards patient autonomy. Respect for the wishes of the patient is a well-established principle of medical ethics. Its scope, though, has been confined to issues of treatment. Recognizing the evaluatively open nature of diagnosis in psychiatry shows that here at least the patients' own values, indeed their experience in general, may be important also in diagnosis.[32]

Even in the most liberal of medical ethics, however, the patient's values are not *all*-important; there must be some negotiation, some weighing of views. And as we have seen, central to the ethical dilemmas involved in psychiatry is the fact that in some circumstances in seems intuitively right to go directly against the patient's express wishes. A full treatment of this would take us into deep metaphysical waters (see next section). But a fourth practical consequence of a value-based model is to give a particular edge to the difficulties faced by the psychiatrist as an expert witness in the courts. Traditionally, the expert is a 'man of science', and it has long been recognized that there is a difficult dividing line between what the psychiatrist legitimately may and may not be an expert in.[33] A value-based model, drawing only on the point made in the last section about the logic of value terms, can help to clarify this question (giving, for example, a more precise understanding of the scientific component of disease concepts.[34] But a value-based model also suggests, contrary to the medical model, that advances in scientific knowledge of brain functioning as such cannot, in principle cannot, resolve these questions finally.

Applying this same consideration to ordinary clinical practice leads to a fifth point: namely, that it shows the place of the multidisciplinary team in a quite different light. In the bioethical–medical model, the importance of the multidisciplinary team is well recognized in relation to practical aspects of implementing treatment. But if questions of value are integral to diagnosis in psychiatry, then the multidisciplinary team, providing as it does a balance of evaluative considerations, is crucial also at the stage of assessment. This is because, while we have no fast and final way of resolving questions of value, one well-recognized way of encouraging bad practice is to allow the values of one person or even of one professional group to become dominant. It is this which is behind the safeguards built into most modern mental health legislation. The Mental Health Act 1983, for example, requires, except in cases of extreme emergency, two medical opinions and the agreement of an Approved Social Worker. In an exclusively scientific medical model all this is accepted by doctors as a temporary expedient necessary only so long as we lack adequate scientific tests for mental disorder. But in a value-based model, the range of values represented by the multidisciplinary team, far from being a concession, is essential. That is to say, it is *logically* essential (though of course not in itself always sufficient) for good practice in psychiatry.

The value-based model of mental illness derived from theoretical ethics thus has a number of directly practical consequences for psychiatric ethics: it shows that diagnosis as well as treatment raises questions of value in psychiatry, that these questions are integral, and that they are not finally resolvable by future scientific advances. It is particularly important to recognize this in cross-cultural psychiatry and in relation to gender issues. The relatively open value judgements involved in psychiatric diagnosis help to explain why psychiatry is especially vulnerable to abuse. This gives a new edge to the meaning of patient autonomy, making it clear that sensitivity to the patient's values and experience is important in diagnosis as well as in treatment. And it shows that the multidisciplinary team is essential to good practice in psychiatry, whatever future developments in brain science may bring.

Taken together these consequences suggest a further, more general consequence, namely that they show psychiatry itself, as a medical discipline, in a quite different and more positive light. In the standard, exclusively scientific–medical model, psychiatry is perceived as trailing behind physical medicine. In a value-based model this picture is reversed, psychiatry in important respects taking the lead. Thus the multidisciplinary team, the patient's perspective, and other aspects of practice shown by the value-based model to be essential in psychiatry, are, surely, just as important in physical medicine. Psychiatry thus provides insights into good practice in clinical medicine generally, which in turn have important implications for medical education.[35] In research, similarly, under the dominance of the medical model, psychiatry is seen as a poor scientific relation of general medicine. In a value-based model, on the other hand, it is no less scientific (although the relevant science – brain science – is much harder to do); but it presents us with the additional intellectual challenges posed by its ethically and conceptually problematic nature.[36]

This change of status, clinically and in research, is important ethically. Raising the status of psychiatry is essential to raising the status of, and hence the care that is provided for, psychiatric patients. It is also essential to the future development of the subject. For it refocuses our research efforts away from the narrowly empirical model appropriate (up to a point) in physical medicine and towards the rich mix of conceptual and empirical issues which, after all, is characteristic of any new and rapidly developing discipline.

Psychiatry and Metaphysics

In the last two sections I have tried to show how a basic point about the logic of value terms from post-war analytical philosophy has important practical implications for psychiatry. In relation specifically to our original problem of consent, this idea has given us new understanding of what we called the line-drawing difficulty. Disagreements over the appropriateness of involuntary treatment in a particular case, in addition to reflecting empirical difficulties (the extent of dangerousness, for instance), may reflect (legitimate) differences of value.

The power of analytical philosophy in psychiatry, indeed the power of the linguistic analytical way of doing analytical philosophy, is shown by the range of results which are generated by this one idea.[37] There are other useful ideas from this tradition: moral descriptivism, for instance, suggests a new and more self-consistent version of the medical model.[38] Indeed the whole debate about the validity of the concept of mental illness can be re-cast as a *forme fruste* of the is–ought debate in ethics.[39] The moves in the is–ought debate can illuminate the debate about mental illness, and, indeed, vice versa: the clinical psycho-pathology of delusions, for instance, the extraordinary range of logical forms which delusions actually take, has important implications for our under-standing of the logical relationship between description and evaluation.[40]

But for all this we are still only on the edge of the potential of philosophy for psychiatric ethics. Metaethics, at least in the post-war period, was concerned mainly with the logic of value terms *simpliciter*. It is thus relevant to the general question of whether a given psychiatric condition is a bad condition to be in. But ethical difficulties in psychiatry are often concerned not so much with whether a condition is a bad condition as with whether it is a bad condition of the particular kind with which medicine is properly concerned. Illness is differ-ent from ugliness, wickedness, foolishness, and so on. The question, then, in psychiatry is, as it is often put, 'mad or bad?', or, as we might add, 'mad or sad?'. The two equivocal cases in the study described above both turned on questions of this kind. No one doubted that both these patients were in a bad condition (sad and suicidal, Case 2; sad and starving, Case 3). The question was whether their bad conditions were of a kind for which specifically medical intervention against their wishes would be ethically justified.

It is this question which connects psychiatric ethics directly with some of the deepest of the metaphysical problems with which philosophy has been con-cerned. We can see this in a general way from the connections between auton-omy, emphasized in bioethics, and a range of topics in the philosophy of mind, including rationality, personal identity, and knowledge of other minds. Thus autonomy assumes rational choice. But rationality, through the window of psychopathology, is a far more complex notion than has traditionally been recognized.[41] In particular it involves non-cognitive as well as the traditionally emphasized cognitive elements.[42] Then again, autonomy assumes a well-de-fined individual whose choices are to be respected. But personal identity, again through the window of psychopathology, is not only a complex notion, but one which is actively constructed, in particular through psychosocial,[43] affective,[44] and developmental processes.[45] Again, moral choices, whether rights-based or utilitarian, assume knowledge of other minds. But this, in conditions ranging from autism through to psychopathy may be defective in a number of different ways.[46]

Elsewhere, I have explored the distinction between illness and other nega-tive evaluative concepts in terms of loss of agency or failure of action.[47] The broad rationale for this is that the essence of the patient's experience of illness, which as we have seen drives the agenda in a value-based model, is incapacity. But incapacity involves loss of agency. Incapacity consists in being unable to do the things which, in the analytical philosopher John Austin's phrase, we would 'ordinarily just get on and do'.[48] Where, therefore, disease is naturally analysed (as in the medical model) in terms of failures of particular *functions*, illness is naturally analysed (in a value-based model) in terms of failures of *action*. This leads to a general account of illness which is broadly consistent with a widely recognized moral feature of illness, namely that it is exculpatory.[49] Its particular significance for psychiatric ethics, though, is that, as against the medical model, it is consistent with and helps to explain the central ethical significance of the psychotic symptom of delusion; and this connects work in this area with a rich resource of philosophical theory on intentionality and the structure of action.[50]

As with metaethics, so with metaphysics, there is clearly a good deal more to be said about all this. I have not touched on the ethical significance of unconscious mental process, for instance, a topic which leads us from philosophy of mind into the philosophy of science. Indeed, forming as it does a relatively seamless whole, there is no part of general philosophy which is not relevant in principle to psychiatry. The particular value of psychiatry to philosophy, on the other hand, is the dowry that it brings, the real world of real people.[51]

Conclusions

In this chapter I have argued from the case of involuntary psychiatric treatment that philosophy is relevant to psychiatric ethics in a variety of ways. Bioethics, as it has developed since the early 1970s, mainly in response to the problems raised by technological medicine, can help to clarify the ethical principles (such as beneficence and respect for autonomy) which lie behind our ethical intuition that involuntary treatment is sometimes justified. To understand the boundary problem, though, the problem of where to draw the line between those cases for which such treatment is justified and those for which it is not, we have had to turn to ethical theory, in particular a feature of the logic of value terms explored by analytical philosophers in the post-war period. This helped to explain the relatively value-laden nature of diagnoses of mental illness, which in turn led to a number of important practical implications for psychiatry. But for a deeper understanding of the boundary problem, it turned out to be necessary to engage with such metaphysical questions as the nature of agency, free will, personal identity and rationality, areas traditionally the concern of general philosophical theory.

If this is accepted, it follows that in psychiatry the distinction between applied and other kinds of philosophy largely disappears. This book is about applied ethics, and, of course, there is more to ethics than philosophy. Anthropology, psychology, law, history, and political theory all have ethical relevance. These disciplines are indeed all highly relevant to psychiatric ethics. But to the extent that philosophy, too, has a contribution to make, we can say that in psychiatry applied philosophical ethics just *is* philosophy.

NOTES

1 This was a report prepared by the Nuffield Council on Bioethics in 1993. The council's terms of reference restrict it to considering ethical problems arising from technological advances.

2 For recent reviews of psychiatric ethics, see Reading Guide.

3 The cases described in this chapter are based on real patients but with biographical and other details changed to ensure confidentiality. They are taken from the questionnaire study referred to in the text, and described more fully in K. W. M. Fulford and R. A. Hope, *Psychiatric Ethics: a Bioethical Ugly Duckling?*

4 Probably the best-known contribution on this subject is T. Szasz's book, *The Myth of Mental Illness*. Involuntary treatment is at the heart of the whole debate about the concept of mental illness; see Reading Guide.

5 See Wing, *Reasoning About Madness*.

6 The revival of casuistry, or case-centred reasoning, in ethics is generally attributed to A. R. Jonsen and S. Toulmin's *The Abuse of Casuistry*. An excellent recent discussion of casuistry in medical ethics is T. H. Murray's 'Medical ethics, moral philosophy and moral tradition'.

7 An important early account of the 'psychiatric treatment' of political dissenters in the former Soviet Union was given by S. Bloch and P. Reddaway in *Russia's Political Hospitals*.

8 In many countries around the world there has been a shift from institutional care of the mentally ill to care in the community. However, this has often been under-resourced, with the result that many long-term psychiatric patients have been neglected, some committing suicide, others (statistically a tiny minority) committing violent crimes including unprovoked and random attacks on strangers. These problems have led to calls for greater control either through additional legal powers, or, as in the UK, through closer supervision in the community. A good historical account of the treatment of the mentally ill is R. Porter's *A Social History of Madness*. A useful recent review is B. Mandelbrote's 'The swing of the pendulum: attitudes to the mentally ill and their management'.

9 See particularly Part II of T. Campbell and C. Heginbotham's *Mental Illness: Prejudice, Discrimination and the Law*.

10 Published by the Department of Health and Welsh Office, *The Code of Practice* is a supplement to *The Mental Health Act 1983*, drawn up in consultation with both mental health professions and patient organizations.

11 See R. A. Hope and K. W. M. Fulford, 'Medical education: patients, principles and practice skills', for a discussion of the strengths and weaknesses of casuistry in medical student education.

12 See Jonsen and Toulmin, *The Abuse of Casuistry*.

13 See Beauchamp and Childress, *Principles of Biomedical Ethics*. For a discussion of the strengths and weaknesses of the principles approach in psychiatry see Fulford and Hope, 'Psychiatric ethics: a bioethical ugly duckling?'.

14 See Fulford, 'Bioethical blind sports'.

15 The Butler Committee was a government committee set up under Lord Butler to review the legal framework for the treatment of mentally abnormal offenders.

16 Arguments for this are set out in Fulford and Hope, 'Psychiatric ethics: a bioethical ugly duckling?'

17 A careful philosophical version of the medical model is developed by C. Boorse in 'On the distinction between disease and illness'. He extends the argument to mental illness in 'What a theory of mental health should be'.

18 See Flew, *Crime or Disease?* Flew examines the whole question of why the mentally ill should sometimes be considered not to be responsible for their actions.

19 See Fulford, 'Concepts of disease and the paradox of patient power'.

20 A particular problem with the medical model is that even those who have argued most strongly for a value-free definition of disease continue to use the term (as it is used in both everyday and medical discourse) with clear evaluative connotations. See Part II of Fulford, *Moral Theory and Medical Practice*.

21 See Fulford and Hope, 'Psychiatric ethics: a bioethical ugly duckling?'.

22 See Boorse, 'What a theory of mental health should be'.

23 A. Duff, in 'Psychopathy and moral understanding', looked in detail at just what psychopathy, understood as a mental disorder, might consist in. Recent work on this topic includes C. Elliot, 'Puppetmasters and personality disorders: Wittgenstein, mechanism and moral responsibility'. For references to Szasz's work, see Reading Guide.

24 An important recent book on ethical theory is J. Dancy's *Moral Reasons*.

25 See Hare, 'Descriptivism' and Urmson, 'On grading'. For a useful review of many of the main philosophical ideas of this period see Warnock, *Contemporary Moral Philosophy*.

26 The whole of disease theory, including diseases defined by reference to the causes of illness, can be derived within the value-based model from the patient's experience of illness. See generally Fulford, *Moral Theory and Medical Practice*, ch. 4.

27 See for example work on the gender biases in schizophrenia research in D. Russell's 'Psychiatric diagnosis and the interests of women' and E. F. Walker and R. R. J. Lewine's 'Sampling biases in studies of gender and schizophrenia'. An important recent review of cultural biases in the diagnosis of severe mental illnesses is L. J. Kirmayer and E. Corin's 'Inside knowledge: cultural constructions of insight in psychosis'.

28 K. Wallace, in 'Reconstructing judgement: emotion and moral judgement', gives a valuable account of the emotive and connative aspects of rationality. J. Radden reviews the relevance of this to psychopathology in 'Rationality and psychopathology'.

29 See Beauchamp and Childress, *Principles of Biomedical Ethics*, p. 84. The emphasis is added.

30 See Bloch and Reddaway, *Russia's Political Hospitals* and Merskey and Shafran, 'Political hazards in the diagnosis of sluggish schizophrenia'.

31 A study of the concepts of illness, disease and mental illness actually in use in the former Soviet Union during the period when abuse of psychiatry was widespread, is reported in Fulford, Smirnoff and Snow, 'Concepts of disease and the abuse of psychiatry in the USSR'.

32 See Fulford, 'Closet logics: hidden conceptual elements in the DSM and ICD classifications of mental disorders'. The importance of the concept of illness in relation to the patient power movement is explored in Fulford, 'Concepts of disease and the paradox of patient power'.

33 A useful review of this is given in the Butler Report, see n. 15 above.

34 See Fulford, *Moral Theory and Medical Practice*, ch. 4.

35 See Hope and Fulford, 'Medical education: patients, principles and practice skills'.

36 See Fulford, 'Mental illness and the mind–brain problem'.

37 See Fulford, 'Philosophy and medicine: the Oxford connection'.

38 See Fulford, *Moral Theory and Medical Practice*, ch. 2. I explore the application of moral descriptivism to involuntary psychiatric treatment in 'Not more medical ethics'.

39 See Fulford, *Moral Theory and Medical Practice*, ch. 3.

40 See Fulford, *Moral Theory and Medical Practice*, ch. 10.

41 See Radden, review article, 'Rationality and Psychopathology'.

42 See Wallace, 'Reconstructing judgement: emotion and moral judgement'.

43 See Harré, 'Emotion and memory: the second cognitive revolution'.

44 See Moore, Hope and Fulford, 'Mild mania and well-being'.

45 See Glover, *I: the Philosophy and Psychology of Personal Identity*.

46 See Hobson, 'Against the "Theory of Mind" ' and *Autism and the Development of Mind*.

47 See generally, Fulford, *Moral Theory and Medical Practice*, Parts III and IV.

48 See Austin, 'A plea for excuses'.

49 Intuitively, illness is an excuse, e.g. for being off work. This has been emphasized in the sociological literature on the nature of illness, an early account being given by T. Parsons in *The Social System*.

50 See Fulford, 'Mental illness and the mind-brain problem'.

51 J. L. Austin, in 'A plea for excuses', pointed to the rich resource of material for philosophical research provided by abnormal psychological states. An example of recent work drawing on this material is K. V. Wilkes's study of multiple personality disorder in *Real People: Personal Identity without Thought Experiments*.

READING GUIDE

Early and still excellent general accounts of the ethical issues arising in all the main areas of psychiatry include *Psychiatric Ethics* (2nd edition) edited by S. Bloch and P. Chodoff, and *Law and Psychiatry: Rethinking the Relationship* by M. S. Moore. Illuminating case histories with careful ethical and legal analysis from a USA perspective are given in *A Casebook in Psychiatric Ethics* published for the Group for the Advancement of Psychiatry. *The Values of Psychotherapy* by J. Holmes and R. Lindley provides a thoughtful account of the ethical framework of the 'talking therapies'.

Empirical work on consent is reported in C. W. Lidz *et al.* (eds), *Informed Consent: a Study Of Decision-making in Psychiatry*, and in chapter 3, subsection II of S. Wear's *Informed Consent: Patient Autonomy and Physician Beneficence within Clinical Medicine*. Valuable insights into the operation of psychiatry from the point of view of the user of services are given in *Experiencing Psychiatry: Users' Views of Services* by A. Rogers, D. Pilgrim and R. Lacey. Although not dealing specifically with psychiatry, G. J. Agich provides a highly relevant discussion of autonomy in *Autonomy and Long-term Care*. Priscilla Aldersen's *Choosing for Children* shows the value of narrative.

Conceptual and ethical aspects of psychiatric diagnosis and disease classification are explored in Sadler, Wiggins and Schwartz's *Philosophical Perspectives on Psychiatric Diagnostic Classification*, in special issues of *Theoretical Medicine* edited by David Mann, and of the *Journal of Medicine and Philosophy* edited by Loretta Kopelman.

A useful review of various theories of the nature of mental illness is A. Clare's 'The disease concept in psychiatry'. Many of the most important classical papers in the debate about the validity of mental illness are to be found in two edited collections: Caplan, Engelhardt and McCartney's *Concepts of Health and Disease*, and R. B. Edwards's *Psychiatry and Ethics*. Clear presentations of the anti-psychiatry and pro-psychiatry extremes in this debate are, respectively, Szasz's *Insanity: the Idea and its Consequences* and Kendell's 'The concept of disease and its implications for psychiatry'. Roth and Kroll's *The Reality of Mental Illness* is a direct reply to Szasz's *The Myth of Mental Illness*. A reconciliation and development of anti- and pro-psychiatry theories is given in my *Moral Theory and Medical Practice*. The medical model in psychiatry is well reviewed by Macklin in 'The medical model in psychoanalysis and psychotherapy'.

Articles on the ethics and philosophy of psychiatry appear periodically in the *Journal of Applied Philosophy*, *Theoretical Medicine*, and the *Journal of Medicine and Philosophy*. Most bioethics journals publish articles on psychiatric ethics, in particular the *Journal of Medical Ethics*. A series of annotated ethical case-studies is published in the *Psychiatric Bulletin* (published by the Royal College of Psychiatrists). A new journal specializing in all aspects of philosophy, ethics and mental health is *Philosophy, Psychiatry and Psychology* (Johns Hopkins University Press).

PART III

The Legal Dimension: Crime and Punishment

11

Crime and Responsibility

Henry Tam

Introduction

In order to reduce crime, we must not only encourage all citizens to act responsibly, but also ascribe responsiblity for wrongdoing accurately. Failure to grasp what it is to be responsible for any given behaviour could lead to innocent people being wrongfully punished, and guilty people allowed to walk free. Every effort directed at cutting back criminal behaviour would miss its target if the the real basis for holding people responsible for their behaviour is not properly clarified and applied through the criminal justice system.

So under what circumstances should a person be held responsible for committing a crime? It would be wrong to assume that just because someone's behaviour has consequences which go against the criminal law, he or she must be responsible for a crime. Take, for example, a nurse who is found to have put a deadly substance in a drink she gave to her patient, leading to the patient's death. On the surface, the nurse has brought about the patient's death and should be held responsible for a serious criminal offence. However, what if it is claimed that in some way or other the nurse 'could not have avoided' putting the substance in the drink? Should she be held responsible, let alone punished, for the latter's death, if she could not have avoided it?

This chapter will show that by analysing how different types of capacity restriction can impact on individuals' responsibility for their apparently criminal behaviour, a clearer picture of how to tackle different causes of criminal behaviour will emerge, and public policies can be adjusted accordingly. Although frustrated policy-makers may at times feel that pleas of 'he could not have done otherwise' should be totally rejected, criminal offences can ultimately only be minimized with the help of a proper distinction between behaviour that should incur punishment and behaviour that should be dealt with by other means.

I will begin by looking at the purpose of holding people responsible for offences which they have a causal role in bringing about. This will help to explain why in certain cases it would be appropriate to take punitive action against the individuals concerned. It will also pave the way for a wider understanding of what alternative strategies should be considered when different types of capacity restriction are involved. One of the crucial lessons to emerge is that if the criminal justice system distinguishes more clearly the different types of capacity restriction, it would be better placed in practice to tackle the root causes of crime.

The Need for Punishment

The question of why offenders need to be punished can be answered in terms of the response which society has to give to those who defy its laws. This contains three inter-related elements:[1]

1 making offenders feel sorry that they have committed the offence;
2 stopping them from re-offending;
3 deterring others from committing a similar offence.

The first element is important because unless criminals genuinely feel sorry about what they have done, they are not likely to appreciate why their attitude towards the rest of society is unacceptable. This element cannot be realized through thoughtless infliction of pain or the inducement of fear. Offenders have to come to recognize, with the help of being made to face up to the outrage and sorrow of their victims if necessary, that they have done something they really should not have done, because of those who were badly affected by it.

The second element is to prevent the offender from offending again. This will involve not just the deprivation of liberty, but also the development of the offender's attitudes and abilities to function as a responsible citizen. Whether they want to or not, criminals should be able to re-enter society – provided they no longer pose a threat to others – with more opportunities to lead a crime-free life. Hardliners who think that this is too soft an element to be included in the penal system would do well to remember that whilst being imprisoned is an unpleasant experience, a high proportion of criminals none the less run the risk of imprisonment again by re-offending, simply because they are not assisted in any way to succeed in living a crime-free life.

The third element is to convey the message that society would not tolerate such offences by anyone else either. This is why punishment needs to be inherently unpleasant, and the unpleasant nature needs to be graded in relation to the extent to which particular types of crime are to be deterred from happening.

For those who have not yet learnt to take their responsiblity seriously, it would be appropriate to emphasize the element of remorse. For those who are simply insensitive to the needs and concerns of others, the emphasis should fall heavily on the severity dimension. But for those who are in fact reluctant offenders anyway, the emphasis should be on helping them manage their lives without resorting to crime again.

Punishment and Responsibility

None of the elements of punishment can be realized if the individual concerned is not in fact responsible for the crime in question. There can be no remorse for something which one has not willingly brought about. One cannot seriously engage in any form of deliberation about not reoffending if one cannot genuinely identify with having committed that offence in the first place. Furthermore, punishment would not be a deterrent for anyone if it is not tied to behaviour which one can control. If one can be 'punished' regardless of whether or not one can influence the course of events in question, then it would be quite arbitrary if one gets picked out for 'punishment', and how one actually behaves becomes irrelevant.

So for anyone who is found to have played a causal role in bringing about an undesirable state of affairs, it is important to determine whether he can really be held responsible for bringing about that state of affairs.[2] If he cannot be held responsible, it is necessary to understand why he none the less caused the damage, and decide what can be done to prevent similar incidents from happening. On the other hand, if the person can be held responsible, we need to ask why he acted irresponsibly, and what could be done to make him act responsibly in the future.

The problem with phrases like 'could not have avoided doing what was done' is that they could imply either that the person concerned was therefore not responsible at all, or that there were understandable excuses for his doing what he did. The former entails a clean acquittal, but the latter leaves open the question of what is to be done about that person. This ambiguity can be resolved and the implications for crime prevention made clearer if we look at the main types of capacity restriction which could be invoked by phrases like 'could not have done otherwise':

1 ignorance;
2 external force;
3 options restrictions.

Ignorance

Suppose a tourist is arrested at the airport after a bag of heroin is found in her suitcase. In fact, unknown to her, someone has tampered with her suitcase and has put the bag of heroin in it. The connection between her action, namely bringing her suitcase back into this country after her trip abroad, and the bag of heroin being smuggled into the country is clearly not something she knew or could do much about. Under such circumstances, it would make little sense to hold her responsible for smuggling heroin. The heroin entered the country not because of, but in spite of, any morally significant character trait in her. Since blame and punishment can only be directed at moral characteristics – otherwise, it would be coherent to think of earthquakes as blameworthy and man-eating sharks as deserving of punishment – and none of the person's moral characteristics has anything to do with the heroin entering the country, the question of responsibility cannot even arise.

Generalizing from this example, it can be said that whenever people's cognitive capacity is restricted by the circumstances in which they find themselves so that they cannot know the criminal effects of their behaviour, then they cannot be held responsible for those criminal effects. In the drug smuggling example, it was the unforeseeable tampering with the person's suitcase which restricted the person's cognitive capacity to realize fully what she was doing. In other cases, it could be one's own lack of knowledge, accidental circumstances which cannot be foreseen, or the temporary disruption of one's cognitive processes (e.g. through an illness) that precludes responsibility from being attributable to the person who had in ignorance brought about something at odds with the criminal law.

It should be pointed out that what is at issue here is not some counter-factual assumption about what the person in question might have done if she had known more. We are not arguing that if the tourist in our drug smuggling example had known that there was a bag of heroin in her suitcase, she would have handed it in to customs. For all we know, if she had known about the heroin, she would have tried to smuggle it through customs. The point is that even if that were true, there would be no basis for holding her responsible for drug smuggling for the simple reason that she did not in fact know that her action would involve the smuggling of drugs. Without the pre-condition of knowing and understanding what she was doing under the description of 'smuggling heroin into the country' she was in no position to make any real decision about the bag of heroin in question.

Is ignorance always a legitimate excuse?

Just because someone is ignorant of the harm he is causing to others, does it necessarily follow that he cannot be held responsible for the harm concerned?

Can we draw a distinction between culpable and non-culpable ignorance? Suppose a driver gets drunk and in his drunken state drives into a child and kills her. It would appear that he could not be entirely innocent in such a situation. But can his ignorance of where he was steering his car or how fast he was driving be entirely irrelevant?

The inclination to condemn the driver could easily obscure a central point, and that is, for what exactly do we want to hold him responsible? If we want to hold him responsible for 'getting himself drunk when he knows that it could lead to dangerous driving', then provided the description is true, the responsibility ascription can be sustained. However, what if the following alternative description were true? The driver got drunk not knowing that the bar owner, who had promised to put him in a taxi, would instead give him the key to his car and let him drive home. Holding the driver responsible for his behaviour under these circumstances would not mean holding him responsible for killing the child, since if the alternative description were true, it would be unreasonable to hold him responsible for killing the child.

There is in fact no such thing as culpable or non-culpable ignorance in itself. The extent to which ignorance can excuse a crime depends on what exactly the person concerned is ignorant about and what he does none the less know about. Drunken drivers should be held responsible for bringing about the death of those they run over regardless of their state of mind at the time of the killing, if crucially they know that getting intoxicated before driving can cause death and yet they choose to do so. By contrast, someone suffering from an unforeseeable blackout while driving who ends up killing a pedestrian cannot be held responsible for causing the victim's death. What one does not know, one cannot be held responsible for.

It could be argued that our approach might encourage some people to remain ignorant when ignorance can protect them.[3] But that is why the criminal justice system must be backed up by an effective education and information programme.

Ignorance, far from blissful, can cause all kinds of undesirable human behaviour, which the criminal law tries to reduce. Since someone who is ignorant cannot coherently be held responsible for his or her behaviour under the relevant description, the solution to ignorance-related offences must lie with the dispelling of the ignorance in question.

This means that young people's education should include teaching about the criminal law, and about what can be harmful and dangerous for oneself and others, and what precautions need to be taken in order to avoid different kinds of undesirable consequences. Public information should cover where formal education leaves off, so that new discoveries about hitherto unknown causal connections can be widely disseminated.

The campaign against drinking and driving is a good example of this approach. Instead of arguing about the *culpability* of people who do not appreciate how badly the consumption of alcohol could cause them to drive, it is much more effective to focus on making the *causal link* between drink–driving and fatal car accidents indisputably clear to everyone.

As far as drug smuggling is concerned, travellers are already warned to watch over their own luggage. But more can still be done in terms of public education to spell out the serious consequences of drug smuggling for those whose lives are wrecked by their addictions, as well as for those who for whatever reason attempt to help with the smuggling of drugs.

A similar approach can be taken in relation to any type of behaviour which is more likely to have morally unacceptable consequences than those who are tempted to engage in it tend to think. For example, a number of recent cases in the UK and the USA have shown ambiguity in both the public mind and the law about what constitutes consent or lack of consent to sexual intercourse: the so-called 'date-rape' issue. (The issue is discussed elsewhere in this volume by Moira Gatens.) Again, both education and public information can be employed to make it clear that the refusal to give consent is final in all forms of sexual relationship. Even judges may benefit from this kind of public information! Rather than leaving the ambiguity about individual interpretations of consents to case-by-case speculation, a general attack on ignorance could remove any doubt as to whose responsibility it is to secure clear consent, and who is to be held responsible if no such consent has been unequivocally given.

External Force

The second main type of capacity restriction which might be invoked by the phrase 'could not have avoided' is what can be called restriction by external force. A full explanation of this concept would require a substantial account of personal identity which would not be appropriate here. But the following brief account can provide a useful sketch of what the notion of the self involves.[4]

A person can conceive of himself as a distinct and autonomous self in so far as his thoughts, feelings, emotions, desires, beliefs, constitute a reasonably co-ordinated whole. He initiates his own action plans, and he responds to external threats and opportunities in terms of his own agenda. He possesses an overall personality, and he accepts his behavioural interactions with others as genuine manifestations of who he is.

On the basis of this account of the self, children can be said to mature as they progress towards the realization and acceptance of who they are in terms of their balanced and co-ordinated personal qualities. Failure to attain a stable self or to sustain one would thus constitute a form of psychological disorder.

Restriction by external force takes place when some force physically or psychologically alien to the self in question, causes individuals to behave in a way unrelated to their personal qualities. For example, suppose a social worker is on her way to take into care a child who is at risk. Before she gets to the child, she becomes seriously ill, collapses in the street and is taken to hospital. She knows that the child is in danger, but by the time she is able to speak again, she learns that the child has been battered to death. The fact that she had not carried out her task of taking the child into care, which would have prevented the child's death, would not imply in such circumstances that she should be held responsible for letting the child die. Indeed if she is plagued by a sense of guilt, we would want to assure her that she was not to be blamed in any way.

What led to the social worker not carrying out her life-saving task was something external to the social worker's self. It did not come about because of anything in her thinking, desires, beliefs, etc. The fact that she was afflicted by this sudden illness is morally irrelevant. However, as in the previous case, the reason why she cannot be held responsible in this situation is not a matter of any counter-factual assumption about how she might have behaved otherwise. Indeed it could even be true that had she recovered in time, she would have resigned because she had simply had enough. But since this was not what in fact prevented her from saving the child, it should have no place in any judgement about her responsibility for the child's death.

In the above example, the external force which made the social worker play an involuntary role in a child's death is in the form of a physical illness. However, it is possible for psychological forces within individuals to cause them to behave in a manner divorced from their true character. Such forces could be said to make them behave in spite of them*selves*. For example, a patient dependent on community care suffers from schizophrenia. Part of him is obsessed with the idea of killing someone to express his frustrations. But it is a part which is alien to *him* in so far as he has a steady enough conception of himself. He perceives the 'murderous will' in his mind as an 'other' self which he wants to eliminate but cannot. If it is this alien part of the patient – and it is by no means easy for psychiatrists and lawyers to reach agreement on case-by-case diagnosis – which causes him to stab a total stranger, then the rationale for not ascribing any responsibility to him for murder would be that the moving force – the obsession to kill – is in a significant sense external to his 'self' and it made him act in spite of his *own* deliberations.

The problem with diminished responsibility

When a person's capacity to act as a responsible agent is restricted by a psycho-logical force within the person, it can be problematic to decide if this is truly a restriction by external force, and if not, what weight to give it in considering the blameworthiness of the person concerned.

The plea of diminished responsibility in murder trials, for example, has frequently aroused suspicion regarding the legitimacy of such a plea. If the accused has carried out the killing, knew what he was doing, and there was no one else who forced him to do it, why should he be let off? There are at least three 'loss of self-control' types of excuse which could be put forward but which would not justify any denial of responsiblity. These relate to the strength, normality or abnormality, and verbal repudiation of the underlying impulse or desire.

Take first the strength of an impulse, and how it might be construed as an excusing factor. Irresistible impulse is in fact a formal defence in law. On the surface, if someone feels an urge to do something and it is so strong that he cannot resist it, it may appear that it would not be fair to hold him responsible for it. But on closer examination we can see that strength is quite irrelevant as a factor. There are all kinds of things about which we feel so strongly that we cannot easily, if at all, alter our psychological states in relation to them. A man, for example, might feel so strongly about wanting to win a tennis tournament that even when feeling exhausted he presses himself to train further; even when his friends ask him to go on a relaxing holiday with them he still insists on more training. This urge or determination to win drives him on and as a result he wins the tournament. It could be said that he won because he had this irresistible desire to win, but it would be absurd to deduce from this that he cannot be regarded as being responsible for his victory. It might be true that in some cases an individual who actually wants to be free from the desire to win tournaments finds that he cannot give it up. But the key lies in whether or not he, as expressed through his highest order desire, wants to get rid of that lower order desire. If he does and finds that he cannot, it is not the strength of the urge to win in itself but the repudiation of that urge which renders it alien and thus relevant to the negation of responsibility. If he identifies with the urge to win then it is part of him, and its strength is not something independent of him but reflects *his* determination. The same distinction applies to criminal offences.

Just as the strength of an impulse is not in itself relevant to whether or not it would negate responsibility, the apparent abnormality of a desire has nothing to do with the issue of responsibility. It is perhaps tempting at times, when faced, for example, with a horrifying murder case motivated seemingly by a perverted desire to seek gratification through the killing of another human being, to put the case in question into a box marked 'abnormal' and assure oneself that it is not something one should worry too much about. But abnormality in this context can only be consistently picked out by either a moral or a statistical approach. If we try the moral route, we would have to label 'abnormal' anything we consider to be immoral. But this would mean that any immoral desire would be by definition an abnormal one. If one then wants to go on to say that one cannot control and thus be held responsible for what is abnormal in one, then we end up with the claim that we are all responsible for our moral acts but never responsible for our immoral ones. The alternative is to use a statistical approach to pick out what is abnormal. But on this basis, a heroic nurse who risks her life to look after a dying child would be abnormal since most people would not be prepared to do such a thing, Once again if abnormality so defined is used to negate responsibility, then the heroic nurse would not be responsible for her admirable deed.

However strong or, in whatever sense, abnormal an impulse or desire may appear to us when it is cited as the underlying cause of a criminal offence, it is only when it can be shown to be something which is genuinely alien to the individual concerned, external to the person's self, that it is a relevant factor for negating responsibility. What is not an integral part of someone's self, especially if that individual has difficulties in sustaining a coherent self, cannot be a basis for how we perceive, blame, or for that matter, praise, that individual. It is of course not always easy to decide if what is claimed to be an alien impulse is really an alien impulse. Mere verbal repudiation of an impulse as alien is certainly not sufficient grounds for negating responsibility. In practice, what must be established is the individual's attitude towards the impulse in question, and what he or she does in the hope of pushing it aside.

It is not difficult to imagine a case in which the son of a rich man has developed an obsessive interest in his father's immense wealth, all of which would pass to him when his father dies. He begins to think about how his father might come to die. He finds himself weighing up the pros and cons of different methods of bringing about his death. Eventually he shoots his father and buries the body on some remote island. He then claims that he has been driven on by this obsessive desire to obtain the inheritance for which he could no longer wait. He says that he disowns that desire and feels deep remorse about his inability to prevent that desire from taking over his life, leading to his father's death. Have we a case of 'external-to-self' restriction which renders him not responsible for his father's death (but calling for psychiatric help), or have we a case of greed masquerading as 'alien desire' (calling for a 'guilty of murder' verdict)? Neither possibility can be dismissed on a priori grounds. The son's attitude towards the allegedly alien desire and what he did about it would be crucial issues to investigate.[5]

Dealing with mental disorder

Whilst it will always be difficult to weigh up the evidence for and against claims of alien desires restricting one's capacity to act, it is important to identify the basic issues so that the plea of diminished responsibility does not become an escape route for those who seek to confuse the judge and jury about the real reasons for their behaviour.

There is no simple correlation between mental disorder and criminal problems. Many people who suffer from mental illness are more likely to be victims of crime rather than perpetrators. But for those who because of their mental disorder could act as causal agents of criminal offences, a number of points are relevant to the way in which they should be treated.

Those who lack a coherent self, or have a relatively coherent self but are none the less plagued by alien impulses and desires, need sympathetic treatment to restore the wholeness of their self. Abuse of the diminished responsibility plea may stir up cynicism about the relevance of mental conditions of those involved in criminal offences. But once the irrelevant features have been identified and removed, it is important to recognize that blame and punishment have no meaning, let alone any effect, for those who are themselves without a stable and coherent self.

Mental disorder can also lead to involuntary body movements or loss of consciousness of what one is doing. In both cases, the relevant kind of capacity restriction would apply (restriction by an external force in the former and restriction by ignorance in the latter) and no criminal responsibility can be legitimately ascribed. The only appropriate action would be to treat the mental disorder concerned and prevent it from causing problems in the future.

A different approach, however, would be required for those who have a dangerous abnormality with which they identify. It would be quite wrong to assume that because they have desires which others find grotesque and repugnant, they must be deeply disturbed by their feelings, and that they should simply be helped with their problems. From their perspective, those desires are an integral part of their being, and anyone trying to remove those desires is in effect trying to destroy their identity. Such people are relatively rare, but when they are encountered it is important to distinguish them from others with mental disorder so that they are not treated in the same way, or allowed to distort our overall perception of mental patients. It is right to see them as what they are: dangerous to and callous about other human beings. And unless it is possible to ensure that they are no longer dangerous, they will have to be kept away from the rest of society. It may be argued that they are not mentally ill, just different from others. In response, it can be pointed out that it is not their difference, but the danger they pose, which makes it necessary to keep them away.

Options Restriction

In cases both of restriction by ignorance and by external force, it can be said that the individual's thinking, attitudes, desires, feelings, etc. are prevented (by ignorance or some external force) from having any intentional bearing on the undesirable outcome concerned. That in essence is why an accused cannot in those cases be held responsible for any criminal offence.

However, 'cognitive' and 'external-to-self' are not the only types of capacity restriction which can be invoked by the phrase 'could not have avoided'. One's capacity to act in the way one would normally like to act can be restricted by being confronted with a narrow range of undesirable options. For example, consider the following pairs of options:

1 Either kill the blackmailer or let him go on blackmailing you.
2 Either drive a truckload of explosives into a crowd or accept the fact that the terrorists who have demanded this would harm your family.
3 Either kill the person who has murdered your friend or leave your friend's death unavenged.

In each of the three aforementioned pairs, the alternative to taking someone's life is something everyone would prefer to avoid having to face. But if circumstances were such that one could not avoid those alternatives – unless one kills would one be responsible for killing? On the basis that neither of the other two types of capacity restriction applies, the answer would have to be yes.

We may feel varying degrees of sympathy for someone who kills because he finds himself in one of the above situations. But the killer would still be accountable in such cases. He weighed the alternative courses of action and after considering them in the light of his *own* thoughts, feelings, desires, etc., he knowingly chose one rather than another. We must not confuse our readiness to reduce our censure of him with the supposition that he is not responsible. How much or how little we blame or condemn him depends on our moral evaluation of his character and judgement as manifested by his choice of action, and this evaluation only makes sense on the assumption that he is responsible. By contrast, when either cognitive or external-to-self restriction applies, the morally undesirable outcome is not a manifestation of the person's character and judgement, and the question of blame simple does not arise.

The fact that options restriction cannot be treated on a par with the other types of capacity restriction can be further demonstrated by comparing the three pairs of options outlined above with the following three pairs of options:

1 Either kill the businessman as asked or turn away the murder contract which would pay you a vast amount of money.
2 Either kill the husband of the woman you are passionately in love with or accept that she would never otherwise leave him.
3 Either kill Jones or wait for probably many more years before he dies and vacates the top job you covet.

Some may find it almost as difficult to avoid the killing option in our second set of examples, but most of us would not hesitate in condemning those who choose to kill in such circumstances. What is at issue in any case is not what moral judgement we ought to pass in such cases, but that the question of moral judgement cannot be bypassed on the ground that the options were 'difficult'.

It is important to make it clear that options restriction is not the kind of capacity restriction that can negate responsibility. Phrases such as 'could not have avoided', when used to invoke options restrictions, should not therefore be accepted as indicative of the absence of responsibility. Failure to understand this point has led to 'incompatibilist' arguments which claim that because we cannot choose what options we have in life – even our own character formation has been causally determined before we had a character of our own to influence – we could not be held responsible for anything. Transposed to social thinking this line of argument leads to the view that no one is ever blameworthy or deserving of punishment.[6] Leaving it unchallenged has allowed it to breed irresponsibility in society. Of course just because an idea has bad social consequences, it does not follow that it is necessarily wrong. On the other hand, once it has been exposed as resting on an equivocal interpretation of the connection between what phrases like 'could not have avoided' seem to invoke, and what really negates responsibility, those same social consequences make it a matter of urgency to reject it.

Circumstantial pressures to commit crime

Although options restrictions cannot be accepted as a basis for the negation of responsibility, they could be relevant where the restrictions concerned generate such circumstantial pressures that anyone sitting in judgement ought to make special allowances for those who have committed an offence in those circumstances. It is none the less important to maintain a clear distinction between those excusing conditions which negate responsibility – which mean that the person accused of having committed a criminal offence is not in fact responsible for the alleged offence and thus has no case to answer for – and those which merely serve as mitigations, where the person accused of having committed a criminal offence is found to be responsible for that offence but who has reasons which may help when it comes to answering for the crime.[7]

Take duress, for example. Certain cases of duress could lead one to think that the offender in question ought to be cleared of all blame. If someone had been told that if he did not help terrorists place a bomb in a building, then his captive family would all be executed, we would be inclined to forgive him, and reserve our blame solely for the real perpetrators of the crime. But this inclination is not justifiable by the sole fact that the offence was committed under duress. The person could have been told that if he did not help the terrorists, bricks would be thrown through his front window. To act out of fear of threatening behaviour is acting out of duress, but fear is not always excusable. And the more serious an offence, the more distressing the fear concerned has to be if its presence is to have any mitigating effects.

Similar observations can be made about other kinds of options restriction such as deprivations. To be deprived of parental love, a stable family life, and minimal financial security, can cut back one's options in life quite significantly. One can sympathize in broad terms with those who have their options narrowed down by circumstances beyond their control, but the exact relevance of this to how any given individual is to be judged in relation to a specific incident depends on the details of the case itself. Unless deprivation prevents a particular individual from developing a coherent self, it offers no grounds for negating responsibility. The balance between what an individual has been deprived of and what he or she has subsequently done may on occasions tip the scales in favour of leniency. But the balance can equally go in the other direction, as when, for example, someone tries to excuse his brutal assault on his neighbours simply on the grounds that they have a happy family and he did not when he was young.

In general it would be as wrong to claim that socio-economic conditions can absolve people from blame for their crimes, as it would be to to claim that they have no bearing on people's propensity to break the law. There are people who would stick to their moral principles whatever pressures they are put under. Some would refuse to commit any crime even if their refusal would cause them to be harmed. But for the majority, the stronger the pressures, the more likely (and the more understandable) it is that they would give in.

It makes good sense, then, for public policies on crime reduction to incorporate action plans to minimize putting people under excessive economic pressures which may prevent them from looking after themselves and their families, or social pressures which diminish their personal dignity. These policies could go hand-in-hand with moves to increase the deterrent effect of crime detection, arrests and imprisonment, so as to cut down the temptation to go against the law. But unless people's options in life are not so restricted as to leave only unpalatable alternatives to crime, we cannot expect them to behave as responsible citizens.

Conclusions

The criminal law exists to deal with certain categories of human behaviour which are deemed undesirable. In order to minimize such behaviour, it is necessary to understand why it takes place, and how it can be avoided. Sometimes this behaviour can occur although the person concerned cannot be held responsible for it. In such cases, rather than trying to change the law so that certain people are penalized even if they were not responsible for any wrongdoing, it would be better to identify other appropriate means to deal with the problem.

In this chapter, I have considered three types of capacity restriction and have argued that since restriction through ignorance prevents a person from knowing the wrongness of his behaviour, and restriction by external force prevents a person from behaving in accordance with his *own* desires as opposed to *alien* impulses and desires, both these types of capacity restriction would negate responsibility. However, it emerged that options restriction, whilst it might serve as a mitigating factor in some cases, would not negate responsibility.

The distinction between different types of capacity restriction then helped clarify different excusing conditions. I have argued that there is no such thing as culpable or non-culpable ignorance in itself. What needs to be established when ignorance is put forward as an excuse is whether or not the person concerned knew that ignorance in those circumstances was likely to cause harm to others.

Loss of self-control as an excuse was found to be valid only if the cause of the loss of control was some form of external-to-self restriction. But if the cause was some non-alien impulse or desire of the person concerned, then however strong, abnormal, or verbally repudiated it might appear, it would not be relevant.

Circumstantial pressures which arise when people's options in life are restricted were found to have no bearing on the issue of absolving responsibility, but their relevance to decisions on leniency was identified and explained.

What then is to be concluded from all this about the problem of crime reduction? I have argued that education and information have a vital role in dispelling ignorance which might otherwise cause harm. Furthermore, I have argued that different approaches are needed when dealing with different types of mental disorder and that practical measures of social improvement have a key role to play in tackling certain crimes which are primarily connected with socio-economic pressures and temptations. The institution of punishment remains, however, to deal with those who have no real excuses for their criminal behaviour, and to ensure as far as possible that they will not again defy the standards of their society as codified in the criminal law.[8]

NOTES

1 Others may see retribution as a fourth distinct element of punishment. Judge Stephen gave one of the most forceful judicial statements of the retributive conception of punishment when he said, 'I think it highly desirable that criminals should be hated, that the punishments inflicted upon them should be so contrived as to give expression to that hatred, and to justify it in so far as the provision of means for expressing and gratifying a healthy and natural sentiment can justify and encourage it' (quoted in Smith and Hogan, *Criminal Law*, p. 6).

2 In order to focus on the issue of responsibility, I have not raised the issue of personal identity in this chapter. It should be noted, however, that whilst an individual may have

been responsible for a crime at a certain time, changes which that individual later undergoes may make it problematic in determining if the individual emerging after the changes can be regarded as morally the same as the one who was responsible for the crime. A useful collection of articles on the problem of personal identity can be found in A. M. Rorty (ed.), *The Identities of Persons.*

3 In order to deter people from wilful neglect of the law, it is sometimes said that ignorance of the law is no excuse. But such a claim cannot be tenable unless it is backed by an effective policy which ensures that the law is known and understood. Such a policy may include the requirement that in specific areas, those concerned must find out what the law says before taking any action. What would be quite unacceptable would be to criminalize certain types of activities, and prosecute offenders without giving them a fair opportunity to discover the changes to the law.

4 Readers unfamiliar with concepts such as 'unity of the self' and 'self-control' can make a start with T. Mischel (ed.), *The Self.*

5 Allowing external-to-self force as a defence may create an opportunity to deceive the jury as to the real motive for a crime. Psychiatrists do not possess any standard method to identify alien desires. However, just as the fact that self-defence can be falsely invoked does not invalidate it as a legitimate defence in law, the fact that alien desires can be falsely ascribed does not mean that they should not be cited as factors which negate responsibility in particular cases.

6 For example, the American lawyer, Clarence Darrow (1857–1938), was renowned for carrying into the courtroom his belief that no one is ever responsible for any wrongdoing. Using incompatibilist arguments and emotive appeals he succeeded in securing the acquittal of many who had been charged with serious crimes.

7 Failure to understand the difference between conditions which negate responsibility and conditions which may serve as mitigation, can lead to misconceived refusal to consider the social causes of crime. The truth of the matter is that the social causes of crime do not excuse crime in the sense of negating the responsibility of those involved, but they must be taken into account in any coherent attempt to prevent as well as to punish crime.

8 I have not raised in this chapter the question of the legitimacy of the criminal law. Of course it is possible that the criminal law of a country may contain elements which are morally unacceptable. How to challenge such elements without undermining the collective basis of law-making would be an important question to consider. See A. M. Bickel, *The Morality of Consent*, and D. Lloyd, *The Idea of Law.*

READING GUIDE

This chapter has focused on the issue of when people apparently involved in criminal activities should or should not be held responsible for the crime in question. A useful starting-point for anyone interested in the underlying moral problems in ascribing responsibility for wrongful behaviour would be J. Feinberg, *Doing and Deserving*; J. Glover, *Responsibility*; and A. Kenny, *Freewill and Responsibility.* All three discuss the key issues within a clear theoretical framework.

Readers who are already familiar with the general arguments would benefit from careful reading of P. Strawson's 'Freedom and resentment' in his *Freedom and Resentment and Other Essays*; H. B. Tam, *A Philosophical Study of the Criteria for Responsibility Ascriptions*, which develops Strawson's ideas into a comprehensive theory of responsibility; M. Klein, *Determinism, Blameworthiness and Deprivation*; and J. Oakley, *Morality and the Emotions*, which analyses the notion of responsibility in the context of his theory of emotions.

Instructive discussions of particular criminal cases can be found in H. L. A. Hart, *Punishment and Responsibility*; and R. A. Duff, *Intention, Agency and Criminal Liability*.

Finally, anyone who is interested in making an in-depth study of the concept of responsibility must tackle the notion of 'the autonomous self'. Interesting observations on this topic can be found in H. Frankfurt, 'Freedom of the will and the concept of person', in G. Watson (ed.), *Free Will*; and R. D. Laing, *The Divided Self*.

CLASSICAL SOURCES

Aristotle: *Politics*
Hegel: *Philosophy of Right*
Bentham: *Of Laws General; Principles of Morals and Legislation*

12

Is Psychopathy a Moral Concept?

Michael Bavidge and Andrew J. Cole

During the nineteenth century psychiatrists began to describe individuals who, although they exhibited grossly abnormal behaviour, did not show other signs of mental illness. For instance, Pinel applied the term *manie sans delire* to individuals who were explosively violent but had no delusional beliefs. The English physician Prichard extended this concept to persons displaying other antisocial behaviours and employed the term 'moral insanity'. Later Maudsley used this category to describe an individual who had 'no capacity for true moral feeling'; 'all his impulses and desires, to which he yields without check, are egoistic, his conduct appears to be governed by immoral motives, which are cherished and obeyed without any evident desire to resist them'.[1]

Even during these early stages the terminology applied to what is now called 'personality disorder' was unstable. Change in the classification of these disorders has continued to be more rapid than in other aspects of psychiatry. The reasons for this constant flux appear to be both medical and philosophical.

First, the range of personality to be encompassed by any classification has never been clear. The early concept of 'moral insanity' applied only to persons who were violent or otherwise criminal. Kraeplin, the great classifier of psychiatric disorders, coined the term 'psychopathic personality' and included categories for eccentrics, liars, and the quarrelsome who might nevertheless remain within the law. Schneider extended the boundary still further to encompass people whose abnormal personality distressed only themselves: the depressive and insecure.[2] Henderson stretched the concept yet again, using the term 'creative psychopath' for individuals who contributed to society by virtue of unusual qualities.[3] These different applications of the concept have left a paradox in modern practice. Contemporary psychiatry follows Schneider in recognizing 'personality disorder' even where only subjective distress is involved. On the other hand, the Mental Health Acts of 1959 and 1983 are closer to Prichard in describing 'psychopathic disorder' in terms of 'abnormally aggressive or seriously irresponsible behaviour'.

Another force for change has been the multitude of classifications put forward. Even modern diagnostic systems, which use standardized interviews and operational definitions to improve their reliability, remain confounded by the infinite potential for variation in personality. The American *Diagnostic and Statistical Manual*, 3rd edition, for instance includes a category 'Atypical, mixed or other personality disorder' for the numerous individuals who do not fit one of the specific diagnostic categories.[4] The number of competing, incompatible and incomplete classificatory systems suggests the conclusion drawn by Schneider: 'Human beings resist precise measurement and, unlike the phenomena of disease, abnormal individuals cannot be classified neatly in the manner of clinical diagnosis.'

Finally unease about the moral status of personality diagnoses has also spurred change. Maudsley noted that moral insanity 'has so much the look of vice or crime that many people regard it as an unfounded medical invention'. This may have spurred the introduction of terminology, such as 'psychopathy', which appears to be purely medical. These changes failed to provide a morally neutral classification of personality disorders. It has proved impossible to introduce neutral terminology that preserves its clinical purity. Instead there has been a recurring need to replace terminology that has become stigmatizing. 'Psychopathy' with its pejorative and legal connotations has been replaced in psychiatric practice by the term 'personality disorder'. Violent and irresponsible dispositions have been variously described as psychopathic, sociopathic, asocial, antisocial and dyssocial, in an apparently vain effort to find morally neutral terminology.[5]

Disquiet with what appears to be a confusion of the clinical with the moral is expressed by Blackburn in 'On moral judgements and personality disorders'.[6] He believes there are ambiguities built into the concept of psychopathy. The ambiguity arises because its defining characteristics have sometimes been taken to be personality disorders, sometimes antisocial behaviour and sometimes hybrids of the two.

The taxonomic confusion at the heart of the concept emerges in two ways. First, the concept makes a conceptual connection between personality disorders and antisocial behaviour whereas the relationship, if any, can only be established by empirical investigation. Building antisocial behaviour into the definition of a personality disorder renders the concept vacuous: it becomes nothing more than a re-description of undesirable behaviour. A respectable clinical notion should begin from an identification of personality disorder which is independent of antisocial behaviour and move to social deviance, relating them as cause and effect.

Second, Blackburn maintains, the concept fuses moral judgement and clinical diagnosis. The melding of moral and clinical attitudes is incompatible with both scientific neutrality and the non-judgemental stance of the clinician. On both grounds, he argues, the concept of psychopathy is unsuitable for any scientific or clinical purposes. It fails to select a homogenous group of people. It does not provide an appropriate target for theoretical or research purposes and it provides no useful guidance to the clinician.

So after 150 years of effort the problem remains. There are periodic calls for the abandonment of the concept of psychopathy, of antisocial personality disorder, or even of personality disorders as a whole. But they keep recurring in some guise or other. The persistence of the concept despite widespread discomfort encourages us to re-examine the taxonomic issues and the pressures on the clinician.

The conceptual link between personality disorder and antisocial behaviour is alleged to be a particular instance of the error of constructing conceptual connections where causal chains are required. Molière's doctor is ridiculed for explaining how opium sends people to sleep by citing its soporific power. He links Y (sending people to sleep) to X (its soporific power) in such a way that X cannot be identified separately from Y and then he goes on to provide a causal explanation of Y in terms of X. If X is just another way of saying Y it cannot also be cited as its cause. The complaint is that the concept of psychopathy first encourages us to define antisocial personality disorder in terms of aberrant behaviour and then goes on to cite the disorder as a cause of the behaviour. Spice is added to the complaint by the thought that it is this causal link which justifies exempting offenders from legal penalties for their crimes. The causal claim is not only spurious, it undermines agency and responsibility.

This criticism is misguided for two reasons. First, explanations of behaviour take many forms, only some of which refer to causes, e.g. 'She did it inadvertently' and 'He gave him the present out of gratitude not self-interest.' These are explanations of behaviour. We understand something important about an action when we know it was done inadvertently or for this rather than that reason. But in neither case are causes cited. No one is saying that it was the inadvertence or gratitude that did it. Likewise, the diagnosis of antisocial personality disorder explains behaviour but personality disorders are not causes. This state of affairs should not be scandalous. Non-causal explanations have played an important role in the development of medicine. Syndromes have often been proposed as explanations for symptoms long before the causes of the condition were discovered. Consumption, for example, was an explanation of progressive wasting and death long before the discovery of the tubercle bacillus.

Second, responsibility is withheld on a variety of grounds which are rarely, if ever, causes of the objectionable behaviour. Saying that someone who is only 3 years old, or someone who is 'barking mad', or someone who is a diplomat ought not to be held responsible for his or her behaviour is not equivalent to saying that it was the extreme youth, the insanity, or the diplomatic status that did it. Similarly the claim that a person suffering from a personality disorder should not be held responsible for his crimes is not equivalent to saying that the personality disorder caused his crime. It may or may not be reasonable to attribute responsibility to someone suffering from a personality disorder but in any case personality disorders are not causes. The issue is whether personality disorder is a good ground for withholding responsibility. What causes can be identified in aberrant behaviour is another question.

So the taxonomic objections to the concept of psychopathy would strike home only if personality disorders were conceived as causes and if reasons for withholding responsibility for objectionable behaviour always cited causes of that behaviour. However, presenting theoretical arguments of this sort does not explain why clinicians retain the notion of personality disorder despite the day-to-day difficulties and pressures that it generates.

Professional Relationships

In England, the forensic psychiatrist works with the legal definition of psychopathic disorder formulated in the Mental Health Act 1983 which stipulates 'abnormally aggressive or seriously irresponsible behaviour'.[7] However, general psychiatry is more often concerned with personality-disordered individuals who are 'a threat to society' in a domestic or day-to-day sense rather than in a legal sense. If the core feature of personality disorder is an abnormality in relating to others it is to be expected that this will manifest itself in everyday interactions. The 'abnormally aggressive or seriously irresponsible behaviour' of psychopathic disorder represents only the tip of an iceberg of distorted relationships and manipulative interactions. The grotesque behaviour which shocks society is the climax of many minor antisocial acts and attitudes. Although these 'atoms' of antisocial behaviour are not the focus of forensic attention, they are familiar to general psychiatrists. Diagnostic criteria for personality disorders include phrases such as:

• tendency to be easily slighted and quick to take offence;
• inadequate rapport in face-to-face interactions . . . e.g. cold, aloof;
• disregard for the truth;
• inappropriate, intense anger;
• insistence that others submit to his or her way of doing things.[8]

Some of the difficulties that may confront professionals in this field are illustrated in the following example.

A man in his mid-forties was brought to the Casualty Department of a hospital because he had been knocking on doors asking for money and directions. He had become aggressive when crossed. The police thought his behaviour odd. He reported to the psychiatrist that he was feeling terribly distressed because of relationship problems. He declared that if he wasn't admitted to hospital he could not be held responsible for his actions and might end up assaulting a complete stranger or throwing himself in front of a car. The man's records showed that this had been a pattern of behaviour since he separated from his wife several months previously, because of violence and alcohol abuse. He had been admitted to psychiatric hospital on several occasions in similar circumstances. He had in the past immediately settled on the ward, socializing cheerfully with other patients. It was decided after discussion with the Senior Psychiatrist that he should not be readmitted to hospital as this would reinforce his inappropriate behaviour and delay the development of more appropriate coping strategies which would require him to take responsibility for his situation. He was offered a consultation the next day. This he angrily rejected stating that nothing was ever done to help him and reiterating that the psychiatrist would be responsible if anyone were to get hurt. As he stormed off, the police made it clear that they believed he should have been 'put away'. Later that night he walked into a psychiatric hospital in another part of town and started to take an overdose in front of the staff.

Cases such as this impose great strains on mental health workers, apart altogether from the threat of physical harm. There is a constant assault on their integrity as persons, as professionals and as members of a therapeutic team. The reasons for this are complex.

At the personal level the professional is faced with someone who invests them with characteristics, thoughts and intentions virtually regardless of the actual circumstances. There may be inappropriate demands and intense, disproportionate anger or hurt when these are denied. Facing such powerful emotions and maintaining a professional stance in these circumstances is extremely demanding. The therapist experiences a natural inclination to react in an everyday manner to these emotions. Anger evokes either submission or aggression, and tears either sympathy or rejection. Containing these immediate responses whilst attempting to be constructive can be exhausting. Support and supervision for the therapist is essential to avoid emotional collapse or 'burnout'. Therapists themselves need opportunities to express emotions evoked by their clients, to be reassured that their behaviour is appropriate and to discuss treatment plans.

Support from colleagues is essential but it does not remove the underlying problem. The intense and difficult interactions with manipulative patients can prove troublesome for teams of professionals. One member of a team may be idealized by the patient whilst others are denigrated. The result may be strong differences of opinion among the team with consequent inconsistencies in approach. Colleagues can find themselves blaming each other for lack of progress whilst the patient's role goes unnoticed.

The behaviour of personality-disordered individuals can sometimes be understood in terms of psychological mechanisms such as transference where the therapist comes to 'stand for' a significant person in the patient's past.[9] However this understanding is more helpful clinically than personally. It may guide treatment but it doesn't diminish the emotional strains inherent in it. This is especially true where the transference feelings are acted out in attacks on the therapist outside the clinical setting. Patients act out their inappropriate and aggressive feelings in a variety of ways that may well include making formal complaints, contacting therapists at home, vandalizing their cars and threatening assault. Although clinicians may understand why patients act in these ways it does not prevent them from being hurt. It may be very difficult for them to be reconciled with patients so that trust is re-established sufficiently for treatment to continue.

Distortions in relationships can subvert professional activity and result in maintaining the dysfunctional status quo. Most doctors are familiar with the patient who asks for a glass of water immediately he is seen, diverting the consultation into meeting need for comfort and delaying a consideration of the problem in hand. Apparently trivial incidents of this sort can herald more serious behaviours such as avoiding any active role in treatment or exaggerating symptoms in order to gain extra help. At an extreme level the patient may threaten to attempt suicide if demands for tablets or appointments are not met. A therapist faced with such clients may strongly wish to give in to their requests. This is a normal response to seeing human distress and it may also seem a prudent way of lessening the risk of suicide. However abdicating control in these circumstances may merely encourage such behaviour, preventing progress and increasing the long-term risks. It is no doubt for this reason that the training of psychotherapists usually includes a recommendation that they set firm limits to the timing, duration and focus of sessions.[10] Sticking to the limits can be very stressful for clinicians who must control their natural responses and live with the risks involved.

Clinicians are required, then, to be professional in their treatment of those who exhibit antisocial personality disorder but they cannot be expected to like them, nor to adopt neutral attitudes to their disruptive, let alone their violent and aggressive behaviour. A study of psychiatrists' attitudes towards personality disorder by G. Lewis and L. Appleby found these patients were regarded as more difficult, less deserving, manipulative, attention-seeking, annoying and in control of their suicidal urges.[11] The authors reached a similar conclusion to Blackburn: the term personality disorder is a pejorative judgement rather than a diagnosis and should be abandoned.

Moral Responses to Personality Disorders

Although it must be acknowledged that psychiatrists may react negatively, both morally and emotionally, to patients with severe personality disorders this is not, of course, a justification for unfair treatment. For example, the all too common assertion that a patient has a personality disorder and therefore does not deserve help is not prognostication but prejudice. Or again, the diagnosis of personality disorder may be made *post hoc* to explain treatment failure and as an excuse for abandonment.[12] This is clinically as well as morally unacceptable. Responses to personality disorders are different from responses to psychiatric illness. We need to understand why this divergence occurs.

Many potentially stigmatizing psychiatric diagnoses at least offer the patient compensatory status as 'ill'. In consequence patients are absolved of much responsibility for their symptoms and relieved of their social and even legal duties. The diagnosis of personality disorder carries little, if any, of this compensation. Ascribing deviant behaviour to an illness which afflicts an individual suggests the patient is a passive victim who would normally act otherwise. This implication does not hold in the case of personality disorder where the deviant behaviour is normal for the patient. In the case of illness there is the hope that acceptable behaviour will return spontaneously after clinical interventions. In the case of personality disorder this is not a realistic expectation, and as a result it is difficult to see personality disorder as an excusing factor analogous to illness.

On the other hand, the ascription of responsibility seems incompatible with the notion of personality disorder as a condition from which the patient suffers and over which he or she has little or no control. The causation of personality disorder has much in common with mental illness. Genetics, neurological damage and childhood experience seem important in both. Lack of discrete onset, a before and after, perhaps obscures the fact that a patient with personality disorder no more asked to be afflicted than did one with a mental illness.

Personality disorders vary widely in both form and severity. They do not all evoke the same level of moral concern. Most of the examples described above refer to individuals with dramatic, explosive or manipulative traits. There are, however, other lifelong and disabling characteristics which involve eccentricity or extreme anxiety. The eccentric group includes people with intense rather obscure interests who do not make relationships and tend to avoid social contacts. Although they remain difficult to relate to and descriptions of their behaviour seem inevitably moral ('easily slighted, cold, aloof') it is possible to see them as suffering from a handicap affecting social interaction. If their behaviour is attributed to a discrete disability this is to treat them as if they were sick. Those who are suffering from extreme anxiety are so clearly 'suffering' and are handicapped in so many functions of everyday life that the role of patient is readily applied to them. So, in cases of eccentricity and anxiety, patient status provides a reason for restraining moral reactions. Of course, the fact that the characteristic behaviour is more solitary and less dangerous and disruptive allows a greater scope for indulgence and indifference.

The ambivalence of our attitudes to personality disorders, in the eyes of some critics like Blackburn, amounts to an intolerable muddle. The persistence of moral terms in the description of the psychopathic personality is seen as a relic of outmoded retributive ways of thinking to which the public may be prone, but to which the health professional ought to be immune. However, it is only possible to deny the fundamental moral dimension of personality disorders by restricting ourselves to a trivial and corrupt notion of moral values. The clinician cannot be a Mrs Grundy let alone a Judge Jefferies. But that says very little. Moral attitudes are not to be identified with moralizing, censoriousness or vindictiveness. Advocating neutrality in the name of professionalism fails to appreciate how deep moral responses go in us, and how fundamentally they structure our personal as well as our social lives.

The fact that people who are disruptive suffer from a personality disorder does not, of course, render their actions less harmful. Nor does it mean that health professionals must cultivate an attitude of indifference towards harmful behaviour. There is, nevertheless, a widespread belief that adverse judgement and reaction ought to be restricted to the consequences of aberrant behaviour but should stop short of the person who engages in it.

This distinction – the sin but not the sinner – is hard to maintain because the problem is seen to lie in the personality of the offenders and in the nature of personal relationships they are capable of maintaining. Concentrating on the person rather than on the consequences of his or her actions is not likely in these cases to have a moderating effect on negative responses. Adopting a professional attitude may mean controlling the feelings that such behaviour evokes, but it does not prevent those responses from occurring, nor does it mean that they are inappropriate.

Finally the determination to adopt a clinical approach does not in itself provide an easily accessible way to handle seriously disruptive behaviour which is an alternative to the layman's. It does little more than suggest that the clinician's relationship to disordered personalities should be modelled on that of the doctor to the patient. It gives no guidelines on how this ideal is to be realized in the face of grotesquely antisocial behaviour.

In these ways, the moral elements in the available attitudes to disordered personalities emerge. No doubt there are aspects of morality, and even more obviously of law, such as desert, responsibility and punishment, which sit uncomfortably with clinical intervention and therapeutic relationships. But even in relation to these heavily loaded concepts the realities of psychiatric practice are unclear. For example, the concept of what people deserve – fundamental in law and morality – seems inappropriate in medicine. A clinician is not comfortable making a distinction between cases deserving of treatment and cases which are not. However, there comes a time when the co-operation of the patient becomes a prerequisite for the initiation or continuation of treatment. In general medicine, the treatment of smokers has raised this issue.

In such cases, the distinction between the co-operative and the uncooperative is likely to be run together with the distinction between the deserving and the undeserving.

Similarly, the attribution of responsibility is generally thought to be the concern of courts and not the business of the clinician. Though the view that disease is not a punishment for wrongdoing took a long time to be accepted, there is now a reluctance to think of illness as anything other than a misfortune, even when the contraction of disease can be traced to behaviour or life-style of the patient. On the other hand, accepting responsibility for one's own actions and facing up to their consequences is regarded as having therapeutic value in many contexts. Firm messages have to be sent to prevent the patient from using therapy as an excuse. The treatment of sexual offenders, for example, is often based on the acceptance by the offender of the true nature of their behaviour and their personal responsibility for it.

Even if the need to attribute responsibility within a therapeutic context is accepted, blame and expressions of disapproval may be thought inappropriate. But this seems neither realistic nor desirable. Subtle, social incentives for desired behaviour are continually produced by clinicians. Control of an interview is maintained by a combination of facilitating nods and phrases when the patient is discussing a relevant topic and of inhibiting silence and gaze aversion to limit digression. Straightforward encouragement is a mainstay of treatment when helping someone to modify unwanted behaviour. Although failure to follow advice should not result in the patient being reproached, it is often necessary to allocate blame in the sense of clarifying where responsibility lies. A man receiving treatment for a violent temper, for example, must be made aware that if he assaults someone it is his, not the doctor's, fault.

One practice that seems completely out of place in the clinic is the infliction of punishment. Certainly the adventitious imposition of harm, which many see as the core of punishment, is incompatible with the therapeutic relationship. There are, however, therapeutic regimes where all sorts of incentives and disincentives are used, sometimes in very systematic ways. In behavioural treatment sophisticated systems of rewards and punishments do not only help the medicine to go down; they are 'the medicine' themselves. Even in institutions which aim to be as informal as possible, disciplinary procedures, such as exclusion from the unit – which are perceived as punishments by those who are subject to them, whatever the official rationale – play a role in setting limits to what is acceptable within the therapeutic regime and in preserving the therapeutic milieu itself.

The desire for a morally neutral terminology in relation to personality disorders is part of a tendency, evident since the Enlightenment, to push for a pure notion of morality uncluttered by non-moral considerations. The factors that have contributed to this trend have been complex: a concern for fairness to individuals, the promotion of autonomy as a value, a preoccupation with the individual's responsibility and obligations. One outcome is that morality seems to pivot on the notion of responsibility.[13] These philosophical considerations have coincided with a social drift away from penal towards therapeutic approaches to deviance, a movement that has been represented as an advance from traditional systems of containment and punishment to enlightened regimes of care and cure. So the focusing of morality on concepts of responsibility and the movement away from responsibility in the care of the personality-disordered reinforce each other. The consequence for psychiatry is that it has come to seem inconsistent to maintain moral attitudes once one has adopted a clinical approach to patients and their behaviour.

An alternative view is that any attempt to deal with antisocial personality disorders must operate within a moral perspective. Even when the disorders do not precipitate spectacular crimes, they threaten personal relations in fundamental ways. The behaviour which is typical of them is incompatible with the moral values and principles embedded in domestic, professional and therapeutic relationships. Because people with personality disorder genuinely have dysfunction in their ability to relate to others, their behaviour cannot help but evoke moral responses and cannot be described except in moral language. The case described above involved a man who is aggressive when he does not get his own way, who plays one set of people off against another, who is histrionic and manipulative, not to mention unreasonable, uncooperative and difficult to deal with. Descriptions such as these, which are given by psychiatrists as well as lay people, are not merely relapses into judgemental attitudes but rather a recognition of the characteristic symptoms.

If this view is correct, the attempt to provide a more satisfactory explanation of psychopathy by disentangling the criteria of social deviance from the criteria of personality disorder will not achieve the desired results. The criteria for the latter are as value-laden as those of the former.

There is an ideal of a morally neutral science and of a non-judgemental therapy, but these ideals cannot be sustained naïvely when the realities of clinical practice are taken into account. If we did not have a concept of psychopathy that straddled the clinical and moral worlds we would have to invent one. The reason is that we cannot avoid taking up a point of view on behaviour at which moral and clinical considerations intersect.

What lies behind the notion that there is something wrong with 'hybrid' concepts? Firstly, the impression arises that there are, or there ought to be, domains of discourse which are simple and therefore unproblematic. Secondly, difficulties seem to be generated by the combination of two or more of these straightforward, univocal ways of talking into one problematic, ambiguous way of talking. It is as if there was nothing wrong with saying that Pele was a good man (if true) and nothing wrong with reporting that he scored a goal in a particular match, but everything wrong with saying that he was a soccer player of great power, flair and courage. However another conclusion is possible: there is nothing wrong with mongrels. It is the pure thoroughbred that is the artificial creation and which proves too sensitive for the robust, problem-solving environment of the clinic.

NOTES

1 Maudsley, *Responsibility in Mental Disease.*
2 Schneider, *Psychopathic Personalities.*
3 Henderson, *Psychopathic States.*
4 American Psychiatric Association, 1987, *Diagnostic and Statistical Manual*, 3rd edn, revised. The most important feature of DSMIIIR is that diagnostic criteria are provided to define clearly the disorders listed. This means that assigning a diagnosis is not merely a matter of clinical judgement, but that the clinician, having elicited the various features exhibited by a patient, must then use the criteria as guidelines for making a diagnosis. Whilst this only has statutory force in the United States of America, it has had a worldwide influence in promoting the concept of diagnostic criteria and possibly increasing diagnostic agreement between psychiatrists of different schools and nations.
5 Tyrer and Stein, *Personality Disorder Reviewed.* This collection of papers by leading researchers into personality disorders discusses the nature, definition and history of the concept of personality disorder. It contains reports on the treatment of personality disorders and their outcomes. It provides an authoritative account of current issues, controversies and developments in this area.
6 Blackburn, 'On moral judgements and personality disorders'. The concept of personality disorder, because of the direct connection with deviant social behaviour of which Blackburn complains, is even more open than ideas of mental illness to the sorts of criticism launched by Thomas Szasz and Michel Foucault. It is an explicitly evaluative concept and is used in situations, court-rooms and elsewhere, when decisions concerning control and compulsion are raised.
7 *Mental Health Act 1983*, 1(2). This Act represents amendments to the 1959 Mental Health Act, which were designed to extend the older Act's basic philosophy that psychiatric care should be provided on a voluntary basis and in the community as far as possible. Some of the major changes safeguard and extend the patient's right to appeal against detention and add new conditions if certain treatments were to be given against the patient's consent. The 1959 Act had defined psychopathic disorder rather illogically as being present only when the patient's condition required or was susceptible to medical treatment. The 1983 Act separated the question of diagnosis from the susceptibility to treatment. This means that individuals who may meet the legal definition of psychopathic disorder cannot be detained in hospital for long periods if treatment is going to be of no benefit. Any antisocial behaviour would therefore have to be dealt with through the criminal justice system.
8 American Psychiatric Association, *Diagnostic and Statistical Manual.*
9 Sandler, Dare and Holder, 'Basic psychoanalytic concepts: 111. Transference'.
10 Murphy and Guze, 'Setting limits: the management of the manipulative patient'.
11 Lewis and Appleby, 'Personality disorder: the patients psychiatrists dislike'.
12 Tyrer, Casey and Ferguson, 'Personality disorder in perspective'.

13 Williams, Bernard, *Ethics and the Limits of Philosophy*. Williams criticizes the philosophical search for 'a voluntariness that will be total that will cut through character and psychological and social determination, and allocate blame and responsibility on the ultimately fair basis of the agent's contribution, no more and no less'.

READING GUIDE

A good general book on this area of applied ethics is *Philosophy in Medicine: Conceptual and Ethical Issues in Medicine and Psychiatry*, by C. M. Culver and B. Gert.

M. Foucault's study *Madness and Civilization: a History of Insanity in the Age of Reason* is one of the best-known discussions of the broad topic of insanity in a social context. Thomas Szasz's attack on the medical model of insanity in *The Myth of Mental Illness* was one of the main influences on the anti-psychiatry movement which is at least partly the inspiration for policies of community-care of the mentally ill. See also *Law, Liberty and Psychiatry* by the same author.

For a contrary view, see *The Reality of Mental Illness*, by M. Roth and J. Kroll, and, on the subject of the treatment of offenders diagnosed as suffering from mental illness, see Antony Flew's polemical *Crime or Disease?*

The issue of compulsory treatment is discussed by K. W. M. Fulford in chapter 10 of this volume and the Reading Guide for that chapter is also relevant to the topics discussed here.

13

Life, Death and the Law

Robert Campbell

Introduction

Medical and health-care ethics are amongst the most widely discussed areas of applied ethics and were, indeed, partly responsible for the resurgence of applied ethics in the early 1970s. The range of issues which can fall under this heading is extremely wide and runs from those which are problematic for any profession – confidentiality, trust, responsibility and professional judgement – to those which are specific to the practice of medicine and the peculiarly intimate relationship between patient and physician, doctor or nurse. Some of the latter have been issues for health-care professionals for as long as there has been a health-care profession and are specifically mentioned in the earliest documents we have relating to this, the writings associated with Hippocrates. The Hippocratic Oath covers, amongst other things, the administration of deadly drugs, procuring abortions, patient confidentiality and the avoidance of sexual misconduct with patients.[1] Other issues have arisen only with the development of modern medical science and technology and our consequent ability to make medical interventions which were simply not possible before: organ donation and transfer, new reproductive technologies, genetic engineering and issues to do with our current capability, in some cases, to delay or even halt the dying process and prolong life beyond what was ever in the past thought possible or even, perhaps, desirable. It is this last issue which will be treated in this chapter.

Active and Passive Euthanasia

The Hippocratic Oath states, 'I will neither give a deadly drug to anybody if asked for it, nor will I make a suggestion to this effect.'[2] The *Declaration of*

Geneva of the World Medical Association (1948, amended 1968) is less specific. It says, 'I will maintain the utmost respect for human life from the time of conception.'[3] The problem is how exactly such principles are to be respected in regard to patients who are dying but in whom the dying process has been delayed or arrested by the intervention of medical technology. It is widely believed that these principles imply that a moral distinction can be drawn between active and passive euthanasia, between actually killing someone, which is proscribed, and allowing someone to die, which may not be, in some circumstances. It is hard to say what this distinction is without begging the question from the outset. But if it is accepted that euthanasia means procuring a 'good' death for someone, for the person's own sake, then active euthanasia must mean intervening to make this happen when it would not otherwise have happened, or at least, not happened then. And passive euthanasia must mean *not* intervening to prevent it from happening when you might have been able to prevent it from happening. Many people seem to think, if they think that euthanasia can be justified at all, that it can be more readily justified if it is passive rather than active. Many people also seem to think that, whereas, in most legal jurisdictions, active euthanasia is strictly forbidden, they do, sometimes, allow that passive euthanasia may be permissible. Both doctors and lawyers talk as if they believe that this is so. The following comments, for example, were reported in a widely discussed case in the United Kingdom:

A. A Down's syndrome child is born with an intestinal obstruction. If the obstruction is not removed, the child will die. Here . . . the surgeon might say 'As this child is a mongol . . . I do not propose to operate; I shall allow nature to take its course.' No one could say that the surgeon was committing an act of murder by declining to take a course which would save the child.

B. A severely handicapped child, who is not otherwise going to die, is given a drug in such amounts that the drug itself will cause death. If the doctor acts intentionally then it would be open to the jury to say: yes, he was killing, he was murdering that child.[4]

There is an important difference between allowing a child to die and taking action to kill it.

No paediatrician takes life; but we accept that allowing babies to die – and I know the distinction is narrow, but we all feel it tremendously profoundly – it is in the baby's interests at times.[5]

This is all most misleading, and should not be taken at face value. The law in this area is complicated, but it is perfectly clear that being passively responsible for someone's death is no defence in law *in itself* to a charge of either murder or manslaughter.[6]

English law, in common with many other legal systems, holds that murder and manslaughter, specifically, are crimes which can be committed either by act or omission. Of course, where a death is caused by someone's action, it is usually relatively easy to identify the responsible agent. He or she is the one who performed the action in question. But who is responsible when someone dies as a result of a failure to act? The responsible agent here is anyone who failed to act *when he or she had a legal duty to act*. According to one authority,[7] this duty can arise either through a contract, a special relationship (such as parent and child or doctor and patient) or where a person has voluntarily undertaken the care of another. Either way, it is clear that health-care teams owe a duty of care to their patients and that wanton or reckless neglect of that duty which results in death can result in a criminal prosecution for murder or manslaughter.

Two more recent cases have focused public opinion again on these issues. On 3 March 1993 Tony Bland died of renal failure in Airedale Hospital, Keighley, West Yorkshire. He had suffered crush injuries in the Hillsborough disaster of April 1989 and had been in a coma ever since. The injuries he had sustained had temporarily deprived his brain of oxygen and the resulting damage had left him in what is known as a 'persistent vegetative state'. Patients in PVS exhibit no awareness of or response to the world around them, though they breathe spontaneously, have a regular heartbeat and occasionally display yawning or chewing movements. Destruction of the neocortex (the 'higher' brain) in such patients means the irreversible loss of consciousness even though an intact brainstem may still maintain respiration and other basic systems vital to physiological integrity.

For three and a half years the life of Tony Bland's body was maintained by artificial hydration and nutrition delivered by naso-gastric tube. Antibiotics administered in the same way protected him from infection. Standard nursing care for such patients is intensive and involves turning every two hours to avoid pressure sores, the manual evacuation of faeces and urine, washing, including the cleaning of nose and eyes which they are often unable to close and the moving and massage of limbs. Under such a regime, PVS patients may well survive for anything from 10 to 30 years.

Tony Bland's parents did not wish this for their son and the Airedale Hospital NHS Trust petitioned the High Court for permission to withdraw artificial hydration and nutrition in November 1992. The case went to appeal in December 1992 and, on 4 February 1993, to the House of Lords. On all three occasions the courts found that it was lawful to discontinue feeding in such cases. The House of Lords ruled that artificial hydration and nutrition was medical treatment, and that a doctor was not under a duty to continue to treat a patient in cases where there was substantial medical agreement that such treatment would be of no benefit to the patient, particularly when that treatment was invasive and had not been consented to. On 22 February, the medical team involved ceased antibiotics and feeding and nine days later Tony Bland died.[8]

There were already decided cases in which it had been held permissible to discontinue treatment which was not beneficial and allow patients to die. What distinguishes the case of Tony Bland from these was that he was not, in any accepted sense, dying. It had also never before been judicially determined that providing food and liquid for a patient, however done, was treatment rather than normal care. Critics of the decision were not slow to suggest that the court had implicitly legitimated euthanasia:

> The Rubicon has been crossed. For all their caveats about future cases also needing to seek the judgement of the courts, the Law Lords' decision that Anthony Bland's doctors can stop feeding him is a definitive turning point. Legalized euthanasia now looms larger.[9]

Many of the judges in the case were also uneasy, though not about the defensibility of the decision they had reached. They were concerned that the legal framework within which they were constrained was generating anomalies which were disturbing. Lord Browne-Wilkinson said that his conclusion would appear to some to be irrational:

> How could it be lawful to allow a patient to die slowly, though painlessly, over a period of weeks from lack of food, but unlawful to produce his immediate death by lethal injection, thereby saving his family from yet another ordeal? [It is] . . . difficult to find a moral answer to that question. But it is undoubtedly the law that the doing of a positive act with the intention of ending a life is and remains murder.[10]

The reason for this remark, or at least for the form which it took, was the conviction on 21 September 1992 of Dr Nigel Cox for the attempted murder of Mrs Lillian Boyes, one of his patients. Mrs Boyes suffered from severe rheumatoid arthritis. Because of the progress of her condition, which was by then critical, she was in so much pain that she could not bear to be touched without screaming. It was described by a professor of rheumatology called as a witness in Dr Cox's trial as the worst such case he had ever read about.[11] When the heroin dose fed to Mrs Boyes by drip in order to relieve her pain failed to do so, Dr Cox first tried an additional heroin injection and then, when that also did not work, an injection of undiluted potassium chloride. Almost immediately Mrs Boyes relaxed sufficiently to be able to hold her son's hand and, minutes later, she died.

Potassium chloride has no pain-killing properties but a dose of the kind administered to Mrs Boyes is certain to kill. Dr Cox was charged with attempted murder. This was ostensibly on the ground that it could not be proved that she died from the potassium injection rather than natural causes because her body had been cremated before an autopsy could be ordered. The charge of attempted murder does, however, if proved, allow the trial judge to avoid the life sentence which is mandatory for murder. Dr Cox was given a suspended twelve-month jail sentence.[12]

Lord Browne-Wilkinson's remarks (above) capture very well the difficulty that these two legal decisions pose, when taken together. Why is it permissible to cease to provide a patient in a PVS with that which he needs to stay alive and not permissible to provide a patient with that which she needs to die? The decisions seem all the more remarkable when one adds that the patient in PVS did not consent to the withdrawal of life-preserving care and the other had repeatedly asked her doctor for the injection he finally agreed to give her. The line apparently endorsed by many of the participants in the debate was that the decision in *Bland* was justified because Tony Bland was not to be killed, but allowed to die, whereas Dr Cox, albeit from indisputably the best of motives, killed Lillian Boyes.

Why, then, did the House of Lords, in the case of *Bland*, authorize the non-treatment of the patient when it was known that it would lead to his death? The arguments were:

1　A doctor is under no duty to continue to treat a patient where such treatment confers no benefit on the patient.
2　Being in a persistent vegetative state with no prospect of recovery is regarded by informed medical opinion as not being a benefit to a patient.
3　The principle of the sanctity of life was not absolute, for example
　　(a)　where a patient expressly refuses treatment, even though death may well be a consequence of that refusal;
　　(b)　where a prisoner on hunger strike refuses food and may not be forcibly fed;
　　(c)　where a patient is terminally ill, death is imminent and treatment will only prolong suffering.
4　Artificial hydration and nutrition required medical intervention for its application and was widely regarded by the medical profession as medical treatment.[13]

It is clear, therefore, that the governing principle here was not that it was permissible to let a patient die so long as he or she was not actually *killed*; rather that *caring* for a patient (in cases where cure was not possible and recovery was extremely unlikely) did not require medical interventions which were of no benefit to the patient. None the less, it is also clear that the treatment in question was not a *disbenefit* to Bland; if it did him no good, it also did him no harm. If doctors were under no duty to continue to treat Bland, they were also under no duty not to. But there was a benefit to Bland's relatives and friends, especially his parents, who were to be spared the grief of continuing to see their son in this exceptionally distressing condition and would, finally, be able to mourn the loss they had suffered two years before. That is not a negligible benefit, by any means, and if, whatever happened, nothing more could be done to harm or benefit Bland himself, it seems right to let the choice of outcome be decided by what would most benefit those closest to him.

But what of *Cox*? It is indeed, hard to see how, on the face of it, this case is to be distinguished from that of *Bland*, without invoking the distinction between active and passive euthanasia. The remarks of Butler-Sloss LJ in the Court of Appeal hearing of *Bland* would seem to do just that.

> The position of Dr Nigel Cox, who injected a lethal dose designed to cause death, was different since it was an external and intrusive act and was not in accordance with his duty of care as a doctor. The distinction between Mr Bland's doctors and Dr Cox was between an act or omission which allowed causes already present in the body to operate and the introduction of an external agency of death.[14]

This was dismissed by some at the time as a 'philosophical nonsense'[15] and it probably is. For not only does the law of homicide clearly provide that omissions as well as acts fall under its scope, there is also no moral reason for supposing that one is less culpable for the bad effects of not doing something one ought to have done than for the bad effects of doing something one ought not to have done. One response to this might well be to dismiss *Bland* as an anomaly and to attempt to reassert that to cause death, whether actively or passively, is always wrong (even if, perhaps, more wrong in some cases than in others).

Suicide and Euthanasia

None the less there is still a difficulty here. For though we might wish to maintain that causing death always ought to be a criminal offence, suicide is legal and thought by most to be unfortunate rather than sinful. But if it is not possible to draw a clear line between *Bland* and *Cox*, how is it possible to draw such a sharp and crucial line between an act performed unaided upon oneself and one where a third party offers assistance or performs it for you?

There are two major traditions of views on suicide. One, which is primarily Judaeo-Christian in origin, sees it as a failing rooted in despair which, in effect, denies that 'all shall be well' and rejects God's plan for oneself. More sympathetic versions of this view see the rejection of God as being both the nature of the act and its punishment; it is self-punishing. The second tradition has Graeco-Roman antecedents and sees suicide as redemptive in certain very specific situations. Where loss of honour has placed one outside civil society then the 'loaded revolver in the library' can be a way of recovering that honour; it is the 'only honourable way out'.

Contemporary western society has an ambivalence towards suicide which can be plausibly attributed to its inheritance of both traditions. On the one hand neither suicide nor attempted suicide is normally subject to direct legal sanction. On the other hand, most social institutions will do their level best to prevent anyone from committing suicide[16] and inciting, assisting or conspiring with a suicide is still often a criminal offence. This ambivalence makes for the drawing of some very fine lines and subtle distinctions. Since the early 1970s, the United Kingdom prison service has maintained a policy of not forcibly feeding hunger strikers even where their life is threatened. Some, most notably Bobby Sands, an Irish Republican prisoner who fasted to death in the Maze Prison in Northern Ireland, have died as a consequence. Whether one calls what Bobby Sands did 'suicide' or something else is not the issue. What is important is the acknowledgement that over this area of their life people have autonomy to live or die as they choose and that it is no business of others to disregard this choice and intervene, even where they can. But it is not thought permissible, on the other hand, to assist them in carrying out that choice either directly or by offering advice or even encouragement.[17] To do so is to move from the legally privileged, but tightly circumscribed, area of suicide into that of euthanasia which, despite the existence in most western countries of societies and pressure groups campaigning for voluntary euthanasia, is still illegal in the UK and in most other legal jurisdictions.

It is not clear, in principle, that this is a defensible position. If it is thought to be permissible, though probably regrettable, that some should find their own lives so intolerable a burden that they wish to end them, why should it be impermissible to assist them in doing so? It is not normally the case that it is wrong to assist someone to do something which it would not be wrong for them to do by themselves. It would seem to be especially harsh to prohibit assisting a suicide when the likely consequences are that potential suicides are denied access to the most painless or effective means of encompassing their wishes. The results are likely to be that the attempt is botched or unnecessarily painful and protracted or even, for some – bedridden or paralysed – not possible at all. But if a rational distinction between the morality of suicide and that of euthanasia cannot be drawn, there must be considerable pressure for the legalization of voluntary euthanasia. And, of course, were that to happen, there would be no need to try to defend the distinction between *Bland* and *Cox*.

The Slippery Slope

But it can be argued that a line must be drawn somewhere, and it is better that it be drawn between suicide and euthanasia, rather than seeking to distinguish between euthanasia of different kinds or in different circumstances. The argument seems to be that there can be forces pulling in particular directions which are resistible from some positions but not from others. Once, in other words, it has been decided that it is possible to end a human life in some cases, it becomes difficult, if not impossible, to resist the pressures to end lives in many other kinds of cases. Another image is of the 'slippery slope'. Once the first step down it is taken, a slide begins which will not stop until the very bottom of the slope is reached. What lies at the bottom is often not spelled out, but for twentieth-century Europeans it is probably Germany in the 1930s and 1940s, Cambodia in the 1970s and Bosnia in the 1990s.[18]

This is a rhetorically persuasive device, but not a theoretically cogent argument. The examples implicity hinted at (or even, occasionally explicitly listed) are real and frightening enough, but generalizing from them must be done cautiously. In the case of Nazi Germany, the progression in the 'euthanasia programme' from putting to death of the terminally ill and in pain, the senile demented, the grossly retarded and the severely disabled to the brutal mass-acres of Jews, gypsies, slavs, socialists and homosexuals was extremely rapid. So rapid, in fact, that it is hard not to believe that the end of the slope was the aim all along, the apparently benign beginnings no more than a propaganda exercise and the 'euthanasia programme' a misnomer from the start.[19] And, in the case of Cambodia and Bosnia (to take only two of many possible recent examples of man's inhumanity to man) there was no progression, no 'slippery slope', at all. Their holocausts began at once, from 'Year Zero'. It is also true that there is an ineluctably self-defining nature to the slippery slope. Where does it begin, and which slopes are slippery and which not? Since 1967 abortion has, in certain circumstances, been legal in the U.K. Though it may be the case that the numbers of legal abortions is greater than some would wish,[20] it has still not been the case that it was the first step down a slippery slope to a holocaust of contempt for the value of innocent human life. Was there a slope which turned out not to be slippery? Was there no slope at all? Or was it so gradual that we have yet to realize our progress down it? There is no reason, in principle, to believe that the move from withdrawing treatment in therapeutically hopeless cases to murdering patients in their beds is any likelier or more irresistible than the move from selectively permitted abortion to wholesale infanticide. It is certainly true that one widely prophesied consequence of the 1967 Act – that abortion would replace contraception as the measure of choice for family planning – has not happened, despite the fact that contraceptive family planning has arguably not been as successful in some areas as it ideally might have been.[21]

None the less, it is the case that legal and moral prohibitions on killing innocent human beings must cut in somewhere and in this extremely morally important area lines may not be drawn cavalierly or arbitrarily. In his article on the slippery slope argument, Bernard Williams suggests that we should dis-tinguish between *reasonable* distinctions and *effective* ones.[22] A distinction may be justifiable on rational grounds, but impossible to enforce. Conversely a distinction may not withstand a great deal of philosophical pressure but, none the less, it may be readily accepted and understood. It is hard to defend the view that there is a material difference in the maturity and experience of someone aged 17 and eleven months and an 18-year-old. But there are obvious advantages in having a clear point at which someone attains the age of majority. So even if distinctions between suicide and euthanasia, or between withdrawing treatment and killing, are hard to justify on moral grounds, there may be good policy reasons for making them as the law and, to some extent, popular morality, currently do.

Consent

One circumstance in which it is evidently true that life-preserving treatment may, indeed must, be withheld is where the patient declines to consent to that treatment. Legally speaking, to treat a patient without her consent is a battery and is legally actionable as such. Why is this so? It is not because patients are thought to be the best judge of their medical situation. Patients are rarely medical experts. Nor is it because medical staff are not generally to be trusted to do the best for their patients.

There are, first of all, good psychological reasons for obtaining a patient's genuine consent to a course of treatment. Such a patient will have a sense of ownership of the decision taken, will be less apprehensive and will retain control over the situation at a point where he or she may well feel both vulnerable and in distress. Such *empowerment* can be therapeutically valuable.

A second reason is that, usually, the decision to treat or not to treat, or to treat in one way rather than another is only partly a medical matter. A physician may, for example, know not merely the national and international data on the relative merits of a radical or a partial mastectomy, a lumpectomy or no treatment at all, he or she may also be able to judge their relative merits in a particular case such as this, in a hospital such as this and with this particular surgical team. But only the woman whose breast and whose life this is can possibly know what degree of risk of recurrence or the spread of secondaries she is prepared to set against the effects of the various forms of surgery. Of course she must first know what the risks are and how the consequences of surgery may be mitigated or compensated for. It is possible that she may need counselling, so that she is dealing with the reality of her condition and not a distorted personal or social mythology. But though the advice of specialists in other fields may help, she is the only specialist on her own life and her views on that topic are at least as valuable as anyone else's. There is, indeed, one respect in which her opinion must carry the most weight. We are all fallible and, within margins set by expertise and experience,[23] all equally likely to turn out to be wrong. But in regard to my own case I have an incentive that all others lack to get it right.

If I am wrong, I bear the consequences. If someone else is wrong about what is best for me, I still bear the consequences.

But there is a third reason which is, arguably, morally more important than either of these. For the patient, just as much as the rest of the medical team, is a moral agent and her plans, wishes and decisions are just as morally important as anyone else's. To disregard her wishes for herself is to assume that someone else's plans and decisions are more important than her own and there is very seldom any moral basis for such an assumption.

It is important to see that these reasons hold whether the patient agrees to a proposed course of treatment or declines it. For it would be a peculiar kind of respect for autonomy if it were exercised only when another person agreed with you. There is, however, one situation in which there is an important lack of symmetry between agreeing to treatment on the one hand, and declining it on the other. For if autonomy matters because it matters that people be able, within limits, to live their own lives, pursue their own plans and make their own mistakes, then it seems odd to respect an autonomous decision which, on the face of it, seems likely to end their life. Declining life-preserving treatment seems to be just such a case. This is reflected in a general reluctance, which appears to exist, to take at face value a refusal of life-sustaining treatment.[24] None the less, without some reason for thinking that such patients are temporarily depressed, or under some illusion, it would be difficult to ground an argument that you knew better than they did whether their life was worth living. But that cuts both ways. If it cannot support a decision to ignore their refusal of treatment, nor can it support a decision to withdraw treatment where they are not able to decide for themselves. The comment made by the judge in *Bland* (Hoffmann, LJ) that

> The court could say from what it had learned of Anthony Bland from those closest to him that, if forced to choose, it was more likely that in his present state he would choose to die than to live.[25]

should not be seen (and perhaps was not intended) as justifying the court's eventual decision.

Nor does a competent patient's right to refuse treatment imply a right to voluntary euthanasia. Your right to decline treatment which might keep you alive is not the same as a right to demand treatment which would kill you. That would, amongst other things, imply a right to coerce medical staff into doing that which they might well have great objections to doing. But it is not clear that that precludes a moral (though not a legal) right to come to an agreement with someone, probably a doctor, who has no such objections. The law has a maxim *Volenti non fit injuria* which means that you are not wronged by something you have consented to.[26] It is on this basis that surgeons are able to perform operations and dentists draw teeth. But it does not apply to criminal injuries.[27] What counts as a *criminal* injury is said to be a matter of degree,[28] but is clearly a matter of policy rather than principle. Injuries incurred during consensual sexual activity have been deemed criminal, but 'manly diversions' such as boxing, wrestling or team contact sports are excluded.[29] This is clearly an example of an 'effective' rather than a 'reasonable' distinction, in Williams's terms. But what it means is that, in law, you may not, in general, consent to an action which causes, or risks causing, you actual bodily harm. A justification for this, though one which is seldom given, is that permitting consent of the victim in such cases to be a defence might make it difficult to pick up on crimes in which the victim's consent was bogus, coerced or in some other way unsatisfactory. There is no difficulty in principle in making this distinction, but in practice one can see that it might, in some cases, be very hard. Devlin makes this point,[30] that in order to defend areas of uncontroversial moral concern, it may be necessary to frame the law so that it covers controversial, or even obviously innocuous, areas as well.

Caring and Curing

It would seem that we are settling on a view that the distinction made by the courts between the legality of the medical team's actions in *Bland* and the illegality of *Cox*, is a distinction made on grounds of policy rather than principle, a line drawn because one needs to be drawn somewhere, rather than one which reason dictates must be drawn *here*. That line has, on one side, various forms of criminal homicide up to and including murder which no one would wish to see legitimated or provided with spurious defences. What, however, lies on the other side of the line? Why not, in other words, if we are concerned that Dr Cox's actions went too far, draw the line much further back and rule that *Bland*, too, was not a legitimate step to take? Many people obviously think that would have been a proper action to have taken, to judge by the public controversy which greeted the decision. What were the imperatives which drove Tony Bland's medical team to request, and the court to grant, permission to withdraw artificial hydration and nutrition?

For most of its history medicine was an art which could ease distress, care for the sick and, on occasions and with some luck, cure some patients. There was very little it could do for most serious illnesses and nothing at all to arrest the process of dying. During the nineteenth century medicine became a science, and began to develop specific treatments for illnesses, which had a high success rate. Even then, however, it has been argued that the science of medicine did less to alleviate disease and lengthen life than better nutrition, housing and public health did.[31] But by the middle of the twentieth century technology had been developed which permitted patients to survive under circumstances which had hitherto been lethal. In many cases, however, we are still unable to cure the underlying condition. It makes sense, therefore, to ask in cases such as that of Tony Bland, whether caring for patients always, invariably, requires that we continue to treat them.

It has been accepted by many that in circumstances where continued treatment offers little prospect of success (in terms of cure or, even, in terms of the significant prolongation of life) and is burdensome to the patient, the patient's family and friends or to the medical team, that such treatment may be discontinued.[32] Even where discontinuing this treatment leads directly to the death of the patient, the Church of England has said that this must not be equated with euthanasia: 'In its narrow current sense, euthanasia implies killing, and it is misleading to extend it to cover decisions not to preserve life by artificial means when it would be better for the patient to be allowed to die.'[33] The Catholic Church's position is that 'if it appears that the attempt at resuscitation constitutes such a burden for the family that one cannot in all conscience impose it on them, they can lawfully insist that the doctor should discontinue those attempts and the doctor can lawfully comply.'[34]

There are circumstances, then, in which care for the patient permits, and may even require, that one ceases to continue to treat him or her. Consider the following:

> a doctor aged sixty-eight [was] dying of an inoperable cancer of the stomach. First it was treated by palliative removal of part of the stomach. Shortly afterwards the patient developed a pulmonary embolism and this was removed by an operation. Again he collapsed with myocardial infarction and was revived by the cardiac resuscitation team. His heart stopped on four subsequent occasions and was restarted artificially. The body lingered on for a few more weeks, with severe brain damage following the cardiac arrest and episodes of vomiting accompanied by generalized convulsions.
>
> This man had been told that he had a stomach cancer; he accepted the diagnosis, which was confirmed by histological examination. Because the cancer had spread to his bones he suffered severe pain that was unrelieved by morphine or pethidine. When his pulmonary embolus was removed he was grateful, but asked that no further attempts should be made to resuscitate him should he require it. The request was not regarded.[35]

As this example, I hope, makes clear, a duty of care does not necessarily imply a duty to treat. Where treatment proves to be of no benefit or involves disproportionate hardship there can be no duty to continue it, even where this will result in the death of the patient.

For Dr Cox the situation was slightly different. He could not cure his patient. For him care involved easing her suffering as far as he was able. What was he to do once that was no longer possible? Treatment was no longer alleviating her pain, but discontinuing it would have made it even worse. In so far as discontinuing Tony Bland's treatment was clearly going to lead to his death and that, had he not died, then the point of doing so would have been lost, then it is difficult to see how what Dr Cox did for Lillian Boyes was morally any different. Indeed, the very Church of England report cited above also allows that it is imaginable that circumstances might exist where killing a patient is the only way of preventing or cutting short great and unbearable pain. It says that such circumstances might arise in wars, or out of the reach of modern medical techniques or in emergencies.[36] Whether that was exactly the situation that Dr Cox found himself in is difficult for outsiders to say, but if it was, then I personally find it very hard to see that he did anything wrong. Why then was he prosecuted? Because a line must be drawn, and the courts found it impossible to draw it anywhere else. But though that line may be both legally enforceable and practically effective, it cannot be said that it is morally defensible.

NOTES

1 See Beauchamp and Childress, *Principles of Biomedical Ethics*, 2nd edn, Appendix II, pp. 329–30.
2 Ibid.
3 Ibid., pp. 330–1.
4 *Obiter dicta* in the case of *Regina* v. *Arthur* (1981), trial transcripts cited by Kuhse in 'A modern myth: that letting die is not the intentional causation of death', *Journal of Applied Philosophy*, 1(1), 1984.
5 Expert testimony from consultant paediatricians in the case of *Arthur* (1981), cited in D. and M. Braham, 'The Arthur case', *Journal of Medical Ethics*, 9, pp. 12–15.
6 English law holds that murder and manslaughter are crimes which can be committed by omission when someone who has a legal duty to act fails to do so. This is why the House of Lords had to establish that there was no legal duty to continue to treat Tony Bland before it could authorize the withdrawal of artificial hydration and nutrition. See *Bonnyman* (1942) 28 Cr App 131; *Pitwood* (1902) 19 TLR 37; *Gibbins and Proctor* (1919) 13 Cr App Rep and *Stone and Dobinson* [1977] QB 354, [1977] 2 All ER 341.
7 Cross and Jones, *Introduction to Criminal Law*, 9th edn, p. 26.
8 Details taken from the *Guardian*, London, 20 November 1992, 4 and 10 December 1992, 5 February 1993, 4 March 1993. See also *Airedale NHS Trust* v. *Bland* (1993), 2 WLR 316; Jennett and Plum, 'The persistent vegetative state'.
9 Melanie Phillips, *Guardian*, 5 February 1993. The letters pages of subsequent editions echoed this point, though equally many took the opposite position.
10 *Guardian*, 5 February 1993, p. 3.
11 Professor David Blake, as reported in the *Guardian*, 17 September 1992, p. 6.
12 The details given of this case were assembled from the *Guardian*, 11–22 September 1992. See also Brahams, 'Criminality and compassion' and 'The critically ill patient', and Campbell 'Declining and withdrawing treatment'.
13 *Bland* (1993) 2 WLR 316.
14 Court of Appeal: *Airedale NHS Trust* v. *Bland*, 9 December 1992.
15 *Guardian*, leader article, 20 November 1992.

16 The United Kingdom Department of Health declared in 1993 that it proposed a reduction in the suicide rate as a target. It is, as yet, unclear on whom the responsibility for delivering this will fall.

17 For example see, in the UK, the Homicide Act 1957, s. 4(2); and the Suicide Act 1961; s. 2(2).

18 The 'slippery slope' (or 'thin end of the wedge') argument has been an influential factor in many discussions of modern medical ethics, presumably because of the combined importance and difficulty of drawing clear and defensible distinctions in this area. For further discussion see D. Lamb, *Down the Slippery Slope*; S. Bok, 'The leading edge of the wedge', *Hastings Center Report*, 1, December 1971; T. Govier, 'What's wrong with slippery slope arguments?', *Canadian Journal of Philosophy*, 12, June 1982; F. Schauer, 'Slippery Slopes', *Harvard Law Review*, 99, 1985 and B. Williams, 'Which slopes are slippery?', in *Moral Dilemmas in Modern Medicine*, ed. Lockwood.

19 See Alexander, 'Medical science under dictatorship'; Lifton, *The Nazi Doctors*.

20 In 1992 there were 153,613 legal terminations of pregnancy in England. This figure shows a rise from 87.6 per thousand conceptions in 1970 to 190.1 per thousand in 1992, but also a steady decline from a peak of 200 per thousand in 1989 (source: Department of Health, *On the State of Public Health 1992*, HMSO).

21 For further discussion of the ethical issues raised by the legal termination of pregnancy, see Hursthouse, *Beginning Lives*; Cohen and Scanlon (eds), *Rights and Wrongs of Abortion*, Feinberg (ed.), *Problem of Abortion*; J. J. Thompson, 'A defense of abortion', *Philosophy and Public Affairs*, 1, 1971; M. A. Warren, 'On the moral and legal status of abortion', *The Monist*, 57, 1973; M. Tooley, 'Abortion and infanticide', in *Philosophy and Public Affairs*, 2, 1972; L. Clarke, 'Abortion: a rights issue?', in Lee and Morgan (eds), *Birthrights*.

22 B. Williams, 'Which slopes are slippery?', in Lockwood (ed.), *Moral Dilemmas in Modern Medicine*.

23 How wide those margins are to be set may well depend on how optimistic or pessimistic one is about the extent of human knowledge, especially, in this kind of cases, in the field of technology and the ability to predict the future.

24 See Brazier, *Medicine, Patients and the Law*, p. 311; also *Re T* [1992] 3 WLR 782, C.A. where the court decided that the refusal was made under the undue influence of the patient's mother and there was reason to believe that the patient did not fully understand its implications and *Re S* [1992] 3 WLR 806 where a court overrode a patient's refusal in the interests of the child she was carrying. *Re S* did cause concern, not least because, despite the decision, both mother and child died. A more recent case, *Re C* (1993) NLJ 1719 has reasserted a patient's right to autonomy and the principle that, *in itself*, refusal of life-sustaining treatment was not evidence of incapacity or ability to make a competent decision in this area.

25 *Guardian*, 10 December, 1992.

26 Though such consent would have to be 'informed', i.e. real and not merely verbal agreement. For further discussion, see Faden and Beauchamp, *A History and Theory of Informed Consent* and Faulder, *Whose Body Is It?*

27 See *Young* (1838) 8 C & P 644; *Cuddy* (1843) 1 Car & Kir 210.

28 See the comments made by Stephen (the trial judge) in *Coney* (1882) 8 QBD 534 at 549.

29 See *Donovan* [1934] 2 KB 498.

30 In *The Enforcement of Morals*, Oxford, 1959.

31 See T. McKeown, *The Role of Medicine*, Oxford, Blackwell, 1979.

32 See Campbell and Collinson, *Ending Lives*, pp. 135–43; also David Sheppard (Bishop of Liverpool) in a letter to the *Guardian*, 27 November, 1992.

33 Church of England's Board for Social Responsibility, *On Dying Well*.

34 Pope Pius XII, *The Pope Speaks*, vol. 4, no. 4, 1957, p. 396.

35 From G. A. Gresham, 'A time to be born and a time to die', in A. B. Downing (ed.), *Euthanasia and the Right to Death*, London, Peter Owen, p. 150.

36 Church of England's Board for Social Responsibility, *On Dying Well*, p. 10.

READING GUIDE

Two useful current texts on medical ethics are John Harris's *The Value of Life* and Beauchamp and Childress's *Principles of Biomedical Ethics*. The latter is comprehensive, sensible and a useful source of case-studies, but is so often quoted and drawn on that it is in danger of becoming the received wisdom. Harris is a good corrective to this, disagreeing, as he does, with Beauchamp and Childress on many substantive theoretical positions. *The Value of Life* is often contentious, but invariably clear and rigorous. Both books are written by philosophers. Good guides to medical ethics written by doctors include Raanan Gillon's *Philosophical Medical Ethics* and W. J. Ellos's *Ethical Practice in Clinical Medicine*. The latter, especially, is an excellent synthesis of well-researched case-studies and perceptively presented philosophical theory.

For those interested in medical law, the best text is probably Brazier, *Medicine, Patients and the Law*, but Mason and McCall Smith, *Law and Medical Ethics* is also a useful source. *Feminist Perspectives in Medical Ethics* by Holmes and Purdy is a timely reminder of the male domination of work in this field and also part of an attempt to redress that balance. Good collections of articles include Arras and Rhoden, *Ethical Issues in Modern Medicine* and Beauchamp and Perlin, *Ethical Issues in Death and Dying*.

There are a number of journals in this area. Of the philosophical ones, the best are *Bioethics*, the *Hastings Center Report*, the *Journal of Applied Philosophy* and *Philosophy and Public Affairs*, though the two last are not exclusively devoted to medical ethics. The *Journal of Medical Ethics* is recognized as pre-eminent by both the medical profession and philosophers and professional journals such as the *British Medical Journal* and the *New England Journal of Medicine* often carry pieces on medical or nursing ethics.

CLASSICAL SOURCES

Plato: *Republic*, Book V; *Phaedo*
Aristotle: *Politics*, Book VII; *Nicomachean Ethics*, Books III and V
More: *Utopia*
Donne: *Biathanatos*
Hume: 'Of suicide'
J. S. Mill: *On Liberty*

14

Ethical Questions Facing Law Enforcement Agents

John Kleinig

Police officers investigating a drug-related murder are led, by slender threads of evidence, to suspect the night-watchman at a housing project. The project superintendent lets them into the watchman's 'quarters', where, concealed behind a picture, they find a weapon that proves to be the murder weapon. The suspect is arrested. When the case is being prepared, the prosecutor advises the police that their entry into the watchman's quarters *may* have been illegal, and, if so, the forensic evidence (their only strong evidence) will be inadmissible in court, resulting in the collapse of their case. The police decide to claim that through the window of the quarters they could see the butt of the weapon, and therefore had reasonable (and thus legal) grounds for entry. Were they justified in doing so?

The suspected accomplice of a notorious hoodlum is giving two detectives a hard time, tendering first one address where they will find the wanted man, then another, and another. It is a hot and humid summer's day, the traffic is terrible, and the detectives are becoming increasingly tired and frustrated. After the third wild goose chase, and an insolent remark by the suspect, one of the officers reacts by giving him a sharp slap. The alleged accomplice lays a complaint, which is taken seriously. If the charge is established, it is likely that the detective will lose his job (and pension). His partner is asked what happened. He knows that in the current political climate the investigating board will be unsympathetic to the trying circumstances. He reports that he saw nothing, but turned around only after he heard a commotion. He did not know what the sequence of events was. Was he justified in protecting his buddy?

An undercover officer who has managed to infiltrate a notorious gang, to the point where he has been accepted as a member, is told to 'punish' a delinquent debtor of the gang leader. He is told where the delinquent is to be found, and ordered to bring back a finger as evidence that the job has been done. The officer knows that if he refuses, his cover will be blown or he himself will be 'punished'. If his cover is blown, the authorities will lose their only real opportunity to bring many of the gang members to justice. On the other hand, if he inflicts the beating and severs the finger, he will be acting illegally and, presumably, immorally. What should he do?

These cases, based on real-life incidents, are just a few of the many in which police must make hard ethical decisions. With some frequency their job places them in situations for which they have been ill-prepared by the ordinary processes of moral nurture and the habits of moral response that develop therefrom. Hence the need for 'law enforcement ethics', not because there is a morality peculiar to law enforcement, but because the police role and the circumstances and conditions under which police must make their decisions are often novel, complex, and time-constrained. The police, however, unlike other social service providers, such as doctors, lawyers, and business people, have not been well served by a debate and literature that takes their concerns and problems seriously. The present chapter is an attempt to take a few steps in that direction. Ideally, it will assist not only police decision-making, but also the assessment of that decision-making by the wider community.[1]

Background

When John Locke enumerated the deficiencies of a 'state of nature' – society without government – he highlighted the need for three complementary institutions: a legislature to draw up common rules for citizens, a judiciary to interpret and apply them, and an 'executive' to enforce them.[2] It is to this last institutional body that so-called 'law enforcement agents' (henceforth 'police') belong, though it is important to note that as our conception of the appropriate role of civil government has evolved, so too has our conception of the role of police. Indeed, at the very inception of modern-day policing – usually associated with the formation of Sir Robert Peel's Metropolitan Police in London in 1829 – the role of police was seen primarily as crime prevention and only secondarily as law enforcement. Nowadays, when police – and government – perform many social service functions along with those more traditionally associated with law enforcement, it is probably better to conceptualize the police role as one of social peacekeeping than as one of law enforcement or crime-fighting.

These initial observations about the police role generate a first tier of ethical questions that police must confront. They are questions concerning the nature, foundations, and limits of police authority. What is it that police are appropriately authorized to do? From where does their authority to do that come? To what extent should their exercises of authority be discretionary? To whom are they accountable, and what mechanisms of accountability are ethically justifiable? These questions are primarily questions of political ethics. They have as their background a recognition that police are generally public officers, agents of governmental authority, and that their function is bound up with larger questions concerning the legitimate functions and limits of government.[3]

Important though they are, this is not the place for an extended exploration of these issues. Here it must suffice to say that in liberal democratic societies police authority is usually claimed to be grounded in or at least dependent on the consent of the governed, and that police are ultimately accountable to the people for the authority they have, for the scope of their responsibility, and for the limits of their discretion. Our primary focus here, however, will be on a second tier of ethical questions that arise for police officers in the course of their work: issues of force, deception, corruption and loyalty. Although these more specific questions tie in with the more general ones I raised, they can be partially negotiated in their own right, and – for the time being – on the basis of broadly shared presumptions.

Discretionary Authority

It will, however, first be useful to consider a few of the issues raised by the police use of discretion, since the exercise of discretion is so central to their work – whether it concerns the provision of some social service, the prevention of crime or the enforcement of law. The topic of discretion bears on the scope of the authority of the police, their interpretation of rules and situations, the priority to be given to competing demands, and the tactics they should use.

The idea of discretion is itself problematic, but is best seen not simply as a capacity that the police have to decide what to do when confronted by a situation or demand that impinges on them, but instead as a normative resource – a privilege, permission or prerogative – to use judgement about how to make a practical determination. As such, discretion has embedded constraints: implicit understandings about the range of choice available to the officer (or department) in question. These constraints may be articulated by reference to institutional, administrative and moral norms, norms that may sometimes be mutually supportive, but which at other times may be in tension.

Questions about the appropriate scope and limits of police discretion tend to be bound up with several other broad issues in policing. One concerns the status of police work, whether policing can be seen as a *profession* whose practitioners should be given wide substantive discretion, or whether police activity should be more tightly controlled by legislation, regulations and supervision. It is generally argued that the kind of knowledge and expertise expected of and possessed by police will not sustain more than a fairly limited discretionary authority, though whether those limitations and provisions for discretionary decision-making should be implemented by means of legislation, judicial review, administrative rule-making or direct supervision is a practical issue which will depend on a great many social factors that are likely to differ from place to place.

For the most part, however, the discretionary authority of police will be a function of both the need to act in situations that are too varied to be fully covered by rules, and the limited resources that will require police to rank or prioritize the demands that are made on them in the light of the various social goals that they are expected to fulfil. Unlike the discretionary judgements of traditional professionals, whose wisdom is usually most appropriately adjudged by peers, it is the citizenry at large to whom police discretionary judgements must be made available for review.

Much of the day-to-day activity of police consists in providing various forms of social assistance: giving directions, directing traffic, attending minor emergencies, listening to gripes, breaking news to families, and so on. But police have powers and responsibilities that extend beyond these matters. They are to a considerable extent the authorized repositories of social force. To them we give the responsibility for ensuring that laws are enforced, that law-breakers are apprehended, and for securing order in situations where it might break down. It is these functions in particular, and the need to fulfil them effectively, that pose some of the most serious ethical problems for police. Police are authorized to use force where it is necessary to achieve their legitimate ends; and in their investigative function they may use a variety of deceptive techniques. The kinds of force and deception that should be available to them, the circumstances under which force and deception may be employed, and the limits that should be placed on their use of force and deception, raise significant ethical questions. But also, because those who violate law and order usually have an interest in avoiding detection or apprehension, police may find themselves offered inducements to compromise their responsibilities. Although the acceptance of bribes and other forms of corruption are clearly wrong, nevertheless there are problematic practices, such as the offering and acceptance of gratuities, and the erection of a 'blue wall of (loyal) silence', that can pose a difficult ethical challenge for police.

The Use of Force

The use of force by any human being against another constitutes an ethical problem. It represents an infringement of the freedom and respect that is due to a being with the capacity to determine his own path in his own way. Although the various pacifist arguments that eschew all resort to force must be taken seriously, I shall here assume that in certain limited circumstances – self-defence, the defence of others, and punishment – the use of force *may* be justified. Whether it *will* be justified in those cases depends on the circumstances of the situation: whether the force used was necessary, proportionate, seemly, and so on. What applies to the use of force generally applies with even greater stringency to the use of deadly force, for here the effects are (or at least threaten to be) irrevocable and a life is extinguished. There is no room for rectifying mistakes, for changes of mind, for remission or pardon, no room for compensating the person who is killed.

The use of force by police is generally justified on much the same general grounds as police authority: a power vested in police by the citizenry, so that their common interests will be more effectively secured than if that power were exercised by individuals as they saw fit. For police to retain that authority, there must be confidence that their use of force on behalf of citizens will be significantly more protective of their common interests than would be the case were each person to retain that right individually.[4]

Vesting police with the right to use force in our behalf is a significant concession, and our assurance that they will exercise it wisely is likely to depend in some measure on the constraints that are placed upon them. Although police will have some discretion about the use of force, that discretion is likely to be fairly limited, lest innocent (or even guilty) people be made to suffer unjustifiably (or excessively). The constraints we place upon them are likely to cover the kinds of force they may use, the occasions on which they may use it, and the amount of force that may be used.

Police departments differ from place to place and from country to country in the kinds of non-deadly force to which they have access. In the United States, which, among democratic countries, is probably distinguished by the very considerable range of forcible techniques and implements that are available to police, forms of allowable non-deadly force have included handcuffs and velcro straps, several types of batons, nets, water cannons, various irritant sprays, choke-holds, stun and laser guns, and dogs.

Excluded from this list are certain kinds of force that have been thought in themselves unacceptable. For example, when police sought to regain alleged evidence hastily swallowed in a drug bust, by having the suspect's stomach pumped, the US Supreme Court considered this use of force 'shocking to the conscience'.[5] The same applies to torture or the 'third degree', which may not only render the extraction of information non-voluntary but also demean the person by treating him in a way that undermines his capacity to make a rational response.

Each of the allowable forms is intended to assist police to achieve their legitimate ends short of the use of deadly force. Yet each has its advantages and drawbacks, each is a source of controversy. Whether police should handcuff every person they arrest is something about which there are significant cultural differences. In the United Kingdom, handcuffing is likely to be the exception rather than the rule, whereas in the United States it is likely to be the rule. And where it is the rule, its necessity might be questioned. Where, for example, a person has been arrested for a non-violent offence, and shows every sign of co-operating, the use of handcuffs might seem to be unnecessary, or at least something for which a discretionary decision might be called for. Yet those who support the rule often claim that the act of arresting a person introduces an element of unpredictability into a person's responses, especially if the person has not previously experienced arrest. Suicide, flight or resistance might be contemplated. Supporters of the rule argue that they are better off with it, even though there will be individual cases in which it might appear unnecessary. Giving officers discretion about when handcuffing is appropriate, they say, will introduce the probability of its discriminatory employment. Minorities and the poor are likely to be seen as greater risks than those who are white and 'respectable'. Obviously, further progress in resolving such issues will depend on an examination of empirical data, training, cultural conditions, and so on.

One additional concern with the use of handcuffs relates to overtightening – often as a means of punishing or getting back at a recalcitrant arrestee. Police can easily get away with claiming that any nerve damage that occurs was brought about by the suspect as he struggled to resist arrest. To circumvent this problem, some departments have experimented with the use of velcro straps.

Similar pros and cons can be advanced in relation to other intermediate uses of force. Ideally, such uses of force should restrain without injuring, so that the person – not yet convicted of any offence – can be 'delivered up' to those institutional processes within the criminal justice system that are more suited to the determination of guilt and innocence. Unfortunately, there is a paradoxical quality to the development and availability of non-deadly coercive techniques. The more risk-free a restraining device, the more easily it can be abused without trace. Mace and stun guns, like truncheons, do not generally cause injury or leave scars, and so it is often complained that they are used abusively. This reinforces the frequently forgotten point that ultimately it is not instruments and techniques that are ethical, but people, and that even though some devices may be inherently more problematic than others, even those that are less problematic will become problematic if their users are not ethical.

The use of deadly force by police has been particularly controversial in the United States, where police are armed as a matter of course, and, until recently, often considered it appropriate to use firearms to apprehend 'fleeing felons'. The 'fleeing felon' privilege, which had its origins in common law, allowed that police, in order to stop suspected criminals who might otherwise escape from apprehension, could seek to prevent their escape by using deadly force. Along with the 'defence of life' privilege, which permitted the use of deadly force where the officer's or some other's life was in danger, it circumscribed the police use of deadly force. The fleeing felon privilege, however, reflected a social and legal environment in which felonies were generally capital offences, and the use of a deadly means probably reflected a situation in which the apprehending officer did not possess a firearm (police officers were not generally armed until late in the nineteenth century) and was in danger of injury during the struggle to apprehend. Recourse to the privilege without 'reinter-pretation' for modern conditions led to many unnecessary injuries and deaths.

In 1985, the US Supreme Court, recognizing the morally problematic character of the fleeing felon privilege, effectively limited the police use of deadly force to those situations in which, given the various interests involved (such as the suspect's right to life, the value of judging people via the normal processes of the criminal justice system, the need to provide a secure environment for citizens, and so on), recourse to it could be judged 'reasonable'.[6] Although the court conducted its analysis in legal terms, the considerations to which it appealed closely mirrored morally significant concerns. The upshot was a restriction on the fleeing felon privilege that all but subsumed it under the provisions of the defence of life privilege. Where the person who is seeking to escape apprehension poses a continuing danger to the lives of others, the use of deadly force *may* sometimes be justified.

There are interesting extensions of these considerations to cover other police practices, such as high speed pursuits. The motor vehicle is sometimes considered to be 'the deadliest weapon in the police arsenal'.[7] Certainly, many more deaths occur as a result of high speed chases than as a result of the use of firearms. So there is an important argument for restricting their use – or at least their continued use after an initial attempt to apprehend a driver – to situations in which the officers have good reason to believe that the offence is serious enough, that the driver of the vehicle has actually committed such an offence, that innocent bystanders will not be unreasonably threatened, and so on. And, as with the use of firearms, there will be an obligation on departments to ensure that officers are properly trained and supervised in their exercise of this option.

In addition to these general considerations, there are many others that need to be taken into account, some at a policy level, others in particular situations. The kinds of firearms or vehicles that may be used by officers, whether warning shots should be fired or the decision to pursue should first be cleared by a dispatcher, whether firearms should be worn when off duty or used from or against a moving vehicle, whether high speed pursuits should be permitted in urban areas, and so on, will need to be considered as part of a more comprehensive ethical inquiry into the police use of deadly force.

The Use of Deception

The increasing constraints on police use of force – in particular, the use of torture and the third degree to extract information – have required that, in order to obtain the information or evidence they need, police have had to find alternative means. Increasingly they have employed deception to achieve their ends. But deception, too, generates significant moral problems.

The background to this concern is the fact that deception is manipulative and erosive of trust. Truthfulness and straightforwardness with others is respectful of their standing as rational agents, capable of making their own judgements and decisions. Those who lie and deceive subvert this capacity in others and treat them simply as means to their own ends. However, although there are a few writers who have eschewed all deception and lying, most consider that the use of deception is sometimes justified. The problem is to establish appropriate limits.[8]

Deception in police work can be considered in relation to various phases of that work: at the broadly investigative stage, before anyone has been taken into custody; at the interrogatory stage, where the person is not free to come and go as he or she pleases; and at the testimonial stage, when the police officer is under oath.[9]

At what I have called the investigative stage, the deception may take many forms: wiretapping, bugging, the use of ruses to enter premises, undercover operations such as stings, decoys, the use of informants, and so on. Here there are problems of targeting, of technique, and of side-effects.

Are people being targeted for, say, political, social or racial reasons? Are they being targeted to determine their corruptedness or only their corruptibility? Is the targeting focused on a person or on a type of offence? Different problems are associated with different questions.[10] In one particularly egregious but legally sanctioned case,[11] disgruntled local residents pressured police to target the owner of a topless nightclub, not because he had broken any zoning law but because they figured that the unwanted bar could be closed only if it could be shown to be the venue for illegal activity. So, over a period of six months an undercover officer was detailed to go on a 'fishing expedition'. He gained the nightclub owner's trust, even to the point of becoming a tenant in his house, and chauffeuring his children. Eventually some evidence of illegal activity was found and the owner convicted. On appeal, the US Supreme Court refused to grant *certiorari*, ostensibly because the owner had 'consented' to the undercover officer's presence in the bedroom where the evidence of illegal activity was found; no constitutional violation was therefore involved. In this case, the targeting was motivated by considerations that had little to do with the occurrence of criminal activity, and the undercover officer was sent on an extended 'fishing expedition' that invaded the target's most private domain.

In other cases, undercover officers have presented targets with inducements, not because any wrong has been done, but to find out whether they would be open to wrongdoing. In extreme cases, such inducements can rebound on the government agents, leaving the defendant with the legal defence of entrapment; but the point of *morally* acceptable deception may be passed before any legal defence is available to the person who fails such a 'test'.[12]

The deceptive techniques used in investigation may be problematic both in themselves and because of their side-effects. Certain exploitations of personal relationships may be inherently problematic, for example, fostering romantic relationships solely to gain information or evidence.[13] Other deceptive techniques may be acceptable in theory, but very problematic in practice, such as sting operations that 'net' innocent people.

It is difficult to provide any simple tests for acceptable investigative deception. However, because of the inherently problematic character of deception, close attention needs to be given to the occasions for its use, the available alternatives, some proportionality between the deception used and the offence to which it is directed, and the costs of its use, not only to the participants but also to the social ethos.

During the interrogatory phase, deception raises some additional problems, for when a person is in custody the likelihood of unfairly or coercively exacted information can be considerable, and there is also the possibility that what is so exacted will not be reliable. Since the criminal justice systems of most liberal democracies seek to establish guilt not by means of coercively exacted confessions, but through a rational accumulation of evidence that will place certain conclusions 'beyond reasonable doubt', the interrogatory situation must be kept free of factors that will compromise this ideal. Is it compromised if an officer attempts to gain information by pretending to be a priest or counsellor? Should the officer be permitted to misrepresent the charges, or likely penalties, or the strength of the case, as a means of extracting information that will be relevant to the state's case? In the United States, the so-called *Miranda* warnings are meant to protect suspects who are in custody by ensuring that what is said is said freely.[14] Suspects are warned that what they say may be used against them, that they have a right to remain silent, and that they may have access to legal representation. A police officer who poses as a priest or counsellor attempts to mislead the suspect about the character of the investigatory situation by suggesting that its intent is spiritual or therapeutic rather than adversarial and accusatory.[15]

Not all deception is ruled out at the interrogatory stage. It may be acceptable for officers to suggest that the evidence they have accumulated is stronger than it really is, in the hope or expectation that a guilty person might consider that no further point would be served by continuing to conceal his guilt. But there is no bright line between those forms of deception that will be morally acceptable and those that will not. Much will depend on the particular circumstances of the case.

At the testimonial stage, however, when police are under oath to tell 'the truth, the whole truth and nothing but the truth', it is generally considered improper for police officers to lie or deceive. Police officers who falsely or deceptively testify before a judge or the court – whether to obtain a search warrant or in the course of a trial – seek to deceive the court: they undermine what is intended to be a rational enquiry.

Yet, as one of the examples at the beginning of this chapter illustrates, it has not been uncommon for police officers to engage in some form of testimonial deception. In the interests of what they see as 'justice', officers sometimes 'massage' their testimony, lest someone they consider guilty be allowed to exploit the stringent requirements for proof of criminal guilt. Often they have been such testimonial deception as the application of a bandaid to sick system, in which opposing lawyers operate as gladiators seeking victory rather than as advocates for justice.

But even though deception may sometimes have a proper place within the police arsenal, as a way of minimizing harm or as a means to justice, its use at the testimonial stage is particularly problematic. Whereas deception that is employed at the investigative or interrogatory stages can be monitored by the courts, lest it be improperly used, permitting it at the testimonial stage would subvert the very institution by means of which we are able to monitor its use during the investigative and interrogatory phases of police work. What is more, the belief that considerations of 'justice' override the need to be truthful in giving testimony assumes that what a particular officer considers to be 'justice' is in fact so. In individual cases, perhaps, an officer will be right, but the somewhat elaborate arrangements that make up our imperfect criminal justice system are there just because, if individuals are permitted to take it into their own hands to decide who is and who is not guilty, then we will do a worse job of it overall than we currently do. Improvements, no doubt, are possible and necessary, but providing for testimonial deception will almost surely be counter-productive. At least, there is a heavy burden on those who think otherwise to show why the system would *generally* work better if testimonial deception were permitted.

Corruption and the Acceptance of Gratuities

Police officers are subject to considerable temptations. Many of those with whom they have to deal are uncooperative, provocative, or in other ways difficult, and the temptation to retaliate is strong. Others have something to hide, and the stakes might be high enough to encourage them to offer attractive deals to officers. On top of this, police officers are often called to situations or given access to places that present them with opportunities for corruption. As a consequence, even though most officers manage to resist such temptations, there is enough failure to constitute misconduct and corruption, the banes of policing.

Although corruption and misconduct *per se* pose no special moral problem (they are clearly wrong), certain other common practices do, and they are thought to pose a problem because of their connection with corruption (or misconduct). The acceptance of gratuities and other gifts is one such practice. In the course of their work, first line officers are often offered free or discounted coffee, meals, or other goods, and in many places it has been the practice for police to accept them. Yet most police departments ban their acceptance, and some go to extraordinary lengths to enforce such bans.

Typically, the argument has been that the acceptance of gifts and gratuities, even if not in itself wrong (though opinions differ on this), will nevertheless lead to various and increasingly serious forms of corruption.[16] Such slippery slope arguments generally take one of three forms.[17] On one view, the acceptance of gratuities itself represents a compromise such that the officer now knows him- or herself to be willing to be less than impartial. And the officer will subsequently find that when confronted by more serious temptations he or she no longer has any *moral* ground for refusal (being already compromised). On a second view, the incremental differences between accepting a free cup of coffee and, say, a bribe are such that any distinction between them will be arbitrary: no significant difference exists between a free cup of coffee, and coffee and doughnuts, between coffee and doughnuts and a free meal, between a free meal and . . . a bribe. On the third view, although there is nothing wrong as such with the acceptance of a gift or gratuity, engaging in the practice tends to create a bond between the officer and the giver that will later make it difficult for the officer to act in an impartial manner. The seeds of compromise have been sown.

The first version of the argument depends on an acceptance of the view that receipt of a gratuity is itself wrong, something first line officers find it very difficult to believe. Whether or not taking an offered gratuity is wrong will depend significantly on the reason why it is taken, and there would appear to be perfectly legitimate reasons for accepting (as well as for offering) a gratuity. It could be offered as an expression of appreciation, and could be accepted as such or as a gracious and welcome act of hospitality and friendship on the part of a member of the community one is commissioned to serve.[18] The second version is formally invalid, because it fails to recognize that there is a *cumulative* significance to the individually insignificant differences, and, although there may be no bright line dividing one case from the other, just as there is no clear line to be drawn between a bald and a hairy person, there is nevertheless a clear distinction to be drawn between cases at one end and those at the other.

The third version has most to be said for it, though its plausibility as an argument will depend on the strength of the connection that can be made at each stage of the downward slide. The available anecdotal evidence suggests that in police circles, at least, there *has been* a problem of apparently trivial practices, such as the acceptance of gratuities, gradually leading a person into serious corruption. Several factors seem to have been involved. There is, for example, no clear way of distinguishing between a gratuity that will 'create' a sense of particular obligation and one that will not: the psychological effect of a gratuity will differ from officer to officer. Moreover, gratuities are often given so that a bond will be created, and the giver will be able to 'rely' on that bond in the event of a relatively small violation that would normally attract a fine.

But even if we begin to enumerate factors that would facilitate slipping on the slope of corruption, they would not show descent to be inevitable. It may well be that most police officers are experienced skiers who know how to handle themselves on slippery slopes. And even if the acceptance of gratuities will in some cases lead to involvement in corruption, it will not follow that the person concerned would – as is often implied – eventually involve himself in active corruption such as extortion, burglary, and drug-dealing. A reply to this, however, might be that because corruption is so damaging to police authority, it is better *policy* that police forgo acceptance of gratuities, lest the few who would find themselves unable to handle the slopes bring whole departments into disrepute and thus undermine the capacity of police to do their work effectively.

There is a different argument for not accepting gratuities, one that does not contain what to many police is the insulting insinuation that they cannot control their tendency to corruption.[19] It is that those businesses (as they usually are) that offer gratuities or discounts tend thereby to attract a disproportionate police 'presence', something the businesses are well aware of, and want to foster, since it adds to their security. However, the presence that is given to these businesses is 'taken' from others that fail to offer such attractions. And so the police presence, intended as a fairly distributed service, and paid for from the public purse, becomes more like a 'fee for service' operation, the greatest amount of service going to those who pay the most attractive premiums.

Loyalty and the 'Blue Wall of Silence'

For a variety of reasons, police culture tends to be characterized by very strong bonds of 'brotherhood'. No doubt the paramilitary organization of policing, with its enforced uniformity, contributes to this, but so too do the sense of dangerousness that pervades police work and the alienation that often exists between police and the community. Loyalty becomes a central feature of police culture. For many police, 'the job' becomes the dominant defining feature of their existence. The loyalty of police to each other is legendary, and the stuff of some of the great stories of police heroism.

But although we recognize the strength that loyalty can give to an organization or group, it may also create serious problems. This has been particularly so in police work (though also in the professions generally), because, coupled with a cynicism that often develops, it may make officers extremely reluctant to deal openly with the misconduct, corruption, and other organizational failures that occur, sometimes allowing them to flourish, but in any case contributing to the alienation between police and community. Accountability is undermined, police work is made less effective, and the whole community suffers.[20]

Police officers, along with many others, tend to view loyalty as a form of commitment that takes precedence over all others. Such a view is encapsulated in Stephen Decatur's famous (or notorious) phrase, 'my country, right or wrong'.[21] Officers who blow the whistle or otherwise choose to testify against their deviant fellows are seen as traitors. Their careers can be ruined and their lives made miserable, or worse.[22] How are we to resolve the tension between a loyalty that enables acts of great courage and heroism and a loyalty that sides with misconduct and corruption?

Briefly, it requires a new understanding of loyalty. Loyalty needs to be earned, and, once given, its claims can be forfeited. Just as an abused child may no longer be bound by loyalty to the sexually abusive parent (even though that loyalty may continue to be demanded), so too may the expected loyalty of fellow officers be forgone if an officer seriously breaches the norms that govern the police role. Such an officer has already betrayed his trust, and others are not bound to condone or conceal what he has done. Officers sometimes fail to appreciate this because their work has made them cynical of the public whose trust they have. They do not see those they serve as worthy of the standards which they are supposed to embody, and so they will not 'sacrifice' one of their own to those they view as hypocritical or wilfully unappreciative.

We can also frame this issue in terms of competing or conflicting loyalties. Police officers, as most of us, will have a variety of loyalties – personal, religious, organizational, political, and so on – and sometimes, though fortunately not too often, these loyalties come into conflict, and a choice has to be made between them. Such choices, however, do not involve a betrayal of one loyalty for another, since the decision is a principled one rather than one made for reasons of convenience or self-interest. When police enter into their work, they take on responsibilities that should develop into – if not reflect – a loyalty to the community they serve along with the loyalty they might owe to their fellow officers. Should those loyalties come into conflict, it need not be supposed that the peer loyalty they feel should take precedence over their wider loyalty to the community.

Conclusion

This brief excursion into some of the ethical questions that confront police has barely scratched the surface of the vast range of hard decisions that they are likely to have to make over the course of a career. Not only will each of the topics covered generate increasingly subtle and difficult questions, but there are many other issues that will come before them. They may have to do with managerial questions, political involvements, industrial action, media relations, and the problematic area of balancing a private and public life. In many circumstances, the situation will be exacerbated by their having to make decisions under severe pressure and time constraints, and often in the face of intense public scrutiny. Police have not always handled such situations well, but neither have they have been given a great deal of assistance. Unlike so many other areas of applied ethics, that relating to the police has received little support, and police have been left to muddle along on their own. Both they and we deserve better.

One of the tragedies of police–community relations has been the fact that police and the community they serve have often felt themselves to be in an adversarial rather than a co-operative relationship. Although there are reasons for that, it behoves those of us who belong to the wider community to recognize the interdependence of police work and communal peace, and to see our critical ethical task not simply as one of fault-finding but of mutual support in a joint enterprise from which we all benefit.

NOTES

1 A considerably expanded discussion of the problems that follow can be found in my *The Ethics of Policing*. See also Elliston and Feldberg (eds), *Moral Issues in Police Work*; Delattre, *Character and Cops*; and Cohen and Feldberg, *Power and Restraint*.
2 Locke, *Second Treatise of Civil Government*, ch. IX.
3 With the growth of privatized and private security and law enforcement services, this issue has become more complex.
4 For a valuable exposition of this argument, and its extension to the use of deadly force, see Jeffrey Reiman, 'The Social Contract and the police use of deadly force', in Elliston and Feldberg, *Moral Issues in Police Work*, pp. 237–49.
5 *Rochin* v. *California*, 342 US 165, 72 S.Ct. 205 (1952).
6 *Tennessee* v. *Garner*, 471 US 1, 105 S.Ct. 1694, 85 L.Ed.2d 1 (1985).
7 See Alpert and Anderson, 'The most deadly force', p. 2.
8 For a general survey and discussion, see Sissela Bok, *Lying: Moral Choice in Public and Private Life*.
9 This division is taken from Skolnick, 'Deception by police'.
10 For further discussion, see Lawence W. Sherman, 'Equity against truth: value choices in deceptive investigations', in Heffernan and Stroup (eds), *Police Ethics*, pp. 117–32.
11 *US* v. *Baldwin*, 621 F.2d 251 (6th Cir. 1980), *cert. denied* 450 US 1045, 101 S.Ct. 1767, 68 L.Ed.2d 244 (1981).
12 An excellent survey and discussion of undercover tactics can be found in Gary Marx, *Undercover: Police Surveillance in America*.
13 See Marx, 'Under-the-covers undercover investigations'.
14 *Miranda* v. *Arizona*, 384 US 476 (1966).
15 Extended discussions can be found in White, 'Police trickery in inducing confessions' and Skolnick and Leo, 'The ethics of deceptive interrogation'.

16 The argument is developed at length in Lawrence W. Sherman, 'Becoming bent: moral careers of corrupt policeman', reprinted in Elliston and Feldberg, *Moral Issues in Police Work*, pp. 253–64.
17 For a comprehensive review of such arguments, see Walton, *Slippery Slope Arguments*.
18 This argued at length by Richard R. E. Kania in 'Should we tell the police to say "Yes" to gratuities?'.
19 See Feldberg, 'Gratuities, corruption, and the democratic ethos of policing', in Elliston and Feldberg, *Moral Issues in Police Work*, pp. 267–76.
20 For a standard discussion of police culture, see Skolnick, *Justice Without Trial*.
21 From a toast, proposed at Norfolk, Virginia, April 1816.
22 For a classic case study, see Maas, *Serpico*.

READING GUIDE

Serious research on police ethics is comparatively recent, though early contributions include Don L. Kooken, *Ethics and Police Service* and David A. Hansen, *Police Ethics*. Scholarly discussion has been largely coincident with the commencement of publication of the semi-annual journal, *Criminal Justice Ethics*, in 1982. Since then, several collections of articles have appeared, most notably Frederick Elliston and Michael Feldberg (eds), *Moral Issues in Police Work*, and William Heffernan and Timothy Stroup (eds), *Police Ethics: Hard Choices in Law Enforcement*. In addition, Howard Cohen and Michael Feldberg, *Power and Restraint: the Moral Dimension of Police Work*, Edwin Delattre, *Character and Cops: Ethics in Policing* (for which a Teaching Guide is available), and John Kleinig, *The Ethics of Policing*, provide coherent overviews of police ethics. A collection of case-studies can be found in Larry S. Miller and Michael C. Braswell, *Human Relations and Police Work* (a Teaching Guide is also available). A useful documentary resource, with an historical and international flavour, is John Kleinig with Yurong Zhang (comp. and ed.), *Professional Law Enforcement Codes: a Documentary Collection*.

PART IV

Economic and Political Dimensions: Politics and Society

15

Is Efficiency Ethical? Resource Issues in Health Care

Donna Dickenson

Introduction

How can we allocate scarce health care resources justly? What sorts of 'delivery systems' should we have? In particular, are markets the most efficient way to deliver health services? Much blood, sweat and ink has been shed over this issue, but rarely has either faction challenged the unspoken assumption behind the corollary claim made by advocates of markets: that efficiency advances the interests of both individuals and society. That is the ethical firepower which the pro-marketeers have tried to commandeer. Anti-marketeers, whilst contesting the effectiveness of market systems of delivery, have largely accepted the proposition that there is something more than a merely prudential obligation to seek efficiency gains, that efficiency promotes distributive justice by minimizing scarcity of resources. But should the opponents of market systems accept the same criteria as the proponents? Is efficiency ethical?

Whether markets *do* necessarily increase efficiency is arguably a matter for economists, although value questions also enter into this apparently factual debate. But the deeper question is whether efficiency is the correct criterion, in terms of social justice and individual needs. This must be the crux of any discussion about resource allocation in applied ethics.

In this chapter I begin by examining the ethical basis of markets, with particular relation to utility and rights. I argue that no individual is morally or rationally obliged to accept the market criterion of greater efficiency if it disadvantages her. I go on to dissect the basis of markets in political theory, in terms of democratic accountability and fairness. Finally, I ask what other means of resource allocation should be considered, in light of the failure of markets to provide a just and analytically satisfying solution.

Markets and Ethics: Utility and Rights

Efficiency is usually presented as an unimpeachable goal with which everyone can agree. As a British Secretary of State for Health put it, 'We all want greater efficiency, don't we?'[1] But actually efficiency is not everyone's primary aim; nor is it a value-free one. Efficiency is a utilitarian goal, one important corollary of maximizing utility for the greatest number. Utility may be maximized by productive efficiency (the most favourable ratio of inputs to outputs) and allocative efficiency (arranging the societal distribution of resources so as to reward the most productively efficient providers). But why can't we all agree with this aim? Whether it is called utilitarian or not, isn't it one which benefits everybody? Why can't efficiency be morally unexceptionable? If efficient allocation of resources is in the best interests of the greatest number, surely everyone must recognize it as right and just?

The great mistake here is *confusing what I would accept on my own behalf with what I would accept in competition with others*, and after all, markets, which are meant to promote efficiency, posit a Hobbesian war of all against all in which competition is the natural state. There is no supposition of altruism in the invisible hand argument.[2]

Like the normative basis of markets, the root of this fallacy about efficiency lies in utilitarianism. John Stuart Mill claimed 'that happiness is a good: that each person's happiness is a good to that person, and the general happiness, therefore, a good to the aggregate of all persons'.[3] It is the jump from the second to the third premiss that is faulty. In the extreme, it might increase the general happiness of a fascist society for a particular race to be exterminated, and in Mill's syllogism it would therefore be a good to the aggregate of all persons, including the members of that race. Clearly that does not mean that each person's happiness or good will have been increased.

The problem is particularly acute when the good in question is health care. It is not clear how I am supposed to benefit from a system which maximizes efficiency if I am one of those denied treatment in the name of overall utility. Perhaps I would prefer improving family doctor services *for myself* to maintaining acute services at my local hospital, if I had a chronic condition which my general practitioner knew and treated well, if I had several small children with lots of coughs or sneezes, or if I were unfamiliar with Pascal's wager! But it does not follow that I would rationally prefer improved GP services *for you*.[4]

'The utilitarian principle is concerned with the interests of the majority, but justice is concerned with the interests of each person equally.'[5] A common philosophical argument against utilitarianism is that it disadvantages minorities.[6] Whatever the merits and demerits of this argument as a general proposition, it has a particular and distinctive force where health issues are concerned. Services for particularly vulnerable groups – the elderly, the mentally ill, those with HIV infection or disability, the dying – may well lose out in market forms of health provision. Women are particularly disadvantaged by low resources for the elderly and the mentally ill, so not only minorities suffer under market forms of provision: women form the majority in those groups. All is rarely rosy for non-acute and community services under any system of health-care resource allocation, but one may doubt whether the market will cure disadvantage; it may well worsen it.

This is not the viewpoint of extreme pro-marketeers. In Coase's theorem,[7] the optimal distribution will naturally occur in a free market, there is no need for either state intervention or reference to rights and entitlements. The pure market automatically produces Pareto optimality, so that no one's lot can be improved without worsening someone else's. A similarly optimal position can only be achieved in rights and contract theories through conscious mechanisms, devices such as the Rawlsian veil of ignorance: there is nothing automatic about it.

If Coase is correct, rights become a commodity like any other. As they say in B-grade detective films, 'Sweetheart, anybody can be bought.' Provided that losers are compensated to some degree, they have no absolute rights, beyond perhaps the implicit initial one to equal concern and respect, the bedrock right in Dworkin.[8] This is an important right, but it does not play a major part in neo-classical economics. Thus market efficiency is judged in neo-classical economic theories, such as Coase's, *not by what rights it actually harms* – since rights are a useless fiction – *but by what utility maximization it potentially offers.* This appears at first to be a natural extension of Benthamite utilitarianism, which saw rights as 'nonsense on stilts'. Modern utilitarians have been less ready to condemn the concept of rights altogether. Many view the social concept of rights as one which adds value to life and enables society to rub along nicely, giving it indirect utility. Thus principles about rights will score high on 'acceptance-utility', according to Richard Hare. They will be chosen 'on the ground that they are the set of principles whose general acceptance in the society in question will do the best, all told, for the interests of the people in the society considered impartially.'[9] But for utilitarians there remains nothing particularly remarkable or sacrosanct about rights in themselves: they are at best a convenient fiction which fulfils a social function in our particular society.

However, although they do not regard rights as absolute, market-based theories use the language of rights very freely. The deepest foundations of the ostensibly value-free pro-market outlook are utilitarian, but in a rather confused and contradictory way, the market also embodies contractarian values and harkens back to classic liberal theorists such as Locke in restricting government intervention. Yet the view that rights are a commodity like any other, and not sacrosanct, would be abhorrent to liberals, as would the market philosophy that those who cannot express their wants in price terms have no rights.[10]

(Perhaps the upshot of claiming to be value-free is that one merely becomes confused about one's real values.)

Furthermore, neo-classical economics posits 'bargain and contract [as] . . . the natural ordering principle.'[11] The main form of conflict resolution in the market is negotiation or haggling, the civilized form of Hobbes's 'warre, as if of every man, against every man',[12] rather than administrative *diktat*, as in hierarchies. Meaningful negotiation requires some semblance of equal power. In classical contract theory, individuals in the state of nature are equal in their power to threaten each other's property, particularly property in the person, to kill each other; this is what motivates them to form the social contract. In current civil society there is clearly no such equality.

Markets and Political Theory: Accountability and Distributive Justice

I have argued that market theory is not value-free, but rests on a shaky construction of opposing ethical viewpoints, utilitarianism and contractarianism. Whether the market is efficient is similarly not merely a question of fact, but also of value. It was over both the efficiency and the desirability of market mechanisms that Marx and Weber differed so radically, and their disagreement was not merely the stuff of statistics but also of political theory. Whereas Marx saw market competition as tending unalterably and balefully towards static concentration and monopoly,[13] Weber presented it as the engine of capitalist dynamism. The market is seen in Weber as a key countervailing power to the state, in Marx as another form of oppression.

These debates are no 'mere' history; as Keynes said, self-styled practical men are usually slaves to some dead theorist.[14] Weber's belief that the top management of socialized or nationalized enterprises inevitably becomes bureaucratic[15] is the intellectual precursor of the proposals in the 1989 UK government white paper *Working for Patients*.[16] Only by injection of mechanisms such as Medical Audit, the Resource Management Initiative and a general NHS management executive, that report implied, could the dead hand of NHS bureaucracy be transformed into the beneficent invisible hand of liberal economics. This was to be done through the creation of an internal market, separating the funding of health care from its provision. Similarly, in Weber the market is seen as a means of democratic accountability, raising an effective barrier against too much power for state officialdom.

But do markets actually empower 'ordinary people' and bestow freedom of choice? Only if they enhance accountability. This requires, first, that information should be decentralized, enabling people to make something approaching a rational decision. In the British system, in practice, patients seem to be getting less information rather than more. This is alleged by some to be deliberate management policy. According to the British Medical Association, consultants have been ordered by managers not to reveal the lengths of hospital waiting lists or the numbers of patients whom they have contracted to treat in each specialism for each year.[17] Patients no longer have the freedom to choose from any hospital or consultant to whom their family physician recommends them: they will be limited to hospitals with whom their doctor (if a fundholder) or their district health authority holds a contract. None of this looks like greater freedom and accountability: rather, less autonomy and more paternalism – though perhaps from managers rather than medics.

This is largely the case in the more market-led US system, where who gets treatment is effectively decided by health-plan managers, hospital administrators, directors of Health Maintenance Organizations, insurance company executives and officials of companies providing insurance plans or HMO membership to their employees. The decision as to whom *not* to treat is made in the first instance on the basis of who is covered by one of these categories, who is not a player in the market; the rest form the 37 million Americans with no health-care provision. The Clinton proposals would bring this group into the decision-making process, but that process would probably remain managerial rather than popular.

Second, in order for markets to empower individuals, purchasing power must be spread along with information. For example, education vouchers, according to their proponents, would enable the educationally disadvantaged to communicate through price mechanisms. The Clinton proposals for a basic benefit package in an insurance-based system also appear to embody this modified-market approach. But much hinges on exactly how comprehensive the benefit package and the resource allocation turn out to be.

In the UK, patients are *less* free under the internal market to choose where they obtain treatment than they were under the old centralized system. In advocating an internal market the Conservative government stressed the freedom of patients to 'shop around'.[18] In practice a considerable or even greater degree of central allocation remains. The district health authority and budget-holding family doctors receive funding for their patients from central government, and then purchase services prospectively from provider hospitals. If a DHA or a fundholder does not have a contract with a particular hospital, patients can no longer ask to be referred there. Allowing patients to 'shop around' would require their home authorities to reimburse them retrospectively; the UK government has not chosen to grasp this particular nettle. Decisions are not actually made by individual 'customers' in the internal-market NHS: rather by district health authorities and fund-holding general practitioners acting on behalf of patients, paternalistically, and arguably less on the basis of beneficence than of cost-effectiveness.[19]

No health-care delivery system will ever abolish paternalism altogether, or achieve the sort of allocation which rational contractors might agree. In health-care markets there will always be particular reasons why consumers rely unduly on doctors, and perhaps in an even more personal and emotional way on nurses. Patients are uncertain about what treatments are available and how well those treatments will work; lack of information is exacerbated by stress, fear, and the thousand natural shocks that flesh is heir to, but against which the model economic man is immune. In addition, some patients may want to shift the burden of risk-bearing on to the health-care professional,[20] although more and more patients now want to take responsibility for their own treatment and to be in a position to give a truly informed consent. (For example, three-quarters of the patients in a recent survey of 262 people seeing a specialist at an out-patients' clinic wanted as much information as possible about their condition, against only 8 per cent who preferred to leave matters in the doctor's hands.[21]

The problem is that although they are 'sold' as promoting autonomy and rational choice, markets in health care actually increase people's vulnerability rather than lessen it. The Clinton proposals do not alter the fundamentally market-based orientation of the US system, and they have been criticized for exaggerating the two-tier structure, leaving the worse-off still vulnerable. Markets in health care increase the uncertainty and risk for the most vulnerable sectors of the community: children in need of specialist services, or patients in intensive care, where the costs are often greatest for those with the worst outcomes.[22] Intensive care unit patients who are later declared 'not for resuscitation' use the most resources of all.[23] As is already occurring in the US under the impact of Diagnosis-Related Groups,[24] hospitals in the UK may decide that limiting the quantity of intensive care beds is a better bet than continuing to treat large numbers of high-cost critically ill patients. But productive efficiency is not the criterion by which doctors or patients should judge critical care, I would argue.

It is becoming increasingly clear in the UK that money is not following many of the most critically ill patients, such as children with leukaemia or cystic fibrosis.[25] Many district health authorities in the UK have taken the easiest route to market, making block contracts with their local hospitals without taking account of the interests of patients with specialist needs beyond the capacity of the district hospitals. The Clinical Standards Advisory Group, set up by the Department of Health to monitor the internal market, has embarrassed the government by reporting that vulnerable children are indeed disadvantaged by the internal market. The principle of competition between hospitals is largely incompatible with justice for acutely ill patients, the committee held.

This is not merely inefficient allocation of resources, which could be rectified by a more sensitive decision-making procedure. The injustice is inherent in a market approach which sets the highest value on efficiency. In terms of cost-effectiveness, it may well be right for purchasers to minimize administrative costs and time spent on deciding special cases. But in terms of justice as fairness it is not.

It is difficult to see how anyone in the Rawlsian original position could consent in advance, behind the veil of ignorance, to a system which would discriminate against children with leukaemia or cystic fibrosis. This is so even if one accepts that it may be rational to accept in advance a greater degree of risk that Rawls allows. Rawls's critics have alleged that it could be perfectly prudent to accept a slave system from behind the veil if the rewards of *not* being a slave were sufficient to offset the risk. But Rawlsian contractors are all adults. If I consent in advance to a system in which I may not grow up to become a contractor, a logical absurdity results.

The fact that internal markets in health care allocate resources unjustly does not mean that previous systems of allocation were just, of course. To a certain extent in the US, and to a much greater extent in the UK, doctors have always voluntarily limited use of resources by patients, from the level of the individual general practitioner (family doctor)[26] to that of the consultant nephrologist limiting kidney dialysis to the under-65s.[27] Life-saving treatment was more strictly rationed for the elderly than for children or neonates, and limited life-enhancing treatments (elective admissions) were ordered more sparingly than life-saving ones. In the mid-1980s, UK doctors were treating far fewer patients for end-stage renal failure than their US counterparts, as well as performing less coronary artery bypass surgery, administering less chemotherapy for tumors they judged unresponsive, and providing fewer referrals to services for the mentally ill and chronically disabled.[28] The difference is that markets claim to be giving more choice and greater accountability; the old system never claimed to be anything but paternalistic.

Less facetiously, public accountability under the UK internal market has been undermined by direct elimination of popular representation. (Elected local authorities' rights to appoint some DHA members were abolished in *Working for Patients.*) Acting in concert or even without mutual consent, these new undemocratically constituted authorities can also put hospitals out of action without public consultation. The Tomlinson Report on the future of London's hospitals, meant to take between three to six years to implement, is already being pre-empted by DHAs' decisions not to enter into contracts with 'doomed' hospitals.[29]

Moreover, even if Londoners who use both hospital and community services heavily – the elderly, for example – were to be 'fully' compensated for the closure of their local hospital by means of equivalent amounts of cash being diverted into GP practices,[30] there would still be questions about their rights having been violated. Not only would the way in which the decision was made matter, in terms of democratic accountability; no Londoner could be certain that tomorrow she might not need treatment in the new operating theatre at St Bartholomew's – to be closed down under the Tomlinson proposals – more urgently than a prescription from her own physician. She might well choose, if she could, to keep the security of greater certainty of treatment in acute cases, matters of life and death. This would be perfectly rational: according to Pascal's wager, a minuscule chance of an infinite loss – as is her death to the individual patient, if not to society as a whole – cancels out a much higher probability of limited gains: treatment for more minor illness by a family doctor. The right to potentially life-saving treatment at a centre of excellence like Bart's cannot be fully compensated by a better level of primary care for chronic or minor illness.[31]

The problem becomes even more acute if the Londoner in this example has only infrequent contact with her own doctor, but does have an immediate and urgent need for the operation at Bart's. Why should she accept the decision to close the operating theatre as just and fair, if it hurts her? As I argued in the first section, no individual is obliged to accept an allocation of resources which disadvantages her, in the name of majority interests.

In this second section I have argued that the interests of the majority are also threatened by market mechanisms, or more precisely, that the market undermines democratic accountability, which is designed to ensure that majority interests *are* served.

Alternative Forms of Resource Allocation

Advocates of the internal market might reply that health needs are a bottomless pit, and that no one's rights are absolute, since demands for health care can be infinitely expandable. If this is so, some form of rationing is inevitable. Of course the *particular* forms of rationing which we are now experiencing are not really inevitable, merely the product of a higher governmental priority on funding other areas than health. But this does not obviate the need for theories of resource allocation, and the market does not have a monopoly there.

Arguments based on rationality or efficiency alone can't get there from here, as it were. Although extreme advocates of pure markets such as Coase claim that moral concepts like rights are superfluous, it is impossible to explain why any individual should accept allocation by market principles, utilitarian dicta about efficiency, or any other distributive mechanism without invoking some theory of justice, entitlements and the social good. Indeed, I have tried to argue that the proponents of the market must acknowledge their own theoretical ancestors, although a cynical wit might doubt whether their pedigree was entirely on the right side of the blanket. In that bloodline there is a certain amount of miscegenation between contract theory and utilitarianism.

Several contending criteria for allocating scarce health care resources[32] have been offered by medical ethicists and political philosophers:

1 *Clinical criteria*, subdivided into:
   (a) *Prognosis*: the resource should go to those with the best chance of recovery (of utilizing the input with maximum productive efficiency);
   (b) *Diagnosis*: the resource should go to those whose clinical need is the most acute, even if their chances of recovery are not great.
2 *Social criteria*, subdivided into:
   (a) *Past merit* or 'social worth';
   (b) *Future merit* or 'potential contribution'.
3 *Equality*: everyone should be treated equally in deciding how to share out the resource, regardless of need or merit, and certainly regardless of ability to pay. This criterion leads to a policy of randomizing allocation, or, less stringently, to allocating resources on a first-come-first-served basis.

In the discussion which follows I shall treat both subdivisions of clinical criteria together, although in emotive terms they pack very different punches. The recent death of 5-year-old Laura Davis, born with short-bowel syndrome, whose prognosis was never anything but poor, illustrates the popular appeal of allocating resource according to need rather than chance of recovery. Those in greatest medical need of a resource by *diagnosis* may well not be the most savable in terms of *prognosis*. This relates to the issue of triage, which will be discussed at greater length when I come to social criteria.

The appeal of a 'purely' clinical set of criteria is that it supposedly bypasses subjective moral considerations and produces an impersonal form of distributive justice. Like the utilitarian calculus to which it is philosophically indebted, it claims to be objective. Some subjectivity may enter in through devices such as 'quality-adjusted life years' (QALYs), or the telephone polling by which members of the Oregon public were asked to rate the importance of various medical procedures for Medicare funding. But broadly speaking, the clinical model interprets the Aristotelian dictum on justice (treating likes alike) by treating as likes those potential recipients 'who are equal with respect to exterior, observable, therapy-related criteria. The criteria are applied unswervingly and damn the implications for general equality.'[33]

Why should there be any implications for general equality? Surely medical need is blind, and decision according to medical need impartial? Unfortunately not: models of allocation according to medical need have been shown in several separate studies to disadvantage patients of the 'wrong' class, race or sex.

The class point is the easiest to see. In a case at the Churchill Hospital in Oxford, the dialysis treatment of Derek Spence, a vagrant kidney patient, was terminated because he was judged not to be fully *compos mentis*, and therefore unable to follow the diet and other requirements for successful treatment. There was considerable conflict over the decision between nurses, who wanted to continue dialysis despite the patient's abusive manner towards them, and physicians, who viewed treatment as a waste of resources. (It has been alleged that medical criteria for allocation generally discriminate against the mentally ill.[34])

This was a case of ending treatment rather than deciding not to initiate it, and might be judged to require higher standards (though not by all commentators, many of whom maintain that there is little ethical difference between terminating care and not offering it in the first place[35]). But the 1986 American case of Baby Jesse illustrates a decision not to initiate treatment, on supposedly clinical justifications which turned out to have an unwitting class bias.

Baby Jesse was a potential heart transplant candidate who met the preliminary criteria on medical grounds. But his parents, unmarried teenagers with a criminal history and drug abuse problems, were judged unlikely to provide the necessary follow-up for the cardiac transplant, such as punctual administration of immunosuppressive medications. The clinicians who rejected Baby Jesse as a transplant candidate were accused of discriminating on social grounds, though they maintained that they were allocating the extremely scarce resource of infant hearts according to purely medical criteria.[36]

Furthermore, it turns out – through one of luck's little ironies – that a purely medical set of criteria for organ allocation benefits whites disproportionately. Histocompatibility makes a successful graft more likely, and for that reason the US Task Force on Organ Transplantation used a criterion for transplants of a six-HLA antigen match and no mismatches.[37] But it is more difficult to obtain six antigen matches in Afro-Caribbeans: statistically, whites are more readily typed by tissue match. Medical advisability is not a straightforward criterion which can eliminate the quirks of chance and avoid questions of justice.

This point emerges most strongly in relation to gender. A study of 87 US treatment centres for end-stage renal failure found that three out of four patients selected for dialysis were male.[38] Ninety-two per cent of those treated were white, but although very slightly disproportionate to the 88 per cent of the population who were Caucasian, this figure was nothing like as skewed as the male–female ratio. All but eight of these centres used mainly 'medical' criteria, and allowed doctors to decide without reference to a lay committee or any other body. This gender bias is all the harder to believe given that women's longer life span means that more potential life-years can be gained by preferring a woman patient to a man of the same age and prognosis. Since women are much more prone to urinary tract infection, which can produce chronic renal failure, there is little reason to think that men made up three out of every four patients who presented with end-stage renal failure. Whether consciously or unconsciously, doctors deciding on the primary basis of 'medical need' were in fact preferring men over women.

This begins to merge into a discussion of social criteria. Even decisions made on ostensibly medical grounds are usually coloured to some extent by social considerations, consciously or unconsciously (as in the case of Derek Spence).

In the study of the 87 centres, which revealed that three-quarters of the scarce resource of dialysis was given to under half of the population (men), leaving the decision up to physicians was actually no guarantee that clinical criteria would predominate. Some centres admitted to administering IQ tests and personality inventories, perhaps trying to add a spurious scienticism to 'gut reactions'.

A related issue in social criteria for resource allocation is triage. The classic example of triage embodied conflict over justice and distribution within the medical profession: between the medical officer in charge of the US North African forces in World War II and a consultant surgeon, over whether scarce penicillin should be given to venereal disease sufferers rather than to men wounded in battle, on the efficiency grounds that the VD victims could be more quickly returned to active service. That the VD victims won out goes against our intuitive sense that those honourably wounded in battle merited the scarce resource more. Deciding in their favour would have been on the grounds of *past merit* or social worth. But the VD sufferers could make a *future contribution* more readily, with less input of scarce medical resource.

The most famous and open use of social criteria was by the Seattle 'God' Committee. In the 1960s Dr Belding Scribner, who had developed a semi-permanent shunt which enabled patients to be dialysed repeatedly without successive surgery, established a secret committee of seven laypersons and physicians to ration use of what was then an expensive and innovatory technique. Preliminary 'medical' guidelines increased the proportion of those rejected for dialysis from one in fifty to one in four, although many of those clinical criteria, as is their wont, were actually highly arbitrary. (No children were accepted, for example, and no patients over 45.) Patients deemed psychologically incapable of coping with the treatment regime were also ruled out.

This left three out of four candidates to be considered for 'social worth'. No criminals or prostitutes were treated; college education, church membership, civic leadership, and high earning capacity all counted in a patient's favour. The members of the committee were rarely in doubt over who was most socially worthy: the clerical representative said, 'Oddly enough, in the choices I have made the correct decision appeared quite clear to me in each case.'[39] The labour leader stated that he gave preference to religious candidates with large families.

Just because social values do often enter surreptitiously into clinical criteria does not mean that we should legitimize them in the operations of such a committee.[40] But many people who would accept that proposition may none the less feel that curtailing health care for the very old is justifiable on the grounds of their minimal *potential contribution* to society. Whereas past merit is unacceptable to almost everyone, many people accept future merit as having some bearing. But should they?

Physicians and nurses owe no less a duty of care to elderly patients than to neonates, but the cost of maintaining the elderly is high. In a time of growing numbers of elderly people and stable or declining spending, we may expect to see an increase in the use of potential contribution as a criterion for rationing scarce resources. As previously 'extraordinary measures' of life support become ordinary, as the interval between terminal diagnosis and death lengthens, 'the death-avoiding therapies . . . can become like food, a kind of medical sustenance the withdrawal of which leads unfailingly to early death'.[41] Further, if we accept curtailing resources for those who can no longer contribute to society, we should be all the more disposed towards cutting short the lives of those who will never be able to contribute much in conventional terms: handicapped neonates, for example.

So far there is, happily, little indication of any such developments in healthcare law. Although some commentators wrongly regarded it as opening the floodgates to mass euthanasia of the 'unfit', the *Bland* decision[42] of 1993 in the UK actually went the other way: regarding nasogastric feeding tubes not as ordinary nursing care, but as an extraordinary medical intervention. Nor was Tony Bland's inability to contribute to society so long as he lay in a persistent vegetative state an issue in the case. The resource issue has weighed more heavily in similar US decisions, since the cost of maintaining the patient must often be borne by the family there (unless it is covered by Medicaid or insurance). But US case law is actually more restrictive than *Bland* in so far as it requires evidence of what the PVS victim would have wanted.[43]

If clinical criteria are unable to remain purely objective, still less, of course, can social criteria for allocation of scarce health care resources escape being ethical judgements. Only the criterion of *equality* overtly recognizes ethical considerations, tackling them head-on through the assertion of equal rights inhering in all patients simply by virtue of their common humanity. Even medical criteria deny this premiss; but after all, people do not choose to be ill (though they may sometimes choose behaviours that lead statistically to illness). Therefore even those with a poor prognosis are victims of discrimination if denied life-sustaining resources in favour of someone with a better clinical outlook. 'Why, after all, should their shorter lives be measured against lives that would have been longer from no merit of their own?'[44] Clinical merit is as much conferred by chance as is social merit, this radical egalitarian argument runs.

The Seattle 'God' Committee members stated that they would have felt irresponsible if they had resorted to a lottery for choosing dialysis recipients. But in legal-ethical terms, lotteries have been held fairer than social criteria when there is conflict of life with life. In *US* v. *Holmes* (1841), the presiding judge ruled that a surviving crew member, Holmes, should not have collaborated with his shipmates in devising and implementing social criteria for deciding who among a shipwreck's survivors should be thrown off a lifeboat in order to lighten its load. Despite his counsel's contention that the crew's method of selection – 'not to part man and wife, and not to throw over any woman' – was more humane than a lottery, Holmes was convicted of unlawful homicide. In the judge's opinion, only casting lots would have been a remedy which the law could sanction: 'In no other way than this or some like way are those having equal rights put on an equal footing, and in no other way is it possible to guard against partiality and oppression, violence and conflict.'[45] Holmes and his shipmates failed to achieve the most efficient or meritorious allocation, in any case: two women jumped overboard to die with their brother.

In this century, several medical ethicists have proposed a modified form of randomized allocation, usually after some debatable elimination through medical criteria of those patients with little or no chance of recovery.[46] What makes this retention of some clinical judgement debatable, of course, is the element of uncertainty in prognosis, of subjectivity in clinical criteria, and of possible benefit to even a terminal patient of a few extra days in which to finish unfinished business. (Indeed, one medical ethicist is willing to give *greater* weight to the desire for life in the patient with a shorter expectation of it.[47]) Thus Rawls writes,

> [W]hen there are many equally strong claims which if taken together exceed what can be granted, some fair plan should be adopted so that all are equitably considered. In simple cases of claims to goods that are indivisible or fixed in number, some rotation or lottery scheme may be the fair solution when the number of equally valid claims is too great.[48]

But could a lottery system ever be practical? A new genetically engineered drug to treat multiple sclerosis, betasteron, is being distributed in the USA through a nationwide lottery involving a waiting list of 57,000 patients. Medical criteria are used initially to restrict eligibility for the lottery: patients must be able to walk at least 100 yards and must have the relapsing-remitting form of the disease. A tracking system guards against attempts by wealthy patients to buy extra lottery tickets. 'Most of my patients are accepting the wait pretty well', commented one neurologist, 'because there is an element of fairness in a lottery'.[49]

As markets publicize resource shortfall and encourage referrals on the 'buy now and avoid the rush principle', however, lotteries tend to attract attention.[50] If it became known that hospitals were allocating life and death on a random basis, through a lottery or first-come-first-served procedure, fewer people might bequeath their kidneys, feeling that their gift of potential life was not being treated with due gravity and gratitude.

Conversely, however, power-holders might do their damnedest to lessen scarcity of medical resources if they had to take their chances in a lottery, rather than being favoured by decision procedures based consciously or unconsciously on social merit. Lotteries have the virtue of putting pressure on authorities to allocate more resource, whereas acceptance of medical or social criteria effectively blames the patient for failure to receive the scarce resource. In 1953 the UK Ministry of Health instituted a national lottery by birth date to allocate what was then the scarce resource of polio vaccine. Many families were able to vaccinate some of their children but not others. The resultant public outcry helped to make the vaccine more widely available.[51]

Elsewhere I have argued that we need to make some exceptions to the principle of randomisation.[52] First, in cases where the scarce resource is nurse time, we must consider the nurse as an autonomous moral agent who can experience regret and remorse. She is not at all the same as an ampoule of penicillin, and we must think about how to respect her as well as the patient. Starting from the principle of equality is generally correct, but the applications are sometimes startling. For example, nurses normally prioritize dying elderly patients on general wards over less acute cases.[53] A dying patient gets more than an equal share of the nurse's scarce time. I think this is right and proper, although it certainly fails the clinical criterion of favourable prognosis or the social one of future contribution, and it invades the egalitarian principle of randomness.

The second area in which exceptions might be argued is the choice between giving the resource to a 70-year-old or a 20-year-old. Most people find the answer obvious enough, but on the whole I am inclined to say they should have equal chances. (I would not agree that the 70-year-old has a *greater* right.) Both may have an equal desire to live, although admittedly that is not the only factor which we have to consider. There is also the good of living beyond 20, and the distress to the younger person's family. But this second argument, about family bereavement, is clearly wrong. We would not say that a 20-year-old with no family should have a lesser claim to the resource than a 20-year-old with hordes of adoring kin.

The good of living beyond 20 is a pricklier issue. In Veatch's view justice as fairness demands,

> that persons be given an opportunity to have well-being over a lifetime equal to that of others. This means that infants, who have had no opportunity for well-being, would get a higher priority than older persons who have had many good years of life.[54]

But what if the years have not been good, or are just becoming so? The fact that people in modern western societies *do* normally live to a statistical average of 70 (longer for women, though this is not taken into account by those who would ration resources by age) says nothing at all about whether they *should* live beyond 70. To argue otherwise is a form of the naturalistic fallacy, the common assumption that something that is natural is also morally right. To put the matter in Rawlsian terms, youth is not a form of desert any more than is intelligence or class.

The third exception to random allocation might be the case of a patient with dependants. Here duty rather than desert is the issue, and the need of others rather than their bereavement. In the case of a mother with young children, Jonathan Glover, though favouring random allocation in many cases, acknowledges that 'refusal to depart from random choice when knowledge about their dependants is available is to place no value on avoiding the additional misery caused to the children if the mother is not the one saved.'[55]

John Harris feels that Glover's preference for saving those with dependants is a form of discrimination favouring parents. '[T]his looks very much like a covert grading of people into the "haves" and the "have-nots" – those who have dependants and those who don't.'[56] Harris even speculates that people might 'acquire' children in order to benefit from 'a relatively cheap form of insurance against a low-priority rating in the rescue stakes'. But having children is extremely expensive, particularly for women, in terms of lost earnings. Nor are children merely a possession, as Harris implies. I would make exceptions to random allocation of scarce resources for mothers and some fathers of dependent children, and for women and some men over 45, the even larger group of carers for elderly or handicapped relatives.

Although markets claim to be both objective and fair, I have argued that they are neither. Allocation by the egalitarian principle of randomization best meets the deontological criterion of respect for persons. Even some consequentialists agree that the fallibility of the utilitarian calculus in life-and-death matters makes random selection the fairest procedure.[57] Although lotteries are not rational in their operations, they are profoundly just.

NOTES

1 Virginia Bottomley, London, March 1993.
2 For an interesting reformulation of economic theory to incorporate altruism, see David Collard, *Altruism and Economy: a Study in Non-Selfish Economics*.
3 John Stuart Mill, *Utilitarianism* cited in Anne Haydock, 'QALYs – a threat', p. 185.
4 A similar argument is made in relation to QALYs (quality-adjusted life years) by John Harris in 'QALYfying the value of life'.
5 Downie, 'Traditional medical ethics and economics in health care', p. 51.
6 The best-known version of this criticism is probably that made by John Rawls in *A Theory of Justice*.
7 Coase, 'The problem of social cost'.
8 Dworkin, *Taking Rights Seriously*. 'In practice economists recommend policies which are only *potential* Pareto improvements. Most economists view actual compensation as irrelevant to optimality' (Hanly, 'The problem of social cost', 1992, p. 80, original emphasis).
9 Hare, *Moral Thinking: Its Levels, Method and Point*, p. 156.
10 For a useful stylized comparison of the normative bases of markets, hierarchies and networks, see Walter W. Powell, 'Neither market nor hierarchy', table 1.
11 E. Miller, 'Economic efficiency', at p. 722, cited in Hanly, 'Problem of social cost', p. 82.
12 Thomas Hobbes, *Leviathan*, Part I, ch. 13.
13 For interpretations of Marx's theory of concentration of production and the resulting crises of capitalism, see: Held, *Models of Democracy*, pp. 111–12; Sweezy, *The Theory of*

Capitalist Development; Mattick, *Marx and Keynes*; and Fine and Harris, *Rereading Capital.*

14 Keynes, *The General Theory of Employment, Interest and Money*, ch. 24, v.

15 Weber, *Economy and Society*, vol. II, p. 1402.

16 HMSO, *Working for Patients*. The 'provider market' in *Working for Patients* is of course only one type of market, in one sector of the economy (the public one) and my discussion does not pre-empt the question of how efficient other types of market may be.

17 Mihill, 'Waiting list facts "denied to patients"'. Northwick Park Hospital in Middlesex wrote to its consultants, 'Patients should . . . never be given information about districts and contracting, and GPs should only be given information on these grounds where absolutely necessary.'

18 This was somewhat different from the 'market socialism' form of internal market envisaged by A. C. Enthoven, who popularized the term 'internal market' in his 1985 paper *Reflections on the Management of the National Health Service.*

19 For further discussion of these two types of reimbursement and the corresponding 'type 1' and 'type 2' forms of the internal market, see Penelope M. Mullen, 'The NHS White Paper and internal markets', p. 19.

20 Mooney and McGuire, 'Economics and medical ethics in health care', p. 8.

21 *Which?* magazine, survey by the Consumers' Association, 7 February 1991.

22 Seitovsky, 'The high cost of dying'. See also Coulton, 'Resource limits and allocation in critical care', p. 88.

23 Younger, Lewandowski, McClish *et al.*, 'The incidence and implications of DNR orders in a medical intensive care unit'.

24 DRGs were introduced by the Reagan administration in 1983 to control Medicare and Medicaid costs by changing payment from retrospective to prospective. The amount paid to hospitals in advance of services rendered is specified by the classification of the patient's illness into one of 467 diagnosis-related groups.

25 This was the conclusion of the Clinical Standards Advisory Group, established in 1991 by the Department of Health as a panel of doctors considering four types of specialist services: neonatal intensive care, cystic fibrosis treatment, care of childhood leukaemia sufferers, and coronary bypass surgery (Mihill, 'NHS policy changes "put patients at risk"').

26 Raanan Gillon, in 'Ethics, economics and general practice', gives many specific examples of this self-restraint.

27 Challah, Wing, Bauer, Morris and Shroeder, 'Negative selection of patients for dialysis and transplantation in the UK'. In this study, a questionnaire containing sixteen case histories of patients with end-stage renal failure was sent to a large number of British and American GPs, consultants and specialist nephrologists for their opinion on the appropriateness of dialysis or transplantation. The UK GPs and consultants rejected a significantly higher number of cases than did the UK nephrologists, although even they rejected a mean of 4.7 cases, against 0.3 for US nephrologists.

28 Aaron and Schwartz, *The Painful Prescription: Rationing Hospital Care.*

29 Sheldon, 'London HAs jump the ministerial gun'.

30 Of course this would be highly problematic: to start, we would also have to weigh in the costs of the 30,000 staff whose jobs are at risk from the London health changes, according to a secret brief allegedly produced by the Department of Health and leaked by the Confederation of Health Service Employees (Travis, 'Hospitals must wait to know fate').

John and Gillian Yudkin, respectively a professor of medicine and a GP, argue further that 'acute hospital beds are merely one of the places where people end up when all else fails . . . [T]here is an overall deficit of 1.6 beds per 1,000 population in inner London, perhaps explaining why most hospitals are on yellow alert and why GPs are having to use the Emergency Bed Service even before the Tomlinson Report is implemented: acute hospital beds are serving a function which is not being provided elsewhere' (letter to the *Guardian*, 21 January 1993).

31 For a similar point in a different context, see Guido Calabresi and Philip Bobbitt, *Tragic Choices*, p. 84.

32 This is what Calabresi and Bobbitt term the 'second-order' question of how to distribute the resource, rather than the 'first-order' determination of how much of it to produce or allocate in the first place (*Tragic Choices*, p. 19).

33 Ibid., p. 184.

34 Pattison and Armitage, 'An ethical analysis of the policies of British community and hospital care for mentally ill people'.

35 The viewpoint of the twenty doctors, nurses, lawyers, ethicists and health-care administrators who produced the Hastings Center, *Guidelines on the Termination of Life-sustaining Treatment and the Care of the Dying*; see p. 130.

36 Veatch, *Death, Dying and the Biological Revolution*, pp. 208–9.

37 US Task Force on Organ Transplantation, *Organ Transplantation: Issues and Recommendations*, p. 87.

38 Katz and Procter, *Social-psychological Characteristics of Patients Receiving Hemodialysis Treatment*, reported in Winslow, *Triage and Justice*, p. 16.

39 Winslow, *Triage and Justice*, p. 15.

40 For the opposite argument, see Leo Shatin, 'Medical care and the social worth of a man'.

41 Baumrin, 'Putting them out on the ice: curtailing care of the elderly', p. 155.

42 *Airedale NHS Trust* v. *Bland*, Law Lords' decision of 4 February 1993, reported in the *Guardian*, 5 February 1993.

43 For example, in the 1990 case of Nancy Cruzan, another PVS victim, the US Supreme Court required 'clear and convincing evidence' of previous statements by the victim concerning withdrawal of life support in the event of an accident.

44 Calabresi and Bobbitt, *Tragic Choices*, p. 182.

45 *US* v. *Holmes*, 26 Fed. Cas. 360 (1841).

46 For example, Veatch (*Death, Dying*, p. 206) thinks that 'people in equal need of an organ ought to have an equal shot at it even if one potential recipient would be more likely to make a socially worthwhile contribution'. Other scholars have proposed some form of randomization in allocating scarce resources, usually either a lottery or a system of first-come-first served; their works include: Winslow, *Triage and Justice*; Paul A. Freund, 'Introduction', *Daedalus*, spring 1969, p. xiii; Childress, 'Who shall live when not all can live?' Outka, 'Social justice and equal access to health care'; Green, 'Health care and justice in contract theory perspective', pp. 111–26; and Dickenson, *Moral Luck in Medical Ethics and Practical Politics*. Most of these texts concern issues around transplantation, but I also extend the principle of equality through randomization to the allocation of nurse time (in my 'Nurse time as a scarce health care resource').

47 Harris, *The Value of Life*, p. 89.

48 Rawls, *A Theory of Justice*, p. 374.

49 Martin Walker, 'Luck of the draw for MS drug', *Guardian*, 8 January 1994.

50 Calabresi and Bobbitt, *Tragic Choices*, p. 189.
51 Hinds, 'On the relations of medical triage to world famine', pp. 38–9.
52 Dickenson, *Moral Luck in Medical Ethics*, p. 64ff.
53 See Veatch and Fry, *Case Studies in Nursing Ethics*, case 23, 'Allocating nursing time according to benefit', p. 84ff.
54 Veatch, *Death, Dying and the Biological Revolution*, pp. 204–5.
55 Glover, *Causing Death and Saving Lives*, p. 222.
56 Harris, *The Value of Life*, p. 105.
57 See, for example, Glover, *Causing Death and Saving Lives*, pp. 218 and 223.

READING GUIDE

Typically the problem of scarce resources is treated as part of the general question of distributive justice by philosophers. Several standard works in medical ethics include chapters under that or a similar title. Utilitarian reasoning is applied in Jonathan Glover's *Causing Death and Saving Lives* and to a lesser extent in John Harris's *The Value of Life*. Both Glover and Harris offer some surprising prescriptions, particularly in relation to rationing by age, although Harris backtracks somewhat to what he calls a 'fair innings' argument.

Largely deontological accounts of distributive justice include the appropriate chapters in Thomas Beauchamp and James Childress, *Principles of Biomedical Ethics* (3rd edition, 1989); Donna Dickenson, *Moral Luck in Medical Ethics and Practical Politics*; and Robert M. Veatch, *Death, Dying and the Biological Revolution*. This last source also illustrates the overlap between distributive justice and the literature on euthanasia and termination of care. Issues about rationing of scarce resources impact on prolonging life when there is little hope of cure.

Health economics tends to take rationing as a proven requirement, in a way that philosophers do not (or at least should not, I would argue). A more philosophical introduction to health economics can be found in chapter 17 of Robin Downie and Kenneth Calman's *Healthy Respect*.

Specific issues within health-care resource allocation frequently come to the fore, attract considerable media attention, and then lapse again into obscurity, In the past particular scrutiny has been paid to kidney transplants, out of all proportion to the number of cases. Issues around arbitrary procedures for deciding on who gets resuscitation, far more important in numerical terms, are now beginning to attract more attention, particularly in relation to recent findings that people with AIDS are more likely to be pressured not to choose resuscitation than are other patients with less stigmatizing illnesses.

An incisive exploration of issues of gender, race and class discrimination in access to health care can be found in Susan Sherwin's *No Longer Patient: Feminist Ethics and Health Care*, chapter 11.

16

Liberty or Community? Defining the Post-Marxist Agenda

Brenda Almond

It is one of the ironies of history that just as defenders of liberty in the western nations were celebrating the triumph of their ideas in Eastern Europe, the cries of 'Viva libertas' were increasingly being drowned by the voices of critics within their own societies. Even erstwhile libertarians, appalled by the crumbling of the social fabric in some of the liberal democracies, are to be found abandoning their creed in favour of the social market and community action.

On the one hand, a form of conservatism is evolving which is authoritarian in essence. Evincing a Burkean contempt for 'the dust and powder of individuality', this new conservatism rejects liberal philosophical traditions, whether Kantian or utilitarian, as egotistical, self-indulgent and socially destructive.[1] Less surprisingly, the left, regrouping after writing off its recent reverses to Stalinism, is returning to the advocacy of state intervention and social engineering under terms it can share with the conservative right, such as community, empowerment and the promotion of autonomy. While the right promote quality control, good housekeeping, and managerial efficiency, the left monitor equal opportunity and health and safety; desirable though all these goals are, the effect of both approaches, however, is to advance new forms of control over the individual in the workplace, the educational institution and the home, diminishing the scope for genuine enterprise, innovation and imaginative creativity.

The new battles against individual freedom are waged on a number of distinct fronts: conceptual, empirical, and moral. At the conceptual level, there is a dispute about the very meaning of liberalism – its essential or defining features. At the empirical level, people disagree about the descriptive features of liberalism, both actual and possible; while at the philosophical level, liberalism is under challenge as an ethical and political ideal: its desirability and inherent morality are no longer fixed features finding general acceptance by all those involved in the debate.

The Concept of Liberalism

Before discussing some of these divisions, it will be useful to make a few preliminary remarks about the concept of liberalism and its historical origins. Intellectually, liberalism is a doctrine associated with western political thought from the seventeenth century to the present day. Its roots lie in the Enlightenment, in responses to religious persecutions and in anti-monarchical sentiments. It found its concrete expression in the institution of parliamentary government in England, and in the French and American Revolutions. In its origins, it is essentially connected with freedom of thought, religion and conscience. It sought to replace the hegemony of tradition and authority with that of reason, and to base political obligation on the free consent of the individual. It preferred law and constitutional guarantees to arbitrary force, and thus favoured the separation of legal, executive and judicial powers. Individual rights as conceived by social contract theorists such as John Locke (1632–1704) and Jean-Jacques Rousseau (1712–78), and then later the principle of utility as expounded by Jeremy Bentham (1748–1832) and John Stuart Mill (1806–73), provide its philosophical foundations; universal suffrage and democracy are its political expression, and the free market its economic basis. It also involves a certain conception of equality; but this is equality before the law, not equality of possessions or advantages.

In the later phases of the development of the notion, however, the individual at the heart of liberal theory was accorded a need, not merely to be respected – to be left free – by others, and in particular by legal authorities, but also to be 'authentic' – to follow his or her own peculiar tastes and inclinations. Thus was social pluralism born out of the commitment to freedom and toleration. It was this second step that provided the basis for the argument that individuality needs bolstering by state provision of various kinds, leading in the end to the welfarist conceptions of liberalism that are current in contemporary thought.

It need hardly be said that this outcome is in conflict with liberalism's starting-point: state support for the individual in any extended sense involves the raising of taxes, itself an invasion – albeit necessary for some purposes – of the individual's right to hold and retain possessions and to enjoy the fruit of his or her labours; it involves, too, support for the expensive bureaucracy needed for the work of taxation and redistribution, thus greatly increasing the role of the state which liberalism was originally concerned to minimize. 'Liberalism', however, still retains some of its association with the classical conception and is, therefore, a term associated, particularly in Britain, with free market economics and libertarianism. In the United States, in contrast, it is most commonly linked to the promotion of welfare, and community or collective action. The labels, then, may be increasingly inappropriate and unhelpful. What is incontrovertible, however, is that political liberalism continues to be the focus for discussion of political ends and goals.

The Critique of Liberalism

Contemporary criticism of liberalism, whether from left or right, arises from a fundamental malaise occasioned by a general decline in the conditions of life in modern liberal societies – the rootlessness of the privatized individual in a mass society, crime, pornography and the decline of the family – in sum, the moral and cultural vacuum to which some versions of pluralistic liberalism appear to lead.

These factors can plausibly be attributed to a central philosophical weakness in the concept of liberalism, at least as it is commonly understood. This is its commitment to neutrality – neutrality, that is, in relation to competing ends or visions of the good. A liberal society, it is often argued, is one that postulates incommensurable values and rights but no positive principles, its only commitment being to what amounts in the end to a position of moral incoherence. This neutralist (or neutered!) conception of liberalism has been put forward by a number of distinguished proponents in recent years. It is, for example, the essence of the influential theory advanced by John Rawls in *A Theory of Justice* that rational principles for society are to be arrived at by a disembodied and depersonalized individual, from a perspective deliberately stripped bare of context, and detached from any substantive conception of the good – a metaphorical 'veil of ignorance'.[2]

Competing conceptions of the good, according to this account of liberal ideology, are the prerogative of individual consumers, and the function of the political system is merely to guarantee their right to choose amongst these ultimate ends. Ronald Beiner describes this as the 'consumer model' of politics, in contrast to non-consumerist conceptions of human fulfilment which attempt to provide a substantive theory of the human good based on community-oriented goals.[3] Indeed, it is Beiner's view that the dominant philosophical understanding of liberalism current in western societies elevates a lack of *ethos* into a principle for living and that, as Allan Bloom pointed out, even religion and sexual orientation become options in the supermarket of 'life-styles'.[4] This 'minimalist moral vision' instantiates. Beiner comments, just one principle or ideal: the elevation of *choice* to the highest good. He goes on to suggest that the way of life centred on choice, mobility and maximal personal freedom is best illustrated by attitudes to the automobile. Here, perversely, private wants are allowed to supersede a wish, that can only be realized collectively, for an environment not dominated by the needs of the motorized style of life. In other words, and more generally, the liberal puts liberty ahead of perfection.

This is an essentially *ethical* understanding of liberalism, that is to say, an understanding of it as a theory embodying personal ideals and individual goals. Its original orientation, however, was *political.* Liberalism was and is a theory concerned with setting limits to the power of the state *vis-à-vis* the individual, but since the state is not the only source of coercion – advertising, manipulation and false consciousness also play a part – Beiner chooses on the whole to leave this meaning aside, characterizing liberalism instead as 'the regime of the modern bourgeoisie', in Jacob Burckhardt's phrase, an 'epoch of money-making and traffic'.[5] This description points also to the more dominant *economic* interpretation of liberalism as, in its classical formulation, the promotion of the free market as a means to the generation of wealth.

One other defining feature must be added to this portrait: liberalism embodies the ideal of the open society: it promotes social and economic mobility, and it is essentially connected with pluralism. As far as this latter point is concerned, Beiner shares Bloom's view that one feature of the plural society, the new politics of groups and alliances, may in fact be interpreted as a search for community in the lonely moral desert created by liberalism: the 'fragmentation and moral anarchy of a liberal-pluralist universe'.[6]

It is interesting to compare this analysis from the left with that offered from a more conservative perspective by the British philosopher, John Gray. In an essay in the London *Times* (11 October 1993), Gray writes that the enterprise culture has destroyed the bonds of trust and community. He attributes this to the mobility needed by a dynamic market economy which conflicts with the ideal of a settled common life. Thus it has produced a 'weakening or dissolution of the ties of community and the generation of a society of strangers'. It has also, he suggests, replaced the 'ethos of service' with the 'meagre morality of contract'. Commenting on the legacy of Thatcherism, Gray says that while people see the culture of choice and wealth creation as a benign legacy, they fear the erosion of the common environment of public institutions and social practices. Hence the ethos of choice needs, he suggests, to be supplemented by 'a concern for conservation and community'.[7]

Previously a sympathetic exponent of John Stuart Mill whose essay *On Liberty* appeared in 1859, Gray, it seems, now views the author of that classic defence of liberty as the confusing source of two distinct varieties of liberalism: classical and revisionary, both of which are flawed. Gray sees Mill's liberalism as marred in general by its 'sentimental religion of humanity and abstract individualism' and identifies as its two fundamental flaws its conception of individuality and the theory of progress it implies.[8] Of the first of these Gray writes, 'the individuality Mill propagates . . . is a shadow cast by the form of life of the rationalist intelligentsia of late bourgeois Europe . . . the life-style of the anomic Bohemians of the world's great cities'.[9] Of the second, he says that

Mill, led astray by his desire to defend 'experiments in living', failed to realize the importance of convention and tradition as conditions of social progress. There *is* a place for experiment in human life, but such experimentation cannot, Gray argues, be conducted on an individual basis; human life is not long enough and the conditions of life are too arbitrary and contingent. Moreover, people's characters and identities are not purely biologically given; they are shaped by cultural influences. This means that if there are to be experiments with aspects of living, these must be conducted by social groups held together by common traditions and practices and be tried, not over a single lifetime, but over several generations. 'A society', Gray writes, 'without strong conventions would unavoidably be chaotic, resembling not so much the Bohemia which our great cities shelter, but rather a Hobbesian state of nature.'[10]

Whilst acknowledging his debt to conservative thinkers such as Michael Oakeshott and liberals such as Isaiah Berlin, Gray nevertheless sees 'foundationalist' liberalism as having failed, and he recommends salvaging from this failure a more 'civil society'. Such a programme, he believes, could be called 'liberal conservatism'. Rather than making the optimistic assumption, then, that the best ideas and traditions will necessarily filter through, whatever people and their rulers do, Gray sees convention and tradition as the essential conditions of progress. Moreover, freedom is not to be judged, he believes, without judging the value of what it is a person is free to do. Like Beiner, Gray says that it is its attempt to be neutral as regards people's choices of the good that is liberalism's great weakness. On this point, both Beiner and Gray acknowledge their debt to Joseph Raz whose own remarks on this subject are worth quoting: 'Since autonomy is valuable only if it is directed at the good it supplies no reason to provide, nor any reason to protect, worthless let alone bad options.'[11]

Possibly exposing himself to a charge of inconsistency, Gray blames liberalism not only for its commitment to neutrality or impartiality in respect of different views of the good, but also for its claim to adopt a universal standpoint. In place of this 'modernism', Gray proposes a turn to a 'postmodernity' that would reject the 'myths of global progress, of fundamental rights and of a secular movement to a universal civilization'.[12] Universalism would give way to particularity, the 'pursuit of a Hobbesian *modus vivendi*' and a politics of 'compromise, bargaining and, in extremity, the judicious use of force to preserve the peace'.[13]

Accepting the kind of sociological account of ideology that sees liberalism as a passing social phenomenon associated with particular historical periods and locations, Gray sees it as having been unfairly privileged, as having been granted an unjustifiable universal status when in fact it is 'only one among the political forms in which human flourishing may occur'.[14] Indeed, elsewhere he argues that Aristotle's ethics, from which this notion of 'flourishing' is derived, is essentially anti-liberal and anti-individualistic. Preferring virtue and community to individualism and anarchy, he says that 'a liberal order under-mines important virtues, including virtues upon which that order itself depends'.[15]

Gray rejects the conception of liberalism, then, which construes it as a historic and cohesive *intellectual* tradition. Nevertheless, he hopes to retain much of the historic inheritance of liberal *practice*. As Karl Marx (1818–83) did, but Mill did not, Gray holds that theory or ideology is secondary, the stepchild of practice. Mill's neglect of the role of institutions in determining both the growth of knowledge and the growth of wealth is described by Gray as a vast lacuna in Mill's thought.[16] But, of course, Gray's criticism has to be placed alongside the consideration that it is no accident, but rather the essence of Mill's liberalism that he gives primacy to the individual, including the eccentric and the genius, and that he emphasizes the power of ideas to change the world.

Liberalism in Practice

In criticizing liberalism from their different standpoints, both Beiner and Gray draw attention to the facts of life in today's liberal societies. So it is worth reflecting briefly on these descriptive aspects before returning to the question of theory. What are liberal societies really like? Since we are in the habit of hearing or reading favourable comparisons between our own societies and the evils of former communist and socialist regimes – their oppression of the individual, their totalitarian imposition of conformity – it is fair to make the point that other comparisons which are less often heard are more favourable to these regimes. In the 1980s it was, for example, safer to walk the streets of Moscow, Warsaw or Prague than those of New York. Today's liberal societies, if one takes the Unites States as typical, are at the mercy of crime, drug syndicates, and sexual exploitativeness. In addition, a mass culture has evolved which is indifferent alike to intellectual and moral virtue. Homelessness, unem-ployment, inflation, the decline of the family, and a painful struggle for the realignment of gender roles confront liberal societies internally, while exter-nally they face environmental and economic threats of global proportions: war, terrorism, AIDS, and the instability caused by the vast disparity in wealth of North and South.

Today's liberal societies are also characterized by the growth of bureaucracy, a creeping managerialism allied to the promotion of economic growth. The British, in particular, have become increasingly familiar with what seem to be inappropriate applications of managerialism to the provision of health, edu-cation, and transport, not always happy developments in which the traveller, the hospital patient, the university student, are all indiscriminately labelled 'customers', while the number of managers constantly threatens to surpass the number of 'real' workers in any of these fields.

Liberal societies are also widely charged with having created identity problems; modern liberal societies are places where people, having had too *much* choice imposed upon them, no longer know who or what they are. In *After Virtue*, MacIntyre sees unfettered individualism as challenging the natural ties of family, neighbourhood, ethnic and national identity, while Michael Sandel in *Liberalism and the Limits of Justice*, insists that choice is meaningless when it is attached to a 'thin' conception of a person.[17] Only a person with some 'thick' identity – gender, class, ethnicity, and a range of abilities, interests, and desires – can meaningfully be associated with the notion of choice. These critics argue, in other words, that we *derive* our identities from the communities to which we belong, whether these are conceived of on a small scale – the family – or on a larger canvas – race, nation, religion, or political group. It is a composite of these roles that actually constitutes our individual identity. This view of morality and a way of life based on who and what one is – one's place in the community – can be traced back to Hegel's (1770–1831) notion of *Sittlichkeit*. There is an echo, too, of F. H. Bradley's (1846–1924) 'My station and its duties'. But MacIntyre takes it further back still, to the Homeric tradition where duties are specific to one's role: as father, wife, child, leader, soldier, etc.

Must Liberalism Fail?

Whatever the ultimate source of these ideas, no resident of an existing liberal society can deny the force of this critique. What, then, to echo another political thinker, is to be done? There is a general tendency, initiated in a seminal paper by G. E. M. Anscombe[18] to turn to Aristotle for a remedy, first in holding that a philosophical psychology or anthropology is a necessary precursor of any theory that would try to specify how society should be run, and second in advocating a shift away from a Kantian emphasis on rights and individual autonomy. As far as the first is concerned, it is argued that the individual can only be *understood* within the context of a community. As far as the second is concerned, it is argued that it is necessary to move from a purely formal moral philosophy preoccupied with rights, interests, and preferences, to a concern with *ethos*: the formation of character and the creation of community. Beiner, for example, writes, 'It would be insane, theoretically and politically, to regard choice of "lifestyles" as a private affair, not a public affair; for if it is not a matter of public concern whether members of a society are good citizens or bad citizens, what *is* of legitimately public concern?'[19] In similar vein, Gray writes, 'There is here an irresolvable conflict between the claim of individuals to live as they please and the defence of that freedom in terms of cumulative moral knowledge of the conditions of human well-being.'[20] (It is worth noting, however, that Gray's optimism about the possibility of moral knowledge is, surprisingly, combined with a more sceptical or 'postmodern' approach to factual and scientific truth.)

The neo-Aristotelian avowal of the ideal of citizenship, bolstered and promoted by positive moral and cultural educational policies, leads Beiner to seek to replace the idea of social and economic rights with that of citizenship and political enfranchisement or empowerment. There is more than an echo in this last condition of the notion of 'authonomy' which is used by Gray as the basis for his advocacy of 'enabling welfare'. It is not, however, a demand for greater wealth. Indeed, Beiner quotes with approval Alasdair MacIntyre's observation, 'A community which was guided by Aristotelian norms would not only have to view acquisitiveness as a vice but would have to set strict limits to growth.'[21]

There are, of course, other conceptions of liberalism, including the atomistic ultraliberalism of the contemporary American philosopher, Robert Nozick.[22] Both Beiner and Gray, however, in the end reject liberalism in any of its forms. Beiner rejects it for its neutral ethical stance and for its far from neutral economic outlook, which endorses economic growth and technological progress. Gray rejects it in the end for its rationalism, its universalism and what he sees as its antipathy to the notion of community. Advocating a social market economy, he writes, 'One of the basic needs of human beings is membership in a community. Such membership will be stable if, and only if, the community is seen to be meeting basic human needs, through the institutions of the market, and, where these fail, through other institutions, such as the enabling welfare state.'[23]

Is liberalism, then, vulnerable to these criticisms? First, let us consider the general view of these critics that rights-based moral theories are unable to deal with the broader environmental and economic ills confronting nation-states, and that a communitarian approach is needed to cope with a new situation in which technology makes our human fate a shared one. Scientific progress has, it is true, made the world a global village in which environmental dangers and global economic forces alike prevent any nation or group from retreating into the private domains of either consumption or conscience. Yet there is no reason to accept that collective problems should not be tackled by appeal to rights. Environmental threats are, in the end, simply new ways in which the actions of some human beings may cause death or harm to others. No appeal to authority, or to metaphysical claims of community, are needed to suggest that it is right to curb irresponsible environmental policies, whether these stem from firms, multinationals or governments. Even the ultraliberalism of Nozick permits this when the logic of its argument is thought through to its conclusion. In other words, whatever the *practical* difficulties, there is no *ethical* objection from a liberal point of view to intervention by states, or even a supra-state, if one could be created and accepted, to protect some individuals against the life-endangering activities of others.

Similar considerations apply, too, to the social evils within liberal societies that have prompted the move to communitarianism. It is only a thoughtless form of libertarianism that demands freedom to peddle dangerous narcotic drugs to the young, or to *use* drugs which make one into a social danger or at least liability; nor does liberalism demand, as Beiner suggests in his book, freedom for some to infect others with a fatal virus (HIV), nor that films or videos should be freely available if they promote murder, cannibalism, or sexual violence. Without departing from the classical liberalism of John Stuart Mill, one may very plausibly argue that a violent pornographic video in the wrong person's hands is equivalent to shouting 'All corn-merchants are thieves' to an angry mob outside a corn-dealer's house at a time of famine.

Positive Liberalism

Even a minimalist interpretation of liberalism, then, will permit – indeed mandate – action on many of the fronts that arouse the concern of communitarians and advocates of civic virtue. As the contemporary British philosopher Anthony Arblaster writes in his seminal account of liberalism, 'We continue to need the best of liberalism' and radicals and socialists, too, can see the value of such liberal ideals as personal liberty, human rights, and equality of status for all regardless of race or sex. But the challenge for communitarians, as Arblaster sees it, is to find a philosophical basis for human rights and freedoms within a more communitarian philosophy, one which stresses the natural sociability of human nature and the interdependence of human beings.

Communitarianism, then, is compatible with a defence of rights and indeed, this element may be needed to curb its potentially totalitarian tendencies. Beiner, for example, writes, revealingly, 'What we need is political philosophy that will no longer take human subjects as the supreme arbiters of their own interests and preferences, but will try to illuminate needs and desires of human life that the subjects themselves may have failed to acknowledge.'[24] This separation of what people *think* they want from what someone else judges that they *ought* to want recalls Rousseau's incipiently totalitarian conception of the citizen 'forced to be free', of which the *terminus ad quem* – although, of course not intended by these authors – is the Gulag and the psychiatric hospital. As Chandra Kukathas writes of Gray's proposals, 'We should be wary of those who peddle autonomy, for we risk trading away our liberties to the people who promise to preserve them.'[25]

Is there available, then, a more positive form of liberalism, capable of providing more of the substance that communitarians see to be missing from the prevailing neutralist conception? In order to answer this question adequately, it is necessary to return to the question of liberalism's essential aspects. At its base, it is simply the idea of the minimal state. But 'minimal' has always included scope for two exceptions: the protection of the individual against internal and external threats, and the enforcement of contracts. I have already argued that the first of these exceptions is fully adequate to justify strong and effective policies to deal with both the macro- and the micro-problems that beset today's liberal societies.

But the second condition, too, could be made to do very much more work than it is usually expected to do. Many of the ills of liberal societies stem from the decline of the family and the breakdown of the contractual elements in human relationships. Almost without notice or comment, it has in effect become, in a modern state, impossible to marry – if by that one means to make a long-term (or even fixed term!) commitment binding on both parties. And states have removed ultimate responsibility for offspring, too, by well-intentioned but ill-devised measures of support for unsupported families. Without advocating a return to the total indissolubility of marriage or the neglect of unsupported children, it is nevertheless possible to propose that some of the ground lost by recent legislation could and should be retrieved. The re-establishment of binding contracts between individuals for such ventures as marriage and parenthood could be the basis for a genuine regeneration of community.

In approaching the problem in this way, the personal ties of family and the naturally evolving ties of neighbourhood can be relied upon to assert themselves if people are given the protection from the actions of others that liberal principles require. It is true that the negative conception of liberalism has laid it open to charges of fractionalization and amoralism. But a positive conception was always truer to the original ideal, for which people have been prepared to sacrifice life and personal liberty. So it is not for us at our present vantage-point to judge that they were deluded. Instead, we should acknowledge that they may have been subsequently misunderstood and betrayed.

In particular, it is only since the mid-twentieth century that the old, and limited, conception of negative rights (to non-interference in life, liberty and possessions) has been widely augmented by the postulation of an obliterating array of so-called 'positive rights' to a variety of sophisticated goods, only realizable in a wealthy and bureaucratized society; it is only in this same period, too, that moral autonomy has increasingly become identified with neutrality and a reluctance to affirm any substantive moral values. The remedy, then, must be to reverse these trends, returning to careful parsimony in the allocation and interpretation of rights, combined with much less parsimony in the area of values. In other words, liberalism is more accurately to be seen not as an ideology of positive rights and negative morality, but as one of negative rights and positive morality.[26]

The retreat from liberalism by so many present-day commentators, then, provides a useful service in exposing the depths of this misunderstanding and the tragic nature of its consequences. There is indeed a liberal dilemma, particularly recognizable in the area of education where any lack of firmness and clarity of principles or ideals is revealed by the litmus test of children's development. But the neutralist conception of liberalism, which linked it to permissiveness and indifference to all that is of value in human life, was always fallacious. Liberalism, in its commitment to reason and to the protection of individuals in the pursuit of their legitimate ends, as well as in its assertion of universal moral concepts, is a rich and substantive tradition, well able to compete with socialism on the one hand and authoritarian traditionalism on the other in the market of ideas.

NOTES

1 See, for example, Alasdair MacIntyre's *After Virtue* and *Whose Justice? Which Rationality?* Roger Scruton sets out a distinctive view of conservatism in *The Meaning of Conservatism*. See also his *The Philosopher on Dover Beach*.

2 Rawls, *A Theory of Justice*. The metaphor of the veil of ignorance is a device for showing how people in the 'original position' might formulate principles for social living that they would be willing to accept whatever social position they later found themselves occupying.

3 Beiner, *What's the Matter with Liberalism?*

4 Bloom, *The Closing of the American Mind*, p. 109, cited in Beiner, *What's the Matter with Liberalism?*, p. 36. Allan Bloom's book is a wide-ranging critique of American society and culture, and in particular of its education policies.

5 Burckhardt, *Reflections on History*, p. 64, cited in Beiner, *What's the Matter with Liberalism*, p. 8, n. 4.

6 Beiner, *What's the Matter with Liberalism*, p. 35.

7 Gray discusses the 'enabling welfare state' in his *The Moral Foundations of Market Institutions*. This is one of a number of publications on controversial issues in politics from the London-based Institute of Economic Affairs, largely critical of welfarist policies and state rather than individual provision. Gray's own views on liberalism have changed over a series of publications on this topic.

8 Gray, *Liberalisms*, p. 230.

9 Ibid., p. 225.

10 Ibid., p. 226.

11 Raz, *The Morality of Freedom*, p. 411.

12 Gray, *Liberalisms*, p. 235.

13 Ibid., p. 235.

14 Ibid., p. 226. This account of liberalism as a transitory and relatively recent phenomenon is best known through Alasdair MacIntyre's *After Virtue* and *Whose Justice? Which Rationality?* In these books, MacIntyre attacks liberal individualism as an unacceptable compound of Kantianism and utilitarianism.

15 Gray, *Liberalisms*, p. 260. Virtue theory, which takes as its starting-point the Greek discussions of the virtues, provides an alternative approach to ethical theory in its modern form. The central idea is that ethics is concerned with character, and that the key ethical question is: what makes a good person? MacIntyre in his works recommends a

return to the Aristotelian tradition as being better able than other theories to meet the common human desire for coherence and meaning in life. See chapter 7 by Jackson in the present volume for a discussion of virtue ethics in relation to business, and the Notes and Reading Guide to that chapter for further guidance on reading in this area.

16 Gray, *Liberalisms*, pp. 227–8.
17 Sandel, *Liberalism and the Limits of Justice*, cited in Beiner, *What's the Matter with Liberalism?*, p. 16, n. 2. See also Sandel's introduction to his edited collection *Liberalism and its Critics*.
18 Anscombe, 'Modern moral philosophy'.
19 Beiner, *What's the Matter with Liberalism?*, p. 22.
20 Gray, *Liberalisms*, p. 244.
21 MacIntyre, *Whose Justice?*, p. 112, cited in Beiner, *What's the Matter with Liberalism?*, p. 164.
22 Robert Nozick's discussion of the way in which a minimal state may be justified, and his argument against proceeding beyond the minimal state, is in *Anarchy, State and Utopia*.
23 Gray, *Moral Foundations*.
24 Beiner, *What's the Matter with Liberalism?*, p. 7.
25 Kukathas, 'Fredom versus autonomy', in Gray, *Moral Foundations*, p. 108.
26 I have discussed the idea of positive liberalism at more length in *Moral Concerns* and in 'Seven moral myths'.

A version of this chapter was first published under the title 'The retreat from liberty' in *The Critical Review*, vol. 8, July 1994. The author thanks the editor and publishers of *The Critical Review* for permission to publish the paper as it appears here.

READING GUIDE

On liberalism, see Anthony Arblaster's comprehensive study, *The Rise and Decline of Western Liberalism*. John Gray provides a briefer account and a useful historical bibliography in *Liberalism* and returns to the theme in *Liberalisms: Essays in Political Philosophy*. See also *Liberalism, Community and Culture* by W. Kymlicka.

Theories of Rights, edited by J. Waldron, is a useful collection of articles on various aspects of rights. For critical discussion of the modern addition of welfare to negative rights, see *What are Human Rights?* by Maurice Cranston and for a specifically ethical focus, see, L. Sumner, *The Moral Basis of Rights*.

The classic defence of free market economics is Adam Smith's *Wealth of Nations*. Contemporary defenders of the free market include F. A. Hayek, author of *The Road to Serfdom* and *The Constitution of Liberty* and Milton Friedman, whose *Capitalism and Freedom* provides arguments for linking these two concepts. See also the following chapter in this volume by Tibor Machan and the accompanying Reading Guide.

For the debate between communitarianism and liberalism, see *Communitarianism and Individualism*, a collection edited by S. Avineri and A. de-Shalit. *Liberals and Communitarians* by S. Mulhall and A. Swift offers clear expositions of the views of the main protagonists in the liberalism–communitarianism debate: Rawls, Sandel, MacIntyre, Taylor, Walzer, Rorty and Raz.

CLASSICAL SOURCES

Hobbes: *Leviathan*
Locke: *Second Treatise on Civil Government*
Paine: *The Rights of Man*
Smith: *An Inquiry into the Nature and Causes of the Wealth of Nations*
Bentham: *An Introduction to the Principles of Morals and Legislation*
J. S. Mill: *Utilitarianism*; *On Liberty*

17

A Defence of Property Rights and Capitalism

Tibor R. 'Machan

The superior freedom of the capitalist system, its superior justice, and its superior productivity are not three superiorities, but one. The justice follows from the freedom, and the productivity follows from the freedom and the justice.

Henry Hazlitt

The concept of freedom, in its socially relevant sense, means the condition of individuals being free from aggression by others.[1] This is the political freedom of the unique American political tradition. It rests on the recognition of every individual's equal moral nature as a self-determined and self-responsible agent, regardless of admittedly enormous circumstantial differences.

By political freedom I mean that no one is an involuntary master or servant of anyone, including the government. In short, when the consent of the governed is the reigning principle, political freedom exists; when it is compromised, political freedom is in peril. Economic freedom implies freedom of trade, in the classical liberal tradition of political economy.

A moral case for a system of community life needs to make clear that such a system supports the ethical life of its members instead of thwarting it. Ethics is a system of principles by which human beings can *choose* to guide themselves to live properly, in line with what is the good life for them. There are competing ethical systems, of course, but not all can be sound. An ethics is sound if it most consistently and completely fulfils the purpose for which ethics is needed, namely, to guide human living towards success in the case of any particular person. A political system is ethically sound if it is in accord with those virtues that bear on community life, that is, if it is just. So the main issue facing someone who considers a political economic system such as capitalism is whether this way of organizing a community, in particular its economic life, is conducive to justice. Here I will only touch on some of the more widely voiced moral questions raised about capitalism, hoping to show that at least from a common-sense ethical framework, one that embraces such virtues as honesty, courage, prudence, justice, generosity, decency, and so forth, capitalism is morally defensible, more so, probably, than its competitors, such as socialism, fascism, the welfare state, communitarianism, etc.

To understand capitalism, one must understand free trade. The nature of free trade is best grasped by noting, first of all, that it is logically dependent on the principle of the right to private property. One cannot trade if one does not own anything. Oddly, Karl Marx clearly identified the function of property rights: 'the right of man to property is the right to enjoy his possessions and dispose of the same arbitrarily, without regard for other men, independently from society, the right of selfishness'.[2] Marx focused on the worst-case scenario, but one should not do that when considering the characteristics of a system of principles. Of course, the right to private property makes free trade possible and thus leaves one free to dispose of one's possessions irrationally. But it also leaves one free to act and trade in accordance with the best judgements one can form – something Marx did not mention. Marx gave us just a fraction of the story. Private property enables one to dispose of one's belongings either responsibly or irresponsibly, so that trade can yield both worthy and unworthy results. Yet, precisely because it is private property, acting in a fashion that brings unworthy results will be less likely, since the harm will first of all befall the owner, not others. Property discourages irrationality and encourages rationality.

It bears noting that most prominent and articulate contemporary defenders of capitalism are economists. This creates a false impression. Economists study the way the free market satisfies human desires, but they ignore the merits of those desires. Nor do they concern themselves with whether the market may be morally justified, whether it is an institution basically in line with human moral values. Economists focus on explaining, describing and predicting the ways of a free market. They insist that economics is value free.

When the most prominent advocates of free market capitalism are economists, it appears that nothing other than efficiency matters about the marketplace. Yet this is going to leave the understanding of the system incomplete, since efficiency must always be judged by reference to some goal, and the goal of prosperity, which economists worry about, is itself controversial. (This lies behind the oft-heard charge that life in capitalist countries is too materialistic and not spiritual enough.) There are, thus, various normative or ethical features of the free society that an economic analysis leaves unexplored. This would not be a problem if economists were not the virtually exclusive defenders of free market capitalism.[3] But their approach does not stress that the market rests on ideas and institutions that are ethical in nature.

For example, freedom of trade presupposes property rights. If no such rights exist, then there is no need for or opportunity to trade. People could just take from others what they want and would not need to wait for agreement on terms. Or, alternatively, if everyone owned everything, no one could ever trade. Everyone's permission would be required for every transaction. For individuals and voluntary associations, such as corporations and partnerships, to set terms of trade presupposes the authority or right to make decisions about property. That is indeed a moral feature and precondition of a free market, not a purely 'descriptive' one.[4]

The moral nature of property rights can be made clear simply enough: if I own something, that means that others *ought to* refrain from thwarting my choice of what to do with it. I am the one who is authorized to set terms, not others. (This is why theft is morally wrong!) This is a moral issue because it involves considerations of how persons ought to choose to act, of what it is right and wrong for them to choose to do.

And, not surprisingly, critics of a free society seem to know all this. They exploit the fact that economists are reluctant to discuss ethical issues by suggesting that something is amiss in their free market theory. Yet, what critics should realize is that precisely because of this value component at the base of market economic theory, the system is demonstrably sound and much of what economists say about it gains support not just from technical economic analysis but also from ethics.

If economists defending the free market-place admitted that at its base we find certain assumptions as to how individuals ought to act and what governments should uphold, they could still proceed to carry on with their technical analysis of how such a system works and why it produces more efficiently than all others. They would simply not address the question as to whether those basic assumptions are ethically sound – let's say, in the spirit of the division of labour. The economist could insist that the job of economics is to study market processes and others should take on the task of figuring out whether a market economy is morally preferable to other systems.[5]

Let us now return to just that task. I have noted that the principle of property rights underlies the market. What are property rights? They are necessary preconditions of genuine free trade and thus of a free market, specifying moral and legal authority for making decisions about socially valued items.

Certainly there are numerous societies in which conditions resembling a structure of private property rights are evident; we might call them a structure of property privileges. In these societies persons are *permitted*, within certain limits, to hold and trade goods and services individually, although the government – the local Coastal Commission, the Federal Communications Commission, the king, or some other powerful group or person – is legally authorized to revoke the privilege. In such societies there is no genuine free market. They have what resembles free markets in the same way a sophisticated zoo can resemble the actual wilds, or some children enjoy limited personal responsibility granted by parents and resembling what is enjoyed by adults. And, of course, the more such privileges become entrenched and depended upon, the more the market will exhibit the tendencies we expect in a free market place. In any case, the right to private property needs now to be considered in some detail, since it is the bedrock of economic freedom.

The Right of Private Property

In order to be moral agents, to make choices about what to do in their lives, persons need to have sovereignty, personal authority, liberty. Such liberty, as understood within the western and, particularly, the American (classical) liberal political tradition, is inseparable from economic freedom and the principle of the right to private property. Why is this so?

Political freedom, as we have seen, means not aggressively intruding upon one another. This is not the restricted freedom of taking part in politics but the broad liberty to live freely among other persons in one's community. Such liberty is a crucial requirement of human dignity, the opportunity to make moral choices and to aspire to moral excellence. What has not yet been made clear is that any opportunity must have a concrete sphere or realm where action can take place. Making effective moral choices in one's life requires, to use Robert Nozick's phrase, 'moral space'.[6]

Very plainly put, the principle of the right to private property serves the purpose of always translating the freedom of personal responsibility into realistic, concrete policies. To the extent that a human polity must be focused on securing the opportunity for individuals to pursue 'the general welfare' – and in so far as the human good must be achieved by all individuals on their own within a concrete realm of jurisdiction or 'moral space' – a good human community must secure for all persons a realm of private jurisdiction. The law of property is that branch of jurisprudence that develops the method for securing for all their proper domain of authority within a highly complex society, one in which what belongs to someone can range from a horse to a sophisticated chemical formula to a musical arrangement.

To the extent that the law of property is not guided by the principle of the right to private property, it departs from this objective. Once this is grasped, the next crucial question that faces us in this connection is how to determine the parameters of the domain of personal authority and thus to justly or correctly assign protection to a set of items or property someone lays claim to.

This is a very complex issue indeed. John Locke's well-known labour theory of property is not adequate as an answer because it is not clear what can count as 'mixing one's labour' with nature. Ideally, if we were to start from scratch, the entrepreneurial theory of property would be best. Described by James Sadowsky, this line of analysis supports the conclusion that 'The owner of property performs an entrepreneurial function. He must predict the future valuation that he and others will make and act or not act accordingly. He is "rewarded" not primarily for his work, but for his good judgment.'[7]

This is consistent with the very basis of personal moral responsibility. That basis lies in one's fundamental choice to think or not to think, to exercise one's rational capacity, one's faculty of reason. The Aristotelian idea that the basic virtue of human life is right reason suggests this, as do several other analyses of what lies at the basis of human morality. In general, since morality presupposes choice, and since all persons are free primarily in their use of their minds, the source of moral merit is, as Sadowsky put it, good judgement. A rational creature would be expected to excel precisely in proportion to his willingness to live by good judgement, and when this good judgement is made with reference to matters of prosperity, it is no less meritorious than when it is made with reference to hygiene, truth-seeking, family matters, career or politics.[8]

Economic freedom is a necessary but not sufficient condition of human excellence. It is a prerequisite of human dignity. It is indispensable for moral agents who must make their way in life in the context of a world the various parts of which may be controlled by different individuals. So as to make certain that each individual has a reasonably clear idea of what parts of reality are within his or her jurisdiction – so that he has, as it were, his moral props in clear focus – a system of private property rights is necessary. Such a system preserves the moral independence – though not, as caricatured by Marx and many others, the social autonomy – of everyone.

Capitalism and Morality

Statists of all stripes have been very eager to undermine the moral legitimacy of capitalism. Economic defenders of the system have tended to avoid the argument, maintaining that on the whole the capitalist system produces greater wealth than do others, a result which everyone seems clearly to prefer.

But this defence is inadequate. We can easily think of circumstances when considerations of prosperity must be traded off so as to achieve other values. We know that no expense must be spared when aiming for some goals. Some economists duck this fact by engaging in economic imperialism, holding that since all values are reducible to wealth, all trade-offs are economic. But this is not so. Friendship is not mainly an *economic* value (i.e. something with a price): if one were to trade it for, say, a rise in pay, one would be acting unethically, not simply losing some valued items. A betrayal will not qualify for an exchange of economic values.[9]

Because the economists have tied their hands about morality, capitalism has been under fire from all sides. It is really something of a tragedy that the most humane, most productive, and most benign system of human economic arrangements would be the target of some of the most morally reprehensible critics: terrorists, Marxist-Leninists, fascists, *et al.* But, to quote Shakespeare, 'Wisdom and goodness to the vile seem vile; Filths savour but themselves.'[10]

Consider some typical and oft-repeated charges against capitalism:

1 Capitalism is anarchic.
2 Capitalism produces waste and trivia.
3 Capitalism caters to the base within us.
4 Capitalism neglects the poor.
5 The workers under capitalism are exploited.
6 The wealthy in capitalism gain special protection against adversity.
7 Capitalism destroys the fine arts.
8 Capitalism abuses the environment.

One could go on, especially if one included charges which are levelled with a particular axe to grind, for example, about inequality of wealth, the disparity of wages paid to different segments of society, and so forth. But these charges presuppose the moral priority of human economic equality, something that rests on intuition rather than argument.[11]

Let us take some time here to respond to some of the moral criticisms of the free market capitalist system. We will see, I think, that in preserving human freedom, especially in the context of commerce, capitalism not only escapes being responsible for moral shortcomings but actually facilitates moral excellence throughout a culture.

Capitalism and Human Excellence

The alleged anarchism of capitalism rests on the view that when free trade or exchange reigns – i.e. producers can freely attempt to interest consumers in their wares, while consumers can freely choose to spend their earnings on items they wish to have – this must result in reckless disregard for what is of real importance in human life.

The charge is plausible, because in a free market-place there is ample opportunity for producing and consuming trivial and even morally odious goods – e.g. pet rocks and pornography – as well as plenty of evil production and consumption. The charge, made by Marxists and conservatives alike, is strengthened by the fact that the alternative offered is always some vision of perfect order, such as humanity fully matured in some distant future (Marx) and society well governed by wise leadership (Plato).

But the reality is that markets are not anarchic but merely reflect the human situation. We are not guaranteed the company of wise and virtuous fellows. We can only choose what we will do about their presence in the neighbourhood. We can trust in the illusion of some future paradise on earth or in the guaranteed, long-range superiority of certain persons, both of which are fantasies. Or we can try to make sure that the effects of other people's foolishness and vice will be limited to their own domain. A system of private property rights can do this better than anything else.[12]

As for the second objection, capitalism does at times produce waste and trivia. But it produces immensely useful items as well, more so than any other system. From the mass production of stereo equipment and prints of the best of humanity's artistic achievements, to hospital instruments and special nutrition for those with health problems, capitalism especially serves both the ordinary and the unique, because its method of production – guided by the price system and other types of knowledge made available via market transactions – informs producers of needs and wants better than any variety of a planned system could.

Moreover, what may seem trivial to some people can be of immense value to others. The reason this is overlooked is that even today many people fail to accord proper standing to individual differences. Thus while most of us may find the various items in tourist traps useless, there can be individuals to whom these can be of value.

As to the pornography or prostitution which could exist in a pure capitalist system, they need not be rationalized as good things on the ground that there is a demand for these, and the consumer is king. Professor Walter Block's book *Defending the Undefendable*, which argued from a free market perspective, makes it appear, quite mistakenly, that nothing else but coercion constitutes evil conduct. Clearly, however, one can betray friends, debase an ideal, lack courage, act imprudently, and do all kinds of moral wrongs without coercing anyone. Even some of the practices that may appear to be justified rebellion, such as littering, could turn out to be mere slothfulness or at least lack of civility.

The defence of human liberty does not require abandoning moral standards – quite the contrary. It is in part so as to enable us to invoke moral standards freely, without the regimentation from others that would rob us of our moral sovereignty, that freedom is vital to every adult. Moral wrongs are no doubt going to be present even in a free society, but it is imperative and clearly possible to combat them on the personal, social, and cultural levels (through the comic arts, editorials, pulpit, and so forth).

Accordingly, capitalism does not just protect the freedom of the base but also that of the noble. It is a prejudice to hold that the market caters to our baser self. Capitalism, by encouraging the rational and responsible use of property, actually meliorates vices like greed, envy, and dishonesty. It is planned economies in which those vices are rife.

As for the poor and the workers, the treatment of workers under early industrial capitalism was not as harsh as Marxist critics have alleged. It is true that England at the end of the eighteenth and the beginning of the nineteenth century was hardly in an ideal state. But the extent of the misery after the introduction of greater economic freedom has been grossly exaggerated. There would have been even greater misery had this system not been introduced. This leads us to believe that there was something radically wrong before the change that has never been given proper attention. While most of the worst restrictions on economic action were removed, many of the enormous feudal land-holdings were left untouched in the name of respect for private property. As we know, these holdings were mostly the result either of conquest or state land-grants. It is extremely doubtful that these holdings could ever have attained their size on the free market. Justice would have dictated the division of these lands among the agricultural workers. Unfortunately this was not done. The result was that a few individuals had votes in the market far beyond their due and were thereby enabled to determine the course of events.[13] With this power at their disposal, it is not surprising that 'capitalists' enjoyed special advantages. But to mistake this for a typically capitalist situation is a serious confusion.

There is another error underlying the charge that capitalism leads to worker exploitation. This is that workers are helpless creatures. The market, however, makes it possible for workers to improve their lot. Marx was influenced by Thomas Malthus's view that the working class will multiply far more rapidly than the income it can generate will support, thus workers will be more and more exploitable, given their numbers. Malthus has been refuted both in theory and by history: enormous numbers of working people in the world have frequently enough found themselves very productively employed, usually when markets were more rather than less free, and when governments did not distort the principles of free trade by domestic and international violation of individual rights. In addition, Marx had little confidence in human creativity and entrepreneurship. Thus he did not allow sufficiently for a sustained rise in the demand for goods and services, based on what human beings could both invent and learn to enjoy or use. The work-force in a capitalist society is, therefore, far from easily exploited. Indeed, it is insulting to workers to think otherwise, and Marx (and later Lenin) had a low opinion of ordinary human beings.

Finally – and this is most difficult for some to accept – many of those who are allegedly exploited have actually placed themselves in a position of weakness. Having failed to develop their skills and talents, they must take what they can get of the limited number of jobs available for the unskilled. Under these circumstances it is arguable that they should be grateful for the opportunity for employment, not protest that they are being mistreated. To proclaim that workers are always exploited, as a class, is to demonstrate an ideological prejudice which ignores the actual characteristic of the different people making up the labour force.

The next charge against capitalism is that it favours the wealthy. In a free society where no special legal privileges are permitted for anyone and where government is constitutionally restricted from regulating economic affairs, the wealthy have only those advantages which come from wealth. These involve the greater ability to purchase various goods and services offered on the free market, an advantage that in a constitutionally limited government does not include political power. Furthermore, wealth gives some only one type of advantage. Personality, character, talent, good will, perseverance, and hard work can often result in far greater success than wealth could provide.

Marx tried to discredit the claim that it was governments in the past – feudalist, mercantilist – which gave lopsided advantages to some select people. When the large joint stock companies had been established, governments clearly favoured them, so that nations might gain wealth, although this proved to be a rather frail strategy. But contrary to Marx, this is not inevitable. Wealth need not become politically influential, unless the legal system opens itself up to this by way of giving governments inappropriate powers.

In any case, without exploring the historical reasons why some firms managed to exercise undue power in the market-place – namely, their special legal privileges – we can point to some matters which could secure general agreement. To begin with, we can note that in the United States, which has had the greatest degree of capitalism in human history, the positions of the wealthy and the poor are not held by one single class or select few. Rather these positions are in constant flux – or at least this has been so in the past, prior to the onset of the massive welfare state – far more than under any other system. This seems to suggest that the wealthy under capitalism have less political or legal power than in other systems.

The charge that capitalism destroys the fine arts because it makes mass culture dominant is also unfounded. Because of the 'noise' of popular culture, the fine arts may not be so visible as are rock and roll, television, and popular literature. But in total quantity, never have so many listened to, viewed, and otherwise experienced great artistic achievements as in capitalist or near-capitalist societies. The mass production of the arts, indeed the finest of them, proves this beyond any reasonable doubt.

As to capitalism's impact to the environment, there is no other system that makes a better effort to avoid the tragedy of the commons, the source of all environmental problems. The tragedy stems from common ownership to resources that will, then, be overused by all those who are convinced that their goals and purposes may be served by these resources without restraint. Since, however, under capitalism property is privately owned, any use of resources would be costly and thus limited. And when property is used to the detriment of neighbours, this would be legally actionable as a form of dumping, trespass, assault, invasion, and so forth. When privatization is impossible or technically difficult, there would be personal injury provisions against pollution. Any activity that is damaging or violates the rights of persons in this sense would have to be prohibited, no less than rape or assault is now. Indeed, the most effective environmentalist public policy flows from a system of private property rights in which both persons and property are supposed to be protected from invasion.[14]

Final Reflections on the Value of Free Markets

It is true that human beings are not perfect. To try to force them to be perfect is futile. Herbert Spencer was right when be observed, 'The ultimate result of shielding men from the effects of folly is to fill the world with fools.'[15] A sign of our imperfection is that we keep returning to the failed effort to perfect one another by means of coercion.

To ask that government, for example, attempt to cure us of our imperfection is to show that one isn't willing to live by one's own evaluations: if the world needs improving, the proper approach is to use whatever skill one has to remedy matters. Censors should try their hands at writing better literature. Critics of waste should produce things of value. Those who fear the base within us should turn to moral education as a way to help out. Those who sympathize with the 'exploited' workers might help by becoming one and seeking remedies.

Capitalism is the political manifestation of the human condition: we are free to do good or evil, and in society we need to keep this in mind. The free market, through the principle of the right to private property, helps us keep this in mind – indeed, institutionalizes it through the law of property.

Democracy itself, which is so much prized even by outspoken critics of the free market, would be impossible without meeting the preconditions of the market-place. This is because democracy requires some secure realm of personal jurisdiction or authority for those who are asked to make their views evident by way of the vote. They need to know that if they are a minority, they will not be at the mercy of vengeful victors who deprive them of their lives, liberty and property. In short, a democratic polity cannot function without capitalism, the system in which private property rights are protected.

Thus, we can conclude, the free market or capitalist system of economic life, provided it is not compromised and, thus, corrupted, is indeed supported by morality and supportive of the ethical life of human beings. To fully appreciate this, however, it is necessary to forgo Utopian politics, whereby the supposedly perfect (community) becomes the enemy of a realistically best system. Unfortunately, too often this habit dominates and, arguably, humanity has suffered serious political and economic failings as a result. Perhaps there will be a chance to improve matters in the future, should the specifically moral merits of free market capitalism become more evident.

NOTES

1 I discuss the different kinds of freedom that are of concern to us in 'Two senses of human freedom'. It needs to be noted here, however, that freedom or liberty in this sense concerns respect for the sovereignty of persons, their realm of authority, not their material or spiritual ability to make headway in life. This latter, rather special, sense of

'freedom' is what is focused upon by those like Karl Marx who stress what they call 'human' as distinct from mere 'bourgeois' freedom. Yet to achieve such 'freedom' – by subjecting others to involuntary servitude – requires the sacrifice of liberty and is, thus, opposed to human morality.

2 Karl Marx, *Selected Writings*, p. 53.

3 I have in mind such eminent economists as Milton Friedman, James Buchanan, Gary Becker, and the late George Stigler, F. A. Hayek and Ludwig von Mises, all of whom stress those aspects of the free market that pertain to its efficiency and eschew concern with whether the system is indeed in accord with, for example, prudence and justice.

4 Some argue that rights should be thought of as meta-normative principles in that they do not directly bear on how one ought to conduct oneself but on the conditions required by everyone in a community for making the choice about how to live. See, for more on this, Douglas B. Rasmussen and Douglas J. Den Uyl, *Liberty and Nature, an Aristotelian Defense of Liberal Order*. The point is not crucial here, however.

5 Something along these lines applies to workers in any applied science, e.g. engineering or building construction. They assume that what is to be done is morally justifiable, though it isn't their province to dwell on that issue.

6 Nozick, *Anarchy, State, and Utopia*, p. 57

7 Sadowsky, 'Private property and collective ownership', p. 123.

8 I explain this further in *Individuals and their Rights*. I draw there on ideas advanced originally in Ayn Rand, in 'The objectivist ethics' in *The Virtue of Selfishness*, although the point has been lurking around in the ethics of numerous philosophers who have stressed the role of reason and choice in the moral life of a human being.

9 Democritus of Abdera wrote, 'The same thing is good and true for all men, but the pleasant differs from one and another.' Quoted in Gordon, *Economic Analysis before Adam Smith*, p. 15.

10 *King Lear*, IV. ii.

11 This doctrine has gained considerable support at the hands of John Rawls, *A Theory of Justice*, in which the role of moral intuitions as the central feature of the foundation of political justice is vigorously endorsed.

12 Some of this is implicit in the Austrian economists' famous discovery of the calculation problem under socialism. See Hoff, *Economic Calculation in the Socialist Society*.

The discovery of serious difficulties with a common ownership policy should be credited to Aristotle (*Politics*, Book II, ch. 3, 1261b34–1261b38). Another version of the point is made in Garrett Hardin, 'The tragedy of the commons'.

Perhaps there is yet another expression of this same difficulty, in connection with the various impossibility theorems showing that rational public choice is not possible in a fully democratic society, one in which citizens may demand the satisfaction of their desires from the government. See Arrow, *Social Choice and Individual Values*, 2nd edn. See also my 'Rational choice and public affairs', as an attempt to spell out the criteria by which we should determine whether something falls within the public domain and is, thus, subject to public policy decision-making. I develop this line of thinking further in my *Private Rights, Public Illusions*.

13 See Sadowsky, 'Private property and collective ownership', p. 124.

14 For a more detailed treatment of this issue, see my *Private Rights, Public Illusions*, ch. 8.

15 Spencer, 'State tampering with money banks', in *Essays*, 1891.

A version of this chapter appeared under the title 'In defense of property rights and capitalism' in *The Freeman*, June 1993. We thank the publisher, Foundation for Economic Education, for permission to publish it here in its present, slightly edited form.

READING GUIDE

Herbert Spencer vigorously argued against state attempts to protect people from the consequences of their own actions, and Ayn Rand's many books defend a similar kind of libertarianism today. Nozick's *Anarchy, State and Utopia* is perhaps the best-known recent defence of the minimal state.

A famous argument concerning the culturally debasing effects of equality is *Democracy in America* by Alexis de Toqueville. J. S. Mill in his classic essay *On Liberty*, while deploring 'the tyranny of the masses', argues that only the most extreme circumstances can justify restriction of liberty by law.

The economist and philosopher F. A. Hayek has strenuously defended liberty and the free market in a number of books, including *The Road to Serfdom* and *The Constitution of Liberty* as has Milton Friedman in *Free to Choose* and many other publications.

Some of the issues treated in this chapter are considered more fully in Tibor R. Machan, *Private Rights, Public Illusions*.

CLASSICAL SOURCES

Plato: *Republic*
Locke: *Second Treatise on Civil Government*
Malthus: *An Essay on the Principle of Population*
Smith: *The Wealth of Nations*
De Tocqueville: *Democracy in America*
Marx: *Capital*

18

Nationalism and Intervention

C. A. J. Coady

The topic of nationalism is intimately connected with the question of the legitimacy of military intervention by one nation in the affairs of another. One interesting fact that joins them (somewhat extrinsically) is worth noting at the start, and that is that many thinkers, of a liberal, 'enlightened' inclination, believed until fairly recently that both nationalism and intervention were bad things, and indeed that, unlike most bad things, they might be on the way to dying out.

What is striking about the 1980s and 1990s is that it is now absolutely clear that neither phenomenon is going away; indeed the incidence of nationalist outbreaks has been remarkably intense, and the incidence of armed, and other, interventions has been equally impressive over a somewhat longer period of time.[1] (Nor, as we shall see, does either upsurge lack influential intellectual support.) Military intervention by one nation in the internal affairs of another is condemned by international law and UN Charter,[2] and many thought it had received its political death blow at the time of Suez when the US pulled the plug on the interventionist efforts of France and Britain. Since then, of course, the United States itself has been a major military intervener in the affairs of other states, directly and palpably, in the cases of the invasions of Grenada, Panama, and the bombing of Libya, more indirectly and contentiously in the case of Vietnam, Cambodia, and Iraq, and more covertly in the case of Nicaragua and other areas of Latin America.

If many intellectuals used to believe, and still are tempted to think, that both nationalism and intervention are predominantly bad things, it is worth noting also that there appears to be a certain philosophical tension in holding to this joint condemnation. What I mean is that one natural way of opposing outside intervention in the affairs of some nation is precisely by placing a high value upon some principle of nationalism which the intervention appears to violate. Michael Walzer has been an eloquent spokesman for this sort of presumption against intervention, i.e., for the idea that states should generally be left alone to sort out their own problems because there is usually 'a fit' between a community and its government, 'a fit' that is mediated by the identificatory emotions and commitments of a community with a common history, language and culture. This national 'fit' may exist even where the regime is corrupt or oppressive, and its moral importance arises from its being part of the political reality that shapes the identities and self-understandings of those who belong to the national community. Where the national community itself, or a significant element within it, wants to overthrow its own dictator, or corrupt government, it should not normally be aided in doing so because there is an intrinsic value to the nation's achievement of liberty by its own efforts. It is integral to the moral and political development of that nation that it should struggle unaided for freedom. But, although this is the general norm, Walzer, and indeed Mill, from whose essay on non-intervention he takes the general shape of his position, allow for intervention to counterbalance other interventions, and to prevent genocide or widespread massacre and denial of human rights.

By way of supplement to this, it is also worth mentioning that some of the leftish defenders of intervention who have emerged in recent years tend also to be strong critics of nationalism who favour a more positive attitude to intervention, not indeed in the cause of aggrandisement, but in the name of human rights. Under this flag, for example, David Luban rejects what he sees as Walzer's 'romance of the nation-state'. Luban wants to reorient traditional Just War theory, and thereby intervention theory, around the idea of protecting human rights, so that respect for existing state polities and sovereignty is given greatly reduced, and essentially derivative, importance. In what follows, I shall argue that nationalism is both too elusive and too dangerous an idea to be relied upon as a support for opposition to interventionist policies, but that we should remain sceptical of the benefits of (military) interventionism on other, more pragmatic, grounds.

First of all, against the suggested connection between nationalism and principled non-intervention, it needs to be remembered that military adventurism is as often fuelled by nationalist concerns, obsessions or delusions on the part of the interveners as inhibited by a respect for the national characteristics of other peoples. A strident pride in one's own national virtue can be, and often has been, an incentive to take a dim view of other political orders, especially when they diverge from the model of political virtue believed to obtain in your own neck of the woods. Jingoism may not be the same as nationalism, but at least the superficial resemblances are strong, so sceptics need some convincing that they are not merely two sides of the one coin. The way in which British sentiments of national pride, regard for 'kith and kin', and reflections upon an heroic past of ruling the waves, promoted and sustained 'the Falklands war' provides a salutary reminder of how these things work in the real world. And the Chinese conquest of Tibet was less a triumph of communist ideology than an assertion of Chinese nationalism. Nor has the United States been conspicuous in recent years for avoiding the connection between national self-glorification and military adventurism, though, in the case of the US, the connection usually goes through an intermediate link of mythologizing in which the nation is seen as uniquely embodying ideals of democracy or freedom that others need to get.

Those who extol the merits of national identity place, as we shall see, a great premium upon virtues such as loyalty, but these have their dark side too, and loyalty is more attractive in close personal relations than in tribal or organizational affiliations, and is there somewhat less prone to the abuses of conformity, mob-thinking, and hatred of the threatening other. Liddell Hart's recollections of Field-Marshal Sir Archibald Montgomery-Massingberd's views on organizational loyalty are worth citing. According to Liddell Hart, Montgomery-Massingberd (not to be confused with the other Montgomery, 'Monty' of Alamein) thought that loyalty was 'a far more important quality for a soldier to possess' than 'brains', and he harped on this attribute in addresses to officers and men to such a degree that it 'came to be a jocular catchword whenever they mentioned him'. What was evident in all the general's emphasis on loyalty, says Liddell Hart, was 'that he regarded criticism not only as disloyalty to the 'establishment' but as detrimental to his own interests, and ambitions, within it'.[3] Nor is the connection between group bonding under such labels as the army or the nation, on the one hand, and individual ambition, on the other, at all unusual. Events in the former Yugoslavia, as in many other outbreaks of national self-assertion, illustrate this vividly.

It is time to be a little more careful about our use of the term 'nationalism'. The varied employments of this term in the literature provide one reason for so much confusion and heat in exchanges on the topic. Some of the variation arises from conflicting interpretations of the term 'nation' which is certainly one of the messier political concepts in use. Other variations come from the different types of moral and political significance attributed to the attachments that nationalism is taken to denote. Some theorists define it in such a way that it can hardly help being a bad thing since it elevates national loyalty above all other moral considerations, in the spirit of 'my country right or wrong'. Others, such as the Israeli philosopher, Yael Tamir, try to distinguish between good and bad nationalisms. Tamir wants to endorse a good form that she calls 'liberal nationalism', but with this, as with other forms of 'good' nationalism, it is hard to avoid making the adjective do all the serious moral work.[4] That people are loyal and passionate about their liberal state or community is no doubt a good thing for them and for the stability and endurance of that sort of state, but we can advance this point without recourse to the currency of nationalism. Other problems arise from the use of 'nationalism' (or 'nation') in such a way as to imply that recognition of national status must involve the granting of full-blown political autonomy. Ernest Gellner, for instance, confidently defines nationalism as 'a political principle which holds that the political and the national unit should be congruent'.[5] Gellner then has little difficulty in showing that, so understood, very few actual sovereign states are nations, at least if 'nation' is understood in terms of ethnic or similarly tribal identifications, and, moreover, the consequences of granting political sovereignty to all who are, or who think of themselves as, nations, would be disastrous.

I doubt that a coherent definition, capable of capturing all the usages of 'nation' or 'nationalism', can be provided. It would have to capture the passionate commitments of Americans to their ethnically and culturally diverse nation as well as the fierce loyalties of native Maoris to theirs (and here I don't mean New Zealand), or the strong attachments some Scots feel to their country, and perhaps Highlanders to theirs. It is hard to resist the thought that what is real here is not the entity but the attachment. This thought is made more seductive by the wealth of evidence that nationalists in fact tend to define themselves by oppositions: opposition to the invader, to the distant imperial centre, to the dominant nearby power, to various forms of excluded 'other' who may be seen as internal representatives of the hated group. Several writers on nationalism have made this point about the reality being created by the attachment. Gellner says that one useful definition of a nation is that 'two men are of the same nation if and only if they *recognize* each other as belonging to the same nation . . . nations are the artefacts of men's convictions and loyalties and solidarities'.[6] Benedict Anderson talks of 'imagined communities' and many commentators have noted the degree of error, confusion, contrivance and manipulation that often goes to make up the objects of nationalist attachment, whether they be items of history, ritual or character. It is symptomatic of all this confusion that writers on nationalism and nations disagree dramatically on the chronology of the phenomenon in question. Many believe that it is a very modern thing, dating it to the eighteenth or even nineteenth century. Others argue that it is as old as human societies themselves. So, William Pfaff sees it as basically a nineteenth-century phenomenon arising from European romanticism whereas Conor Cruise O'Brien finds powerful expressions of it in the Bible.[7]

Given all these different conceptions and attendant confusions, there may be little point in providing a restrictive definition that ungenerously narrows, or a broad one that too permissively widens, the terms of discussion. Our sketch of the conceptual geography of the debate should suffice for our purposes. One thing that must be noted however is a deep ambiguity in the idea of a nation that any discussion must register. This is between a nation understood as a political entity and one understood as a racial, religious, tribal or ethnic group. These two understandings of 'nation' are importantly different, though they are often confused, and it is worth seeing how different they are, while keeping in view certain underlying similarities. Let us call the ethnic sense *NE* and the political sense *NP*. In the *NE* sense, countries such as Australia and the United

States are not nations at all, and it is very hard to find a clear case of a country that *is* a palpable nation in this sense. In the *NP* sense, they are paradigm cases. The term 'culture' is sometimes used to explicate the *NE* sense of nation, but it might just as easily be cited in connection with the *NP* sense. Although the United States and Australia are, in a sense, multicultural states, there is also an equally clear sense in which they have overarching national cultures that strike foreign visitors with great force. When the French or Japanese or Australians lament the swamping of their societies by American culture, it is clear enough what they mean, and it has no direct reference to the ethnic cultures within the USA. For this reason, the term 'culture' should be used with great care; if any term is even more opaque than 'nation', it is 'culture'.

We must turn now to a discussion of the sort of moral underpinning that is usually offered for the status of national sentiment and attachment. This underpinning proceeds by way of a claim about morality and a related claim about personal identity. The claim about morality concerns the importance of particularities for the moral life, and especially the particular attachments that go with a certain use of the personal pronouns 'my' and 'our'. This is clearest with relationships like friendship, kinship or love. And its significance is thought to be a major problem for utilitarianism and other forms of consequentialism. We might recall in this connection the furore created by the anarchistic rationalist William Godwin's insistence that if the great theologian and sage Archbishop Fénelon and his no-account valet were trapped in a flaming building and only one of them could be rescued, the rescuer would be obliged to save Fénelon even if the valet were his own father, brother or benefactor. Even the valet, if thinking soundly in this fundamentally utilitarian way, should acquiesce, for he would be acting unjustly if he preferred his own life to the far worthier Fénelon. Actually, my version of the example is taken from later editions of Godwin's book where it was toned down because of the outcry occasioned by the first edition. There, the competitor with Fénelon for rescue is a chambermaid who is imagined to be the rescuer's wife or mother. The utilitarian temper and its distance from the common-sense morality is well caught by Godwin's comment: 'What magic is there in the pronoun 'my' to overturn the decisions of everlasting truth? My wife or mother may be a fool or a prostitute, malicious, lying or dishonest. If they be, of what consequence is it that they are mine?'[8]

Non-consequentialist moral thinking, by contrast, tends to emphasize the fact that ethics is concerned not only with impersonal outcomes but very centrally with the quality of actions by agents whose identities as moral beings are bound up with emotions and dispositions dependent to a high degree upon attachments of precisely the particularist kind that Godwin dismisses. The pronoun 'my' functions here not to register property rights (as certain views of the family, both conservative and radical mistakenly assume) but as an indicator of identification. This is part of the point behind the common-sense attitude to the special moral obligations generated by friendship and kinship towards which utilitarian theory is either dismissive or (in its more complex forms) awkwardly accommodating. The claim, mentioned earlier, about personal identity is then offered partly as an explanation of these moral intuitions, and partly as an expansion of them. As explanation, it tries to show that the privileged moral status of these attachments stems from the way in which they serve to constitute, or help constitute, an individual's sense of him- or herself. They seem to me to have a certain amount of success in this explanatory enterprise (though they cannot be the whole story), but, emboldened by this partial success, they then tend to link up with an even grander enterprise, about which I am much more suspicious.[9]

The grander enterprise claims that individuals' identities are constituted, or partly constituted, not only by their intimate connection to family and friends but by their culture, or their society or their tribe, or their nation or (in some versions) their state. Without wanting to deny some influence to these factors in how a person lives and understands their life, I think that the talk of identity here is overblown, at least as a claim about how people *must be* in order to have a serious identity and a rich moral life. To take the *NE* sense of 'nation', some people do build their lives emphatically around racial or tribal or national identifications, but this is not inevitable and I very much doubt that it is usually morally desirable. It is a curious fact that the identification is often invested with greatest passion and significance where it no longer genuinely represents a reality of daily life, as in the case of expatriate groups who cling to myths, beliefs and symbols that frequently no longer resonate in their homelands and have merely artificial relevance in their present environment. There is a psychology at work here somewhat like that described by G. K. Chesterton with reference to those who 'long for the old feasts and formalities of the childhood of the world' yet have no relish for the living rituals of their own time, and who, had they lived 'in the time of the maypole would have thought the maypole vulgar'.[10] Sometimes a fair degree of this sort of attachment is harmless, as in a delight in the cuisine, geography, fauna, art or folk songs of one's ancestral homeland; often it is harmful, as, I think, it too frequently is in the political passions and activities of expatriate communities, such as Irish Americans or Australian Croatians, and more alarmingly in the fracturing activities of various tribal affiliations in Africa, of which the activities of the Zulu Inkatha movement has been a prominent sign, though more recently eclipsed by the tragic divisions in Rwanda and other parts of Africa. I do not of course deny that ethnic or nationalist feelings and sentiment are sometimes powerfully felt; my view is that they have a strong tendency to be harnessed, manipulated, and often created in the cause of wreaking havoc on people and institutions perceived as 'outsiders'. Nations in the *NP* sense will sometimes coincide with nations in the *NE* sense, though nowadays this is rare. In any event, the nation (*NP*) can certainly give rise to powerful unifying emotions and commitments even where it is, as so often, a composite of many nations (*NE*). This was true of many of the unifying nationalist movements of the nineteenth century, such as the Italian, and it remains true today of ethnically diverse nations such as India, Australia and the United States, though all of these are also subject to certain disintegrating tendencies, as indeed is modern Italy.

Some degree of special attachment to one's country and its political and cultural institutions is not only generally harmless, but is probably a good thing, up to a point, as long as those institutions and attachments are in fact valuable (or at least not vicious). The attachment is likely to be most valuable when the nation or the group of whatever kind is actually suffering persecution or oppression precisely because it is (or is believed to be) a group of that kind. In the United States, it is not surprising that fantasies about 'the African nation' should take root, even though, by any account of 'nation' there is clearly no such thing.[11] In my country, proud identification by people of indigenous descent with 'the aboriginal nation', though somewhat absurd when one considers the diversities and hostilities of the original tribal inhabitants of Australia, is not only understandable in the light of historic and continuing injuries which *presumed* such a group identification, but clearly has some positive political, psychological and moral advantages. Where the oppressed band together under group labels, it is easy to sympathize with them, but, even here, the bonding carries the characteristic dangers, as is so evident in the American phenomenon entitled 'The Nation of Islam', where genuine identification with a tragic past and a legitimate attempt to repair present misfortune have been distorted by fantasy and hatred into alarming extremes of racism. We should recognize the inevitability of these invocations of national identity and sentiment, and countenance what positive aspects they possess, without forgetting their delusional, destructive and harmful sides. The primary task is not to canonize these attachments, but to keep them from getting out of hand. Recent attempts by philosophers and other theorists to give a palatable face to nationalism can only make this task of restraint more difficult to achieve.

There is one other confusion that can obstruct discussion here, especially in connection with the problem of intervention. This is the confusion between national independence and popular sovereignty. The latter notion is basically that of a certain sort of involvement in political processes, and can be characterized as the idea that those who are ruled should have a significant say in how they are ruled; it goes very naturally with democracy, but is perhaps compatible with a benign, consultative autocracy, or even a benign consultative imperium. It has no need to invoke the nation, in either the *NE* or *NP* sense. There seems no reason why a group of 'rootless cosmopolitans' living together in a territory cannot engage in such self-rule without invoking a 'self' that has the thick emotional and moral connotations beloved of nationalists. Even such cosmopolitans may rightly want to resist invasions or interventions from those who want to destroy or degrade their political arrangements, and could resist them as attacks upon popular sovereignty. On the other hand, it is all too sadly clear that one can have national independence in the absence of anything resembling popular sovereignty.

Given this view of nationalism, what do we say of intervention? (By intervention here I am going to mean some form of armed intervention in a conflict within the confines of another state. The Gulf War therefore will not be a pure case of intervention since it was avowedly a response to a request by one state for aid in repelling an invasion into its territory by another. Of course, intervention can mean non-military interference, and it can mean non-military intervention in a non-military crisis. Both raise important issues that I will here have to ignore.) I have a bias against intervention, but it should by now be clear that it doesn't come from a deep respect for nationalism or national independence *per se*. Rather it comes from a general desire to limit the resort to war. The workings of this desire are apparent in the development of traditional Just War theory which I see as becoming progressively more restrictive over the centuries as the horror and futility of so much warfare become abundantly more evident.

The medieval tradition of the Just War theory stems primarily from St Augustine and is very well presented in Jonathan Barnes's chapter, 'The Just War' in the *Cambridge History of Later Medieval Philosophy*.[12] With respect to the *jus ad bellum*, as the account of the conditions under which it was permissible to go to war was often called, the medieval theory was generally more permissive than modern theory though sometimes the differences are only terminological. The classical theory, as both Barnes and Johnson make clear, tended to allow a wider range of causes than a modern theory like Walzer's or any theory that could be extracted from the UN Charter and its declaration of rights. The medieval theory is restrictive – the Prince cannot wage war as he pleases nor conduct it as he likes – but it envisages more legitimate causes for military intervention than self-defence, which is what the modern idea of outlawing 'aggression' comes down to. As Grotius put it, 'the sources from which wars arise are as numerous as those from which law suits spring.'[13] Barnes asks whether the medieval theory sanctioned what he calls 'humanitarian wars' (what I shall call 'altruistic wars') such as one waged against a government which is injuring its own citizens.[14] He replies that the letter of the theory appears to countenance this but that the spirit is against it, and he quotes Suárez approvingly as saying, 'what some assert that sovereign kings have power to punish injuries over the whole world is altogether false, and confounds all order and distinction of jurisdictions'.[15]

This raises both an interesting historical and an interesting substantive ethical question, one which, as the Tanzanian invasion of Amin's Uganda, the Vietnamese invasion of Pol Pot's Cambodia, and the recent desperate scenarios in the former Yugoslavia and in Somalia show, is very much a contemporary issue. On the historical question, it is worth noting that Barnes quotes one of the very late medieval theorists, Suárez, to make his point about the spirit of the theory. It is possible to argue, however, that by the time of the Spanish theologians, Suárez and Vitoria, the spirit of the theory had begun to change quite a bit and partly under their influence. Although self-defence had always loomed large, perhaps largest, as a legitimate ground for resort to war, it is clear, for instance, that earlier medieval thinking about the morality of war allowed room, among the morally permissible causes for war, for various 'injuries' of a religious nature so that a war to return some heretical peoples to orthodoxy or, even in some circumstances, to conquer heathens was at least a candidate for a just war. Aquinas is not explicit about the legitimacy of 'holy war', though his silence is significant, and his formulations permissively broad. St Bernard of Clairvaux, however, ardently supported the Second Crusade, and, of course, was not alone in doing so. Writing to the clergy and people of England, Eastern France and Bavaria he called upon them in ringing terms to smite 'the enemy of the Cross' in the Holy Land.

> Now is the acceptable time, now is the day of abundant salvation. The earth is shaken because the Lord of heaven is losing his land, the land in which he appeared to men, in which he lived amongst men for more than thirty years; the land made glorious by his miracles, holy by his blood . . . for our sins the enemy of the Cross has begun to lift his sacrilegious head there, and to devastate with the sword that blessed land, the land of promise.[16]

Both Vitoria and Suárez and later Grotius are anxious to remove wars of religion from the category of just wars and so it is plausible to see them as standing at the beginning of a move towards a somewhat more restrictive attitude to the *jus ad bellum*. Indeed it is a plausible hypothesis that, with the exception of such aberrations as the occasional re-emergence of the holy war tradition, powerfully resurgent in seventeenth-century England, for instance, and the *raison d'état* theory of the nineteenth century, the evolution of Just War theory has been towards a more and more cautious and prohibitive attitude towards war. The current ban on 'aggressive war' and the absolute prohibition of 'intervention' can, I think, for all its obscurity, be seen as the outcome of such a development. This is why I find the increased readiness to resort to intervention (at least where the costs to the interveners appear slight) a depressing development. The international system of states may be no great shakes, but a strong burden of proof rests on those who argue for its disturbance by external violence.

Perhaps this proof can sometimes be provided; we should be very clear, however, about the difficulties that stand in its way. In the case of intervention we have, in addition to the bias against all forms of warfare except clear cases of self-defence, further complicating factors of an epistemological and psychological kind. These are related to certain facts about national culture but require no sanctification of it. The epistemological factors concern the difficulties involved in knowing enough about what is going on in foreign countries to be confident that an intervention on behalf of one group in a struggle is actually in favour of a just cause, and, moreover, where it is, that it is actually likely in the long run to promote the cause rather than set it back. I am not sceptical about the abstract possibility of such knowledge, but I am somewhat sceptical about its ready availability to the national leadership of prospective interveners. This is not only because the facts are intrinsically difficult to ascertain (though often they are), but because the task of ascertaining them is not going to be given to impartial academic investigators, but more often to impassioned partisans of one sort or another. Sometimes passion helps you get at the truth, but more often it obscures it, especially in the details that often matter most, when it comes to strategy and tactics.

As for psychology, the existing attachment to the matters beloved of advocates of nationalism (local culture, traditional practices and affiliations) militate not only against foreigners understanding local circumstances, but also tend to create resentment and hostility against even the most benevolent agents of intervention, especially the longer their intervention lasts and the more power it removes from local initiative. The plight of the UN intervention in Somalia illustrates this problem, though there are other factors involved there as well. Similarly British troops were welcomed with cheers and tears of joy by beleaguered Catholics in Ulster in the 1960s, but these attitudes soon disappeared. This point about the dangers of 'length of intervention' lies behind the idea that there is something to be said for a test of 'swiftly in, swiftly out' for humanitarian intervention, but it is much easier to see in retrospect that this criterion has or has not been satisfied than it is in advance. It is a well-known fact about the psychology of warfare that the belligerent powers usually believe that their wars will be brief. 'Home before Christmas' was the comforting slogan that departing troops cried on their way to the front at the start of World War I, and something similar has often been on the lips of troops and their leaders before conflagrations that endured for years. Sometimes, no doubt, the troops can be 'home before Christmas' or the equivalent. This was true of the Gulf War, though it is far from clear that the speed of that enterprise contributed to a particularly successful outcome for the persecuted minorities of Iraq whatever value it had for the Kuwaitis.

What then of the excruciating problems posed by the likes of Haiti, Somalia and Bosnia? This is not the place to make detailed political analyses of volatile contemporary crises, but I shall offer a few brief comments for illustrative purposes on aspects of the Bosnian tragedy. I do not think that the national aspirations of the Bosnian Muslims nor those of the Serbians, Croats, Macedonians, or whatever, morally demand military intervention by NATO, the UN, or the US. But the case for the prevention of gross human rights violations (like shelling of civilians in Sarajevo, or persistent murderous persecution in Haiti) is far more appealing. If politics fails to prevent such deeds, then it is right to consider interventions such as aerial attacks, but even here several considerations count against such action. The killing of the people in the Sarajevo market early in 1994 created a wave of revulsion world-wide, and a concomitant desire to do something to prevent further such outrages. In particular, there were outcries for aerial bombardment of the Serbian-occupied hills around the city. In the event, the credible threat of aerial bombardment worked to bring an important respite to Sarajevo's inhabitants. But it is unclear that the implementation of that threat would have produced morally and politically acceptable results. We need to ask some tough questions about any such implementation. How long will bombardments have to be kept up, and how can we avoid brief intervention turning into prolonged occupation and partisan warfighting? It is worth recalling that the civilians who died in the market were killed by a mortar grenade, and mortars are highly mobile, easily operated, offensive weapons that do not need to be installed in mountainsides, and can be brought back after bombardments have ceased. I understand that the mountainsides to have been bombed included Serbian-controlled villages. Were their civilian populations to be the direct or 'collateral' victims of the intervention? How can we avoid intervention's merely strengthening the nationalist will, on all sides, to continue the conflict (and make UN protective forces targets)? Since slaughter of civilians is going on all through the region and by all sides, how is it possible to extend the principle of preventing such slaughter in an impartial, and at the same time controllable, way?

In this connection, Conor Cruise O'Brien has usefully drawn attention to the disabling effects of viewing international politics through the lens of a television camera.[17] The world is full of violations of human rights, many of them perpetrated by nationalists, but we ignore most of them because they are not on our television screens. Where were (or are) the calls for intervention in Burma to prevent the massacres and oppressions of students and other dissidents? What about the Indonesian record in East Timor, or the gross (though so far bloodless) denial of civil rights to the Indian population of Fiji in the name of native Fijian nationalism? In these untelegenic countries we not only discount military intervention, we do nothing politically either. Nor does such curious selectivity operate only in the wake of television; it is a remarkable fact that modern nation-states will spend huge sums of government money to address by military means social and political problems in other countries when they are not prepared to devote comparable sums to the relatively peaceful resolution of their own staggering domestic problems. In the USA, the problems of urban degradation, drug addiction and violent crime come readily to mind.

Yet political and moral isolationism is no real solution to problems of genocide, civil war, and political disintegrations abroad. There may indeed be no solutions to some of these problems, at least in the short term, and realistic recognition of this will be preferable to salvational fantasies, especially military ones. None the less, there do seem to be some signs that the international community is groping towards better ways of trying to deal with such problems. One notable feature of modern interventions is the growing tendency towards multinational, often UN-authorized, intervention. This gets around the ban on one nation's intervention in the affairs of another, by making intervention collective, legally sanctioned by a wider community, and generally more like policing. On the whole, this seems a good development, though it has its ambiguities. It may make the epistemological and psychological problems, discussed earlier, slightly more tractable in so far as it brings a wider perspective to bear upon the realities of the target country, and helps reduce local fears of a neo-colonial presence by the rescuers. But it must be admitted that the recent record is very patchy.

One problem concerns the difficulty of separating the characteristic UN roles of watchdog, protector of civilians, maintainer of truces, from the more interventionist activities of punishing wrongdoers, settling the conflict and making a new political order. One can easily merge into the other; this was part of the lesson of the UN's intervention in Somalia. None the less, although something like the traditional UN peace missions will continue to have an important role to play, even where they risk some version of the usual problems of intervention, the real challenge to our political imagination and will may be to devise new strategies and institutional forms of international co-operation in order to prevent or swiftly correct, where possible, such disasters as attended the dissolution of Yugoslavia. World government has been much out of favour with political theorists, but this is partly because it has been conceived in too monolithic a fashion.

Powerful international institutions are actually one of the most striking facts of late twentieth-century life, and it should not be beyond human ingenuity to devise more satisfactory international political forms that will minimize fears of a totalitarian world government, but enable effective arbitrational, judicial and, if necessary, military procedures to be deployed as acts of international justice. This would eliminate any need for recourse to 'altruistic' military interventions by individual powers, and would provide a morally superior alternative. Of course, it lies in the future, and it will not come cheap, but it already has some embryonic presence. We should frame our responses now with this ideal in mind. Thomas Hobbes was confident that the civil state was a work of reason to deliver individuals from the violence of the state of nature. The international order is not a state of nature, but it has anarchic features, and it is surely time to exercise that reason to make the international order less impotent and to deliver suffering human beings from the ravages of unjust political violence, even, or perhaps especially, where that violence flies a national flag.

NOTES

1 The resurgence of nationalism has caught some theorists napping. That admirable publication, *A Companion to Contemporary Political Philosophy* (edited by R. E. Goodin and P. Pettit), a publication that aims at a certain comprehensiveness on matters of

political philosophy, has no entry on nations or nationalism. Its editors say in the Preface that they have not included nationalism because 'it hardly counts as a principled way of thinking about things' (p. 3). They go on to complete the rout by saying of 'theism, and fascism' that they 'would seem to play only a marginal role in the contemporary world'.

2 For a good statement of the standard position in international law, see G. Graham, 'The justice of intervention'. For newer developments, see Paul Kahn, 'From Nuremberg to the Hague: the United States position in Nicaragua v. United States and the development of international law'.

3 Liddell Hart, *Memoirs of Captain Liddell Hart*, p. 103.

4 Tamir, *Liberal Nationalism*.

5 Gellner, *Nations and Nationalism*, p. 1.

6 Ibid., p. 7.

7 See O'Brien's review of Pfaff and of Tamir in his essay, 'The wrath of ages: nationalism's primordial roots'.

8 Godwin, *Enquiry Concerning Political Justice*, p. 42. (See Introduction, p. xxx for details of alterations in later editions.)

9 Someone who consciously makes the jump that concerns me here is David Miller in 'The ethical significance of nationalism'. The target for his pro-nationalist attempt at persuasion is precisely someone with the position I am advancing, namely (as he puts it at p. 659), 'someone who is willing to entertain particularist commitments but believes that there is something fishy about nationality'.

10 The quotes are from Chesterton's 'Christmas and aesthetes' in *Heretics*, reprinted in *The Essential G. K. Chesterton*, p. 74.

11 For an excellent discussion of Africa and its diverse cultural, political, religious and tribal loyalties, see Appiah, *In My Father's House*.

12 See also Holmes, *On War and Morality*, chs 4 and 5.

13 Grotius, *De jure belli et pacis*, II, i, ii, p. 171.

14 J. Barnes, 'The just war', p. 778. The term 'humanitarian war' seems first to have been used in international law to refer to military interventions for the purpose of protecting one's own nationals endangered in a foreign country, though Barnes's use and my use of 'altruistic war' is much wider, and somewhat differently motivated, since it includes fighting on behalf of the foreign nationals endangered in their own country. See Kahn, 'From Nuremberg to the Hague', p. 45, n. 161.

15 Barnes, 'The just war', p. 779.

16 See Holmes (ed.), *War and Christian Ethics*, p. 88.

17 O'Brien, 'The wrath of ages', p. 148.

This paper grew out of work done when I was Laurance S. Rockefeller Visiting Fellow in Ethics and Public Affairs at Princeton University Center for Human Values in 1993–4. I should like to thank the Center for a stimulating environment, and Arthur Kuflik, Debra Satz and Judith Lichtenberg for helpful input to the evolution of this paper.

READING GUIDE

For general discussions of nationalism, Ernest Gellner's *Nations and Nationalism* and E. J. Hobsbawm's *Nations and Nationalism since 1780* are worth reading. For an absorbing interpretation of the philosophical background, favourable to nationalism, there is Sir Isaiah Berlin's 'The bent twig: on the rise of nationalism', and for an interesting, more recent defence of a moderate version of nationalism I recommend Yael Tamir's *Liberal Nationalism*. Michael Walzer's *What It Means To Be an American* is a discussion of the specific problems of national identity in the United States.

On intervention, the *locus classicus* is J. S. Mill's, 'A few words on non-intervention', which is discussed and elaborated in Michael Walzer's *Just and Unjust Wars*. Walzer's book is the best modern discussion of Just War theory, though since its publication in 1977 there have been many good books and articles on moral issues to do with war, notably Robert Holmes's vigorous defence of pacifism in his *On War and Morality* and Jenny Teichmann's *Pacifism and the Just War*. David Luban's critique of Walzer's position, in his articles 'Just War and human rights' and 'The romance of the nation-state', is worth particular attention, as is Walzer's reply to his critics in 'The moral standing of states'. Just War theory is also discussed in chapter 20.

CLASSICAL SOURCES

de Vitoria: *De Indis et de jure belli*
Suárez: *Selections from Three Works*
Grotius: *De jure belli et pacis*

PART V

International and Global Dimensions: Extending the Moral Community

19

Rich and Poor

Jennifer Trusted

Is Poverty Inevitable?

'For ye have the poor always with you.'[1] This biblical quotation is a reminder that poverty is not a recent moral or practical problem peculiar to contemporary society. Acknowledgement of poverty, along with pity and indifference have also always been with us and our attitude to poverty and the degree to which we condone, or at least tolerate, poverty amid plenty has not changed radically in twenty centuries. However, today there are two new factors which strongly influence current response: first, the general recognition that there is no divinely established social order and therefore no moral right to affluence. This is accompanied by a general view that gross economic inequalities are distasteful, if not obscene and that they should be eliminated. Second, those living in the developed countries of the western world are now aware of poverty in far-away places, a poverty that may be far greater than that which they have near to home. Later I shall return to discuss the biblical sentence in its original context but at this point I want to present it in today's common secular form of 'the poor are always with us'.

In the light of these new factors let us consider our current views of the sense and significance of 'the poor are always with us'. If we assume that, at least in practice, some people will inevitably have more money than others, then it follows that there will always be some people who have less. It could be maintained that those with less than the mean, or perhaps less than the median, are poor so that it then becomes trivially true that the poor are always with us.

Such a trite truism is worth stating because it makes us reflect on the statement's underlying assumption, the assumption of the inevitability of poverty. Should that assumption be questioned? For since inequality itself is not *logically* inevitable, can we not, indeed should we not, eliminate it? This question admits of no simple answer: first, there is no known human (even primate) society where inequalities are not present and (so far as we know) they have always been present. Therefore even if differences are not logically necessary perhaps they are, in practice, a necessary characteristic of human social life and will continue to be so. Second, even if inequalities were not inevitable, so that there was at least a possibility of eliminating them, would that be advantageous? *Should* they be eliminated? For it may be the case that though *gross* inequalities are unacceptable some degree of inequality is beneficial. It may be that the most disadvantaged would indeed be worse off in a society aiming for strict egalitarianism. In addition, and perhaps more important, such a society might be neither a just nor a free society.

There is no doubt that the question merits serious consideration but in this chapter I shall discuss neither the possible achievement nor the possible moral desirabilty of complete egalitarianism. I wish to consider moral issues that we face today rather than those relating to some potentially possible, potentially Utopian (or potentially hellish) future.

Relative and Absolute Poverty

Some would argue that it is more helpful to understand the phrase 'the poor are always with us' not as a truism following inevitably from unequal distribution of wealth but as a general description of human societies, where some members are (and have always been) unable or barely able to support themselves and their dependents. These are the poor. On this interpretation the poor are not necessarily those with less than the mean (or median) and nor does poverty have to be an inevitable feature of human society. Therefore in considering poverty and its problems we need to decide whether to adopt a relative concept of poverty related to the general affluence or whether it would be more helpful to treat poverty as an absolute condition, related to subsistence. Though, as we shall see, both concepts involve problems, we can at least contend that in either case poverty need no longer be seen as an inevitable and therefore unchangeable feature of every human society. For moral and possibly practical economic reasons, gross inequalities or a generally low standard of living should be and can be reduced; and we can work for their elimination with some hope of success.

In his paper 'Poverty; absolute or relative?' Beverley Shaw argues that to accept a relative definition of poverty (so that poor citizens in the West are judged to be *in poverty*, even though they are not living at bare subsistence level) will lead to a failure to distinguish the two notions of poverty. Such a failure will promote what he considers a possibly dubious cause of social egalitarianism and will also reduce concern for those who are poor in an absolute sense and who live near to starvation.[2]

If we take an overt absolutist position and say that poverty is to be conceived in terms of subsistence, then those who are inadequately fed and housed would be 'the poor' regardless of what fraction of their community they represent. In certain societies we might have to conclude that some, perhaps many, of those above the mean were poor, and in other societies we might need to go even further and say that all (or almost all) its members were poor.

However, appealing as the adoption of an absolute standard of poverty may be, I shall argue that, in the end, we must take a relativist view and assess individual poverty in comparison with the general affluence of the society being studied.[3] Moreover although this does almost certainly entail arguing for modified egalitarian policies – and I shall discuss this later – it does not inevitably lead to a lack of concern for the completely destitute. Indeed I suspect that concern for the badly off in the affluent West will encourage general concern about poverty.

On the relativist view the problem is to decide firstly what scale of inequality is to be taken as too gross to be tolerable? Ten per cent, 50 per cent or 80 per cent less than the mean? Is there perhaps a concealed absolutism in that the percentage chosen might depend on the level of general affluence? A second problem, or another aspect of the first problem, arises in considering what is to be taken as an acceptable level of subsistence. That level is not fixed: it will vary not only in time (though here I shall be concerned solely with the current situation) but also in place. What would be thought barely adequate nourishment in the UK would be thought ample in Somalia. What may be regarded as totally unacceptable accommodation in the UK would be thought more than comfortable in large parts of India. Hence although an absolute criterion of poverty can have initial appeal, because it appears to give a simple standard that simplicity is misleading.

There can be no purely absolute standard; at least to some extent poverty must be related to a given society and the concept of poverty will alter according to the society considered.

Defeatism and Selfishness

It is worth noting that 'the poor are always with us' has been used in a defeatist way to excuse any attempt to help the poor. It has been argued, even by those who do not take the sentence as a tautology, that it is pointless to try to alter circumstances. Such people believe, or say they believe, that relief efforts are a labour of Sisyphus – and can change nothing. The implication is that the problem is so great that nothing anyone does can make a significant difference and therefore since no action is worthwhile there is no need to feel guilty about giving no help. But almost always this is an excuse for selfishnes; as James Fishkin points out this attitude masks an indulgence in self-serving cynicism.[4]

There is also a different excuse for apathy which is primarily directed against a relativist assessment of poverty. Here, the implication is that well-to-do and relatively well-to-do people may be compassionate when faced with abject destitution but are not prepared to sympathize with complaints about a lack of technological consumer goods, that is, a lack of the relatively common 'luxuries' that are seen as part of everyday life in the affluent West. In the UK, for example, there are dismissive references *ad nauseam* to those on income support expecting colour television sets and spending money on cigarettes and liquor.

Certainly most of the relatively poor (those in the West) along with most of the well-to-do, spend unwisely; perhaps it is not surprising that those living quite close to (though not quite at) subsistence level look for easy and un-demanding relaxation. There is a social problem here that does not lie within the scope of this essay. I allude to the dismissive references, which are at least to some extent based on fact, only because (in general) those who make them do not do so in order to highlight any social or psychological problem but to provide a convenient excuse for their lack of charity. I maintain that it does not follow that because there is horrific poverty and destitution in various parts of the world that we need not be concerned with a different order of poverty and deprivation in our own country. Moreover, as I indicated earlier, I suspect that those who disregard the plight of the poor in their own country, as being no matter of moment, are not particularly concerned with the even greater desti-tution overseas.

Compassion and Guilt

Most people, with the possible exception of psychopaths, do feel considerable compassion for the unfortunate, not only for unfortunate human beings but also for non-human animals. Moreover the compassion may be elicited not only by poverty but by awareness of pain and suffering, or bereavement or disap-pointment. Here, while we are concerned with poverty in general, it is as well to bear in mind that there are forms of deprivation not directly related to lack of money. However, a characteristic of economic poverty, perhaps not found so markedly with other kinds of deprivation, is that it is much more likely that it can be relieved, or ameliorated; at least we know what needs to be done as a first step.

Compassion is almost universal and, as I have implied, even those who do nothing and give little feel the need for some excuse for their inaction. This is shown, as I said earlier, in their defeatist welcome of 'the poor are always with us' (usually by those who have not considered whether this is a concealed tautology or a factual statement) and their dismissal of the existence of 'real' poverty in the West. The very selfish may thus completely stifle what little compassion they have, and most of us are selfish enough to moderate our compassion (even though it is not completely suppressed) because at bottom we know we could do and give more. Suppressed compassion is inevitably attended by guilt.

But many people genuinely do want to help. Admittedly the desire is often transitory, the response to a television programme, for example about a sick child overseas. It may well take the form of agitating that *someone else* undertake a mission of mercy, but it is still there. There are indeed exceptional people who devote their lives to others, both at home and in distant countries but most of us do very little and give relatively little and therefore feel guilty about what we know is a trivial response. One major problem for the fortunate is how much more they should give and what else they should do. They feel compassion. But is compassion enough? What is their duty?

I have argued elsewhere that we should not be overwhelmed by the misery in the world around us; we cannot help everyone.[5] In his assessment of utilitarianism the same point is made by Bernard Williams:

> The demands of utilitarianism for maximum welfare production are boundless. There is no limit to what a person might be doing to improve the world, except the limits of time and strength. Moreover, because the relations of possible states of affairs to any given person's actions are indeterminate, the demands are boundless in the further sense that there are often no clear boundaries between the demands on me and the demands on someone else.[6]

By contrast some philosophers, for example Peter Singer, have argued that we have a moral duty to help those in need to the limits of our ability. In other words we are morally obliged to give so much that we reduce our standard of life to only just above the point where our gift would cause as much suffering to ourselves (and any dependents) as those we seek to relieve.[7] This is to expect a saintly concern for the welfare of others for it is to assert that morality *demands* heroic sacrifice. Singer himself appreciates that few will sacrifice on such a scale and suggests that it would be realistic to propose donating one tenth of income to the starving. However, Singer regards this as a purely practical approach; literally, half a loaf is better than no bread; in moral terms there should be complete sacrifice.[8]

In his essay 'Judgement Day' Louis Pascal at first appears to take the same view as Singer. He writes,

> If you are part of that small portion of humanity who are to a significant degree happy, and if your happiness is to any extent at all dependent upon material goods or leisure time, then your happiness is bought at the expense of the misery, degradation, and the lives of your fellow human beings. How many people had to die and how many people

had to suffer in order for you to enjoy that wealth and leisure? How many people could you have saved had you not preferred your comfort to their lives?[9]

However Pascal comes to the conclusion that aid in the form of food or medical technology (with the exception of birth control devices) must encourage further population growth and thus must exacerbate the problem. He concludes that, apart from countries about to achieve population stablization, all aid should be cut off 'and the sooner the better'.[10]

Garrett Hardin takes a similar line which is outlined by Singer as follows:

> we in the rich nations are like the occupants of a crowded lifeboat adrift in a sea of drowning people. If we try to save the drowning by bringing them aboard our boat will become overloaded and we shall all drown. Since it is better that some survive than none, we should leave the others to drown. In the world today, according to Hardin, 'lifeboat ethics' apply. The rich should leave the poor to starve, for otherwise the poor will drag the rich down with them.[11]

Fishkin is close to Singer in admitting a moral obligation to help but, unlike Singer, he is not prepared to accept that we are morally obliged to make heroic sacrifices; he believes that there must be a cut-off point for heroism.[12] He does not discuss the extent of morally obligatory sacrifice: whether it should be 5 per cent, 10 per cent, 50 per cent, or more of the disposable income.[13] He is concerned with the moral problem that follows from accepting that we all do have a general obligation to help those in need.

He writes as though the problem has arisen relatively recently in that it is only in the last few decades that we have come to be aware of deprivation overseas. But, as remarked at the start of this chapter, there has always been acute poverty. It has been present through all recorded history. Poverty in feudal times was terrible and was no less so after the Industrial Revolution in the West – far greater than private individuals, or even private charities, could assuage. In the early twentieth century Leonard Woolf had been a British Government District Officer in Ceylon. When he returned to England he did some social relief work in London and wrote,

> There was no doubt about the poverty in the east end of London in 1912; I would rather have lived in a hut in a Ceylon village than in the poverty stricken, sordid, dilapidated, god-forsaken hovels of Hoxton. And the moment I stood in their grim rooms and began to speak to the dejected inhabitants, whose voices and faces revealed nothing but the depths of their hopelessness, I realized my hopelessness and helplessness there . . . in Hoxton one was confronted by some vast, dangerous fault in the social stucture, some destructive disease in the social organism, which could not be touched by paternalism or charity or good works.[14]

There is still poverty in the UK but social and political changes have made some improvement. Even so there is room for further improvement and it is possible that a radical restructuring of the methods for coping with relative poverty – in the Third World as well in the West – is needed.

On the empirical evidence available it does not seem that socialism and a socialist (communist) economy will help. Thomas Nagel suggests that we all must take a different attitude to the underprivileged and then we might come to accept a social system in which it is not the case that 'rewards do *not* depend on productive contribution, and in particular that some people receive much more of the social product than they contribute'.[15] He argues that there must be a notion of negative responsibility on the part of society for failing to arrange support and he contends: 'The sense that benefits not provided, which could be provided, are being *withheld* from the poor, will seem unnatural only if one rejects the assumption of negative responsibility.'[16]

It might be thought ridiculously Utopian to suggest that members of a modern western capitalist society could come to accept that reward was not tied to contribution but, apart from the fact that Nagel is not suggesting that there should be *no* correlation of talent and effort with reward, he points out that in this century there have been very deep changes in personal attitudes:

> Transformations in the tolerance of inequality can occur. In the United States, during my lifetime, and in other Western countries, there has been such a change in attitudes toward overt racial and sexual discrimination . . . I hope I am not too optimistic in believing that most white males in North America or Western Europe today would feel uncomfortable about being awarded a job or admission that excluded blacks or women, or held them to higher qualifications. Most potential beneficiaries of such discrimination do not want it reinstated and would not, if it occurred, simply count themselves fortunate to be on the winning side of the racial or sexual divide. They would feel benefits gained in this way were tainted, even dishonourable. Formerly that was not generally true; the legal abolition of overt discrimination – practised, enforced, or protected by the state – has had a deep mental effect, which gives the legal result stability.[17]

Nagel is considering the underprivileged in the West (the relatively poor) but the same change in attitude in relation to people in less affluent countries, and to their economies is needed. In the long run this is a matter of policy and, in the long run it requires not only a change in the West but also a change in the attitudes of those rich (sometimes super-rich) nationals of the Third World countries themselves. Such changes have yet to come but it is worth bearing in mind that charity can be nothing but a temporary panacea.

In relation to charity Fishkin maintains, like Singer, that we do have a positive general obligation to help others in need, that is, to show what he calls *minimal altruism*, namely, that if we can save a human life at minor cost, we are obliged to do so.[18] There seems to be no question that, on moral grounds, a relatively small, for most of us an insignificantly small, donation should be made to save another human being from starvation. But there are tens, possibly hundreds, of thousands of starving people, and, as Fishkin points out, it is this which is the basis of our moral problem. That problem arises when we face large-scale poverty for, by accepting the principle of minimal altruism as well as maintaining that we are not morally obliged to make heroic sacrifices, we arrive at an impossible moral position:

> small scale sacrifices, if large enough in number, add up to heroic totals. And our usual criteria for differentiating obligations and supererogatory acts of heroism are inadequate for this kind of case. Yet these same criteria are adequate when smaller numbers are involved. A small number of minor sacrifices would not add up to anything significant. And if the sacrifices were more than insignificant to begin with, then a principle of minimal altruism would not obligate us to make them. It is only when the numbers are large enough that a principle of minimal altruism can entail requirements for sacrifice so great that they add up to heroic proportions.[19]

Fishkin admits that he has no easy answer to the problem[20] and that he cannot formulate a coherent moral position. He concludes that the admission of a principle of general obligation must lead to the breakdown of the basic structure of individual morality. Yet he does not wish to reject that principle, in order to maintain a coherent position. He writes,

> we could maintain the basic structure in its entirety but give up the notion of general obligation. I believe that this is, in its own way, equally troubling. For it would seem a denial of our common humanity not to admit some general obligations to perform actions on behalf of any other person, even a total stranger.[21]

Considering the moral consequences of our actions, Fishkin gives a choice:

> must we then defend the notion that the world is in a morally preferable state: (a) when we live in comparative luxury and frivolity while some people starve, as opposed to (b) when we efficaciously sacrifice as much as we can – in time, effort, amd resources – to ensure that no one, or as few persons as possible, is starving?
> . . . Either the *a* alternative . . . is a morally better state of the world (the state in which we continue our way of life and others starve) or *b* is really better, and we are then obligated to do what we can to see that as few starve as possible.[22]

He thinks that the general obligation to save life (at minimum risk to oneself) must be retained and that it is morally indefensible to treat a comfortable cultured life-style as sacrosanct. Thus, though conceding the coherence of the position taken by Jan Narveson, namely, 'the importance of the kind of life we have set out to live is greater than the amount of suffering preventable by depriving ourselves of the means to live it',[23] he condemns it.

That condemnation is interesting, for it is clear that most of us do regard the kind of life we have set out to live as more important than donating large sums to famine relief. In this context there can be no doubt that actions speak louder than words. The question is whether we are immoral through failing in our duty, that is, in disregarding the general obligation to save life.

Duty and Benevolence

I should like to suggest another way to resolve this problem, and thus to maintain a coherent moral position. It does not necessarily mean that we avoid condemnation for selfishness but it does avoid the accusation of failing in our *duty*. This solution involves replacing the concept of general *positive obligation* by a concept of general *benevolence*.

To act benevolently is to act not out of a sense of moral obligation but through charity or love for one's fellows. Just as there are general and particular obligations so there is general and particular charity. I suggest that positive obligations are always particular obligations: those we have explicity (and perhaps legally) contracted or those which we accept implicitly as parents, children, spouses and friends. It does not follow that we then have no moral obligations to strangers for we certainly have a general negative obligation to avoid harming them through injury, verbal abuse, various types of discrimination (e.g. racial and sexual discrimination), dishonesty and fraud. In addition I suggest that we do have moral obligations to those strangers whom we directly encounter, albeit by chance. It is in this context that we acquire a duty (assuming no great risk to ourselves, i.e. minimal altruism) to save a child we see drowning or to pull a baby from the flames, to feed the starving man who comes to our door and, like the Good Samaritan, to comfort someone in distress. I would maintain that proximity does indeed make a difference, a difference so great that when we encounter distress personally, general positive benevolence involves a particular moral obligation to help.

In so far as we understand compassion as an aspect of benevolence we may feel morally obliged to help strangers far away but this is a matter of personal choice, not a universal moral law. This is not, of course, to say that we should ignore distant misfortune, nor is it to say that those who respond are misguided, but I do maintain that their response to distant suffering arises from compassion, and that this is as an aspect of benevolence and not a matter of duty.

Such a view of duty may be disputed and it is therefore necessary explicitly to defend it, for duty is not a simple concept. As I have just indicated, in everyday life positive duties are particular duties; they are related either to obligations incurred through accepting a role in a community (voluntary or paid) whereby others can rely on the carrying out of appropriate tasks, or to fulfilling commitments made by promises and contracts.[24] But acceptance of a duty, as a moral obligation, should not be only a matter of conforming to social rules and social custom; the social situation counts for one aspect of duty but there should also be the *wish* to act morally.

Following the Kantian analysis of moral action, if we are to act purely from moral motives we must act autonomously and not as a result of social pressure. But Kant's view of morality is based solely on the purely rational acceptance of a moral principle, whereas I suggest that we should acknowledge not only that society but also our own emotions can and do influence us. Nor, I suggest, is it necessary to accept Kant's view that moral action is entirely divorced from pleasure, the pleasure of being benevolent. Kant writes,

> To help others where one can is a duty, and besides this there are many spirits of so sympathetic a temper that, without any further motive of vanity or self-interest, they find an inner pleasure in spreading happiness around them and can take delight in the contentment of others as their own work. Yet I maintain that in such a case an action of this kind, however right and however amiable it may be, has still no genuinely moral worth. It stands on the same footing as other inclinations – for example the inclination for honour . . . for its maxim lacks moral content, namely the performance of such actions, not from inclination, but *from duty* . . . when no longer moved by any inclination . . . [he] does the action for the sake of duty alone; then for the first time his action has its genuine moral worth. Still further: if nature had implanted little sympathy in this or that man's heart . . . would he not still find in himself a source from which he might draw a worth far higher than any that a good-natured temperament can have? Assuredly he would. It is precisely in this that the worth of character begins to show – a moral worth and beyond all comparison the highest – namely, that he does good, not from inclination, but from duty.[25]

Kant stresses that moral worth lies in acting according to the principle of duty and not in the purpose to be attained by it.[26] Thus he would have acknowledged no moral worth in benevolence and compassion *per se* nor in an active desire to relieve suffering. Kant relates duty to his Categorical Imperative: 'I ought never to act except in such a way *that I can also will that my maxim should become a universal law*'.[27]

However it does not follow, even with such a stern view of moral obligation, that Kant would have regarded heroic sacrifice as morally required by his Categorical Imperative. It could be reasonably argued, for instance, that the maintenance of a cultivated life-style, allowing the possibility of philosophic criticism, was also subject to the universal law. There is scope for argument (and perhaps an agreement to differ) as to whether the Categorical Imperative can accommodate a limitation of sacrifice – a cut-off point for heroism.

Ought Implies Can

There is also another restriction: Kant said it is a duty to help others where one can and this is clearly in accord with his Categorical Imperative. But quite apart from any conflict with a life-style, there is some restriction on that imperative in that we cannot act in accord with the impossible. Williams says,

> The fact that moral obligation is a kind of practical conclusion explains several of its features . . . it is an obligation to do something – and the action must be in the agent's power . . . If my deliberation issues in something that I cannot do, then I must deliberate again.[28]

Williams points out that the question of what is in an agent's power is complex because if we grant that we are partly or wholly determined there are psychological as well as physical factors that need to be considered. But here I shall confine discussion of the agent's power to a consideration of the fact that no single individual can possibly help all those who need help. In that case, if the concept of moral duty is only applicable to cases where there is economic power to act, then, even within her own quite restricted social group, no person can help all those in need and therefore no person can be morally obliged to help everyone even in that group.

Who to Help

We have particular obligations to those we know and to those whom we directly encounter. In many ways Kant's rational but emotionless understanding of the nature of duty is helpful in establishing a framework to study the nature of moral obligation. But it cannot help us to decide between obligations any more than can the utilitarian thesis that, in effect, rules it a duty to maximize happiness (or minimize unhappiness). Whichever of these two ethical theories we favour we have to appeal to some other standard in order to rank duties. We cannot fulfill even our particular obligations and we need a guide as to *which* of the many large cases we shall favour. In my view it is here that the Kantian dismissal of inclination as a moral motive is incorrect.

I suggest that we have a stronger *duty* to help those near to home and that our obligations, explicit and implicit, are greater to those nearest to us. This is supported by most people's strong inclination to help those close to them. In addition I suggest a pragmatic reason in that a moral duty becomes stronger if we think that our actions will be effective.

To develop these points further: firstly there is no doubt that we are more concerned with the welfare of those closest to us: family, personal friends, neighbours and fellow citizens. Quite apart from the genetic/evolutionary aspects of altruism there is another important factor operating in human societies. For the nearer the relationship the more readily we can appreciate that what we do personally, in the way of gifts and direct help will have beneficial practical results.

Then, in relation to efficacy, we know that aid sent far away is more likely to be wasted by being wrongly directed or being misappropriated. Aid given close at hand may also be wasted but the opportunity for waste is much less. Moreover we can often see what good is done. This is not necessarily a mere manifestation of self-righteousness but rather a genuine pleasure in relieving distress, a pleasure arising from our sympathy for others. This pleasure adds to the moral value of giving rather than, as Kant maintained, detracting from it. In other words the old adage 'It is better to give than to receive' is true. At the very least it is just as good to give as to receive; I maintain strongly that duty done cheerfully and willingly is more valuable both to those who give and to those who receive.

How Should Aid Be Directed?

Compassion urges support for more than our relatives and friends and it may be directed to support international agencies or to established national and local charities. In the latter case there is the advantage that the voluntary offer of time and effort rather than money need not involve abandoning a person's livelihood or deserting family and friends. People can do their regular work whilst sacrificing some of their leisure (time they might have spent on amusements and in congenial company) in order to help those in need. Thus people can play their part as ordinary citizens as well as giving something extra to those in need. The former is not to be regarded as of no relevance here because it is as ordinary citizens that people contribute to the general wealth, both through the work they do and through the taxes they pay.

But even without active participation in charitable works there is still much that can be done through gifts of money and goods. An argument for giving help at home rather than elsewhere is that there it is possible to choose the particular areas of distress to relieve. There is no demerit in showing favouritism; it is impossible for even the wealthiest individual to help everyone and by choosing those needs for which we feel especial sympathy we are more likely to make greater sacrifices. It is obvious that such voluntary and perhaps considerable sacrifice can and will be made more readily if there is some active personal interest and involvement. This is *not* to advocate seeking out only the 'deserving poor' (indeed we may feel more sympathy for the undeserving rogue), but it is to oppose the Kantian view that there is no special moral goodness in helping those to whom we are emotionally attached. I suggest that moral value attaches to and is to be found in taking active pleasure in our good works. It shows no less compassion to help those causes which we personally desire to promote; our moral duty to help others need not and perhaps should not be regarded as a heavy burden.

The Danger of Preferences

Would this mean that certain forms of distress would receive scant attention? Children in distress, victims of terrorist attacks, and dramatic natural calamities, environmental dangers and certain diseases might get a lot of attention whereas the old and senile, the mentally ill and the mentally retarded, newly released prisoners and drug addicts might be ignored. Quite apart from some especially heart-rending forms of deprivation there are, undoubtedly, fashions in charities; at present cancer relief and ecology are prime favourites. However though it is undeniable that certain charities attract funds more readily than others I do not think that this is a relevant objection when we are considering personal generosity. Here preferences are to be encouraged. It is in the field of government aid through taxation that the less popular causes should be helped.

Political Action

This brings me to a second reason for suggesting that there is a duty to give prior attention to the needs of those close at hand, for these are the people whose needs we can directly affect with our votes at national and at local level. In relation to the narrow constituencies of local politics there is the possibility of exerting considerably influence at the ballot box and perhaps, too, some additional effect through personal contact with local councillors.

In western democracies people can also seek to influence their national government by voting for political parties and politicians most likely to promote help for the needy. Yet relief of poverty is not just a question of giving money; as I argued earlier, charity is nothing more than a panacea and will generally be transitory and inadequate. Some of the structural changes that Leonard Woolf thought were necessary have been implemented in the UK and in some other western countries. However, there is likely to be a need for some fundamental changes in personal attitudes of the kind proposed by Nagel, involving a relaxation of the relation between rewards and productive contribution. Our problems may remain unless the concept of negative responsibility on the part of society becomes generally acceptable.

Even if Nagel's suggestions are dismissed there can be no doubt that deep changes are necessary in notions of responsibility and social structure in all countries. But what influence can western voters have on political and social policies in other countries? Indeed most would agree that even to attempt to do this through a policy involving sticks and carrots would be morally objectionable. This is a practical as well as a moral problem. In many countries well-meaning attempts to provide aid, even with no political overtones, have not always been welcomed and sometimes aid workers are rebuffed. Nevertheless, one way of influencing the Third World is to change western attitudes to the unfortunate in all countries; example will be more powerful than any precepts.

Now of course it will be said that, bad as conditions are at home, problems are relatively trivial as compared with many misfortunes overseas. As argued earlier, such an opinion need not be voiced as a consequence of selfishness, but because those whose compassion is so deeply stirred by deep distress feel that to offer any limited help to those who are, undeniably, far better off is to support what are comparatively frivolous enterprises. Surely, they argue, if children are dying of starvation we should give all that we can to them, even if we cannot be sure that all money will be properly used and even if it may be inadequate. Is it not frivolous and almost irresponsible to support local charities for cancer research, or housing aid, or telephone advice and sympathy for the near-suicidal, or gifts to an old people's home here and to ignore the destitute overseas? How much more frivolous and irresponsible to contribute to music scholarships or to the repair of ancient monuments or a national arts-collection fund? What these examples suggest is that it is necessary for each of us to choose our obligations and that we are not bound to regard preservation of life itself as the most outstanding obligation. It can be just as much an obligation to make life worth living.

Our Debt to the Future

Our debt to future generations involves not only preservation of the natural environment but also preservation of a wonderful cultural heritage: its music, its literature and its art. There was poverty, serfdom and slavery in ancient Egypt, in ancient Greece, in China, in India, in Aztec America and in Renaissance Italy. Yet our lives benefit from their arts and are unaffected by their social distress. We must not only preserve what we received but also add to and develop that heritage. Yet the creativity which produces art, then and now, is at least in part a result of the patronage and leisure enjoyed by a privileged few. The same must be acknowledged for learning and advances in learning. This is not to advocate elitism, for the pleasure produced by the gifted few can be shared by the many.[29]

Though the final plea for consideration of quality is made by metaphorical appeal to a biblical text, that text is intended to illustrate the secular position: bare existence is *not* enough and is hardly worth having. There is also a need for the enrichment of human life beyond mere subsistence. The case is put in the full quotation:

> There came unto him a woman having an alabaster box of very precious ointment, and poured it on his head, as he sat *at meat*.

But when his disciples saw *it*, they had indignation, saying, To what purpose *is* this waste?

For this ointment might have been sold for much, and given to the poor.

When Jesus understood *it*, he said unto them, Why trouble ye the woman? for she hath wrought a good work upon me.

For ye have the poor always with you; but me ye have not always.

For in that she hath poured this ointment on my body, she did *it* for my burial.

Verily I say unto you. Wheresoever this gospel shall be preached in the whole world, *there* shall also this, that this woman hath done, be told for a memorial of her.[30]

NOTES

1 Matthew 26: 11.
2 Shaw, 'Poverty: absolute or relative?', p. 35.
3 The European Union has adopted a relative view when assessing the poverty of entire countries, counting a country as poor if it has less than half the average income of the countries of the EU at any particular time. However this is of dubious value since the average must be based on suspect figures and also can mask vast individual differences within any country. As will be seen from the text, the relativist view favoured here is the assessment of poverty (or lack of poverty) of *individuals* in relation to the society in which they live.
4 Fishkin, *Limits of Obligation*, p. 6.
5 Trusted, 'The problem of absolute poverty'.
6 Williams, *Ethics and the Limits of Philosophy*, p. 77.
7 Singer, 'Famine, affluence and morality', p. 33.
8 Singer, *Practical Ethics*, p. 181.
9 Pascal, 'Judgement Day', p. 114.
10 Pascal, 'Judgement Day', p. 119.
11 Singer, *Practical Ethics*, p. 175.
12 Fishkin, *Limits of Obligation*, p. 5.
13 In fact I think that the percentage must depend on the means of the donor; clearly it is easier to give a large percentage of a large income than to give quite a small percentage from an income which provides only modest comfort.
14 Woolf, *Beginning Again*, p. 100.
15 Nagel, *Equality and Partiality*, p. 99.
16 Ibid., p. 101.
17 Ibid., pp. 96–7.
18 Fishkin, *Limits of Obligation*, p. 3.
19 Ibid., pp. 6–7.
20 Ibid.
21 Ibid., p. 33.
22 Ibid., pp. 75–6.
23 Quoted by Fishkin, *Limits of Obligation*, p. 77, from Narveson, 'Aesthetics, charity', p. 551.
24 Williams, *Ethics and the Limits of Philosophy*, p. 27.
25 Kant, *The Moral Law*, pp. 63–4.

26 Ibid., p. 65.
27 Ibid., p. 67.
28 Williams, *Ethics and the Limits of Philosophy*, p. 175.
29 I would argue that the view is one of perfectionism rather than elitism. The distinction is made by Derek Parfit in his paper 'Overpopulation and the quality of life.'
30 Matthew 26: 7–13.

READING GUIDE

Apart from the books and articles referred to in the text two general books on social justice are those by John Rawls, *A Theory of Justice*, and Robert Nozick, *Anarchy, State and Utopia*. These are important texts in their own right but certain chapters are especially relevant here. In Rawls, see particularly chapters 5 and 6 and in Nozick, chapter 7, 'Distributive justice'.

A book concerned especially with Third World problems and adopting a Kantian perspective is Onora O'Neill's *Faces of Hunger*. The issues are also set out succinctly by Nigel Dower in his contribution to *A Companion to Ethics*, edited by P. Singer, chapter 23, 'Justice and the Third World' and is treated in depth in his book *World Poverty: Challenge and Response*.

Both in the article mentioned in the text, 'Famine, affluence and morality' and in chapter 8 of *Practical Ethics*, 2nd edn, Peter Singer offers an interesting treatment of these issues from a utilitarian moral position. He provides a useful, detailed and extensive bibliography in connection with this chapter. There is also a selection of relevant papers in *Moral Problems*, edited by J. Rachels.

See also *The Limits of Obligation* by James Fishkin; *World Hunger and Moral Obligation* edited by W. Aiken and H. LaFollette; and *International Justice and the Third World*, edited by R. Attfield and B. Wilkins.

CLASSICAL SOURCES

Hume: *A Treatise of Human Nature*, Book III, part II
Malthus: *An Essay on the Principle of Population*
Smith: *An Inquiry into the Nature and Causes of the Wealth of Nations*

20

War, Terrorism and Ethical Consistency

Gerry Wallace

There is a wide moral consensus that although the waging of war can sometimes be justified terrorism is always wrong. This orthodoxy is challenged from two diametrically opposed positions. For the pacifist both war and terrorism are absolutely wrong and for the same reason: they involve violence. The apologist for terrorism also rejects the conventional view but arrives at the opposite conclusion to the pacifist: for him both war and terrorism are capable of moral justification. These two approaches, otherwise totally different, are alike in one important respect: they imply that the orthodox moral view is ethically inconsistent. The pacifist condemns both the violence of war and the violence of terrorism. The apologist for terrorism argues that if just wars are possible then terrorism as a form of war can be justified.

Whether or not the conventional view is ethically consistent is the subject of this paper. Ethical consistency is, of course, a complex matter in its own right[1] and war and terrorism introduce additional difficulties. Orthodoxy allows that violence can be justified but insists that whatever justifies war cannot justify terrorism. So we must ask: what is the moral basis of the conventional attitude to war? Is terrorism a form of war? Indeed, what is terrorism? What concept of terrorism underpins the orthodox position? Does terrorism involve an evil in addition to those of war? If so, what is it?

Just War Theory

Orthodox moral thinking about the morality of war would seem to be mainly based on Just War theory, a way of thinking about the morality of war originally codified by medieval writers such as Thomas Aquinas and Franciscus de

306 *International and Global Dimensions*

Vitoria.[2] In accordance with Just War theory, war is only justified when two extremely general conditions are satisfied: it must be undertaken for a just cause (*jus ad bellum*) and be prosecuted by just means (*jus in bello*).

Although this might seem platitudinous, it reminds us that a war can be appraised morally from two different standpoints: first, under what conditions is going to war to be justified and, second, how must warfare be conducted if it is to be morally acceptable? However, when we turn to more detailed statements of the theory we see that the just war approach is essentially a humane way of thinking about war rather than a set of precise and agreed rules. Scientific theories can be stated definitively, moral theories only rarely so. In the present case, within a broad consensus, we find different writers and institutions offering a variety of interpretations. For Aquinas three conditions are necessary if waging war is not to be 'sinful'. First, the authority of the sovereign by whose command the war is waged is required. Second, there must be a just cause; those who are attacked must deserve the attack on account of some fault. Third, war must be waged with the rightful intention of advancing good and avoiding evil.[3]

Although it is not unusual for commentators to gloss 'sinful' as 'morally wrong' we need to remember that for Aquinas the concept of sin necessarily involves a reference to God's will, something which secular moral language lacks. This makes little difference to Aquinas's second and third conditions but it probably does to the first. For Aquinas, the sovereign's authority is morally required because only he or she can legitimize the killing that war involves and the sovereign has a duty to God not to abuse this power.[4] But a secular interpretation is also possible. Aquinas might be making a conceptual rather than a moral point to the effect that collective violence against a state only *constitutes* war when undertaken on the authority of the sovereign. Accordingly a terrorist group such as the IRA. or PLO. would be logically incapable of waging war for want of the necessary authority.

For Aquinas, the question of when war may be justified brings with it a background of kingdoms in conflict, a perspective that needs to be modified if it is to fit modern political institutions where the norm is the nation-state (commonly a republic and sometimes a democracy). The transition is complicated by the fact that Aquinas's first condition seems, without more ado, to make rebellion and civil war unjustifiable. The question, then, for anyone who thinks that rebellion and revolution *are* sometimes morally justified, as many contemporary Just War theorists and upholders of the orthodox view do, is whether the theory can be modified without at the same time legitimizing terrorist violence. Since the resort to terrorism, like civil war and revolution, commonly occurs in conditions where the legitimacy of the state is disputed, the question has important implications for the moral comparison between war and terrorism.

Aquinas's other two conditions – just cause and rightful intention – also require elucidation. What kinds of 'fault' justify attack? What is it to conduct war with a 'rightful intention'?

'Just cause' is commonly understood as implying a 'wrong received' which entitles the victim to use force to defend itself and to prevent further attacks. Within the Just War tradition, however, disagreement arises over the extent to which *punitive* action as distinct from *self-defensive* action is legitimate. Aquinas's formulation, couched in terms of 'faults' which 'deserve' attack, appears to support the former reading but contemporary theorists – as well as the UN Charter – define 'just cause' in terms of the use of force in response to aggression solely for the purpose of national self-defence. More importantly for our purposes, there is a conflict between the UN Charter and the 'self-defence' version of just cause when restricted to nation-states. The latter implies that any form of warfare – and, thus, terrorism when conceived of as war – is unjustifiable except when it is waged by a nation-state. In contrast Article 7 is less restrictive: commenting on the definition of 'aggression' it asserts that nothing in the definition 'could in any way prejudice the right to self-determination . . . of *peoples* . . . forcibly deprived of that right' (my emphasis). On this interpretation it is not merely nation-states, still less kingdoms, that can have just cause but also peoples.

Contemporary Just War theorists explicate Aquinas's 'rightful intention' by means of a number of principles.[5] War must be a last resort, undertaken out of necessity and with some hope of success. It must not only be a proportionate response but waged with proportionality whilst respecting non-combatant immunity, an admirable attempt to limit the evils of war. Only when other means of resolving the conflict have failed may war be unleashed. Even then just war is not revenge; there must be some prospect of the overall moral situation being improved, or at least prevented from degenerating further. It must be a necessary means to attaining those ends, in proportion to the original wrong and proportionality must govern the conduct of war; massacre and over-kill, no matter how just the cause or heinous the original offence, are never justified.

Despite their other differences, upholders of the Just War theory normally accept some form of the non-combatant immunity principle according to which the targeting of non-combatants (or innocents) is forbidden even if more good than evil will result. It is often said that terrorism is wrong because it inevitably violates this principle and that if terrorism *is* a form of war, it is a necessarily unjust form. We shall return to this point later but it is worth noting that within the Just War tradition there is room for disagreement over who or what may be legitimately targeted. Are political rulers legitimate targets? Are clearly foreseen but unintended civilian casualties – so called 'collateral damage – acceptable? Is the maker of the bullet immune to attack but not the soldier who fires it? What about off-duty military personnel?[6]

However, though these problems of application are important, it is sufficient for our purposes to note that within the Just War tradition a fundamental distinction exists between who may be targeted and who may not; and considerations of consequence can never, or only in exceptional circumstances, supplant this.

Innocent Immunity

The idea that terrorism is wrong because it violates the non-combatant/innocent immunity principle would provide a *rationale* for the orthodox position. War is just, other things being equal, when the principle is respected. Since, *ex hypothesi*, terrorism always violates the principle, it can never be justified. Two questions arise. Is targeting the innocent in war always morally impermissible? If it is not, does this provide the apologist for terrorism with a model for justifying terrorism?

Let us approach these questions by considering some situations in which, it is said, the non-combatant/innocent principle can be ignored. The bombing of Hiroshima and Nagasaki at the end of World War II is commonly defended on the grounds that although it involved the deliberate killing of innocent people it brought the war to an early end and with fewer casualties.[7] The notion of 'innocents' in this context is relatively uncontroversial; targeting cities meant that non-combatants of all kinds were attacked: women, children, the disabled and the feeble-minded, in other words, people who posed no threat whatsover to Allied forces. Does this provide a plausible moral analogy for the apologist for terrorism?

There are, I suggest, two reasons why it does not. First, the idea that civilian deaths are justified provided they reduce combatant casualties to a minimum has little relevance to the typical terrorist situation where such considerations do not usually arise. Second, the crude form of calculation involved leads to morally repellent conclusions in other contexts so it would be unconvincing for the apologist to rely on it in the present one. For instance, killing an innocent person would not be justified even if this enabled doctors to acquire the organs required to save the lives of seriously ill patients; the aggregation involved is morally repugnant.

So if the utilitarian calculation is to be plausible it must satisfy a number of other requirements of Just War theory. The resort by Britain to area bombing in 1940–1 ('terror' bombing, as it was sometimes called), that is, the deliberate targeting of civilians by attacks on residential areas of German cities, is perhaps a more persuasive example.[8] France had been defeated and the USA had not entered the war. British civilians were being killed in large numbers by Luftwaffe attacks on British towns and cities. For a variety of reasons Britain's own airforce was incapable of mounting successful strategic bombing missions against German targets.[9] The army had been vanquished and the navy severely weakened by submarine warfare. In these desperate and exceptional circumstances area bombing was a last resort aimed at destroying the morale and will of the German people and averting invasion and defeat by a power committed to racism and genocide.

To defend area bombing in these extreme circumstances is not to imply that it would be justified if other options were available – as was the case with the horrific bombing of Dresden and other German towns later in the war. Nor are civilian deaths being 'traded off' against military ones, something clearly at odds with the Just War tradition. The crucial appeal is to the idea of determining *which* innocent deaths will occur in circumstances where it is certain that *some* will. This reminds us that the absolute prohibition on targeting innocents, which Just War theory is often taken to involve, entails that a nation or people must be prepared to suffer innocent deaths without replying in kind. This remains true even when this is the *only* response open to it which has any chance of success. Noble though this may be, it is by no means obvious that retaliation which has some defensive potential is incompatible with waging war with 'rightful intention', especially when such restraint makes the victory of an evil regime like Hitler's Germany more likely.

Let us suppose for the purposes of argument that the principle of innocent/ non-combatant immunity is open to question in the kind of extremely perilous war situation we have described, under the conditions specified and when the beneficiary of restraint is a regime as evil as the Nazi one. Does it offer the apologist for terrorism a model for the justification of terrorism? In other words, if we are doubtful about innocent immunity in these extreme and highly specific circumstances must we be prepared to countenance the possibility of 'justified' terrorism in equally extreme circumstances?

There is little doubt that the resort to terrorism can satisfy the 'good cause' criterion. Communities can certainly face threats to their survival as grave as those Britain encountered in 1940. A tribe, ruler or government may set about exterminating a community or people as has happened to the Marsh Arabs and Kurds in Iraq in the 1980s and early 1990s and to many others elsewhere. So if terrorism is always wrong it must be for some other reason. Nor is it convincing to locate the wrongness of terrorism in a lack of legal legitimacy; as we have already noticed, the UN Charter recognizes that a people as well as a nation-state has a right to self-defence. The crucial question is whether terrorism – which for the moment we are assuming is a form of war that ignores the innocent immunity principle – is ever a morally acceptable form of communal self-defence.

If Britain's recourse to area bombing in 1940–1 was justified this was because five conditions were satisfied. (1) It was a measure of last resort; there was no effective military alternative and appeasement had failed. (2) It was an act of collective self-defence. (3) It was a reply in kind against a genocidal aggressor.

(4) It had some chance of success. (5) It was an attempt to determine which innocent deaths would occur in conditions where it was certain that some would. Remove any of these features and the case is considerably weakened. How closely can terrorism mirror these conditions?

Terrorism may occur in situations where it is not unreasonable to regard it as a measure of last resort. A people may be brutally oppressed by a genocidal regime and ignored by the world community or given no material assistance. There is a deep reluctance to acknowledge that terrorism can succeed in achieving its objectives and it is often condemned on the ground that no matter how just the cause it is bound to be counter-productive, produce pointless suffering and fail to satisfy condition (4). Comforting though this belief may be, it is hard to square with the brutal efficiency of terrorist campaigns in a number of colonial situations.

Nevertheless, we are not immediately forced to concede that the case for terrorism can be as strong as that for Britain's resort to area bombing in 1940. It must also be shown that conditions (1) and (4) can be satisfied *simultaneously*. If terrorism is to be a last resort the people or community involved must be confronted by an evil and powerful oppressor immune to moral argument, passive resistance and any form of opposition short of terrorism. So quasi-military responses such as guerrilla warfare or armed resistance must be ruled out as impossible or pointless; otherwise, they are to be preferred as morally better alternatives. But in these circumstances, how can a campaign of terrorism have any likelihood of ending the oppression? It is definitive of the last resort defence that powerlessness is confronted by brutal, unfeeling oppression. Given the nature of the hypothesized oppressor, the chances of succees are minimal; cruel and extensive 'counter-terrorist' measures are the almost certain outcome.[10]

So this way of defending terrorism – conceived of as a form of war which disregards the innocent immunity principle – is unconvincing because it is extremely unlikely that conditions (1) and (4) can be satisfied simultaneously. Furthermore, it is important to remember that the terrorist's primary concern is rarely collective self-defence; liberation and social justice are the usual watch-words so the analogy with physical survival in war is, at best, attenuated. This is damaging because, whatever its defects, it is hard to think of a more promising analogy from the apologist's point of view than one based on considerations of collective self-defence in perilous circumstances when the beneficiary of restraint is a regime given to genocide. That the orthodox view can withstand the comparision is evidence of its robustness.

The Nature of Terrorism and the Orthodox View

The orthodox view must obviously rest on a conception of what terrorism *is*. So far we have assumed that it is a form of war which by its nature violates the innocent/non-combatant immunity principle prominent in the Just War approach. This conception is an amalgam of two common definitions, one of which sees terrorism as a form of war, the other as necessarily involving attacks on the innocent. As we have seen, when it is approached in this way, a strong defence can be offered for the orthodox view. The trouble is that the hybrid conception is at best contentious and more probably inadequate. For some philosophers (e.g. Primoratz) the targeting of innocent people is indeed an essential feature; for others (e.g. Hare) it is not.[11] C. A. J. Coady believes that 'terrorism' as a matter of definition should be reserved for acts that are morally unjustified, whereas for Khatchadourian and Hare it is an open question whether terrorism is wrong by definition.[12] More generally, terrorism has been characterized as a form of war (Hughes), a form of crime or even as essentially ambiguous as between war and crime (Gilbert).[13] Whether assassination is terrorism or terrorism necessarily involves terror are further sources of disagreement.[14]

The idea that terrorism is a form of war rests, I believe, on a confusion between acts of terrorism and campaigns of terrorism. It is only plausible to regard the latter – the sort of thing waged by the IRA, the PLO or ETA – as a form of war. But there are also 'one-off' acts of terrorism. It has been suggested that Lockerbie was in revenge for the (accidental) shooting down of an airliner by the US Navy in the Gulf. Lockerbie was certainly an act of terrorism but it was not a war nor a form of war. Assassinations are also examples of 'one-off' acts which, according to circumstances, can be acts of terrorism.

In response to those, like Primoratz, who say that whether we are dealing with campaigns or acts of terrorism the crucial point is that innocent people are the targets, we must ask: Is this is a defining characteristic of terrorism?[15]

It is clear that terrorism is not always targeted on non-combatants; for instance, in Northern Ireland, IRA attacks on British soldiers have been routinely described as terrorist attacks even when those soldiers are on duty and aware of the possibility of attack. Further, when they are involved in counter-terrorist operations, it is surely tendentious to describe them as non-combatants. In reply, it might be said that though perhaps technically combatants, their rules of engagement are not those appropriate to a war situation and so morally speaking they are innocent. But, if we ignore the particular contingencies of the Northern Ireland situation (and the deployment of the SAS in it), it would be foolish to generalize and conclude that *whenever* troops are attacked by terrorists they will always be innocent in this sense. So we cannot rule out the possibility that in some situations terrorist attacks may be on those who are not innocent from a Just War point of view.

The notions of innocent and non-combatant are by no means synonymous and come from different areas of moral justification. Innocence is to be contrasted with guilt; the implication being that the wrongness of killing innocent people is akin to the injustice of punishing someone in whom there is no fault.[16] With the notions of combatant and non-combatant, the focus is on self-defence and the wrongness of killing signifies the absence of a threat rather than the absence of guilt. The term 'legitimate target' is used – perhaps sometimes with deliberate ambiguity – to cover both combatants and the guilty.

Whatever the complexities of the notion of 'innocence', the victims of terrorist violence are often innocent people; the indiscriminate nature of much terrorist violence makes it incompatible with any coherent account of what it is to be a 'legitimate target', 'at fault' or 'guilty'. This fact, plus the frequency of such attacks, leads naturally to the conclusion that it is of the essence of terrorism that its targets are innocent people. Furthermore, when terrorism is defined in these terms, there is a convincing *rationale* for the orthodox view; it is not of the essence of war that innocent people are attacked (though, of course, they often are) but it is a necessary feature of terrorism.

So the idea that terrorism is inevitably bound up with attacks on innocents must be taken seriously. Yet, the problem remains: how, if this is so, can attacks on on-duty soldiers be deemed to be attacks on innocents in the Just War sense? The Prevention of Terrorism Act (1984) definition allows that on-duty soldiers and those who are not members of the public can be terrorist targets because violence can be used against them for political ends: 'In this act unless the context otherwise requires . . . "terrorism" means the use of violence for political ends, and includes any use of violence for the purpose of putting the public or any section of the public in fear . . .'

An explanation of the attractions of defining terrorism in terms either of the innocence of its targets or in the broader way favoured by the Prevention of Terrorism Act is that the everyday concept of terrorism involves an ambiguity.[17] The notion of a 'terrorist attack' is a wide one and covers any attack by terrorists in pursuit of their cause. Thus attacks by, for instance, the IRA on soldiers, civilians, property, politicians or even symbolic targets have all been correctly described as terrorist attacks. With this variety and usage in mind it would not be surprising if we arrived at a definition of terrorism that was very wide and found no necessary connection between terrorism and the innocence of its targets.[18]

But a different approach is possible. We might concentrate our search for a definition on the question: What makes an organization like the IRA or PLO a terrorist organization *in the first place*? Would the IRA be a terrorist organization if it had restricted itself to attacks on symbolic targets or empty government buildings? Surely not. Welsh nationalist groups who have destroyed empty holiday cottages belonging to English people are not normally described as terrorists. Nor would attacks on symbolic targets by animal liberationists attract the label 'terrorist'. Therefore, the IRA would not have been a terrorist organization if it had restricted itself to symbolic targets, though in view of its *actual* history these are now described as 'terrorist attacks'!

The situation would be less clear had the IRA merely targeted armed soldiers. The mode, circumstances and purpose of the attacks together, perhaps, with an historical analysis of the Northern Ireland situation would be crucial. Parallels could be drawn with the French Resistance or guerrilla forces; arguments could be mustered either way. The important point is that there would be room for dispute whereas given the *actual* history of the IRA there can be no serious doubt that is a terrorist organization.

A *possible* explanation of the linguistic situation is that the IRA became a terrorist organization by pursuing its political goals through attacks on the public: putting bombs in shops, railway stations and the like; by committing what might be called 'acts of terrorism'. In similar fashion, we can be sure that those responsible for Lockerbie were terrorists because this is what they became by that act. Acts of terrorism in this sense are also, of course, terrorist attacks but not all terrorist attacks are acts of terrorism; for example attacks on symbolic targets are not.

This suggests that some of the confusion about how terrorism is to be defined, illustrated by the abundance of definitions on offer, can be explained by the failure to clarify the relationship between 'acts of terrorism' in the above sense and 'terrorist attacks'. Broad definitions will naturally arise when we concentrate on 'terrorist attack', narrower ones when we reflect on what makes a group a terrorist group in the first place.

Let us now consider the implications of the distinction for the orthodox view that war can be just but terrorism can never be. If the orthodox view relies on a definition of terrorism grounded in the usage of 'terrorist attack' it will not be very convincing; it would imply that while war, with all its horrors, can sometimes be justified, a terrorist attack on, for instance, a symbolic target must be wrong. On the other hand, if the orthodox view is underpinned by a narrower definition, focused on whatever it is that *makes* an organization a terrorist organization, it may be more plausible. For instance, if it were the case that terrorism in this narrow sense necessarily involved attacks on the public – and so was contrary to Just War doctrine – the difference between war and terrorism would be clear and the orthodox view ethically consistent.

Complications

Although this way of defending the orthodox view against the charge of inconsistency has its attractions, it also has its difficulties. Obviously the orthodox view must rest on some conception of terrorism; if that conception is incompatible with uncontroversial examples of terrorism, consistency is bought at a price.

Initially it may be plausible to suppose that an organization becomes a terrorist organization by attacking the public in pursuit of its political and moral goals but on consideration it must be rejected; there are other ways in which this can happen. Attacks on politicians and rulers even when politically motivated do not necessarily amount to terrorism; Guy Fawkes and his co-conspirators were guilty of treason not terrorism; Julius Caesar was assassinated though not by terrorists. But attacks on rulers and politicians can amount to terrorism; the attempt to assassinate Mrs Thatcher in her hotel at Brighton is incontestably an example of terrorism. What is the distinguishing factor?

The distinction between what I have called 'acts of terrorism' and 'terrorist attacks' offers a possible explanation. Guy Fawkes and his co-conspirators did not attack the public and so were not a terrorist group. Their attempt to blow up the king was not therefore an attack *by* terrorists. By contrast, the IRA, prior to its attack on Mrs Thatcher, had attacked the public and thus was a terrorist organization and its assassination attempt was, therefore, an attack by terrorists. Unlike the Guy Fawkes episode, it is properly described as a 'terrorist attack'.

Although the distinction provides an explanation of the difference between the two cases, it implies, implausibly, that the attack on Mrs Thatcher was terrorism only in a secondary sense; an attack *by* terrorists rather than an act of terrorism *simpliciter*. Yet surely an organization could *become* a terrorist organization by resorting to political violence of this kind? Further, it would be unconvincing to defend the thesis by insisting that Mrs Thatcher was really a member of the public. Nor is it plausible to suppose that the difference lies in the fact that Mrs Thatcher was an innocent target but Julius Caesar and James I were not. Language is not being guided by a detailed knowledge of history, still less a weighing of innocence and guilt.

Consider the following example. A prominent member of a government guilty of genocide is captured by members of a hitherto non-violent, anti-government group. They torture him and threaten to continue to do so unless his colleagues publicize their grievances. It is surely reasonable to conclude that the group has resorted to terrorism *irrespective of the guilt or innocence of their captive*. And it would equally be an act of terrorism whether their captive was a soldier guilty of carrying out the government's policies with exceptional cruelty or simply a member of the public chosen for the purpose at random.

The implication is that targets are irrelevant for the purposes of defining terrorism: civilians, politicians, combatants, the guilty or innocent can all be victims of terrorism. From which it in turn follows that the orthodox view cannot to be defended by arguing that the targets of terrorism, unlike those in a just war, are *necessarily* innocent or non-combatants; though, of course, often they are. Nor is the point affected by the observation that in a sense terrorism commonly involves two kinds of targets: those who are attacked and those, such as the government or public, whom the attack is meant to coerce or influence.

Conclusion

An examination of what is uncontroversially regarded as terrorism does not offer complete support for the orthodox view that war may be justified but terrorism is inevitably morally wrong. Although a definition of terrorism in terms of the nature or combat status of its targets highlights something of great moral significance about many episodes of terrorism, other instances of terrorism are neglected. If it is to be plausible and consistent the orthodox view, therefore, needs to be supported by a more thorough account of the nature of terrorism.[19]

The apologist has a harder task. As we have seen, in the conditions of oppression and powerlessness where a campaign of terrorism might seem to be justified as a last resort, it is almost inconceivable that it will improve matters. Nor can such apologists take much comfort from the fact that attacks on symbolic targets can count as 'terrorist attacks'; if they restrict themselves to these cases they are ignoring the real issue of how political coercion involving killing and maiming (often innocent) people can be ever justified. An apologia in accordance with Just War theory will require, *as a first step*, evidence that situations can occur in which simultaneously there is 'good cause' for terrorism, some chance of success but no better moral alternative.

NOTES

1 See Williams, 'Ethical consistency'.
2 Aquinas, *Summa Theologica*, parts IIa and IIae; Franciscus de Vitoria, *De Indis et de jure belli*.
3 Aquinas, *Summa Theologica*, part II sect. 2 q. 40.
4 See also Anscombe 'War and murder': 'The right to attack with a view to killing is something that belongs to rulers and those they command to do it . . .' and 'The deliberate choice of inflicting death in a struggle is the right only of ruling authorities and their subordinates.'
5 See Lackey, *Ethics of War and Peace*.
6 For a discussion of non-combatant immunity and military necessity see Michael Walzer, *Just and Unjust Wars*.
7 For the dangers of 'computational morality' see S. Hampshire, 'Morality and pessimism', in *Public and Private Morality*.
8 I have discussed this example in some detail in 'Area bombing, terrorism and the death of innocents'. Also in this connection see John C. Ford SJ, 'The morality of obliteration bombing'.

9 For an official account of the conversion to area bombing see Sir Charles Webster and Noble Frankland's *The Strategic Air Offensive Against Germany 1939–45*, vol. 1.
10 For a more detailed version of the argument see my 'Terrorism and argument from analogy'.
11 Igor Primoratz takes the first view in 'What is terrorism?' and R. M. Hare the latter in 'On terrorism' in his *Essays on Political Morality*.
12 See Coady, 'The morality of terrorism', Khatchadourian, 'Terrorism and morality' and Hare, 'On terrorism', in *Essays on Political Morality*.
13 See Hughes, 'Terrorism and national security' and Gilbert, 'Terrorism: war or crime?'.
14 Teichman, 'How to define terrorism', Wilkins, *Terrorism and Collective Responsibility*.
15 Primoratz, 'What is terrorism?'
16 For a discussion of the absolute wrongness of killing innocents see Nagel, 'War and massacre'.
17 It would also explain why Teichman ('How to define terrorism') offers two definitions.
18 For example, Wilkins (*Terrorism and Collective Responsibility*, p. 6) gives an extremely wide definition: terrorism is the attempt to achieve political, social, economic or religious change by the actual or threatened use of violence against persons or property; the violence employed in terrorism is aimed partly at destabilizing the existing political or social order but mainly at publicizing the goals or cause espoused by the terrorists; often, though not always, terrorism is aimed at provoking extreme counter-measures which will win public support for the terrorists and their cause; terrorism will be perceived by its practitioners as an activity aimed at correcting grave injustices which would otherwise be allowed to stand.
19 I explore a possible definitional strategy in 'The language of terrorism'.

READING GUIDE

War and Moral Responsibility, edited by M. Cohen *et al.*, contains papers on the morality of war written from a number of radically different standpoints as do *War and Morality*, edited by R. Wasserstrom, and *Values in Conflict*, edited by Burton M. Leiser. Kai Nielsen's 'Violence and terrorism: its uses and abuses' is to be found in the last of these and offers a robust defence of the view that 'revolutionary terrorism' might sometimes be justified. Diametrically opposed to this is Paul Wilkinson, who defines 'political' terrorism in terms of 'the systematic use of murder' (in *Terrorism and the Liberal State*).

Walzer's *Just and Unjust Wars* is a classic statement and defence of the Just War approach amplified and illuminated by detailed consideration of a number of historical case-studies. *The Ethics of War and Peace* by Douglas Lackey provides a thorough discussion of the principles underlying the Just War approach. Just War theory is also discussed in chapter 18.

Stuart Hampshire in 'Morality and pessimism', in *Public and Private Morality* (edited by him) spells out some of the dangers of unrestrained consequentialism in reasoning about war. Alan Gewirth argues for the absolute nature of certain moral rights in 'Are there any absolute rights?', in *Theories of Rights*, edited by J. Waldron.

Applied Philosophy: Morals and Metaphysics in Contemporary Debate, edited by Brenda Almond and Donald Hill, has six papers on terrorism, war and conflict, including a powerful defence of contingent pacifism by Richard Norman.

CLASSICAL SOURCES

Grotius: *De jure belli et pacis*
Hobbes: *Leviathan*
Machiavelli: *The Art of War*
Hegel: *Philosophy of Right*

21

Enlarging the Community: Companion Animals

Stephen R. L. Clark

Wisdom, Ordinary Decency and Human Rights

One of the roots of philosophical humanism is to be found in Stoicism. This is not to say that Stoics all thought that all men were created equal, endowed by their creator with equal rights to life, liberty, and the pursuit of happiness.[1] On the contrary, the mass of suffering humanity were slaves, and morally incapable. The wise, if anyone was wise, owned everything: they alone, whatever their social standing amongst the unconsidered many, were free, royal and possessing all things. But even those who were not wise could come to see their kinship. Some respect is owed to any human being, of whatever class or race or gender. 'The mere fact that someone is a man makes it incumbent on another man not to regard him as alien'.[2] Nothing, by contrast, is owed to what is less than human. No bargain can be made between human and non-human, and everything non-human may be used solely for human purposes. Pigs, it was said, are only walking larders, with a soul to keep them fresh in place of salt. Anyone who expressed sympathy for brutes must be something of a brute. This is the dogma that was, unfortunately, endorsed by Augustine, Thomas Aquinas, Spinoza, Kant and any number of self-justifying moderns. Moderns, unlike their predecessors, feel no qualms at adopting as their goals exactly the 'bestial' purposes the older moralists deplored. Stoics certainly thought it right to use brutes for good human ends, but would not therefore have endorsed their use to create, or test, cosmetics or minor drugs or luxury foods. Someone with such tastes would be no better than the brutes themselves.[3] Moderns have also usually forgotten that even the wise owned nothing *absolutely*, since they 'own' it only in a sense that allows the gods and their peers to own it too: as Thomas Jefferson insisted, in line with the common law of England and ancient ethics, we have no claim upon the land itself, but only on its lawful fruits.[4] Nothing, said Locke, was given to man to spoil or destroy.[5] The point preceded Locke: this is what an early Muslim legal scholar, Abu al-Faraj, says: 'People do not in fact own things, for the real owner is their Creator; they only enjoy the usufruct of things, subject to the Divine Law'.[6]

Stoic ethics culminate in a firm division between the human and the less-than-human, as well as between the wise and foolish. But it is grounded in natural impulses shared with other animals.[7] 'The Stoics say that an animal has self-preservation as the object of its first impulse . . . The first thing appropriate to every animal is its own constitution and the consciousness of this. For nature was not likely either to alienate the animal itself, or to make it and then neither alienate it nor appropriate it'.[8] Nature also ensures that each sort of animal will be similarly attached to what is needed for its survival, including other creatures of appropriate kinds. 'We are an animal, but a gregarious one which needs someone else as well. For this reason too we inhabit cities; for there is no human being who is not part of a city'.[9] Hierocles also identifies what are, as it were, different circles around each of us, to whose inmates we are variously attached.

> The first and closest circle is the one which a person has drawn as though around a centre, his own mind . . . The second one further removed from the centre but enclosing the first circle . . . contains parents, siblings, wife, and children. The third one has in it uncles and aunts, grandparents, nephews, nieces and cousins.[10]

The widest circle is that of the whole human race, and our duty is to try and respect the people of each as if they belonged to the next inner circle, drawing them closer in until we mind as much about distant strangers as about ourselves (or as near as we can manage: 'for no-one agrees with [the Stoics] that the appropriation is equal – that is contrary to plain fact and one's self-awareness'[11]).

Oikeiosis, or appropriation, is the process whereby creatures are 'attached' to what matters for their preservation. That same process helps to constitute their very being. An entity is something whose parts co-operate in furthering their common survival. A human individual will generally need friends and family even to survive as a single organism, but those associates are not merely instrumental goods. Even the foolish are not wholly self-absorbed, or else the 'self' they are attached to is larger than their individual bodies. We 'identify' with larger wholes. The wise will also choose what nature has appropriated to them, but for a grander reason. Ordinarily foolish people, like other creatures, do what comes naturally, because that's what they feel like doing. The wise may do exactly the same things (to the outward eye), but do them because they see they should. Lacking that perception, and suffering from many sicknesses, 'some will do wrong, while others will perform right actions:

for these are natural to them'.[12] Only the wise know why this or that is needed for the world to be, and do it because they know that God or Fate or Nature will have it so.

My concern here is not with the wise, nor with that aspect of right reason that requires us never to complain, never to regret, never to be surprised.[13] 'If I actually knew that I was fated to be ill,' said Chrysippus, 'I would even have an impulse to be ill. For my foot too, if it had intelligence, would have an impulse to get muddy.'[14] Once they have understood what the world requires of them, the wise would wish it. The mind of the wise is the very mind of God, for they identify themselves entirely with the world. Since we do not understand, and are attached to smaller wholes than the great world itself, we strive to follow such impulses as preserve what is appropriate to us. No Stoic would seek to blame us when we act in ways that lead to personal disaster, but the disaster – or what to us is disastrous – will still come. What is it that we had best preserve, and how should we do it? Epictetus's advice runs as follows:

> Consider who you are: in the first place a human being, that is, someone who was nothing more authoritative than moral purpose, but subordinates everything else to this and keeps it free from slavery and subordination . . . Furthermore you are a citizen of the world and a part of it, not as one of the underlings but one of the foremost constituents. For you are capable of attending to the divine government and of calculating its consequences. What then is a citizen's profession? To regard nothing as of private interest, to deliberate about nothing as though one were cut off [i.e. from the whole] . . . Next keep in mind that you are a son . . . next know that you are also a brother . . . next if you are a town councillor, remember that you are a councillor; if young, that you are young, if old, that you are old; if a father, that you are a father. For each of these titles, when rationally considered, always suggests the actions appropriate to it[15].

The classes to which we belong are not merely descriptive, but normative. By knowing what we are, we can tell at once what we should do. Sometimes Stoics emphasized the primacy of universal law, world-citizenship. 'There will not be a different law at Rome and at Athens, or a different law now and in the future, but one law, everlasting and immutable, will hold good for all peoples and all times.'[16] Only those obedient to that one law can really be free, or friends: 'all who are not virtuous are foes, enemies, slaves and estranged from one another, including parents and children, brothers and brothers, relations and relations'.[17] Only the virtuous will even manage to fulfil their lesser duties, as town councillors or parents. The rest of us, being vicious, cannot console ourselves that we manage to be good parents, or good councillors despite being failures on the wider stage. At other times the Stoics could agree that we could, and should, do our lesser duties even without a firm grip on right reason. Nature requires us to identify with family and friends and cities, and think ill of those who fail to. The wise may justify their local loyalties by reasoning them out from the first principles of cosmic citizenship; the rest of us are loyal long before we even glimpse the possibility of wisdom.

Amongst the loyalties we actually and historically form are ones toward domestic or working animals. A child's affection for a cat or dog or horse is not very different from her affection for her human friends and family. She values its company and reciprocal affection, demands that others care for it, and could easily resent occasional bids for solitude or independence. Those who work with 'animals' are usually, and naturally, attached to them even when they have put 'childish things' away. They come to see, more or less knowledgeably, with the others' eyes, and allow them more or less of liberty to go their own way when it suits them. Dogs, cats and horses are the commonest non-human creatures to elicit, and partly reciprocate, affection, in the settled West. But cows, pigs, hawks, snakes, spiders all have their admirers, here and elsewhere. It seems indeed to be a species characteristic that we readily adopt small (smallish) creatures and rear them in our midst, expecting them to learn enough of our ways to be called 'tame'. It is no contradiction to add that we frequently betray what trust they have in us.

Stoics, of course, do not usually mention such attachments. There may be reasons why we should detach ourselves from them, and form 'adult' loyalties instead. People who go on loving 'animals', at the expense of more 'mature' relationships, are thought to be 'social inadequates' even if they do no harm to anyone. If we were more Stoic we might add that people who go on loving chance-met friends at the expense of larger loyalties are more dangerous still, while also suspecting that those who *profess* to follow larger loyalties and betray their friends are more likely to be villains. What is strange is that moralists of this stamp do not even recognize the fact of human–animal attachment, except as a stage in education. Maybe youngsters who never learn to love and take responsibility for a 'pet' will be less able to manage more mature relationships. Maybe children who abuse those animals in their power will, dreadfully, go on to abuse such humans as they can. Here in Britain, at least, we instruct our children to be 'kind to animals', and hope they will go on to be kind to human beings. But even in Britain, and even disregarding those who unashamedly oppress both wild and domestic animals, those who are 'too kind' are judged sentimentalists, and scorned.

The species characteristic which allows us to 'tame' the young of other species (and eventually to breed more easily tameable varieties) no doubt has a neo-Darwinian explanation. Hominids who could identify with other animals in this way had a better chance of managing them: hunters could guess which way they'd run or how to get the help of other hunting species; pastoralists and farmers could appreciate good health and beauty in the creatures whose milk or meat or labour they required; even traders and industrialists found it easier to be courteous towards their neighbours, strangers and competitors because they had had practice disentangling other creatures' aims, and been in the habit of liking such dissimilar beings. Whatever the wise do, many of us feel friendly toward strangers because they remind us of our pets!

It is not improbable that our ancestors selected other creatures for those infantile features that please us in our young: cuteness and an affectionate intelligence. Delighting in those things, we bred ourselves, and our domestics, to display them. Civilized human and domestic non-human animals alike are 'tame': we are tied by affection and obedience to our stations. For most of human history most people never matured beyond that point: we stayed loyal to our superiors and did not expect ourselves to be self-movers, independent agents. For most of human history most human beings have been slaves or wives or children. For most of human history there was no reason to expect that different rules applied to humans and non-humans. 'Non-human animals are in part *constitutive* of human societies: any adequate specification of societies as structures of social relationship or interaction must include reference to non-human animals as occupants of social positions and as terms in social relationships.'[18] 'The ox is the poor man's slave', said Aristotle, accurately insisting that in human society there were always parents and children, men and women, free and slaves.[19] Even the 'free' (the self-owned) – except in such self-governing cities as Aristotle thought were best suited to a core human nature – rarely ruled themselves or thought of themselves as having 'rights' to do so.

Affections that bind associates together, in brief, can easily be manifested in strongly domineering forms that give little liberty to those who are, sincerely, 'loved'. Those affections pay no heed to species boundaries. What has happened to ensure that so many moralists now think it 'obvious' that all and only *human* beings are really owed 'respect', and that the actual affections felt between human and non-human should be disregarded?

Deconstructing Humanism

Humanism decrees that every 'human being' is of a 'rational' kind that merits a respect far greater than we could reasonably give to any non-rational creature. We can make explicit bargains with such rational creatures, but not with the non-rational. Because we *can* do this, some say, we should behave as if we have already agreed to treat each other 'decently' (though no such actual agreement to be decent could affect us if we weren't already decent). The historical fact is, of course, that we have more reason to suspect that our ancestors made bargains with wild dogs than that they made a bargain with all human strangers. Dogs can be domesticated; strangers cannot always be enslaved, or bargained with. The Stoic response, which was also Spinoza's, was that every human being was attached, by nature, to the nature common to all human beings. The point was not merely that we are gregarious animals, but that in liking what we come to realize we are bound to like, to admire, to seek to preserve the nature we have in common with all other humans. Why we should not equally admire the nature we have in common, say, with all mammals, remains moot.

The character or set or related characters which has usually been identified as the human essence is a capacity to speak a human language, to make choices about one's future, to organize communal actions in accordance with some freshly negotiated plan, to recognize oneself as one creature amongst many, having a history, a character, a hope of change.[20] '*Homo sapiens*' names a species uniquely and universally endowed with language, self-consciousness and a capacity for life under the law in a community of the like-minded. Aristotle's dicta that humans are political animals, animals with language, animals capable of recognizing and acting upon general principles all amount to the same thing, a picture of humanity that identifies human beings as something unlike all other animals (though Aristotle, as I shall point out, was not committed to the view that *all* human beings are like that). Some have added that the capacity to make tools to alter the environment, and to organize the labour of so doing, makes a crucial difference.

Ancient moralists might have agreed that there were human beings who deserved respect (the wise, the saintly, the heroic), yet felt no impulse to respect the mere fact of a shared 'humanity'. Some might have added that we should love even the greatest wretch or villain, but not because their nature (or ours) had merited such love. We have inherited the idea that conspecifics share 'the same nature', that a biological species is a natural kind, with its very own 'essence'. In coming to love, or at least respect, any fellow human being (as being a human being) we are bound to love or at least respect all other humans. We may, of course, be irrationally and personally attached to some particular human beings, and feel indifferent to others who are, 'objectively', just like them (that is, no impartial judge would notice any important difference). But it is a mark of rationality to be moved instead (or at least as well) by characters that do not depend on any such irrational attachment. 'Rational' moralists of this kind, like the Stoic wise man, may deduce a duty to care for 'their own family and friends', but would not accept a personal attachment as a really 'moral' reason for that care. 'Rational' moralists, correspondingly, deny that any attachment to tame animals could count against their duty to humankind.

Not all our conspecifics can actually join the conversation that identifies us all, importantly, as human. Some are too young, too old, too foolish or too damaged. Most of us prefer to believe, or to pretend, that even those who cannot, in fact, converse with us still *could* if things were different, and are owed the same respect as human beings without those disabilities. Some recent moralists have suggested that this is superstition, and that those who can't converse should not be treated as if they could. 'Becoming a person' (which is to say, a creature that can have real rights) is a slow, socially determined happening. Creatures that aren't (yet) persons may be treated gently, but are not wronged by being imprisoned or killed. It seems indeed that Aristotle's notion of a 'natural slave' is still alive and well: such slaves have no will of their own, and are rather helped than otherwise by being treated as means to their owners' goals.

Did Aristotle contradict himself by holding both that there was a universal human essence, and that there were some 'humans' (biologically so called) who were not fully moral agents? The truth is that he did not think there was an 'essence of humanity', shared by all members of the species. Human beings *in general* have to decide what to do, and those of us who wonder how best to live must obviously decide on our own answers. It doesn't follow that those who can't decide, who lack that power, aren't *human*, nor that we owe them nothing. We may even owe them such assistance as we can to overcome their disability: children should be brought up to be the agents they could not have been without our care; if those incapable of moral agency could possibly be cured, they should be. I doubt if Aristotle thought they could: their defects were deep-rooted. Other humanists have held that creatures not of our own species cannot be cured of moral imbecillity (of not being agents), because the mechanism is not even potentially there, but that our conspecifics always could be. Whether this distinction is a real one, who can say? My purpose is rather to bury 'humanism' than praise it, but without adopting the new 'personism' in its place.

Humanism, traditionally understood, demands the real existence of a natural kind, humanity. The problem is that biological species are not natural kinds. Modern biologists point out that the classes identified in folk biology have often turned out to have no single character in common, nor even to have a common ancestor they do not share with creatures from another class. 'Fishes' does not name a well-defined biological kind, any more than 'weeds' (the things we call fishes are not members of any single biological group, or *taxon*). But even recognized biological *taxa* do not have essences strictly so called. There is no character that a thing has to have if it is to count as a member of a particular biological *taxon* except the historical character of being a member, by descent, of a named set of populations. A species, in modern terms, is not a set of creatures with a shared and essential nature, but a set of interbreeding populations. It seems to follow that if we consider human beings as a biological class we cannot expect that all such creatures share a nature. Maybe all humans presently known to us can talk, or live under negotiated agreements with their fellows, just as all reptiles have three-chambered hearts: but there is nothing to say they must. We might yet discover a genuinely human tribe that has lost the gift of language properly so-called.[21] There is no single nature that species members certainly display. 'Humans' might even turn out to be a merely nominal class, like weeds or fishes, identified as such only because a given community chooses to do so. If it does identify a real species (as seems likely) that species is simply a collection of creatures united by genealogical relationships, not phenomenal or genetic resemblances.[22]

Consider an analogy. 'Mammalism', so to call it, does play a part in the choices that we make: furry creatures with faces get a better deal than scaly ones (unless they are rats). But even if we elevated this subjective preference to the point of objective principle (as it might be: all really 'moral' beings must respect all creatures that are cuddly and care for their young) it would surely be odd to deny respect to non-mammals that did the same, and respect what are technically mammals even though they didn't. It would be odder still to go on being mammalists when we had found out that, strictly, there were no mammals (any more than fishes). And that, unfortunately for humanists, is the point.

On the one hand, it is not easy to see why a shared nature should count for quite so much. Even if the reason why I value a particular companion would also, in other circumstances, give me reason to value a quite different one, it does not follow that I should now value that other being just as much, or do as much for her or to her. It might even happen that the fact of a shared nature is a reason to be very wary of that other: those who share a nature may be real competitors. From which it might follow that I will naturally be attached to those sufficiently unlike me, or unlike those I am at first attached to, not to be rivals. Of course, if I had been born across a border I would be just as attached to those I now oppose: why should I therefore not oppose them? If Nature or God or Fate can require me to love *this* woman, *this* country, *these* cats and *these* children maybe I will thereby understand the feelings of my enemies for *their* loved ones. Will I therefore love them too?

On the other hand, even if a shared nature does give some reason for a wider respect or loyalty than at first we feel, what reason do we have to suppose that all our conspecifics have any such shared nature? If species are not natural kinds, then neither is humankind a kind. Consider a possible future – maybe that imagined by Olaf Stapledon on a future Neptune, after the great migration. In that age, he fantasized, the then human species evolved to fill many different niches. Amongst the descendants of our human stock were (will be) sea-squirts, grazers, pack hunters, porpoises, bats and creatures recognizably like 'us'.[23] Practically all the 'animals' of that future world were (will be) hominid. Maybe several different contemporaneous species could be speakers, though with somewhat different innate speech-patterns. Even in our world 'species-barriers' (which is to say, bars against interbreeding) are not as clear, nor as consistent, as popular thought supposes. What reason could there be on Neptune to attach ourselves entirely to 'our species' or 'our bloodline'? Why not acknowledge instead that every creature, whether on Neptune or on Earth, is like and unlike 'us', and we may be profitably and reasonably attached to any?

Why, in short, do modern humanists mind so much about descent, despite the fact that most of them acknowledge no importance in lineage or race? It is absurd, so most would say, to honour members of a particular royal line merely because they're 'royal' by descent, although they show no sign of any shared nobility of character or admirable competence. It is positively wicked to reserve all rights to members of one particular ethnic group, our own. Why is it less absurd, less wicked, to honour only 'human beings' when we no longer believe they share an admirable nature, and cannot identify a natural boundary between one 'species' and the next? Both reason and natural affection require more of us than that.

A Partial History

In our beginnings as a species personal attachments to our relatives and friends served well. We liked each other's company, and could fairly readily devise joint projects that were profitable to all. None of us were strong enough to force unwilling partners; from which it does not follow that we didn't manage to manipulate each other's motives. These small groups were made up of males and females, parents and children, conversationalists and tamed animals. We even managed to form larger unions, recognizing an advantage in seeking spouses from elsewhere and sharing out the land over which we wandered. We invented complex patterns of intermarriage, and rules to restrain ourselves from over-hunting, over-grazing a land we shared with other human and non-human groups. In those days we did not suppose that we were anything but 'animals', and easily attributed a kind of speech to other animals with whom we sought to be on good terms. If we quarrelled too much, we went away.

There is no need to exaggerate. That life (which surviving hunter-gatherers still maintain) was not idyllic. Neither was it 'solitary, poor, nasty, brutish and short'.[24] When we settled down to farm the land, and fence it off from wild things, we started on the road to empire. We needed to defend 'our land', and to co-ordinate the manifold activities that were required for irrigation, trade and storage of our surplus. The result was that we could no longer rely on personal attachment and egalitarian exchange to keep the peace. We established rules of ownership, caste structures and embodied deities to make it possible for us to deal predictably with strangers. The world itself was moralized, in that the preferred order of society was projected on the cosmos, and social order founded on it. That moral order, largely now neglected by our moral theorists, governed, and still governs, a large part of the world. People know their places, and treat each as place-holders more than friends. Non-human members of the wider order may have higher status than many of the humans, because hardly any human being (not even the priests or kings) is 'free' to choose. Acting otherwise than one's station requires is not a proof of personal agency, but a failing to be expiated, and so no mark of a superior status. Here too there is no need to exaggerate. Serfdom allowed more people than ever before to crowd together, and live in something like tranquillity: it was not, and mostly is not, Hell on Earth. But neither is such civilization all that we could wish.

Both hunter-gatherer society and the empires have left their mark within our ethical tradition, the 'inherited conglomerate'. We value personal freedom, personal attachment, but we also acknowledge (grudgingly) such duties of obedience as civilized society required. Humanism is the attempt to recreate equality amongst the mass of humankind while still insisting upon immovable divisions between the different servants of empire. In the earliest ethic co-operation between people, dogs, horses, cattle was a sort of bargain; in the later, and imperial, version cattle, slaves, serfs, officers were all duty-bound to serve the Law. Industrial society creates new demands, making it difficult to enforce such powerful divisions of caste, sex and status. Our ethical systems, briefly, are historically formed adjustments to expanding populations, changing indus-tries.[25] In Patterson's words:

> An industrial society cannot work if people do not change from traditional to more regulated rhythms of work; people must learn to get to work on time, whatever sacred views they may hold about the correct relationship between the rising of the sun and the rising of the human spirit; they must acquire greater literacy, however much such literacy undermines traditional cosmologies; they must acquire specialized skills, however satisfying the activities of the materially self-sufficient person; they must recognize the rights of women to greater independence outside the household economy, however dearly held the traditional sexist views on the matter; they must abandon traditional conceptions of ritual purity with respect to other groups if a modern transportation system is to work; they must accept the rules of bureaucratic structures; they must be willing to migrate from the regions of their birth; they must increasingly abandon familial favoritism in favour of generally accepted standards of competence; they must forego the preservation of a large number of extended kin-ties; and they must accept the inevitable drift toward a more secular view of the world.[26]

Recognizing the historical and economic causes of ethical change, we need not simply acquiesce in them.[27] It is all too easy to believe that the ethical system created by and for a particular age is 'deeply rational', and that all those who move away from it are wrong. The alternative is to recall that ethical assump-tions change, and can be changed. We do not absolutely have to continue rationalizing the 'inherited conglomerate', though we should certainly remem-ber what forces lie behind our illusion of ethical progress.

Ethical Conclusions

By the Stoic account, those who are wise respect the wisdom manifested in a providential universe. Ordinarily decent people, unable or unwilling to follow Chrysippus's advice, should instead attempt to play their parts as parent, spouse, craftsman or citizen. Because irrational creatures cannot make or keep a contract (so it is said), there are no mutual agreements, no laws, between

328 *International and Global Dimensions*

beasts and human beings. But such decent people will still be moved by personal attachments that transcend species boundaries, and may reasonably conclude that there are, after all, bargains to be made between us. Theories about our real natures helped our ancestors to move away from egalitarian and multi-species compacts. When we settled down to fence and farm the land we made up castes and offices to divide us from each other, and from the wild things round about. As our empires grew in size we could no longer rest content with personal attachments: citizens from across the empire must be treated decently, merely because they're citizens (of one class or another). Industrial society, requiring greater mobility, greater adaptability among its workers, saps residual caste loyalties, while separating most of us still more from the beasts (except such domestic artefacts as we still allow).

Reason may help to teach us otherwise. We can come, we have come, to many agreements with non-human creatures. There is no essential boundary between human and non-human. Our ethics rest as much on sentiment and personal attachment as on any reasoned argument about what things like us should do. We may also be forced to realize that our lives and loves depend upon the living earth, made up of many million creatures and kinds of creatures whom we cannot afford to treat as worthless. It is easy now to despise those human tribes who thought all strangers were their enemies or prey, who failed to see the promise of a greater friendship. In learning that those strangers were, after all, 'like them', they came to feel a certain respect for them that gradually permitted a degree of personal attachment between older enemies. But a more secure affection, and respect, came with the understanding that the strangers were *not* like them. The living earth, the promise of a greater friendship, often depends upon unlikeness.

Those who are wise, by Stoic rules, will welcome what there is, and not demand that everything be like themselves before they love it. Even ordinarily decent people, vicious and ill-informed as all of us, not being wise, must be, may come to believe themselves members of a wider city, compound of many species. Greek colonists convinced themselves (as later Europeans also did) that they need keep no bargains with barbarians (who could not be expected to keep any bargains); they thereby proved themselves more treacherous than any of their prey. The history of humanism is of betrayal. It may be that we have the reason, and the material opportunity, to learn better ways. Hunters, agriculturalists and industrialists alike can contribute moral insights: our descendants, if we are lucky, may believe we did as well.

NOTES

1 On the philosophical background to this claim see Wills, *Inventing America*, pp. 229ff.
2 Cicero (*On Ends* 3.63), in Long and Sedley (eds), *Hellenistic Philosophers*, 57F: vol. I, p. 348.

3 See Clark, 'Humans, animals and "animal behavior" ', in Miller and Williams (eds), *Ethics and Animals*, pp. 169ff. It is of course a strange conceit to suppose that beasts have any interest in such things.

4 White, *Philosophy of American Revolution*, p. 223.

5 Locke, J. Second Treatise 31, in *Two Treatises Government*, p. 332.

6 Mazri, Al-Hafiz 'Islam and ecology', *Islam and Ecology*, p. 7.

7 See Clark, *The Nature of the Beast* and Benton, *Natural Relations*.

8 Diogenes Laertius (*Lives of the Philosophers* 7.85), in Long and Sedley (eds), *Hellenistic Philosophers*, 57A: vol. I, p. 346.

9 Hierocles (1st century AD), in Long and Sedley (eds), *Hellenistic Philosophers*, 57D: vol. 1, p. 347: on this notion of 'city' see Clark, 'Good and bad ethology and the decent *polis*', in Loizou and Lesser (eds), *Polis and Politics*, pp. 12–22.

10 Hierocles, in Long and Sedley (eds), *Hellenistic Philosophers*, 57G: vol. 1, p. 349.

11 Anonymous commentator on Plato's *Theaetetus*, in Long and Sedley (eds), *Hellenistic Philosophers*, 57H: vol. I, p. 359.

12 Alexander (*On Fate* 205), in Long and Sedley (eds), *Hellenistic Philosophers*, p. 391.

13 Cicero (*Tusculan Disputations* 5.81), in Long and Sedley (eds), *Hellenistic Philosophers*, 63M, vol. I, p. 397.

14 Epictetus (*Discourses* 2.6.9), in Long and Sedley (eds), *Hellenistic Philosophers*, 58J: vol. I, p. 356.

15 Epictetus (*Discourses* 2.10ff), in Long and Sedley (eds), *Hellenistic Philosophers*, 59Q: vol. I, p. 364.

16 Cicero (*Republic* 3.33), in Long and Sedley (eds), *Hellenistic Philosophers*, 67S: vol. I, p. 433.

17 Diogenes Laertius (*Lives of the Philosophers* 7.32), in Long and Sedley (eds), *Hellenistic Philosophers*, 67B: vol. I, p. 430.

18 Benton, *Natural Relations*, p. 68.

19 Aristotle, *Politics*, 1.1253b5ff.

20 Some of this material appeared in Clark, S. R. L., 'Philosophical anthropology', in Becker and Becker (eds), *Encyclopedia of Ethics*, vol. II, pp. 963–4.

21 The chances are that there are no recognizably human beings whose ancestors *never* spoke; we have the features that we do because the ancestors of all of us began to speak long before we were recognizably human, and had no patience with offspring that failed the test. See Miller, 'The Wahokies', in Singer and Cavalieri (eds), *The Great Ape Project*, pp. 230–6.

22 See Clark, 'Is humanity a natural kinds?'.

23 Stapledon, *Last and First Men*, pp. 277f.

24 See Lee and De Vore (eds), *Man the Hunter* and Sahlins, *Stone Age Economics*.

25 See Clark, S. R. L. 'Companions on the way'.

26 Patterson, *Ethnic Chauvinism*, p. 186.

27 See Wood, 'Marx against morality'.

READING GUIDE

This chapter deals with the natural roots of morality, and our attitudes to creatures of another species. Our duties, or lack of them, to 'animals' have been examined on the one side by Peter Singer in *The Expanding Circle*, Tom Regan in *The Case for Animal Rights*, Stephen Clark in *The Moral Status of Animals*, Mary Midgley in *Animals and Why They Matter* and James Rachels in *Created from Animals*. The contrary position is represented by Raymond Frey in *Rights, Killing and Suffering*, and Peter Carruthers in *The Animal Issue*. Related issues about animals have been addressed by Vicki Hearne in *Adam's Task: Calling Animals by Name*, Barbara Noske in *Humans and Other Animals*, and Carol Adams in *The Politics of Meat*.

The biological roots of morality have been discussed in a volume edited by C. S. Stent, *Morality as a Biological Phenomenon*, and by Stephen Clark in *The Nature of the Beast*.

Stoic, and other ancient approaches to the question are discussed by Daniel Dombrowski in *The Philosophy of Vegetarianism* and by Richard Sorabji in *Animal Minds and Human Morals*. Porphyry's *On Abstinence*, the oldest full-scale defence of animals, is available in a translation by Esmé Wynne-Tyson.

For an account of the influence of Descartes's views on animals, see L. C. Rosenfeld: *From Beast-machine to Man-machine*. See B. Rollin, *The Unheeded Cry* for a history of twentieth-century thought on animal consciousness.

A collection edited by Peter Singer, *In Defence of Animals*, deals with several of the moral and political issues; another, edited by Peter Singer and Paola Cavalieri, *The Great Ape Project*, grounds a political movement for granting rights to other species of ape on biological discoveries of the abilities of those other apes and the nature of species differentiation.

CLASSICAL SOURCES

Porphyry: *On Abstinence from Animal Food*
Plutarch: *Are Beasts Rational?*
Montaigne: *Collected Essays*

22

Ethics and the Environment: the Global Perspective

Robin Attfield

I

Ecological problems are problems which arise from human dealings with the systems of the natural world. Familiar (or rather, notorious) examples include pollution, the depletion of resources, the destruction of species and of wilderness and the growth of deserts. At first, in the 1960s and 1970s, these often seemed relatively small, localized problems, but by now it is difficult to resist the view that both their spread and their significance are global, and that nothing less than the future of the planet is at stake. In part, of course, these problems have a scientific character. But science and technology alone cannot solve them, because they concern what *ought* to be done, and tackling them involves values and ethical principles. So they turn out to be every bit as relevant to applied philosophy as the issues discussed in previous chapters, if not more so.

There is another connection between these problems and philosophy. Many different accounts have been given by philosophers of the relation of the natural world to humanity and to human faculties. Thus for Plato the material world was at best an imperfect embodiment of the Ideas which are the proper objects of knowledge; and later, for Descartes, it was a machine entirely lacking the consciousness which gives the human mind its essential and distinctive character. Neither of these approaches, plausibly, allow the interdependence of humanity and the natural world (or perhaps we should say 'the rest of the natural world') to be taken seriously. Thus ecological problems call for a good deal of traditional philosophy of mind and epistemology and much traditional metaphysics to be radically revised. One environmental philosopher has even suggested that the entire history of philosophy presents an almost comprehensive disincentive to the development of preservationist attitudes in society, and that nothing less than a comprehensive overhaul of the philosophical tradition is required.[1] Even if this overestimates the role of philosophy as a barrier to sensitive thought and practice, it powerfully conveys the importance of a metaphysic which takes nature seriously, and of a social philosophy which fosters the well-being of nonhuman nature as well as of humanity.

II

Meanwhile in ethics the new awareness of environmental issues gives rise to the need for a theory which accounts for the problematic nature of ecological problems, and which requires a revaluation of the values which might seem to be sufficient for most inter-human dealings. For environmental issues bring to light duties which are not duties *to* anyone or anything, being focused rather on whichever people (or other creatures) happen to live in the late twenty-first and subsequent centuries. Again, they plausibly bring to light values in nature: valuable states, the value of which is not valuable for or to any consciousness, but which is simply valuable for the creatures concerned, and from no point of view but that of the universe.

Certainly traditional ethical theories are poorly suited to coping with ecological issues. Most accounts of duty represent duty as owed to someone or other, and suggest that, without such a legatee or recipient, there are no duties. This in turn would suggest that we have no duties where people of over a century hence are concerned, for in the nature of the case we cannot identify who will be alive then, or therefore find individuals who are the focus of present obligations. (Besides, it is up to the current generation and its successors to decide who shall then live; so our duties cannot originate from what is owed to people whose future existence is preordained already.) Yet it is increasingly accepted that we hold the planet in trust for a sequence of generations unborn, and have a responsibility for the state in which we pass it on. So a different understanding of duty (and of responsibility) is clearly needed.

Again, traditional theories of ethics take into account the interests and feelings of humanity, God or the gods and (at most) sentient animals only; the suggestion that there is independent value in the lives of other living creatures or other species strains traditional theories such as utilitarianism and Kantianism to breaking point. Yet this very belief about value seems unavoidable to account for many people's reactions to the destruction of species, whether sentient or not; and its rejection implies that the world was valueless before conscious life appeared, a view which many find unappealing and some find arrogant. So the constituency of morality turns out to be wider than has often been supposed; more creatures count morally than many of our traditions allow. At the same time our map of where intrinsic value is to be found must also be redrawn.

III

Difficulties such as these led the American naturalist Aldo Leopold to propose a new ethic (the 'land ethic'), recognizing an enlarged moral community extending to the entire biosphere and all the creatures interacting therein. Indeed he went so far as to suggest that the criterion of ethical rightness is the contribution of an action to promoting the integrity, stability and beauty of the biotic community.[2] While this particular proposal could have unintended totalitarian implications, many have been inspired by it to recognize a need to enlarge the scope of ethics.

One reason why this was a salutary development is that environmental concern, as it gained strength from the 1960s onwards, often throve on local protests, and was thus liable to adopt limited perspectives. While it was not always committed to the NIMBY syndrome ('Not in My Back Yard'), it was often prone to be concerned with the quality of life of prosperous people in the West, and maybe of their children, and to stop there. The vital need for a wider perspective prompted the Norwegian philosopher Arne Naess to write 'The shallow and the deep, long-range ecology movement', the latter movement including in its concerns the Third World, the more distant human future, and the needs of non-human creatures.[3] While Naess commended these concerns for their own sake, and for the sake of the self-realization of all the affected creatures (whether human or non-human), the kind of long-term and global perspective which he advocated has increasingly been recognized as required by self-interest; attached as many of us may be to a locality, nothing less than the planetary biosphere supplies an adequate conception of 'the environment' if our shared environment is to remain intact.[4] The need to avoid environmental myopia also prompted Richard Routley, an Australian philosopher, to present to a World Congress the case for a new, environmental ethic, in which values in nature and the case for their preservation would be recognized.[5]

IV

What Naess was advocating turned out to be 'the Deep Ecology platform'; underpinned by a plurality of possible metaphysical commitments (from Buddhism through Christianity to the tenets of Spinoza), principles were advocated, all of them ultimately supportive of self-realization, including simple living, avoidance of waste, recycling and, eventually, a reduction of the human population.[6] Initially Naess and his followers seemed to be advocating a value-theory of the intrinsic value of natural creatures, species and ecosystems, and a related preservationist ethic, based on belief in 'the equal right of all creatures to live and blossom' (biotic egalitarianism); but when Richard Routley (now Sylvan) pointed out some of the inconsistencies, Naess's expositor Warwick Fox was able to claim that the principal supporters of the Deep Ecology platform were not teaching a value-system or an ethic at all, but were instead advocating a changed conception of the self and an enlarged identification with nature, and employing the language of value and of principle simply to express this. They were also advocating rejection of traditional dualisms in which selves are regarded as metaphysically distinct from each other and from their objects, holding that if the ontological and psychological message takes root, there is no need to theorize about values or obligations.[7]

But much of this platform conflicts with the beliefs of those initially inclined towards 'deeper' rather than 'shallower' positions. To many (including Sylvan), deeper positions essentially concern values, which supply grounds for policies and for priorities between them; distinctions between objects are indispensable if a scientific understanding of the world is to be possible; identification with nature is far from the only motivation for preserving it; and what is amiss with biotic egalitarianism is not that it expresses environmentally sensitive attitudes, but that a more coherent value-theory is needed to underpin action, whether collective or individual.[8] Yet another problem (albeit one which probably is not perceived as such by Sylvan) concerns whether, in urging a diminution of the human population, it may undervalue human life.

Naess's case is at its strongest where he rejects the view that only human interests count, and stresses that some more impartial perspective is indispensable; indeed this may be the real message underlying biotic egalitarianism. As Leopold stressed, human beings can no longer behave as if they were the conquerors of nature, and may need to adopt the role of plain citizen, and a member of the biotic community. Yet these stances are far from distinctive to Deep Ecology; while those who have attempted to derive a new ethic from, for example, Leopold's criterion of rightness as loyalty to the biosphere, have found difficulty in avoiding treating individuals as having instrumental value only. (At best their value would be instrumental in upholding the balance of nature; at worst in subverting it. In the latter case this value would be both instrumental and negative too.[9]) Just here totalitarian implications flood in. Clearly some different principles need to be resorted to.

V

A defensible principle governing relations between species has been advanced by Peter Singer, the principle that equal interests should receive equal consideration.[10] This principle avoids species-bias; to the extent that the principle goes along with (sometimes) giving human beings priority, it does so not because they are human beings, but because of distinctive interests such as their interest in the exercise of autonomy. Singer is not advocating equality of treatment, since this would involve denying equality of consideration when cases are relevantly different from each other. But the distinctive interests of non-humans, such as the interest of chickens in spreading their wings and the interest of pigs in rooting, will also carry weight.

Such principles, however, have come in for criticism. Deep Ecologists object that they are insufficiently holistic, and fail to recognize the intrinsic value of species and ecosystems; others object at the way they draw the line at creatures with consciousness or with sentience; and yet others criticize them for insufficiently protecting individual interests against the aggregated interests of other creatures. This latter view is adopted by upholders of animal rights, who maintain that the only basis on which the maltreatment of individual animals can be adequately forestalled is through the recognition of rights which cannot normally be overridden, however much good can be achieved by infringing them. Nothing short of such rights, they hold, can underpin practices such as conscientious abstention from consuming animal flesh. One of the foremost advocates of this case is Tom Regan.[11]

Yet it is not clear that this approach is preferable to Singer's consequentialism. Thus when rights conflict, appeal must in any case be made beyond them to something like interests. Again, absolutist principles may not deserve the strength of support which rights theory would bring them. And consequentialists can themselves support some kind of non-absolutist rights theory, strong enough, perhaps, to protect individuals in most circumstances. Regan's position is also just as liable as Singer's to holist criticisms, and also to the criticism that it restricts moral concern to creatures which are subjects of a life, i.e. which have a point of view. While holist criticisms are unconvincing, and there seems no clear justification for ascribing intrinsic value to species and ecosystems, the view that only sentient lives have independent value appears almost as arbitrary as the humans-only view rejected above. But if so, the solution would not seem to lie in an extension of rights theory to plants, let alone bacteria. Theories of rights, with their stress on identifiable, atomistic individuals, are peculiarly unsuited to environmental problems, not least for the reasons mentioned previously concerning the largely unidentifiable character of future generations, and our responsibilities in their regard which persist none the less.

Thus a wider range of interests (including those of nonsentient creatures) should be taken into consideration than Singer does; moving in this direction seems far preferable to jettisoning interests and basing ethics on non-derivative rights, or again to making ecosystems which somehow give value to their members ethically central. So if the Equal Interests Principle can be interpreted so as to cope satisfactorily with inter-species conflicts, this would seem the best approach. (I have attempted such an interpretation in *The Ethics of Environmental Concern.*[12]) At the same time, if value of some non-instrumental kind is to be recognized throughout the realm of living creatures, the Cartesian dualism of mind and matter, in which matter is inert and mechanistic, needs to be superseded by a metaphysic which allows material systems to think and feel, an epistemology which recognizes material objects as intersubjectively real and not the mere products of human ideas, and an aesthetic which takes seriously natural value as well as the value of cultural artifacts.

VI

If morality requires a wider range of creatures to be taken into account, the question arises of whether the same principles apply to creatures of the wild as to domesticated creatures, which can be regarded as the products of culture as much as of nature. Some writers, such as Holmes Rolston III, are so eager to uphold policies of letting-be when areas of wilderness are in question, as to maintain that different principles apply to the distinct realms of nature and of culture. The issue of whether human agents should intervene to save animals at risk is to turn on whether humanity has already assumed responsibility for the animals in question, whether by breeding them or perhaps by altering their environment in a way which puts them at risk. (Thus releasing water from a dam could put caribou at risk of drowning.) Otherwise nature should be left to take its course; this is the way to maintain the adaptiveness and fitness of the species concerned.[13]

Support for this distinction is to be found from Eugene C. Hargrove, who advocates for the natural world what he terms 'therapeutic nihilism'.[14] Wilderness is best served by leaving well alone, and this policy is the one likeliest to restore it after human interventions. Granted Hargrove's activism as a preservationist and educationalist, it must be clear that he does not in the same way apply therapeutic nihilism to the realm of culture, except in limited medical contexts. Hargrove's reasons include the uncertainty of interventions with the natural world ever proving beneficial, and this is certainly a good general reason for caution. Such caution, however, is justified wherever interventions are likely to miscarry, and would not seem to uphold treating nature and culture as realms which are ethically distinct.

Rolston's concern for preserving the adaptedness and fitness of wild creatures may be treated similarly; it has its place, but is far from the only ethically relevant factor in decisions about saving endangered animals. Nor do humanitarian considerations cease to matter when wild creatures are in question. It would, admittedly, be disastrous if human beings regarded themselves as entitled or authorized to police the natural world (say) to minimize suffering; but this could not in any case be our responsibility if predators and thus predation are to be allowed to flourish, something which is manifestly one of the goals of those concerned to preserve wild creatures, even though it must sometimes be overridden by the need to protect, for example, human life. Letting-be, then, is often justified; but its justification will depend on all the circumstances (such as the uncertainty of the consequences for complex biological systems or the impact on predators), and not on a strict nature–culture dualism.

Besides, there will sometimes be a case for actively seeking to restore a natural system, e.g. by returning a 'creamed' species to its erstwhile environment. While the outcome will *ex hypothesi* not be in all respects wild, and will in some ways be the result of human planning, this does not seem to vitiate it as a policy, particularly where a similar array of flourishing creatures emerges to the array which there once was before humanity intervened in the first place. The restoration of wolves to Yellowstone and of Caledonian forest to tracts of the Scottish Highlands plausibly counts as an enrichment, and may thus be preferable to policies of letting-be or therapeutic nihilism. There is, certainly, a risk that the outcome will be moulded by arrogance and ignorance, a danger not sufficiently heeded by restoration ecologists such as Losin;[15] but it cannot be assumed, with Rolston, that restored ecosystems are a mistake,[16] or that they will necessarily comprise artefacts and thus be valueless (thus Eric Katz[17]). It is implausible to hold, with Katz, that moral standing and intrinsic value depend on their bearers being the unalloyed products of evolution. If this were so, domestic animals would have no moral standing, and, contrary to what has already been argued, could be treated by people in any way they please. It is much better to accept that the many natural creatures adopted into human culture should be respected, and that like consideration should be accorded to like interests whatever their origins and wherever they are located.

VII

But is this truly an environmental ethic? Manifestly it is arrived at by 'extensionism', i.e. by reasoning outwards from cases where interests are already recognized as deserving consideration. This, however, has been criticized for omitting respect for those systems on which all living creatures depend, a principle not likely to be arrived at on an extensionist basis, but nevertheless (supposedly) vital.[18] Here it should be granted that the units which need to be conserved are often ecosystems, without which wild creatures could not live the kind of life which is natural to them. It should also be granted that modern environmental problems will not be understood if ecosystems are not taken into account, and equally if we are unready to recognize that there is a shared planetary environment, a system of systems, which stands to be disrupted or upheld. What is much more dubious is that this shows these systems to have intrinsic value; in that the systems support the flourishing of such creatures, and in that this flourishing is of intrinsic value, the systems should rather be regarded as having instrumental value, albeit in very high degree.

VIII

This move already serves to rescue environmental ethics from intractable problems concerning priorities between systems and their members. But Janna Thompson has recently maintained that any environmental ethic which acknowledges values-in-nature beyond the realm of sentient creatures must fail to be credible and persuasive. For no such ethic can justify locating intrinsic value in nonsentient creatures without committing itself to absurdities such as the intrinsic value of machines and crystals. Worse still, no such ethic can yield clear guidance for action, since it is implicitly committed to recognizing intrinsic value in everything.[18]

Yet there is a considerable difference between those beings which are capable of injury, disease and health, and those which can be damaged and (in some cases) repaired, but which are ineligible for being injured or healed. It is implausible to maintain that if the former have a good of their own, and moral standing therewith, so equally do the latter, whether they be machines, crystals, species or ecosystems. And it is arbitrary to recognize the moral standing of sentient creatures (e.g. wolves and snakes), but to reject that of those further creatures which are capable of disease, injury and of health (e.g. mangroves and cedars). Thus it is in no way inconsistent to recognize the moral standing of nonsentient living creatures (e.g. trees) but not to recognize such standing for nonliving entities such as rocks and rivers (even when the nonliving entities are systems, themselves largely composed of living creatures).

As for the capacity of such an ethic for giving practical ethical guidance, this will not be impeded but fostered by the inclusion in its purview of the whole range of interests which ought to be considered, present and future, human and nonhuman. This makes it possible to determine how strong are the interests at stake when it is proposed, for instance, to cut down a forest; for the equal interests principle allows the weight of the interests at stake when an action or policy is under consideration to be compared. Such an ethic is thus capable of giving highly specific guidance. True, that guidance will not always condemn cutting down a forest, as on occasion that is what the balance of interests will favour. But it should not be assumed (with Katz[20]) that an environmental ethic will invariably favour preservation. For if an environmental ethic is comprehensive enough to take seriously the whole range of ethical considerations, then it cannot be guaranteed beforehand that its deliverances will always take the form which preservationists (or any other lobby) would prefer.

Thus the criticisms both of philosophers sceptical of environmental ethics (such as Thompson) and of philosophical holists (such as Katz) can both be resisted. There is an all-or-nothing aspect to both these positions, and also a tendency not to be sufficiently self-critical about the platform (and its foundations) from which the criticisms are launched. At the same time the discussion of these criticisms serves to bring out the importance of a genuinely inclusive, comprehensive ethic which is capable of sifting competing cases. One attempt at producing a decision-making method with these characteristics consists in the method of 'comprehensive weighing', a method devised with a view to the resolution of environmental conflicts, and committed to taking into account all affected interests and to weighing them appropriately.[21] Unfortunately this method adopts (like Thompson) a sentience-only view of moral standing; but there is nothing to prevent it being extended to take into account the interests of other living creatures (which could be identified and represented by human proxies). Further development of this method is projected.

IX

A further reasonable challenge to an environmental ethic is whether it provides for sustainability; for, without sustainable systems of production and provision for the preservation of most ecosystems on a sustainable basis, the lives of future generations will be at best endangered, and at worst forestalled. There are, certainly, some problems about making this notion explicit;[22] but these may be resolved if a sufficient range of bearers of intrinsic value is allowed to inform accounts of what is to be sustained.

The kind of environmental ethic which is defended here does not underwrite every form of sustainable process; thus some forms of whaling could conceivably be sustainable, but would still be precluded by an ethic which pays sufficient heed to the interests of whales, and to their comparability to the interests of human beings. But where the perennial availability of resources is at issue and does not pose ethical problems like those raised by whaling, there is every reason to conclude that an environmental ethic does what is required, and also that alternative ethical systems are in danger of failing to do so, through undervaluing some of the beings which ought to be preserved.

At the same time, an environmental ethic of the kind I have described will uphold those forms of sustainable development which deserve to be upheld. For its adherents have no choice about recognizing the needs of human beings living in situations of deprivation and 'underdevelopment', as well as the likely needs of their successors (including the need for a sustainable environment); if we give due weight to non-human and to future interests, we are already committed to giving full consideration to human needs of both the present and the future. Such an ethic is unlikely to require that human beings be debarred from areas of wilderness, particularly in the Third World; instead it is likely to commend practices in which human beings live in harmony with their environment, whether they live in the Third World or in the developed countries.

X

In conclusion, to meet the contemporary challenges human beings need a comprehensive and discriminating ethic, and not just a new account of the self and self-realization (valuable as that may be). But such an ethic needs to be harnessed to a metaphysic which avoids the kind of disparagement of the material world which afflicts philosophical systems such as Cartesianism. Versions of idealism and of relativism which make the reality or the value of that world depend on human perceptions also seem to belittle it beyond necessity. Likewise an aesthetic is needed which provides for appreciation of nature as well as of art.

Some philosophers maintain that it is also essential to regard the natural world as in no way the product of design; only thus (they claim) can it be autonomous.[23] But if the value of creatures turns not on their origins but on having a good of their own, their createdness would not detract from their value; at the same time a belief in creation and a respect for fellow creatures could be crucial in inspiring the kind of world-view which environmental problems show to be urgently needed.

NOTES

1 Hargrove, *Foundations of Environmental Ethics*. For another view, see Attfield, 'Has the history of philosophy ruined the environment?' and *Environmental Philosophy: Principles and Prospects*.
2 Leopold, *A Sand County Almanac*.
3 Naess, 'The shallow and the deep, long-range ecology movement'.
4 This point is well argued by Nigel Dower, 'The concept of the environment', in Attfied and Belsey (eds), *Philosophy and the Natural Environment*.
5 Routley, 'Is there a need for a new, an environmental ethic?'.
6 Naess, 'A defence of the Deep Ecology movement'; 'The Deep Ecology movement'.
7 Sylvan, 'Critique of Deep Ecology'; Fox, 'Approaching Deep Ecology: a response to Richard Sylvan's critique'. If Fox is right and Deep Ecology has no value-theory and no ethic, this must count seriously against Deep Ecology, which, like other positions, must in the end supply reasons with which to defend practices and policies if it is to cut any ice.
8 The same criticism applies to the different, biocentric egalitarianism of Paul Taylor, *Respect for Nature: a Theory of Environmental Ethics*.

9 For such an attempt to base an ethic on the ideas of Leopold, see J. Baird Callicott, *In Defense of the Land Ethic*.
10 Singer, *Practical Ethics*, 2nd edn, ch. 1.
11 Regan, *The Case for Animal Rights*.
12 Attfield, *Ethics of Environmental Concern*, 2nd edn, ch. 9.
13 Rolston, *Environmental Ethics*.
14 Hargrove, *Foundations of Environmental Ethics*.
15 Losin, 'Faking nature' and 'The Sistine Chapel debate: Peter Losin replies'.
16 Rolston, ' The wilderness idea reaffirmed'.
17 Katz, 'Artifacts and functions'. Perhaps, however, Katz has a point in claiming that artifacts have (at any rate) less value when we reflect on the possibility of animals being genetically engineered so as to lack the capacity for feeling; what is objectionable about such a practice lies in generating creatures of constricted powers and fulfilments when creatures of ampler powers and fulfilments, such as natural animals are, could have been generated instead.
18 Thus e.g. Rodman, 'Four forms of ecological consciousness reconsidered'.
19 Thompson, 'A refutation of environmental ethics'.
20 Katz, 'Artifacts and Functions', penultimate page.
21 Attfield and Dell (eds), *Values, Conflict and the Environment*.
22 Holland, 'Natural capital'. After tackling problems about the criteria of sustainability, this essay boldly claims that we all presuppose that nature is good, in that on the natural world our entire being depends. Holland is not, of course, committed to leaving nature unmodified, but would favour a 'bias towards the natural' which would favour preservation in cases of doubt.
23 See Elliot, 'Ecology and the ethics of environmental restoration'; Katz 'Artifacts and functions'; and, in another way, Hargrove, *Foundations of Environmental Ethics*.

READING GUIDE

Aldo Leopold's *A Sand County Almanac* pioneered new approaches while conveying a love of the community of the land. In his essay 'The shallow and the deep, long-range ecology movement', Arne Naess developed some of the philosophical implications. The related Deep Ecology position is most coherently expressed in Warwick Fox's *Toward a Transpersonal Ecology*. The history of traditional attitudes to nature is discussed in John Passmore, *Man's Responsibility for Nature*; these matters plus normative issues are reassessed in Robin Attfield, *The Ethics of Environmental Concern*, of which the second edition (1991) surveys the recent literature. A wide range of philosophical positions and approaches is to be found in Robin Attfield and Andrew Belsey (eds), *Philosophy and the Natural Environment*.

Holmes Rolston's *Environmental Ethics* (not to be confused with the journal with that same name) exuberantly covers the main issues from a deep (but objectivist) perspective; an anthropocentric perspective is found in Eugene C. Hargrove's *Foundations of Environmental Ethics*. A range of more Leopoldian, ecocentric perspectives is presented in J. Baird Callicott's *In Defense of the Land Ethic*.

Other writers defend a much greater concern for individual creatures. While Peter Singer's *Practical Ethics* stops short at the interests of sentient creatures, Tom Regan's *The Case for Animal Rights* recognizes rights, but only in creatures which are conscious subjects.

Egalitarian and biocentric approaches are found both in Paul Taylor, *Respect for Nature* and in Robin Attfield, *Environmental Philosophy: Principles and Prospects*.

CLASSICAL SOURCES

A splendidly detailed account of historical attitudes to nature is to be found in Keith Thomas, *Man and the Natural World: Changing Attitudes in England, 1500–1800*. The view of human beings as stewards of nature may be found in Sir Matthew Hale, *The Primitive Origination of Mankind*, London, 1677. One kind of ecological awareness was present in Thomas Malthus, *An Essay on the Principle of Population* (1798), and another in Friedrich Engels, *Dialectics of Nature* (1873–82).

Bibliographies

INTRODUCTION

Almond, B. and Hill, D. (eds), *Applied Philosophy: Morals and Metaphysics in Contemporary Debate*, London, Routledge, 1991.

Gaita, R., *Good and Evil: an Absolute Conception*, London, Macmillan, 1991.

Graham, G., *Living the Good Life: Introduction to Moral Philosophy*, New York, Paragon, 1990.

Hare, R. M., *Moral Thinking: its Levels, Method and Point*, Oxford, Clarendon Press, 1981.

Hume, D., *A Treatise of Human Nature*, ed. E. C. Mossner, Harmondsworth, Penguin Books, 1985 (first published 1739 and 1740).

Kant, I., *Groundwork of the Metaphysics of Morals*, trans. by H. J. Paton and published as *The Moral Law*, London, Hutchinson, 1948.

Moore, G. E., *Principia Ethica*, Cambridge, Cambridge University Press, 1993 (first published 1903).

Norman, R., *The Moral Philosophers*, Oxford, Oxford University Press, 1983.

Popper, K., *The Open Society and its Enemies*, 5th rev. edn, London, Routledge, 1966 (first published 1945).

Rachels, J. (ed.), *Moral Problems*, 3rd edn, New York, Harper & Row, 1979.

Singer, P. (ed.), *Applied Ethics*, Oxford, Oxford University Press, 1986.

——, *Practical Ethics*, 2nd edn, Cambridge, Cambridge University Press, 1993.

Skillen, A., 'Welfare State vs. Welfare Society?', in Almond and Hill (eds), *Applied Philosophy*.

Talmon, J., *The Origins of Totalitarian Democracy*, London, Secker & Warburg, 1952.

Von Wright, G. H., *The Varieties of Goodness*, London, Routledge & Kegan Paul, 1963.

Winkler, E. R. and Coombs, J. R. (eds), *Applied Ethics*, Oxford, Blackwell, 1993.

CHAPTER 1   TROUBLE WITH FAMILIES?

Aiken, W. and LaFollette, H. (eds), *Whose Child? Children's Rights, Parental Authority and State Power*, Totowa, NJ, Rowman & Littlefield, 1980.

Aristotle, *The Politics, Oeconomica*, in R. McKeon (ed.), *The Basic Works of Aristotle*, New York, Random House, 1941.

Barrett, M. and Macintosh, M., *The Anti-Social Family*, London, Verso/New Left Books, 1982.

Berger, B., Carlson, A. and Davies, J., *The Family: Is It Just Another Lifestyle Choice?*, London, Institute of Economic Affairs, 1993.

Blustein, J., *Parents and Children: the Ethics of the Family*, Oxford, Oxford University Press, 1982.

Butler, S., *The Way of all Flesh*, Harmondsworth, Penguin Books 1982.

Butler J., *Fifteen Sermons*, in *The Works of Joseph Butler*, ed. W. E. Gladstone, Oxford, Clarendon Press, 1896.

de Beauvoir, S., *The Second Sex*, trans. and ed. H. M. Parshley, Harmondsworth, Penguin Books, 1972.

Dennis, N., *Rising Crime and the Dismembered Family*, London, Institute of Economic Affairs, 1993.

Ehrenreich, B. and English, D., *For Her Own Good: 150 Years of the Experts' Advice to Women*, London, Pluto Press, 1979.

Engels, F., *On The Origin of the Family, Private Property and the State*, London, Lawrence & Wishart, 1972 (first published 1884).

Epictetus, *Encheiridion* in *Arrian's Discourses of Epictetus*, London, Heinemann, 1978.

Firestone, S., *The Dialectic of Sex*, New York, Bantam Books, 1971.

Godwin, W., *Enquiry Concerning Political Justice*, ed. K. Cadell Carter, Oxford, Clarendon Press, 1971.

Hardyment, C., *Dream Babies: Child Care from Locke to Spock*, Oxford, Oxford University Press, 1984.

Hughes, J., 'The philosopher's child', in *Feminist Perspectives in Philosophy*, ed. M. Whitford, and M. Griffiths, Basingstoke, Macmillan, 1988.

——, 'Thinking about children', in G. Scarre (ed.), *Children, Parents and Politics*, Cambridge, Cambridge University Press, 1989.

Jaggar, A. and Rothenburg, P. (eds), *Feminist Frameworks*, 2nd edn, New York, McGraw-Hill, 1984.

Laing, R. D., *Sanity, Madness and the Family*, London, Tavistock, 1970.

Midgley, M., 'Rights talk will not sort out child-abuse: comment on Archard on parental rights; *Journal of Applied Philosophy*, 8(1), 1991.

—— and Hughes, J., *Women's Choices: Philosophical Problems Facing Feminism*, London, Weidenfeld, 1981.

Nietzsche, F., *Thus Spake Zarathustra*, trans. R. J. Hollingdale, Harmondsworth, Penguin Books, 1969.

O'Neill, O. and Ruddick, W. (eds), *Having Children: Philosophical and Legal Reflections on Parenthood*, Oxford, Oxford University Press, 1979.

Okin, S. M., *Women in Western Political Thought*, London, Virago, 1980.

——, *Justice, Gender and the Family*, New York, Basic Books, 1989.

Plato, *Republic* and *Laws* in *The Collected Dialogues*, ed. E. Hamilton and H. Cairns, Princeton, NJ, Princeton University Press, 1961, or see *Republic*, 2nd edn, trans. D. Lee, Harmondsworth, Penguin Books, 1974.

Rousseau, J.-J., *Émile or On Education*, trans. B. Foxley London, Dent/Everyman, 1966 (first published 1762).

Scarre, G. (ed.), *Children, Parents and Politics*, Cambridge, Cambridge University Press, 1989.

Skinner, B. F., *Walden Two*, New York, Macmillan, 1962.

Sommers, C., 'Philosophers against the family', in C. Sommers and F. Sommers (eds), *Vice and Virtue in Everyday Life*, 2nd edn, San Diego, Calif., Harcourt Brace Jovanovich, 1989.

Williams, B., 'Persons, character and morality', in *Moral Luck: Philosophical Papers 1973–80*, Cambridge, Cambridge University Press, 1981.

Wollstonecraft, M., *A Vindication of the Rights of Woman*, Harmondsworth, Penguin Books, 1978 (first published 1792).

CHAPTER 2   LOVE AND PERSONAL RELATIONSHIPS

Almond, B., 'Human bonds', *Journal of Applied Philosophy*, 5, 1989.

Aristotle, *Ethics*, rev. edn, trans. H. Tredennick, Harmondsworth, Penguin Books, 1976.

Baker, R. and Elliston, F. (eds), *Philosophy and Sex*, Buffalo, NY, Prometheus, 1984.

Bataille, G., *L'Érotisme*, Paris, Les Éditions de Minuit, 1957.

de Beauvoir, S., *The Second Sex*, trans. and ed. H. M. Parshley, Harmondsworth, Penguin Books, 1972.

Dilman, I., *Love and Human Separateness*, Oxford, Blackwell, 1987.

Fisher, M., *Personal Love*, London, Duckworth, 1990.

Foucault, M., *The History of Sexuality*, trans. R. Hurley, Harmondsworth, Penguin Books, 1981.

Gilbert, P., *Human Relationships*, Oxford, Blackwell, 1991.

Gregory, P., 'Against couples', *Journal of Applied Philosophy*, 1, 1984.

——, 'The two sides of love', *Journal of Applied Philosophy*, 3, 1986.

——, 'Eroticism and love', *American Philosophical Quarterly*, 25, 1988.

Plato, *Symposium* and *Phaedrus* in *The Collected Dialogues*, ed. E. Hamilton and H. Cairns, Princeton, NJ, Princeton University Press, 1961.

Rougemont, D. de, *Les Mythes de l'amour*, Paris, Éditions Albin Michel, 1961, repr. 1972.

Singer, I., *The Nature of Love*, vol. 1, *Plato to Luther*, 1984; vol. 2, *Courtly and Romantic Love*, 1984; vol. 3, *The Modern World*, 1987; Chicago and London, University of Chicago Press.

Scruton, R., *Sexual Desire*, London, Weidenfeld & Nicholson, 1986.

CHAPTER 3   BETWEEN THE SEXES: CARE OR JUSTICE?

Aristotle, *Nicomachean Ethics*, trans. H. Tredennick, rev. edn, Harmondsworth, Penguin Books, 1976.

de Beauvoir, S., *The Second Sex*, trans. and ed. H. M. Parshley, Harmondsworth, Penguin Books, 1972 (first published 1949).

Dworkin, A., *Intercourse*, London, Secker & Warburg, 1987.

Friedman, M., *What Are Friends For? Feminist Perspectives on Personal Relationships and Moral Theory*, Ithaca, NY, Cornell University Press, 1993.

Game, A. and Pringle, R., *Gender at Work*, Sydney, Allen & Unwin, 1983.

Gatens, M., *Feminism and Philosophy: Perspectives on Difference and Equality*, Cambridge, Polity Press, 1991.

Gilligan, C., *In a Different Voice: Psychological Theory and Women's Development*, Cambridge, Mass., Harvard University Press, 1982.

Haavind, H., 'Love and power in marriage; in H. Holter, *Patriarchy in a Welfare Society*, Oslo, Universitetsforlaget, 1984.

Held, V., *Feminist Morality: Transforming Culture, Society and Politics*, Chicago, University of Chicago Press, 1993.

Kymlicka, W., *Contemporary Political Philosophy: an Introduction*, Oxford, Oxford University Press, 1990.

Lacey, N., 'Theory into practice? Pornography and the public/private dichotomy', in A. Bottomley and J. Conaghan (eds), *Journal of Law and Society*, Special Issue: Feminist Theory and Legal Strategy, 1993.

Landes, J., *Women and the Public Sphere in the Age of the French Revolution*, Ithaca, NY, Cornell University Press, 1988.

Kittay, E. and Meyers, D. (eds), *Women and Moral Theory*, Totowa, NJ, Rowman & Littlefield, 1987.

Lloyd, G., *The Man of Reason: 'Male' and 'Female' in Western Philosophy*, 2nd edn, London, Methuen, London, Routledge, 1993 (first published 1984).

MacKinnon, C., *Feminism Unmodified: Discourses on Life and Law*, Cambridge, Mass, Harvard University Press, 1987.

Marcus, S., 'Fighting bodies, fighting words: a theory and politics of rape prevention', in J. Butler and J. W. Scott, *Feminists Theorize the Political*, London and New York, Routledge, 1992.

McCloskey, D. N., 'Some consequences of a conjective economics', in M. A. Ferber and J. A. Nelson, *Beyond Economic Man: Feminist Theory and Economics*, Chicago, Chicago University Press, 1993.

Noddings, N., *Caring: a Feminist Approach to Ethics and Moral Education*, Berkeley, Calif., University of California Press, 1984.

Okin, S. M., *Justice, Gender and the Family*, New York, Basic Books, 1989.

Pateman, C., *The Sexual Contract*, Cambridge: Polity Press, 1988.

——, *The Disorder of Women*, Cambridge: Polity Press, 1989.

Rawls, J., *A Theory of Justice*, Oxford, Oxford University Press, 1971.

Roiphe, K., *The Morning After: Sex, Fear and Feminism*, London, Hamish Hamilton, 1994.

Rossi, A., *Essays on Sex Equality*, Chicago, University of Chicago Press, 1970.

Rousseau, J.-J., *Émile*, trans. B. Foxley, London, Dent/Everyman, 1966 (first published 1762).

Ruddick, S., *Maternal Thinking*, New York: Ballantine, 1989.

Saxonhouse, A., 'Aristotle: defective males, hierarchy, and the limits of politics', in M. L. Shanley and C. Pateman, *Feminist Interpretations and Political Theory*, Cambridge, Polity Press, 1991.

Solomon, R. and Higgins, K., *The Philosophy of (Erotic) Love*, Lawrence, Kan., University Press of Kansas, 1991.

Young, I. M., *Justice and the Politics of Difference*, Princeton, NJ., Princeton University Press, 1990.

CHAPTER 4 CHILDREN WHO RUN: ETHICS AND HOMELESSNESS

Abrahams, C. and Mungall, R., *Runaways: Exploding the Myths*, London, National Children's Home Central Office, 1992.

Aiken, W. and LaFollette, H. (eds), *Whose Child? Children's Rights, Parental Authority and State Power*, Totowa, NJ, Rowan & Littlefield, 1980.

Almond, B., 'Education and liberty', *Journal of Philosophy of Education*, 25, 1991.

——, 'Rights', in Singer (ed.), *A Companion to Ethics*.

Archard, D., *Children: Rights and Childhood*, London, Routledge, 1993.

Bell, D., *Communitarianism and its Critics*, Oxford, Clarendon Press, 1993.

Berger, B., Carlson, A. and Davies, J., *The Family: Is It Just Another Lifestyle Choice?*, London, Institute of Economic Affairs, 1993.

Blustein, J., *Parents and Children: the Ethics of the Family*, Oxford, Oxford University Press, 1982.

Button, E., *Rural Housing for Youth*, London, Centrepoint, 1992.

Dennis, N., *Rising Crime and the Dismembered Family*, London, Institute of Economic Affairs, 1993.

Dingwall, R., Eekelaar, J. and Murray, T., *The Protection of Children*, Oxford, Blackwell, 1983.

Harré, R. and Gillett, G., *The Discursive Mind*, London, Sage, 1994.

Harris, J., 'The political status of children', in K. Graham (ed.), *Contemporary Political Philosophy*, Cambridge, Cambridge University Press, 1982.

'Homelessness: the facts', Shelter Fact Sheet 1991, London, Shelter.

Holt, J., *Escape from Childhood*, Harmondsworth, Penguin Books, 1974.

Hutson, S. and Liddiard, M., *Youth Homelessness: the Construction of a Social Issue*, Swansea, Macmillan, 1994.

Jones, J., *Young People in and out of the Housing Market: Working Papers 1–5*, Edinburgh, Centre for Educational Sociology at the University of Edinburgh and Scottish Council for the Single Homeless, 1994.

Kant, I., *Groundwork of the Metaphysics of Morals*, trans. by H. J. Paton and published as *The Moral Law*, London, Hutchinson, 1948.

Midgley, M., 'Rights talk will not sort out child abuse', *Journal of Applied Philosophy* 8(1), 1991.

O'Neil, O. and Ruddick, W. (eds), *Having Children: Philosophical and Legal Reflections on Parenthood*, Oxford, Oxford University Press, 1979.

Parker, M., 'The growth of understanding', unpublished Ph.D. thesis, University of Hull, 1992.

Rawls, J., *A Theory of Justice*, Oxford, Oxford University Press, 1971.

Scarre, G. (ed.), *Children, Parents and Politics*, Cambridge, Cambridge University Press, 1989.

Shotter, J., *Conversational Realities*, London, Sage, 1993.

Singer, P. (ed.), *A Companion to Ethics*, Oxford, Blackwell, 1991.

Strathdee, R., *No Way Back*, London, Centrepoint, 1992.

——, *Children Who Run*, London, Centrepoint, 1993.

Tucker, A., 'In search of home', *Journal of Applied Philosophy*, 10, 1994.

Vygotsky, L. S., *Mind in Society*, Harvard, Harvard University Press, 1978.
Williams, B., *Ethics and the Limits of Philosophy*, London, Fontana, 1985.

CHAPTER 5   EDUCATION: CONSERVING TRADITION

Arnold, M., *Culture and Anarchy*, London, Smith, Elder, 1882.
Callan, E., *Autonomy and Schooling*, Montreal, McGill-Queen's University Press, 1988.
Carr, D., *Educating the Virtues*, London, Routledge, 1991.
——, 'Recent work in the philosophy of education', *Philosophical Books*, 35, 1994.
Chesterton, G. K., *What's Wrong with the World*, London, Cassell, 1910.
Churchland, P., *Matter and Consciousness*, Cambridge, Mass., MIT, 1984.
Cohen, B., *Means and Ends in Education*, London, George Allen & Unwin, 1982.
Cooper, D., *Illusions of Equality*, London, Routledge & Kegan Paul, 1980.
——, *Authenticity and Learning: Nietzsche's Educational Philosophy*, London: Routledge & Kegan Paul, 1983.
—— (ed.), *Education, Values and Mind: Essays for R. S. Peters*, London, Routledge & Kegan Paul, 1986.
Crittenden, P., *Learning to be Moral*, London, Humanities Press, 1990.
Curtis, B. and Mays, W. (eds), *Phenomenology and Education*, London Methuen, 1978.
Davidson, D., *Essays on Actions and Events*, Oxford, Clarendon Press, 1980.
Dearden, R. F., 'Philosophy of education, 1952–82', *British Journal of Educational Studies*, 30, 1982.
Dennett, D., *The Intentional Stance*, Cambridge, Mass., MIT, 1989.
Dewey, J., *Democracy and Education*, New York, The Free Press, 1966 (first published 1916).
——, *Experience and Education*, London, Collier Macmillan, 1966.
Donagan, A., *The Theory of Morality*, Chicago, University of Chicago Press, 1977.
Geach, P., *Mental Acts*, London, Routledge & Kegan Paul, 1958.
Gewirth, A., *Reason and Morality*, Chicago, University of Chicago Press, 1978.
Gutmann, A., *Democratic Education*, Princeton, NJ, Princeton University Press, 1987.
Haldane, J., 'Religious education in a pluralist society: a philosophical perspective', *British Journal of Educational Studies*, 34, 1986; reprinted in L. J. Francis and A. Thatcher (eds), *Christian Perspectives for Education*, London, Fowler Wright, 1990.
——, 'Metaphysics in the philosophy of education', *Journal of Philosophy of Education*, 23, 1989.
——, 'Chesterton's philosophy of education', *Philosophy*, 65, 1990.
——, 'Applied ethics', in N. Bunnin and E. James (eds), *The Blackwell Companion to Philosophy*, Oxford, Blackwell, 1994.
Hamlyn, D. W., *Experience and the Growth of Understanding*, London, Routledge & Kegan Paul, 1978.
Harris, J., 'Recent work in the philosophy of education', *Philosophical Quarterly*, 33, 1983.
Harris, K., *Education and Knowledge*, London, Routledge & Kegan Paul, 1979.
Hirst, P., *Knowledge and the Curriculum*, London, Routledge & Kegan Paul, 1974.
Kant, I., *Pedagogical Lectures*, trans. A. Churton as *Kant on Education*, London, Kegan Paul, Trench, Trübner & Co., 1899.
Langford, G., *Education, Persons and Society: a Philosophical Enquiry*, London, Macmillan, 1985.

——, *Educating Reason: Rationality, Critical Thinking and Education*, London, Macmillan, 1985.

MacIntyre, A., *After Virtue*, London, Duckworth, 1981.

——, *Whose Justice? Which Rationality?*, London, Duckworth, 1988.

——, *Three Rival Versions of Moral Inquiry*, London, Duckworth, 1990.

Morris, V. C., *Existentialism in Education*, New York: Harper & Row, 1966.

Nagel, T., *The Possibility of Altruism*, Oxford, Oxford University Press, 1970.

——, *Equality and Partiality*, New York, Oxford University Press, 1991.

Nozick, R., *Anarchy, State and Utopia*, Oxford, Blackwell, 1974.

O'Hear, A., *Education, Society and Human Nature: an Introduction to the Philosophy of Education*, London, Routledge & Kegan Paul, 1981.

——, 'History of philosophy of education', in T. Honderich (ed.), *The Oxford Companion to Philosophy*, Oxford, Oxford University Press, 1994.

Peters, R. S. *Authority, Responsibility and Education*, London, George Allen & Unwin, 1959.

——, *Ethics and Education*, London, George Allen & Unwin, 1966.

——, (ed.), *The Concept of Education*, London, Routledge & Kegan Paul, 1967.

——, (ed.), *Philosophy of Education*, Oxford, Oxford University Press, 1973.

Plato, *Republic*, trans. R. Waterfield, Oxford, Oxford University Press, 1993.

Rawls, J., *A Theory of Justice*, Oxford, Oxford University Press, 1971.

——, *Political Liberalism*, New York, Columbia University Press, 1993.

Rousseau, J.-J., *Émile, or On Education*, trans. A. Bloom, New York, Basic Books, 1979.

Scheffler, I., *The Language of Education*, Springfield, Ill., Thomas, 1960.

Seigl, H., *Educating Reason: Rationality, Critical Thinking and Education*, London, Routledge & Kegan Paul, 1988.

Strike, K., *Liberal Justice and the Marxist Crique of Education*, London, Routledge, 1989.

Taylor, C., *Sources of the Self* Cambridge, Cambridge University Press, 1990.

——, *Multiculturalism and the Politics of Recognition*, Princeton, NJ, Princeton University Press, 1992.

Walker, J. and Evers, C., 'Towards a materialist pragmatist philosophy of education', *Education and Perspectives*, 11, 1984.

Walzer, M., *Spheres of Justice*, Oxford, Blackwell, 1985.

White, J., *Education and the Good Life*, London, Kogan Page, 1990.

White, P., *Beyond Domination: an Essay in the Political Philosophy of Education*, London, Routledge & Kegan Paul, 1983.

CHAPTER 6   ETHICS, LAW AND THE QUALITY OF THE MEDIA

Barendt, E., *Freedom of Speech*, Oxford, Oxford University Press, 1985.

Belsey, A. and Chadwick, R. (eds), *Ethical Issues in Journalism and the Media*, London, Routledge, 1992.

Birkinshaw, P., *Freedom of Information: the Law, the Practice and the Ideal*, London, Weidenfeld & Nicolson, 1988.

Calcutt, Sir D., *Review of Press Self-Regulation* (Cm 2135), London, HMSO, 1993.

Central Intelligence Machinery, London, HMSO, 1993.

Christians, C. G., Rotzoll, K. B. and Fackler, M., *Media Ethics: Cases and Moral Reasoning*, 3rd edn, New York, Longman, 1991.

Elliott, D. (ed.), *Responsible Journalism*, Beverly Hills, Calif., Sage, 1986.

Ewing, K. D. and Gearty, C. E., *Freedom under Thatcher: Civil Liberties in Modern Britain*, Oxford, Oxford University Press, 1990.

Finer, S. E. (ed.), *Five Constitutions*, Harmondsworth, Penguin Books, 1979.

House of Commons National Heritage Select Committee, *Privacy and Media Intrusion*, London, House of Commons, 1993.

Jansen, S. C., *Censorship: the Knot that Binds Power and Knowledge*, Oxford, Oxford University Press, 1988.

Keane, J., *The Media and Democracy*, Oxford, Polity Press, 1991.

Klaidman, S. and Beauchamp, T. L., *The Virtuous Journalist*, New York, Oxford University Press, 1987.

Lee, S., *The Cost of Free Speech*, London, Faber & Faber, 1990.

Lichtenberg, J. (ed.), *Democracy and the Mass Media*, Cambridge, Cambridge University Press, 1990.

Lord Chancellor's Department, *Infringement of Privacy*, London, Lord Chancellor's Department, 1993.

MI5: the Security Service, London, HMSO, 1993.

Mill, J. S., *On Liberty* (and other works), ed. Stefan Collini, Cambridge, Cambridge University Press, 1989.

Milton, J., *Areopagitica, a Speech of Mr John Milton for the Liberty of Unlicensed Printing, to the Parliament of England*, London, 1644.

Peak, S. (ed.), *The Media Guide 1994*, London, Fourth Estate, 1993.

Report of the Committee on Privacy and Related Matters (Chairman: Sir David Calcutt) (Cm 1102), London, HMSO, 1990.

Robertson, G. and Nichol, A., *Media Law*, 3rd end, Harmondsworth, Penguin Books, 1992.

Sieghart, P., *The Lawful Rights of Mankind: an Introduction to the International Legal Code of Human Rights*, Oxford, Oxford University Press, 1985.

Stephenson, H., *Media Freedom and Media Regulation: an Alternative White Paper*, Birmingham, Association of British Editors, Guild of Editors and International Press Institute, 1994.

Thornton, P., *Decade of Decline: Civil Liberties in the Thatcher Years*, London, National Council for Civil Liberties, 1989.

CHAPTER 7   RECONCILING BUSINESS IMPERATIVES AND MORAL VIRTUES

Bok, S., *Lying*, Hassocks, Harvester Press, 1978.

——, *Secrets*, Oxford, Oxford University Press, 1984.

Callahan, J. (ed.), *Ethical Issues in Professional Life*, New York, Oxford University Press, 1988.

Foot, P., *Virtues and Vices*, Berkeley, Calif., University of California Press, 1978.

Fox, R. M. and DeMarco, J. P. (eds), *New Directions in Ethics*, New York, Routledge, 1986.

Galbraith, J. K., *The Affluent Society*, 4th edn, Harmondsworth, Penguin Books, 1987.

Geach, P. T., *The Virtues: the Stanton Lectures, 1973–74*, New York, Cambridge University. Press, 1977.

Hayek, F. A., 'The non-sequitor of the "Dependence Effect"', in T. L. Beauchamp and N. E. Bowie (eds), *Ethical Theory and Business*, 2nd edn, Englewood Cliffs, NJ, Prentice-Hall, 1983.

Iannone, A. P. (ed.), *Contemporary Moral Controversies in Businesss*, New York, Oxford University Press, 1989.

Jackson, J., 'Honesty in marketing', *Journal of Applied Philosophy*, 7, 1990.

——, 'Preserving trust in a pluralist culture', in J. Mahoney and E. Vallance (eds), *Business Ethics in a New Europe*, Dordrecht, Kluwer Academic Publishers, 1992.

MacIntyre, A., *After Virtue*, London, Duckworth, 1981.

Nash, L. L., *Good Intentions Aside*, Boston, Mass., Harvard Business School Press, 1990.

Slote, M., *Goods and Virtues*, New York, Oxford University Press, 1983.

——, *From Morality to Virtue*, New York, Oxford University Press, 1992.

Wallace, J. D., *Virtues and Vices*, Ithaca, NY, Cornell University Press, 1978.

CHAPTER 8 THE GENE REVOLUTION

Anderson, W. F., 'Human gene therapy: scientific and ethical consideration', in R. F. Chadwick (ed.), *Ethics, Reproduction and Genetic Control*, rev. edn, London, Routledge, 1992.

Annas, G. J. and Elias, S. (eds), *Gene Mapping: Using Law and Ethics as Guides*, New York, Oxford University Press, 1992.

Beauchamp, T. L. and Childress, J. F., *Principles of Biomedical Ethics*, 3rd edn, New York, Oxford University Press, 1989.

Brenner, S., 'The human genome: the nature of the enterprise', in Chadwick, Bock and Whelan (eds) *Human Genome Analysis*, pp. 6–12.

British Medical Association, *Our Genetic Future*, Oxford, Oxford University Press, 1992.

Chadwick, D., Bock, G. and Whelan, J. (eds), *Human Genetic Information: Science, Law and Ethics*, Chichester, John Wiley, 1990.

Chadwick, R., 'Justice in priority setting', in R. Smith (ed.), *Rationing in Action*, London, BMJ, 1993, pp. 85–95.

——, Coli, D., Husted, J., Ngwgna, C., Ndray, S., Shickle, D., Pogliana, C. and Ten Have, H., *Ethical Implications of Human Genome Analysis for Clinical Practice in Medical Genetics* with *Special Reference to Genetic Counselling*, Cardiff, Centre for Applied Ethics, 1993.

Clarke, A., 'Is non-directive genetic counselling possible?', *The Lancet*, 338, 1991, pp. 998–1001.

—— (ed.), *Genetic Counselling: Practice and Principles*, London, Routledge, 1994.

Clothier, C. M. (Chairman), *Report of the Committee on the Ethics of Gene Therapy*, London, HMSO, 1992.

DE Wachter, M., *Experimental (Somatic) Gene Therapy: Ethical Concerns and Control*, Maastricht, Institute for Bioethics, 1993.

Draper, E., 'Genetic secrets: social issues of medical screening in a genetic age', *Hastings Center Report*, 22 (Special Supplement), 1992, pp. 15–8.

Dworkin, G., *The Theory and Practice of Autonomy*, Cambridge, Cambridge University Press, 1988.

Green, R., 'Method in bioethics: a troubled assessment', *Journal of Medicine and Philosophy*, 15, 1990, pp. 179–97.

Holm, S., 'Genetic engineering and the north–south divide', in A. Dyson and J. Harris (eds), *Ethics and Biotechnology*, London, Routledge, 1994.

Ignatieff, M., *Scar Tissue*, London, Chatto & Windus, 1993.

Keller, E. F., 'Nature, nurture, and the Human Genome Project', in Kevles and Hood (eds), *The Code of Codes*.

Kevles, D. J. and Hood, L. (eds), *The Code of Codes: Scientific and Social Issues in the Human Genome Project*, Cambridge, Mass., Harvard University Press, 1993.

Knoppers, B. M., *Human Dignity and Genetic Heritage*, Montreal, Law Reform Commission of Canada, 1991.

Lippman, A., 'Prenatal genetic testing and screening: constructing needs and reinforcing inequalities', in Clarke (ed.), *Genetic Counselling*, pp. 142–86.

Macer, D., *Shaping Genes*, Christchurch, New Zealand, Eubios Ethics Institute, 1990.

Nuffield Council on Bioethics, *Genetic Screening: Ethical Issues*, London, Nuffield Council on Bioethics, 1993.

Pembrey, M., 'Embryo therapy: is there a clinical need?', in D. R. Bromham, M. E. Dalton and J. Jackson (eds), *Ethics in Reproductive Medicine*, London, Springer-Verlag, 1992.

Royal College of Physicians, *Prenatal Diagnosis and Genetic Screening*, London, Royal College of Physicians, 1989.

——, *Ethical Issues in Clinical Genetics*, London, Royal College of Physicians, 1991.

——, *Purchasers' Guide to Genetic Services in the NHS*, London, Royal College of Physicians, 1991.

Shuster, E., 'Determinism and reductionism: a greater threat because of the Human Genome Project?', Annas and Elias (eds), *Gene Mapping*, pp. 115–27.

Skene, L., 'Mapping the human genome: some thoughts for those who say there should be a law on it', *Bioethics*, 5(3), 1991, pp. 233–49.

Zwart, H., 'Rationing in the Netherlands: the liberal and communitarian perspective', *Health Care Analysis*, 1(1).

CHAPTER 9 ETHICAL DECISION-MAKING IN SCIENCE AND TECHNOLOGY

Barnes, B. and Edge, D. (eds), *Science in Context Readings in the Sociology of Science*, Milton Keynes, Open University Press, 1982.

Bell, D., *The Coming of Post-Industrial Society: a Venture in Social Forecasting*, Harmondsworth, Penguin Books, 1976 (first published in USA 1973).

Blunden, E., *Shelley: a Life Story*, London, Collins, 1946.

Borgmann, A., *Technology and the Character of Contemporary Life: a Philosophical Enquiry*, Chicago, University of Chicago Press, 1984.

Carson, R., *Silent Spring*, London, Hamish Hamilton, 1962.

Commission of the European Communities, *Proposals for Council Decisions concerning the Specific Programmes implementing the Fourth Framework Programme for Research. Technological Development and Demonstration Activities (1994–1998)*, COM(94)68 final, Brussels, 30 March 1994, p. 465. The objectives come under the proposed Specific Programme entitled 'A European programme of targeted socio-economic research for growth, employment and social integration'.

Daniels, N., *Reading Rawls*, Oxford, Blackwell, 1975.

Dawkins, R., *The Blind Watchmaker*, Harlow, Longman Scientific and Technical, 1986.

Feyerabend, P., *Science in a Free Society*, London, Verso Editions/NLB, 1982 (first published 1978).

Franklin, B., *The Autobiography of Benjamin Franklin & Selections from his Writings*, with an introduction by Henry Steele Commager, New York, Random House, The Modern Library, 1944.

Herman, R., *The European Scientific Community*, Harlow, Longman, 1986.

Huxley, J., *Essays of a Humanist*, London, Chatto & Windus, 1964.

Johnson, D. G., 'Do engineers have social responsibilities?', in *Journal of Applied Philosophy*, 9(1), 1992, pp. 21–34.

Lakatos, I. and Musgrave, A., *Criticism and the Growth of Knowledge*, Cambridge, Cambridge University Press, 1970.

Lewis, H. W., *Technological Risk*, New York, Norton, 1990.

Lindemann, R., 'The trophic-dynamic aspect of ecology', *Ecology*, 23(4), 1942, pp. 399–418.

Locke, D., *A Fantasy of Reason*, London, Routledge, 1980.

Owens, S., *Energy-conscious Planning*, London, Council for the Protection of Rural England, June 1991.

Popper, K., *The Poverty of Historicism*, 2nd edn, Routledge & Kegan Paul, London, 1961.

——, *Objective Knowledge: an Evolutionary Approach*, rev. edn, Oxford, Clarendon Press, 1979 (first published 1972).

——, *In Search of a Better world: Lectures and Essays from Thirty Years*, trans. L. Bennett, with additional material by M. Mew, London, Routledge, 1992.

Porter, R. (ed.), *Man Masters Nature: 25 Centuries of Science*, London, BBC Books, 1987.

Priestley, J., 'Experiments and observations on different kinds of air', in *Joseph Pricitley: a Collection of his Work*, London, 1934.

Rawls, J., *A Theory of Justice*, Oxford, Oxford University Press, 1971.

Roberts, C., *The Scientific Conscience: Reflections on the Modern Biologist and Humanism*, New York, George Braziller, 1967.

Sarch, L., *The Effects of Patent Protection on Plant Biotechnologies in Developing Countries*, Luxembourg, STOA, Directorate-General for Research, European Parliament, 1994.

Shelley, M. W., *Frankenstein or, the Modern Prometheus*, repr. with an introduction by R. E. Dowse and D. J. Palmer, Dent, London, 1963 (first published 1818).

Shiva, V., *Monocultures of the Mind: Perspectives on Biodiversity and Biotechnology*, London, Zed Books, 1993.

Wynne, B., *Empirical Evaluation of Public Information on Major Industrial Accident Hazards*, Luxembourg, Community Documentation Centre on Industrial Risk, Institute for Systems Engineering and Informatics, Joint Research Centre of the European Communities (ISBN 92-826-4402-2), 1992.

Yearley, S., *Science, Technology and Social Change*, London, Unwin Hyman, 1988.

CHAPTER 10 PSYCHIATRY, COMPULSORY TREATMENT AND THE VALUE-BASED MODEL OF MENTAL ILLNESS

Agich, G. J., *Autonomy and Long-term Care*, Oxford, Oxford University Press, 1993.

Alderson, P., *Choosing for Children: Parents' Consent to Surgery*, Oxford, Oxford

University Press, 1990.

Anzia, D. J. and La Puma, J., 'An annotated bibliography of psychiatric medical ethics', *Academic Psychiatry*, 15, 1991, pp. 1–7.

Austin, J. L., 'A plea for excuses', *Proceedings of the Aristotelian Society*, 57, 1956–7, pp. 1–30. Reprinted in A. R. White (ed.), *The Philosophy of Action*, Oxford, Oxford University Press, 1968.

Beauchamp, T. L. and Childress, J. F., *Principles of Biomedical Ethics*, 3rd edn, Oxford, Oxford University Press, 1989.

Bloch, S. and Chodoff, P., *Psychiatric Ethics*, 2nd edn, Oxford, Oxford University Press, 1991.

—— and Reddaway, P., *Russia's Political Hospitals: the Abuse of Psychiatry in the Soviet Union*, Southampton, Camelot Press, 1977.

Boorse, C., 'On the distinction between disease and illness', *Philosophy and Public Affairs*, 5, 1975, pp. 49–68.

——, 'What a theory of mental health should be', *Journal of Theory Social Behaviour*, 6, 1976, pp. 61–84.

Butler, Rt Hon., the Lord (Chairman), *Report of the Committee on Mentally Abnormal Offenders*, Cmnd. 6244, London, HMSO, 1975.

Campbell, T. and Heginbotham, C., *Mental Illness: Prejudice, Discrimination and the Law*, Aldershot, Dartmouth Publishing Co., 1991.

Caplan, A. L., Engelhardt, T. and McCartney, J. J. (eds), *Concepts of Health and Disease: Interdisciplinary Perspectives*, Addison-Wesley, 1981.

Clare, A., 'The disease concept in psychiatry', in P. Hill, R. Murray and A. Thorley (eds), *Essentials of Postgraduate Psychiatry*, New York, Grune & Stratton, 1979.

Dancy, J., *Moral Reasons*, Oxford, Blackwell, 1992.

Department of Health and Welsh Office, *Code of Practice: Mental Health Act 1983*, London, HMSO, 1993.

Duff, A., 'Psychopathy and moral understanding', *American Philosophical Quarterly*, 14(3), 1977, pp. 189–200.

Edwards, R. B. (ed.), *Psychiatry and Ethics: Insanity, Rational Autonomy, and Mental Health Care*, New York, Prometheus Books, 1982.

Elliot, C., 'Puppetmasters and personality disorders: Wittgenstein, mechanism and moral responsibility', *Philosophy, Psychiatry and Psychology*, 1(2), 1994, pp. 91–103.

Flew, A., *Crime or Disease?*, New York, Barnes & Noble, 1973.

Fulford, K. W. M., *Moral Theory and Medical Practice*, Cambridge, Cambridge University Press, 1989.

——, 'Philosophy and medicine: the Oxford connection', *British Journal of Psychiatry*, 157, 1990, pp. 111–15.

——, 'Bioethical blind spots: four flaws in the field of view of traditional bioethics', *Health Care Analysis*, 1, 1993, pp. 155–62.

——, 'Mental illness and the mind–brain problem: delusion, belief and Searle's theory of intentionality', *Theoretical Medicine*, 14, 1993, pp. 181–94.

——, 'Closet logics: hidden conceptual elements in the DSM and ICD classifications of mental disorders', in Sadler, Wiggins and Schwartz (eds), *Philosophical Perspectives on Psychiatric Diagnostic Classification*.

——, 'Not more medical ethics', in K. W. M. Fulford, G. Gillett and J. M. Soskice (eds), *Medicine and Moral Reasoning*, Cambridge, Cambridge University Press, 1994.

——, 'Concepts of disease and the paradox of patient power', in K. W. M. Fulford, S. Erser and T. Hope (eds), *Essential Practice in Patient-centred Healthcare*, Oxford, Blackwell, forthcoming.

—— and Hope, R. A., 'Psychiatric ethics: a bioethical ugly duckling?', in R. Gillon and A. Lloyd (eds), *Principles of Health Care Ethics*, Chichester, John Wiley & Sons, 1993.

——, Smirnoff, A. Y. U. and Snow, E., 'Concepts of disease and the abuse of psychiatry in the USSR', *British Journal of Psychiatry*, 162, 1993, pp. 801–10.

Glover, J., *I: the Philosophy and Psychology of Personal Identity*, Harmondsworth, Penguin Books, 1988.

Group for the Advancement of Psychiatry, *A Casebook in Psychiatric Ethics*, New York, Brunner & Mazel, 1990.

Hare, R. M., 'Descriptivism', *Proceedings of the British Academy*, 49, 1963, pp. 115–34, reprinted in R. M. Hare, *Essays on the Moral Concepts*, London, Macmillan, 1972.

Harré, R., 'Emotion and memory: the second cognitive revolution', in A. Phillips Griffiths (ed.), *Philosophy, Psychology and Psychiatry*, Cambridge, Cambridge University Press, 1995.

Hobson, R. P., 'Against the "theory of mind"', *British Journal of Developmental Psychology*, 9, 1991, pp. 33–51.

——, *Autism and the Development of Mind*, Hillsdale, NJ, LEA Inc., 1993.

Holmes, J. and Lindley, R., *The Values of Psychotherapy*, New York and Oxford, Oxford University Press, 1989.

Hope, R. A., 'Ethical philosophy as applied to psychiatry', *Current Opinion in Psychiatry*, 3, 1990, pp. 673–6.

—— and Fulford, K. W. M., 'Medical, education: patients, principles and practice skills, in R. Gillon and A. Lloyd (eds), *Principles of Health Care Ethics*, Chichester, John Wiley & Sons, 1993.

Jonsen, A. R. and Toulmin, S., *The Abuse Of Casuistry: a history of Moral Reasoning*, Berkeley, Calif., University of California Press, 1988.

Kendell, R. E., 'The Concept of disease and its implications for psychiatry', *British Journal of Psychiatry*, 127, 1975, pp. 305–15.

Kirmayer, L. J. and Corin, E., 'Inside knowledge: cultural constructions of insight in psychosis', in X. F. Amador and A. S. David (eds), *Insight and Psychosis*, New York, Oxford University Press, forthcoming.

Kopelman, L. M., 'Moral problems in psychiatry', in R. Veatch (ed.), *Medical Ethics*, Jones & Bartlett, 1989.

—— (ed.), 'Philosophical issues concerning psychiatric diagnosis', *Journal of Medicine and Philosophy*, 17(2), 1992.

Lidz, C. W., Meisel, A., Zerubavel, E., Carter, M., Sestak, R. M. and Roth, L. H. (eds), *Informed Consent: a Study of Decision-making in Psychiatry*, London, Guildford Press, 1984.

Macklin, R., 'The medical model in psychoanalysis and psychotherapy', *Comprehensive Psychiatry*, 14(1), 1973, pp. 49–69.

Mandelbrote, B., 'The swing of the pendulum: attitudes towards the mentally ill and their management', *British Journal of Psychiatry Review of Books*, 3–5, January 1994.

Mann, D. (ed.), 'Theoretical issues in psychiatry', *Theoretical Medicine*, 12(1), March 1991.

Merskey, H. and Shafran, B., 'Political hazards in the diagnosis of sluggish schizophrenia', *British Journal of Psychiatry*, 148, 1986, pp. 47–56.

Moore, M. S., *Law and Psychiatry: Rethinking the Relationship*, Cambridge, Cambridge University Press, 1984.

Moore, A., Hope, T. and Fulford, K. W. M., 'Mild mania and well-being', *Philosophy, Psychiatry and Psychology*, 1, forthcoming.

Murray, T. H., 'Medical ethics, moral philosophy and moral tradition', in K. W. M. Fulford, G. Gillett and J. M. Soskice (eds), *Medicine and Moral Reasoning*, Cambridge, Cambridge University Press, 1994.

Nuffield Council on Bioethics, *Genetic Screening: Ethical Issues*, London, Nuffield Council on Bioethics, 1993.

Parsons, T., *The Social System*, Glencoe, Ill., Illinois Free Press, 1951.

Porter, R., *A Social History of Madness: Stories of the Insane*, London, Weidenfeld & Nicolson, 1987.

Radden, J., review article: 'Rationality and psychopathology', *Philosophy, Psychiatry and Psychology*, 1, forthcoming.

Rogers, A., Pilgrim, D. and Lacey, R., *Experiencing Psychiatry: Users' Views of Services*, London, Macmillan, 1993.

Roth, M. and Kroll, J., *The Reality of Mental Illness*, Cambridge, Cambridge University Press, 1986.

Russell, D., 'Psychiatric diagnosis and the interests of women', in Sadler, Wiggins and Schwartz, *Philosophical Perspectives on Psychiatric Diagnostic Classification*.

Sadler, J. Z., Wiggins, O. P. and Schwartz, M. A., *Philosophical Perspectives on Psychiatric Diagnostic Classification*, Baltimore, Md., Johns Hopkins University Press, 1994.

Szasz, T. S., *The Myth Of Mental Illness*, New York, Hoeber, 1961.

——, *Insanity: the Idea and its Consequences*, New York, John Wiley & Sons, 1987.

Urmson, J. O., 'On Grading', *Mind*, 59, 1950, pp. 145–69.

Wallace, K., 'Reconstructing judgement: emotion and moral judgement', *Hypatia*, 8, 1993, pp. 61–83.

Walker, E. F. and Lewine, R. R. J., 'Sampling biases in studies of gender and schizophrenia', *Schizophrenia Bulletin*, 19(1), 1993, pp. 1–7.

Warnock, G. J., *Contemporary Moral Philosophy*, London, Macmillan, 1967.

Wear, S., 'Empirical studies of informed consent', ch. 3, subsection II in *Informed Consent: Patient Autonomy and Physician Beneficence within Clinical Medicine*, Dordrecht, Netherlands, Kluwer Academic Publishers, 1993.

Wilkes, K. V., *Real People: Personal Identity without Thought Experiments*, Oxford, Clarendon Press, 1988.

Wing, J. K., *Reasoning about Madness*, Oxford, Oxford University Press, 1978.

CHAPTER 11   CRIME AND RESPONSIBILITY

Ackrill, J. L., *Aristotle's Ethics*, London, Faber & Faber, 1973.

Audi, R., 'Moral responsibility, freedom, compulsion', *American Philosophical Quarterly*, 11, 1974.

Becker, L. C., *On Justifying Moral Judgements*, London, Routledge & Kegan Paul, 1973.

Bickel, A. M., *The Morality of Consent*, New Haven and London, Yale University Press, 1975.

Buxton, R., 'Circumstances, consequences and attempted rape', *Criminal Law Review*, 30, 1984.

Chisholm, R. M., 'He could have done otherwise', *Journal of Philosophy*, 64, 1967.

Davidson, D., *Essays on Action and Events*, Oxford, Clarendon Press, 1980.

Duff, R. A., *Intention, Agency and Criminal Liability*, Oxford, Blackwell, 1990.

Feinberg, J., *Doing and Deserving*, Princeton, NJ, Princeton University Press, 1970.

Fingarette, H., 'Responsibility', *Mind*, 75, 1966.

Fischer, J. M., 'Responsibility and control', *Journal of Philosophy*, 79, 1982.

Frankfurt, H., 'Freedom of the will and the concept of person', repr. in G. Watson (ed.), *Free Will*, Oxford, Oxford University Press, 1982.

Gendin, S., 'Insanity and criminal responsibility', *American Philosophical Quarterly*, 10, 1973.

Glover, J., *Responsibility*, London, Routledge & Kegan Paul, 1970.

Hacker, P. M. S. and Raz, J. (eds), *Law, Morality and Society*, Oxford, Clarendon Press, 1977.

Hall, J., *General Principles of Criminal Law*, Indianapolis, Ind., Bobbs-Merrill, 1960.

Harris, J., *Violence and Responsibility*, London, Routledge & Kegan Paul, 1980.

Hart, H. L. A., *Punishment and Responsibility*, Oxford, Clarendon Press, 1968.

Houlgate, L. D., 'Knowledge and responsibility', *American Philosophical Quarterly*, 5, 1968.

Kenny, A., *Freewill and Responsibility*, London, Routledge & Kegan Paul, 1978.

Klein, M., *Determinism, Blameworthiness and Deprivation*, Oxford, Oxford University Press, 1990.

Laing, R. D., *The Divided Self*, Harmondsworth, Penguin Books, 1965.

Lloyd, D., *The Idea of Law*, Harmondsworth, Penguin Books, 1974.

Mischel, T. (ed.), *The Self*, Oxford, Blackwell, 1977.

Morris, H. (ed.), *Freedom and Responsibility*, Stanford, Calif., Stanford University Press, 1961.

Oakley, J., *Morality and the Emotions*, London, Routledge, 1993.

Pritchard, M. S., 'Responsibility, understanding and psychopathology', *The Monist*, 57, 1974.

Rorty, A. M. (ed.), *The Identities of Persons*, London, University of California Press, 1976.

Siegler, F. A., 'Voluntary and involuntary', *The Monist*, 51, 1968.

Smith, J. C. and Hogan, B., *Criminal Law*, London, Butterworths, 1988.

Schoeman, F. (ed.), *Responsibility, Character and the Emotions*, Cambridge, Cambridge University Press, 1987.

Strawson, P. F., 'Freedom and resentment', in *Freedom and Resentment and Other Essays*, London, Methuen, 1974.

Tam, H. B., *A Philosophical Study of the Criteria for Responsibility Ascriptions*, Lampeter, Edwin Mellen Press, 1990.

Ten, C. L., *Crime, Guilt and Punishment*, Oxford, Oxford University Press, 1987.

Watson, G. (ed.), *Free Will*, Oxford, Oxford University Press, 1982.

Will, F. L., 'Intention, error and responsibility', *Journal of Philosophy*, 61, 1964.

Young, R., 'Autonomy and the "Inner Self"', *American Philosophical Quarterly*, 17, 1980.

CHAPTER 12   IS PSYCHOPATHY A MORAL CONCEPT?

American Psychiatric Association, *Diagnostic and Statistical Manual of Mental Disorders*, 3rd edn, Washington, American Psychiatric Association, 1987.

Blackburn, R., 'On moral judgements and personality disorders', *British Journal of Psychiatry*, 153, 1988, pp. 505–12.

Culver, C. M. and Gert, B., *Philosophy in Medicine: Conceptual and Ethical Issues in Medicine and Psychiatry*, Oxford, Oxford University Press, 1982.

Flew, A., *Crime or Disease?*, New York, Barnes & Noble, 1973.

Foucault, M., *Madness and Civilization: a History of Insanity in the Age of Reason*, New York, Random House, 1973.

Henderson, D. K., *Psychopathic States*, London, Chapman & Hall, 1939.

Lewis, G. and Appleby, L., 'Personality disorder: the patients psychiatrists dislike', *British Journal of Psychiatry*, 159, 1988, pp. 44–9.

Maudsley, H., *Responsibility in Mental Disease*, London, Kegan Paul & Trench, 1885.

Mental Health Act 1983, London, HMSO, 1983.

Murphy, G. E. and Guze, S. B., 'Setting limits: the management of the manipulative patient', *American Journal of Psychotherapy*, 14, 1960, pp. 30–47.

Roth, M. and Kroll, J., *The Reality of Mental Illness*, Cambridge, Cambridge University Press, 1986.

Sandler, J., Dare, C. and Holder, A., 'Basic psychoanalytic concepts: III. Transference', *British Journal of Psychiatry*, 116, 1970, pp. 667–72.

Schneider, K., *Psychopathic Personalities*, 9th edn, trans. M. W. Hamilton, London, Cassell, 1950.

Szasz, T., *The Myth of Mental Illness*, New York, Hoeber, 1961.

——, *Law, Liberty and Psychiatry: an Enquiry into the Social Uses of Mental Health Practices*, New York, Macmillan, 1963.

Tyrer, P. and Stein, G., *Personality Disorder Reviewed*, London, Gaskell, 1993.

——, Casey, P. and Ferguson, B., 'Personality disorder in perspective', *British Journal of Psychiatry*, 159, 1993, pp. 463–71.

Williams, B., *Ethics and the Limits of Philosophy*, London, Fontana, 1985.

CHAPTER 13   LIFE, DEATH AND THE LAW

Alexander, L., 'Medical science under dictatorship', *New England Journal of Medicine*, 241, 1949.

Aristotle, *Politics*, trans. T. A. Sinclair, Harmondsworth, Penguin Books, 1981.

——, *Nicomachean Ethics*, trans. D. Ross, Oxford, Oxford University Press, 1980.

Arras, J. and Rhoden, N. (eds), *Ethical Issues in Modern Medicine*, 3rd edn, Mountain View, Calif., Mayfield Publishing Co., 1989.

Beauchamp, T. L. and Childress, J. F. (eds), *Principles of Biomedical Ethics*, 2nd edn, Oxford, Oxford University Press, 1983.

Beauchamp, T. L. and Perlin, S. (eds), *Ethical Issues in Death and Dying*, Englewood Cliffs, NJ, Prentice-Hall, 1978.

Brahams, D., 'Criminality and compassion', *Law Society Gazette*, 35, September 1992.

——, 'The critically ill patient', in Cribb and Tingle (eds), *Nursing Law and Ethics*.

Brazier, M., *Medicine, Patients and the Law*, Harmondsworth, Penguin Books, 1987.

Brock, D., *Life and Death: Philosophical Aspects of Biomedical Ethics*, Cambridge, Cambridge University Press, 1991.

Campbell, R., 'Declining and withdrawing treatment', in Cribb and Tingle (eds), *Nursing Law and Ethics*.

—— and Collinson, D., *Ending Lives*, Oxford, Blackwell, 1988.

Church of England National Assembly (Board for Social Responsibility), *On Dying Well*, London, Church Information Office, 1975.

Cohen, M. and Scanlon, T. (eds), *The Rights and Wrongs of Abortion*, Princeton, NJ, Princeton University Press, 1974.

Cribb, A. and Tingle, J. (eds), *Nursing Law and Ethics*, Oxford, Blackwell, forthcoming.

Cross, R. and Jones, P. A., *Introduction to Criminal Law*, 9th edn, London, Butterworths, 1980.

Culver, C. M. and Gert, B., *Philosophy in Medicine*, Oxford, Oxford University Press, 1982.

Donne, J., *Biathanatos*, ed. E. W. Sullivan II, Newark NJ, University of Delaware Press, 1984 (written 1608).

Ellos, W. J., *Ethical Practice in Clinical Medicine*, London, Routledge, 1990.

Faden, R. and Beauchamp, T. L., *A History and Theory of Informed Consent*, Oxford, Oxford University Press, 1986.

Faulder, C., *Whose Body Is It? The Troubling Issue of Informed Consent*, London, Virago Press, 1985.

Feinberg, J. (ed.), *The Problem of Abortion*, 2nd edn, Belmont, NY, Wadsworth Publishing Co., 1973.

Gillon, R., *Philosophical Medical Ethics*, London, Wiley & Sons, 1986.

Glover, J., *Causing Death and Saving Lives*, Harmondsworth, Penguin Books, 1977.

Harris, J., *The Value of Life*, London, Routledge, 1985.

Hastings Center, *Guidelines on the Termination of Life-sustaining Treatment and the Care of the Dying*, Briarcliff Manor, NY, Hastings Center, 1987.

Holmes, H. B. and Purdy, L. M. (eds), *Feminist Perspectives in Medical Ethics*, Bloomington, Ind., Indiana University Press, 1992.

Hume, D. 'Of suicide', in P. Singer (ed.), *Applied Ethics*, Oxford, Oxford University Press, 1986 (Hume's essay first published 1777).

Hursthouse, R., *Beginning Lives*, Oxford, Blackwell, 1987.

Jennett, B. and Plum, F., 'The persistent vegetative state: a syndrome in search of a name', *The Lancet*, 1, 1972, pp. 734–7.

Kennedy, I., *The Unmasking Of Medicine*, London, Allen & Unwin, 1981.

Ladd, J., *Ethical Issues Relating to Life and Death*, Oxford, Oxford University Press, 1979.

Lamb, D., *Down the Slippery Slope*, London, Croom Helm, 1988.

Lee, R. and Morgan, D. (eds), *Birthrights*, London, Routledge, 1989.

Lifton, R. J., *The Nazi Doctors: Medical Killing and the Psychology of Genocide*, New York, Basic Books, 1986.

Lockwood, M. (ed.), *Moral Dilemmas in Modern Medicine*, Oxford, Oxford University Press, 1985.

Mason, J. K. and McCall Smith, R. A., *Law and Medical Ethics*, 3rd edn, London, Butterworths, 1991.

Mill, J. S., *On Liberty*, Harmondsworth, Penguin Books, 1982 (first published 1859).

More, Sir Thomas, *Utopia*, trans. P. Turner, Harmondsworth, Penguin Books, 1965 (first published 1516).

Plato, 'Phaedo', in *The Last Days of Socrates*, trans. H. Tredinnick, Harmondsworth,

Penguin Books, 1959.

——, *Republic*, trans. F. M. Cornford, Oxford, Oxford University Press, 1941.

President's Commission for the Study of Ethical Problems in Medicine and Biomedical and Behavioural Research, *Deciding to Forgo Life-sustaining Treatment*, Washington, US Government Printing Office, 1983.

Weir, R. (ed.), *Ethical Issues in Death and Dying*, New York, Columbia University Press, 1986.

——, *Abating Treatment with Critically Ill Patients*, Oxford, Oxford University Press, 1989.

CHAPTER 14   ETHICAL QUESTIONS FACING LAW ENFORCEMENT AGENTS

Alpert, G. P. and Anderson, P. R., 'The most deadly force: police pursuits', *Justice Quarterly*, 3(1), March 1986, pp. 1–14.

Bok, S., *Lying: Moral Choice in Public and Private Life*, New York, Pantheon, 1978.

Cohen, H. S. and Feldberg, M., *Power and Restraint: the Moral Dimension of Police Work*, New York, Praeger, 1991.

Criminal Justice Ethics, published semi-annually, John Jay College of Criminal Justice, 899 Tenth Avenue, New York, NY 10019, USA.

Delattre, E., *Character and Cops: Ethics in Policing*, Lanham, Md., University Press of America & American Enterprise Institute, 1989.

Elliston, F. A. and Feldberg, M. (eds), *Moral Issues in Police Work*, Totowa, NJ: Rowman & Allanheld, 1985.

Hansen, D. A., *Police Ethics*, Springfield, Ill., Charles C. Thomas, 1973.

Heffernan, W. C. and Stroup, T. (eds), *Police Ethics: Hard Choices in Law Enforcement*, New York, John Jay Press, 1985.

Kania, R. R. E., 'Should we tell the police to say "Yes" to gratuities?', *Criminal Justice Ethics*, 7(2), Summer/Fall, 1988, pp. 37–49.

Kleinig, J. I. with Zhang, Y. (comp. & ed.), *Professional Law Enforcement Codes: a Documentary Collection*, Westport, Conn., Greenwood Press, 1993.

——, *The Ethics of Policing*, Cambridge, Cambridge University Press, forthcoming.

Kooken, D. L., *Ethics and Police Service*, Springfield, Ill., Charles C. Thomas, 1957.

Locke, J., *Two Treatises of Government*, rev. edn, introduction and notes by P. Laslett, New York, Mentor, 1965 (first published 1690).

Maas, P., *Serpico*, New York, Viking, 1973.

Marx, G., *Undercover: Police Surveillance in America*, Berkeley, Calif., University of California Press, 1988.

——, 'Under-the-covers undercover investigations: some reflections on the state's use of sex and deception in law enforcement', *Criminal Justice Ethics*, 11(1), Winter/Spring 1992, pp. 13–24.

Miller, L. S. and Braswell, M. C., *Human Relations and Police Work*, 2nd edn, Prospect Heights, Ill., Waveland Press, 1987.

Skolnick, J., *Justice Without Trial: Law Enforcement in a Democratic Community*, 2nd edn, New York, John Wiley, 1975.

——, 'Deception by police', *Criminal Justice Ethics*, 1(2), Summer/Fall 1982, pp. 40–53.

—— and Leo, R., 'The ethics of deceptive interrogation', *Criminal Justice Ethics*, 11(1), WinterSpring 1992, pp. 3–12.

Walton, D. N., *Slippery Slope Arguments*, Oxford, Clarendon Press, 1992.

White, W. S., 'Police trickery in inducing confessions', *University of Pennsylvania Law Review*, 127, January 1979, pp. 581–621.

CHAPTER 15   IS EFFICIENCY ETHICAL? RESOURCE ISSUES IN HEALTH CARE

Aaron, H. J. and Schwartz, W. B., *The Painful Prescription: Rationing Hospital Care*, Washington, DC, Brookings, 1984.

Airedale NHS Trust v. *Bland*, Law Lords' decision of 4 February 1993, reported in the *Guardian*, 5 February 1993.

Baumrin, B., 'Putting them out on the ice: Curtailing care of the elderly', *Journal of Applied Philosophy*, 8(2), 1991, pp. 155–60.

Calabresi, G. and Bobbitt, P., *Tragic Choices*, New York, Norton, 1978.

Challah, S., Wing, A., Bauer, R., Morris, R. W. and Shroeder, S. A., 'Negative selection of patients for dialysis and transplantation in the UK', *British Medical Journal*, 288, 1984, pp. 119–22.

Childress, J. F., 'Who shall live when not all can live?', in S. Gorovitz (ed.), *Moral Problems in Medicine*, 2nd edn. Englewood Cliffs, NJ, Prentice-Hall, 1978.

Coase, R., 'The problem of social cost', *Journal of Law and Economics*, 3, 1960, pp. 1–44.

Collard, D., *Altruism and Economy: a Study in Non-selfish Economics*, Oxford, Martin Robertson, 1978.

Coulton, C. J., 'Resource limits and allocation in critical care', in S. J. Younger (ed.), *Human Values in Critical Care Medicine*, New York, Praeger, 1986.

Dickenson, D., *Moral Luck in Medical Ethics and Practical Politics*, Aldershot, Gower, 1991.

——, 'Nurse time as a scarce health care resource', in G. Hunt (ed.), *Ethical Issues in Nursing*, London, Routledge, 1994.

Downie, R. S., 'Traditional medical ethics and economics in health care: a critique', in G. Mooney and A. McGuire (eds), *Medical Ethics.*

—— and Calman, K. C., *Healthy Respect: Ethics in Health Care*, London, Faber & Faber, 1987.

Dworkin, R. M., *Taking Rights Seriously*, Cambridge, Mass., Harvard University Press, 1977.

Enthoven, A. C., *Reflections on the Management of the National Health Service*, London: NPHT, 1985.

Fine, B. and Harris, L., *Rereading Capital*, London, Macmillan, 1979.

Freund, P. A., 'Introduction', *Daedalus*, spring 1969, p. xiii.

Gillon, R., 'Ethics, economics and general practice', in Mooney and McGuire (eds), *Medical Ethics.*

Glover, J., *Causing Death and Saving Lives*, Harmondsworth, Penguin Books, 1977.

Green, R. M., 'Health care and justice in contract theory perspective', in R. M. Veatch and R. Branson (eds), *Ethics and Health Policy*, Cambridge, Mass., Ballinger Publishing, 1976.

Hanly, K., 'The problem of social cost: Coase's economics versus ethics', *Journal of Applied*

Philosophy, 9, 1992, pp. 77–84.

Hare, R. M., *Moral Thinking: its Levels, Method and Point*, Oxford, Clarendon Press, 1981.

Harris, J., 'QALYfying the value of life', *Journal of Medical Ethics*, 13(3), September 1987, pp. 117–23.

——, *The Value of Life*, London, Routledge, 1985.

Hastings Center, *Guidelines on the Termination of Life-sustaining Treatment and the Care of the Dying*, Briarcliff Manor, NY, Hastings Center, 1987.

Haydock, A., 'QALYs – a threat', *Journal of Applied Philosophy*, 9, 1992, pp. 183–8.

Held, D., *Models of Democracy*, Cambridge, Polity Press, 1987.

Hinds, S., 'On the relations of medical triage to world famine: an historical survey', in G. R. Lucas and T. W. Ogletree (eds), *Lifeboat Ethics: the Moral Dilemmas of World Hunger*, New York, Harper & Row, 1976.

HMSO, *Working for Patients*, London, HMSO, 1989.

Katz, A. H. and Procter, D. M., *Social-Psychological Characteristics of Patients Receiving Hemodialysis Treatment for Chronic Renal Failure*, Washington, DC, Department of Health, Education and Welfare, 1969.

Keynes, J. M., *The General Theory of Employment, Interest and Money*, London, Macmillan, 1936.

Mattick, P., *Marx and Keynes*, Boston, Mass., Porter Sargent, 1969.

Mihill, C., 'NHS policy changes "put patients at risk"', *Guardian*, 7 July 1993.

——, 'Waiting list facts "denied to patients"', *Guardian*, 11 February 1993.

Mill, J. S., *Utilitarianism*, London, Dent, 1910 and subsequent reprints (first published 1861).

Miller, E., 'Economic efficiency', *Journal of Economic Issues*, 24(3), pp. 719–32.

Mooney, G. and McGuire, A., 'Economics and medical ethics in health care: an economic viewpoint', in Mooney and McGuire (eds), *Medical Ethics*.

—— and —— (eds), *Medical Ethics and Economics in Health Care*, Oxford, Oxford University Press, 1988.

Mullen, P. M., 'The NHS White Paper and internal markets', *Financial Accountability and Management*, 6, 1990, pp. 33–50.

Outka, G., 'Social justice and equal access to health care', *Journal of Religious Ethics*, 2, 1974, pp. 11–32.

Pattison, S. and Armitage, P., 'An ethical analysis of the policies of British community and hospital care for mentally ill people', *Journal of Medical Ethics*, 12, 1986, pp. 136–42.

Powell, W. W., 'Neither market nor hierarchy', *Research in Organizational Behaviour*, 12, 1990, pp. 295–336.

Rawls, J., *A Theory of Justice*, Cambridge, Mass., Harvard University Press, 1971.

Seitovsky, A. A., 'The high cost of dying: what do the data show?', *Milbank Memorial Fund Quarterly*, 62, 1984, pp. 591–608.

Shatin, L., 'Medical care and the social worth of a man', *American Journal of Orthopsychiatry*, 26, 1966, pp. 96–101.

Sheldon, T., 'London HAs jump the ministerial gun', *Health Services Journal*, 7, 1993.

Sherwin, S., *No Longer Patient: Feminist Ethics and Health Care*, Philadelphia, Pa., Temple University Press, 1992.

Sweezy, P., *The Theory of Capitalist Development*, New York, Monthly Review Press, 1942.

Travis, A., 'Hospitals must wait to know fate', *Guardian*, 12 February 1993.

US v. Holmes, 26 Fed. Cas. 360, 1841.

US Task Force on Organ Transplantation, *Organ Transplantation: Issues and Recommendations*, Washington, DC, Department of Health and Human Services, 1986.

Veatch, R. M., *Death, Dying and the Biological Revolution: Our Last Quest for Responsibility*, rev. edn, New Haven, Conn., Yale University Press, 1989.

—— and Fry, S. T., *Case Studies in Nursing Ethics*, Philadelphia, Pa., J. B. Lippincott Co., 1987.

Weber, M., *Economy and Society*, 2 vols, Berkeley, Calif., University of California Press, 1978.

Which? magazine, 7 February 1991.

Winslow, G. R., *Triage and Justice*, Berkeley, Calif., University of California Press, 1982.

Younger, S., Lewandowski, W., McClish, D. *et al.*, 'The incidence and implications of DNR orders in a medical intensive care unit', *Journal of the American Medical Association*, 253, 1985, pp. 54–7.

CHAPTER 16   LIBERTY OR COMMUNITY? DEFINING THE POST MARXIST AGENDA

Almond, B., *Moral Concerns*, Atlantic Highlands, NJ, Humanities Press, 1987.

——, 'Seven moral myths', *Philosophy*, 65, 1990, pp. 129–36.

Anscombe, G. E. M., 'Modern moral philosophy', *Philosophy*, 33, 1958.

Arblaster, A., *The Rise and Decline of Western Liberalism*, Oxford, Blackwell, 1984.

Avineri, S. and de-Shalit, A. (eds), *Communitarianism and Individualism*, Oxford, Oxford University Press, 1992.

Beiner, R., *What's the Matter with Liberalism?*, Berkeley, Calif., University of California Press, 1992.

Bentham, J., *An Introduction to the Principles of Morals and Legislation*, London, Athlone Press, 1990 (first published 1789).

Bloom, A., *The Closing of the American Mind*, New York, Simon & Schuster, 1987.

Burckhardt, J., *Reflections on History*, trans. M. D. Hottinger, London, George Allen & Unwin, 1943.

Cranston, M., *What are Human Rights?*, London, Bodley Head, 1973.

Friedman, M., *Capitalism and Freedom*, Chicago, Chicago University Press, 1962.

Gray, J., *Liberalism*, Milton Keynes, Open University Press, 1986.

——, *Liberalisms: Essays in Political Philosophy*, London, Routledge, 1989.

——, *The Moral Foundations of Market Institutions*, London, IEA Health and Welfare Unit, 1992.

Hayek, F. A., *The Constitution of Liberty*, London, Routledge, 1960.

——, *The Road to Serfdom*, London, Routledge, 1976 (first published 1944).

Hobbes, T., *Leviathan*, ed. C. B. Macpherson, Harmondsworth, Penguin Books, 1981 (first published 1651).

Kukathas, C., 'Freedom versus autonomy', in Gray, *Moral Foundations*, pp. 101–14.

Kymlicka, W., *Liberalism, Community and Culture*, Oxford, Oxford University Press, 1989.

Locke, J., *Two Treatises of Government*, rev. edn, introduction and notes by P. Laslett, New York, Mentor, 1965 (first published 1690).

MacIntyre, A., *After Virtue*, London, Duckworth, 1981.

——, *Whose Justice? Which Rationality?*, Notre Dame, Ind., University of Notre Dame

Press, 1988.

Mill, J. S., *On Liberty*, Harmondsworth, Penguin Books, 1982 (first published 1859).

Mulhall, S. and Swift, A., *Liberals and Communitarians*, Oxford, Blackwell, 1992.

Nozick, R., *Anarchy, State and Utopia*, Oxford, Blackwell, 1974.

Paine, T., *The Rights of Man*, ed. T. Benn, London, Dent/Everyman, 1993 (first published 1791, 1792).

Rawls, J., *A Theory of Justice*, Cambridge, Mass., Harvard University Press, 1971.

Raz, J., *The Morality of Freedom*, Oxford: Oxford University Press, 1986.

Rousseau, J.-J., *The Social Contract*, trans. M. Cranston, Harmondsworth, Penguin Books, 1968 (first published 1762).

Sandel, M., *Liberalism and the Limits of Justice*, Cambridge, Cambridge University Press, 1982.

—— (ed.), *Liberalism and its Critics*, Oxford: Blackwell, 1984.

Scruton, R., *The Meaning of Conservatism*, 2nd edn, London, Macmillan, 1984.

——, *The Philosopher on Dover Beach*, Manchester, Carcanet, 1990.

Smith, A., *An Inquiry into the Nature and Causes of the Wealth of Nations*, ed. K. Sutherland, Oxford, Oxford University Press, 1993 (first published 1776).

Sumner, L. W., *The Moral Foundations of Rights*, Oxford, Clarendon Press, 1987.

Waldron, J. (ed.), *Theories of Rights*, Oxford, Oxford University Press, 1984.

CHAPTER 17 A DEFENCE OF PROPERTY RIGHTS AND CAPITALISM

Aristotle, *Politics*, trans. T. A. Sinclair, rev. edn, T. J. Saunders, Harmondsworth, Penguin Books, 1984.

Arrow, K. J., *Social Choice and Individual Values*, 2nd edn, New York, Wiley, 1963.

Block, W., *Defending the Undefendable*, New York, Fleet Press, 1976.

Friedman, M. and R., *Free to Choose*, Harmondsworth, Penguin Books, 1980.

Gordon, B., *Economic Analysis before Adam Smith*, New York, Barnes & Noble, 1976.

Hardin, G., 'The tragedy of the commons', *Science*, 162, 1968, pp. 1243–8.

Hayek, F. A., *The Constitution of Liberty*, London, Routledge, 1960.

Hayek, F. A., *The Road to Serfdom*, London, Routledge & Kegan Paul, 1976.

Hoff, T. J. B., *Economic Calculation in the Socialist Society*, Indianopolis, Ind., Liberty Press, 1981.

Locke, J., *Two Treatises of Government*, rev. edn, introduction and notes by P. Laslett, New York, Mentor, 1965 (first published 1690).

Machan, T. (ed.), *The Libertarian Alternative*, Chicago, Nelson Hall, 1974.

——, 'Rational choice and public affairs', *Theory and Decision*, 12, 1980, pp. 229–58.

——, *Individuals and their Rights*, La Salle, Ill., Open Court Publishing Co., 1989.

——, 'Two senses of human freedom', *The Freeman*, 39, 1989, pp. 33–7.

——, *Private Rights, Public Illusions*, New Brunswick, NJ, Transaction Books, 1994.

Malthus, T., *An Essay on the Principle of Population*, 1803 edn, ed. D. Winch, Cambridge, Cambridge University Press, 1992.

Marx, K., *Karl Marx: Selected Writings*, ed. D. McLellan, Oxford, Oxford University Press, 1977.

Mill, J. S., *On Liberty* in *Three Essays*, ed. R. Wollheim, Oxford, Oxford University Press, 1975.

Nozick, R., *Anarchy, State and Utopia*, New York, Basic Books, 1974.

Rand, A., *The Virtue of Selfishness*, New York, New American Library, 1961.

Rasmussen, D. B. and Den Uyl, D. J., *Liberty and Nature, an Aristotelian Defense of Liberal Order*, La Salle, Ill., Open Court Publishing Co., 1991.

Rawls, J., *A Theory of Justice*, Cambridge, Mass., Harvard University Press, 1971.

Sadowsky, J., 'Private property and collective ownership', in Machan (ed.), *The Libertarian Alternative*.

Smith, A., *An Inquiry into the Nature and Causes of the Wealth of Nations*, ed. E. Cannon, New York, 1937 (first published 1776).

Spencer, H., *Essays: Speculative and Practical*, New York, Humboldt, 1885.

CHAPTER 18 NATIONALISM AND INTERVENTION

Anderson, B. R., *Imagined Communities: Reflections on the Origin and Spread of Nationalism*, London, Verso, 1983.

Appiah, A., *In My Father's House: Africa in the Philosophy of Culture*, Oxford, Oxford University Press, 1992.

Barnes, J., 'The just war', in N. Kretzmann, A. Kenny and J. Pinborg (eds), *The Cambridge History of Later Medieval Philosophy*, Cambridge, Cambridge University Press, 1982, pp. 771–84.

Berlin, I., 'The bent twig: on the rise of nationalism', in *The Crooked Timber of Humanity*, New York, Knopf, 1991.

Chesterton, G. K., *The Essential G. K. Chesterton*, ed. P. J. Kavanagh, Oxford, Oxford University Press, 1987.

Gellner, E., *Nations and Nationalism*, Oxford, Blackwell, 1983.

Godwin, W., *Enquiry Concerning Political Justice*, vol. 1, New York, Alfred A. Knopf, 1926.

Goodin, R. E. and Pettit, P. (eds), *A Companion to Contemporary Political Philosophy*, Oxford, Blackwell, 1993.

Graham, G., 'The justice of intervention', *Review of International Studies*, 13, 1987, pp. 133–46.

Grotius, H., *De jure belli et pacis*, vol. 2, trans. F. W. Kelsey, Oxford, Oxford University Press, and London, Humphrey Milford, 1925.

Hegel, G. W. F., *Philosophy of Right*, Indianapolis, Ind., Bobbs-Merrill, 1965 (first published 1821).

Hobsbawm, E. J., *Nations and Nationalisms since 1780*, Cambridge, Cambridge University Press, 1992.

Holmes, A. F. (ed.), *War and Christian Ethics*, Michigan, Baker Book House, 1991.

Holmes, R. L., *On War and Morality*, Princeton NJ, Princeton University Press, 1989.

Johnson, J. T., *Ideology, Reason, and the Limitation of War: Religious and Secular Concepts 1200–1740*, Princeton, NJ, Princeton University Press, 1975.

Kahn, P. W., 'From Nuremberg to the Hague: the United States position in Nicaragua v. United States and the development of international law', *Yale Journal of International Law*, 12, 1987, pp. 1–62.

Liddell Hart, B. H., *The Memoirs of Captain Liddell Hart*, vol. 1, London, Cassell, 1965.

Luban, D., 'Just War and human rights', *Philosophy and Public Affairs*, 9, 1980, pp. 160–81.

——, 'The romance of the nation-state', *Philosophy and Public Affairs*, 9, 1980, pp. 392–7.

Machiavelli, N., *The Art of War*, a rev. edn of the Ellis Farneworth trans., with intro. by N. Wood, Indianapolis, Ind., Bobbs-Merrill, 1965.

Mill, J. S., 'A Few Words on non-intervention', in *Collected Works of John Stuart Mill*, vol. XXI, Toronto, University of Toronto Press, 1984, pp. 111–24.

Miller, D., 'The ethical significance of nationalism', *Ethics*, 68, 1988, pp. 647–62.

O'Brien, C. C., 'The wrath of ages: nationalism's primordial roots', *Foreign Affairs*, 72(5), 1993, pp. 142–9.

Pfaff, W., *The Wrath of Nations: Civilization and the Fury of Nationalism*, New York, Simon & Schuster, 1993.

Suárez, F., *Selections from Three Works*, vol. 2, Oxford, Oxford University Press, and London, Humphrey Milford, 1944.

Tamir, Y., *Liberal Nationalism*, Princeton, NJ, Princeton University Press, 1993.

Teichmann, J., *Pacifism and the Just War*, Oxford, Blackwell, 1986.

Vitoria, F. de, *De Indis et de jure belli reflectiones*, ed. E. Nys, Washington, Carnegie Institute of Washington, 1917.

Walzer, M., *Just and Unjust Wars*, New York, Basic Books, 1977.

——, 'The moral standing of states: a reply to four critics', *Philosophy and Public Affairs*, 9, 1980, pp. 209–29.

——, *What It Means To Be an American*, New York, Marsilio, 1992.

CHAPTER 19   RICH AND POOR

Aiken, W. and LaFollette, H. (eds), *World Hunger and Moral Obligation*, Englewood Cliffs, NJ, Prentice-Hall, 1977.

Attfield, R. and Wilkins, B. (eds), *International Justice and the Third World*, London, Routledge, 1992.

Cooper, D. E. and Palmer, J. (eds), *The Environment in Question*, Routledge, London, 1992.

Dower, N., *World Poverty: Challenge and Response*, York, Ebor Press, 1983.

——, 'Justice and the Third World', in Singer (ed.), *Companion to Ethics*.

Fishkin, J. S., *The Limits of Obligation*, New Haven, Conn., Yale University Press, 1982.

Kant, I., *Groundwork of the Metaphysics of Morals*, trans. by H. J. Paton and published as *The Moral Law*, London, Hutchinson, 1948.

Laslett, P. and Fishkin, J. (eds), *Philosophy, Politics and Society*, 5th series, New Haven, Conn., Yale University Press, 1979.

Malthus, T., *An Essay on the Principle of Population*, 1803 edn, ed. D. Winch, Cambridge, Cambridge University Press, 1992.

Nagel, T., *Equality and Partiality*, Oxford, Oxford University Press, 1991.

Narveson, J., 'Aesthetics, charity, utility and distributive justice', *The Monist*, 56, 1962.

Nozick, R., *Anarchy, State and Utopia*, Oxford, Blackwell, 1974.

O'Neill, O., *Faces of Hunger*, London, Allen & Unwin, 1986.

Parfit, D., 'Overpopulation and the quality of life', in Singer (ed.), *Applied Ethics*.

Pascal, L., 'Judgement Day', in Singer (ed.), *Applied Ethics*.

Rachels, J. (ed.), *Moral Problems*, 3rd edn, New York, Harper & Row, 1979.

Rawls, J., *A Theory of Justice*, Oxford, Oxford University Press, 1971.
Singer, P., 'Famine, affluence and morality', in P. Laslett and J. Fishkin (eds), *Philosophy, Politics and Society*.
—— (ed.), *Applied Ethics*, Oxford, Oxford University Press, 1987.
—— (ed.), *A Companion to Ethics*, Oxford, Blackwell, 1991.
——, *Practical Ethics*, 2nd edn, Cambridge, Cambridge University Press, 1993.
Shaw, B., 'Poverty: absolute and relative?', *Journal of Applied Philosophy*, 5, 1988.
Trusted, J., 'The problem of absolute poverty: what are our moral obligations to the destitute?', in Cooper and Palmer (eds), *The Environment in Question*.
Williams, B., *Ethics and the Limits of Philosophy*, London, Fontana, 1985.
Woolf, L., *Beginning Again*, London, Hogarth Press, 1964.

CHAPTER 20 WAR, TERRORISM AND ETHICAL CONSISTENCY

Almond, B. and Hill, D., *Applied Philosophy: Morals and Metaphysics in Contemporary Debate*, London, Routledge, 1991.
Anscombe, G. E. M., 'War and murder', in R. Wasserstrom (ed.), *War and Morality*, Belmont, Calif., Wadsworth, 1970.
Aquinas, T., *Summa Theologica*, ed. T. Gilbey, London, Blackfriars and Eyre & Spottiswoode, 1963–75.
Coady, C. A. J., 'The morality of terrorism', *Philosophy*, 60, 1985.
Cohen, M., Nagel, T. and Scanlon, T. (eds), *War and Moral Responsibility*, Princeton, NJ, Princeton University Press, 1974.
Ford, J. C., 'The morality of obliteration bombing', in Wasserstrom, *War and Morality*.
Gallie, W. B., *Understanding War*, London, Routledge, 1991.
Gewirth, A., 'Are there any absolute rights?', *Philosophical Quarterly*, 31, 1981.
Gilbert, P., 'Terrorism: war or crime', *Cogito*, 3, 1989.
Graham, K., *The Battle of Democracy*, Brighton, Wheatsheaf Books, 1986.
Hampshire, S. (ed.), *Public and Private Morality*, Cambridge, Cambridge University Press, 1978.
Hare, R. M., *Essays on Political Morality*, Oxford, Oxford University Press, 1989.
Hegel, G. W. F., *Hegel's Philosophy of Right with Marx's Commentary*, ed. H. P. Kainz, The Hague, Nijhoft, 1974.
Hobbes, T., *Leviathan*, Oxford, Blackwell, 1960.
Honderich, T., *Violence For Equality*, Harmondsworth, Penguin Books, 1980.
Hughes, M., 'Terrorism and national security', *Philosophy*, 57, 1982.
Khatchadourian, H., 'Terrorism and morality', *Journal of Applied Philosophy*, 5(2), 1988.
Lackey, D. P., *The Ethics of War and Peace*, Englewood Cliffs, NJ, Prentice-Hall, 1989.
Laqueur, W., *Terrorism*, London, Weidenfeld & Nicholson, 1977.
Leiser, B. M., *Values in Conflict*, New York, Macmillan, 1981.
Machiavelli, N., *The Art of War*, a rev. edn of the Ellis Farneworth trans. with intro. by N. Wood, Indianapolis, Ind., Bobbs-Merrill, 1965.
Nagel, T., 'War and massacre', *Philosophy and Public Affairs*, 2, 1972.
Nielson, K., 'Violence and terrorism: its uses and abuses', in B. M. Leiser (ed.), *Values in Conflict*.
Norman, R., 'The Case for Pacifism', in Almond and Hill (eds), *Applied Philosophy*, and in

Journal of Applied Philosophy, 5, 1988.

Primoratz, I., 'What is terrorism?', *Journal of Applied Philosophy*, 7, 1990.

Singer, P., *Practical Ethics*, 2nd edn, Cambridge, Cambridge University Press, 1993.

Teichman, J., 'How to define terrorism', *Philosophy*, 64, 1989.

Thompson, J., *Justice and World Order*, Routledge, London, 1992.

Wallace, G., 'Area bombing, terrorism and the death of innocents', *Journal of Applied Philosophy*, 6, 1989.

——, 'Terrorism and the argument from analogy', *International Journal of Moral and Social Studies*, 6, 1991.

——, 'The language of terrorism', *International Journal of Moral and Social Studies*, 8, 1993.

Wasserstrom, R. (ed.), *War and Morality*, Belmont, Calif., Wadsworth, 1970.

Walzer, M., *Just and Unjust Wars*, London, Allen Lane, 1977.

Webster, Sir Charles (with Noble Frankland), *The Strategic Air Offensive Against Germany 1939–45*, vol. 1, London, HMSO, 1961.

Wilkins, B. T., *Terrorism and Collective Responsibility*, London, Routledge, 1992.

Wilkinson, P., *Political Terrorism*, London, Macmillan, 1974.

——, *Terrorism and the Liberal State*, 2nd edn, London, Macmillan, 1986.

Williams, B., 'Ethical consistency', *Proceedings of the Aristotelian Society*, 39, 1965.

CHAPTER 21 ENLARGING THE COMMUNITY: COMPANION ANIMALS

Adams, C., *The Politics of Meat*, New York, Continuum, 1990.

Becker, L. C. and Becker, C. B. (eds), *Encyclopedia of Ethics*, New York, Garland Press, 1992.

Benton, T., *Natural Relations*, New York and London, Verso Books, 1993.

Carruthers, P., *The Animal Issue*, Cambridge, Cambridge University Press, 1992.

Clark, S. R. L., *The Moral Status of Animals*, Oxford, Oxford University Press, 1984.

——, 'Humans, animals and "animal behavior"', in Miller and Williams, *Ethics and Animals*.

——, *The Nature of the Beast*, 2nd edn, Oxford, Oxford University Press, 1984.

——, 'Is humanity a natural kind?', in Ingold (ed.), *What is an Animal?*

——, 'Apes and the idea of kindred', in Singer and Cavalieri, *Great Ape Project*.

——, 'Good and bad ethology and the decent *polis*', in Loizou and Legger (eds), *Polis and Politics*.

——, 'Companions on the way', *Philosophical Quarterly*, 44, 1993.

Dombrowski, D., *The Philosophy of Vegetarianism*, Amherst, Mass., University of Massachusetts Press, 1984.

Frey, R., *Rights, Killing and Suffering*, Oxford, Blackwell, 1983.

Hearne, V., *Adam's Task: Calling Animals by Name*, New York, A. A. Knopf, 1986.

Ingold, T. (ed.), *What is an Animal?*, London, Unwin Hyman, 1988.

Khalid, F. and O'Brien, J., *Islam and Ecology*, London and New York, Cassell, 1992.

Lee, R. B. and De Vore, O. (eds), *Man the Hunter*, Chicago, Aldine Atherton, 1972.

Locke, J., *Two Treatises of Government*, rev. edn, introduction and notes by P. Laslett, New York, Mentor, 1965 (first published 1690).

Loizou, A. and Lesser, H. (eds), *Polis and Politics: Essays in Greek Moral and Political*

Philosophy, Aldershot and Brookfield, Vt, Gower Press, 1991.

Long, A. A. (ed.), *Problems in Stoicism*, London, Athlone Press, 1971.

—— and Sedley, D. (eds), *The Hellenistic Philosophers*, Cambridge, Cambridge University Press, 1987.

Mazri, A.-H. B. A., 'Islam and ecology', in Khalid and O'Brien (eds), *Islam and Ecology*.

Midgley, M., *Animals and Why They Matter*, Harmondsworth, Penguin Books, 1983.

Miller, H. B., 'The Wahokies', in Singer and Cavalieri (eds), *Great Ape Project*.

—— and Williams, W. H. (eds), *Ethics and Animals*, Clifton, NJ, Humana Press, 1983.

Montaigne, *Collected Essays* (trans. J. Florio 1603), London, Dent/Everyman, 1910, Book III, ch. 12.

Noske, B., *Humans and other Animals*, London, Pluto Press, 1989.

Patterson, O., *Ethnic Chauvinism*, New York, Stein & Day, 1977.

Plutarch, *Moralia*, trans. H. Cherniss and W. C. Helmbold, London and Cambridge, Mass., Loeb Classical Library, vol. 12, Heinemann, 1949 and later.

Porphyry, *On Abstinence from Animal Food*, trans. T. Taylor, London, Centaur Press, 1965.

Rachels, J., *Created from Animals*, Oxford, Oxford University Press, 1990.

Regan, T., *The Case for Animal Rights*, London, Routledge, 1983.

—— and Singer, P. (eds), *Animal Rights and Human Obligations*, Englewood Cliffs, NJ, Prentice-Hall, 1989.

Rollin, B., *The Unheeded Cry*, New York, Oxford University Press, 1989.

Rosenfield, L. C., *From Beast-machine to Man-machine*, New York, Octagon Books, 1968.

Sahlins, M., *Stone Age Economics*, London, Tavistock, 1972.

Stapledon, O., *Last and First Men: Last Men in London*, Harmondsworth, Penguin Books, 1972 (first published 1930).

Singer, P., *The Expanding Circle*, Oxford, Oxford University Press, 1981.

—— (ed.), *In Defence of Animals*, Oxford, Blackwell, 1989.

——, *Animal Liberation*, 2nd edn, New York, 1990 (first published 1975).

—— and Cavalieri, D. (eds), *The Great Ape Project: Equality Beyond Humanity*, London, Fourth Estate, 1993.

Sorabji, R., *Animal Minds and Human Morals*, London, Duckworth, 1994.

Stent, G. S., *Morality as a Biological Phenomenon*, Berlin, Dahlem/Abakon, 1978.

White, M., *The Philosophy of the American Revolution*, New York, Oxford University Press, 1978.

Wills, G., *Inventing America: Jefferson's Declaration of Independence*, New York and Toronto, Random House, 1979.

Wood, A., 'Marx against morality', in P. Singer (ed.), *A Companion to Ethics*, Oxford, Blackwell, 1991.

CHAPTER 22 ETHICS AND THE ENVIRONMENT: THE GLOBAL PERSPECTIVE

Attfield, R., *The Ethics of Environmental Concern*, 2nd edn, Athens and London, University of Georgia Press, 1991.

——, 'Has the history of philosophy ruined the environment?', *Environmental Ethics*, 13, 1991, pp. 127–37. Also in *Environmental Philosophy: Principles and Prospects*.

——, *Environmental Philosophy: Principles and Prospects*, Aldershot, Avebury, 1994.

—— and Belsey, A. (eds), *Philosophy and the Natural Environment*, Cambridge, Cambridge University Press, 1994.

—— and Dell, K., (eds), *Values, Conflict and the Environment*, Oxford, Ian Ramsey Centre and Centre for Applied Ethics, Cardiff, 1989.

Callicott, J. Baird, *In Defense of the Land Ethic*, Albany, NY, State University of New York Press, 1989.

Carson, R., *Silent Spring*, London, Hamish Hamilton, 1962.

Clark, S. R. L., 'The rights of wild things', *Inquiry*, 22, 1979, pp. 171–88.

Elliot, R., 'Ecology and the ethics of environmental restoration', in Attfield and Belsey (eds), *Philosophy and the Natural Environment*. pp. 31–43.

—— and Gare, A. (eds), *Environmental Philosophy*, St Lucia, University of Queensland Press; Milton Keynes, Open University Press; University Park, Pa., Pennsylvania State University Press, 1983.

Engels, F., *Dialectics of Nature* [1873–82], republished in *Collected Works*, vol. 25, London, Lawrence & Wishart, 1987.

Fox, W., 'Approaching Deep Ecology: a response to Richard Sylvan's critique of Deep Ecology', *Environmental Studies Occasional Paper* 20, Hobart, University of Tasmania, 1986.

——, *Toward a Transpersonal Ecology: Developing New Foundations for Environmentalism*, Boston and London, Shambhala, 1990.

Goodpaster, K. E., 'On being morally considerable', *Journal of Philosophy*, 75, 1978, pp. 308–25.

Guha, R., 'Radical American environmentalism and wilderness preservation', *Environmental Ethics*, 11,1989, pp. 71–83.

Hale, Sir Matthew, *The Primitive Origination of Mankind*, London, 1677.

Hargrove, E. C., *Foundations of Environmental Ethics*, Englewood Cliffs, NJ, Prentice-Hall, 1989.

Holland, A., 'Natural capital', in Attfield and Belsey (eds), *Philosophy and the Natural Environment*.

Katz, E., 'Artifacts and functions: a note on the value of nature', *Environmental Values*, 2(3), 1993, pp. 223–32.

Leopold, A., *A Sand County Almanac and Sketches Here and There*, New York, Oxford University Press, 1949.

Losin, P., 'Faking nature – a review', *Restoration and Management Notes*, 4, 1986, p. 55.

——, 'The Sistine Chapel debate: Peter Losin replies', *Restoration and Management Notes*, 6, 1988, p. 6.

Lovelock, J. E., *Gaia: a New Look at Life on Earth*, Oxford, Oxford University Press, 1979.

McCloskey, H. J., *Ecological Ethics and Politics*, Totowa, NJ, Rowman & Littlefield, 1983.

Malthus, T. R., *An Essay on the Principle of Population*, 1803 edn, ed. D. Winch, Cambridge, Cambridge University Press, 1992.

Mannison, D., McRobbie, M. and Routley, R. (eds), *Environmental Philosophy*, Canberra, Australian National University, 1980.

Meadows, D. H., Meadows, D. L., Randers, J. and Behrens, W. W., III, *Limits to Growth*, London, Pan, 1972.

Midgley, M., 'Duties concerning islands', in Elliott and Gare (eds), *Environmental Philosophy*.

Naess, A., 'The shallow and the deep, long-range ecology movement: a summary', *Inquiry*, 16, 1973, pp. 95–100.

——, 'A defence of the Deep Ecology movement', *Environmental Ethics*, 6(3), 1984, pp. 265–70.

——, 'The Deep Ecology movement: some philosophical aspects', *Philosophical Inquiry*, 8, 1986, pp. 10–31.

Partridge, E. (ed.), *Responsibilities to Future Generations*, New York, Prometheus Books, 1981.

Passmore, J., *Man's Responsibility for Nature*, 2nd edn, London, Duckworth, 1980.

Regan, T., *The Case for Animal Rights*, London, Routledge & Kegan Paul, 1983.

Rodman, J., 'Four forms of ecological consciousness reconsidered', in Scherer and Attig (eds), *Ethics and the Environment*.

Rolston, H., III, *Environmental Ethics: Duties to and Values in the Natural World*, Philadelphia, Pa., Temple University Press, 1988.

——, 'The wilderness idea reaffirmed', *The Environmental Professional*, 13, 1991, pp. 370–7.

Routley, R., 'Is there a need for a new, an environmental ethic?', *Proceedings of the XVth World Congress of Philosophy*, Varna (Bulgaria), 1973, pp. 205–10.

Scherer, D. and Attig, T. (eds), *Ethics and the Environment*, Englewood Cliffs, NJ, Prentice-Hall, 1983.

Singer, P., *Practical Ethics*, 2nd edn, Cambridge, Cambridge University Press, 1993.

Sprigge, T. L. S., 'Are there intrinsic values in nature?', in B. Almond and D. Hill (eds), *Applied Philosophy*, London, Routledge, 1991, pp. 37–44.

Stone, C., *Should Trees Have Standing?*, Los Altos, Calif., William Kaufman, 1974.

Sylvan (formerly Routley), R., 'A critique of Deep Ecology', *Radical Philosopy*, 40, 1985, pp. 2–12 and 41, 1985, pp. 10–22.

Taylor, C. C. W. (ed.), *Ethics and the Environment*, Oxford, Corpus Christi College, 1992.

Taylor, P., *Respect for Nature: a Theory of Environmental Ethics*, Princeton, NJ, Princeton University Press, 1986.

Thomas, K., *Man and the Natural World: Changing Attitudes in England, 1500–1800*, London, Allen Lane, 1983.

Thompson, J., 'A refutation of environmental ethics', *Environmental Ethics*, 12(2), 1990, pp. 147–60.

VanDeVeer, D., 'Interspecific justice', *Inquiry*, 22, 1979, pp. 55–79.

Wenz, P., *Environmental Justice*, Albany, NY, State University of New York Press, 1988.

Index